The Japanese Theatre

The Japanese Theatre

From Shamanistic Ritual to Contemporary Pluralism

REVISED EDITION

BENITO ORTOLANI

PRINCETON UNIVERSITY PRESS
PRINCETON, NEW JERSEY

Published by Princeton University Press, 41 William Street,
Princeton, New Jersey 08540
In the United Kingdom: Princeton University Press,
Chichester, West Sussex

Originally published by E. J. Brill, Leiden, The Netherlands; revised edition, with corrections
and a new preface, published by Princeton University Press, 1995

Library of Congress Cataloging-in-Publication Data
Ortolani, Benito.
The Japanese theatre : from shamanistic ritual to contemporary
pluralism / Benito Ortolani.— Rev. ed.
p. cm.
Includes bibliographical references and index.
ISBN 0-691-04333-7
1. Theater—Japan—History. I. Title.
PN2921.O78 1995   94-23504
792'.0952—dc20

The publisher would like to acknowledge the author of this volume for providing the
camera-ready copy from which this book was printed

Princeton University Press books are printed on acid-free paper
and meet the guidelines for permanence and durability of the Committee on Production
Guidelines for Book Longevity of the Council on Library Resources

First Princeton Paperback printing, 1995

Printed in the United States of America

3 5 7 9 10 8 6 4 2

CONTENTS

Contents

PREFACE TO THE REVISED EDITION

This revised paperback edition offers a few improvements over the original hardcover book of the same title, published in 1990 by E. J. Brill in Leiden, the Netherlands, and now for some time out of print. A number of specialists in the field of Japanese theatre reviewed that publication favorably, also providing suggestions that have been incorporated into the present edition, as much as the strict limits imposed by the publishers allowed. I am grateful to all of them, in a special way to James Brandon, Karen Brazell, Susan Matisoff, Thomas Rimer, and Andrew Tsubaki. Darko Suvin kindly contributed a number of entries for the bibliography, helping thus to make it the most complete reference tool now available for works about the Japanese theatre written in western languages. The recent research published until 1994 was taken into consideration, especially in the sections about Zenchiku's theories of the *nō*, the performances sponsored by the Jesuit missionaries during the second half of the sixteenth century/beginning of the seventeenth, and the contemporary post-*shingeki* movement. The section about Chikamatsu and *Kanadehon Chūshingura* was moved to the chapter dedicated to the puppets, and an analysis of *junsui kabuki* (plays written for *kabuki* only) was introduced in the chapter about *kabuki*. The quality and the size of the illustrations were substantially improved.

It is my hope that this paperback edition published by Princeton University Press will reach a wide audience, including many students and theatre practitioners, and thus contribute to the process of nurturing genuine esteem and understanding for non-western cultures. Japan's theatrical tradition should no longer be treated as exotic and cut off from the rest of the planet, but as a substantial and integrated part of world theatre that began and developed with more ties to Indian, Chinese, Korean, and European traditions than so far acknowledged, and which is now projecting creative waves of influence on world performance of a size and importance never previously attained.

INTRODUCTION

The history of the Japanese theatre suggests a few similarities with the history of the English stage. Both insular countries, while still in a primitive phase of civilization, were exposed to the theatrical traditions of powerful empires—Rome in the West and China in the East. The Roman legions brought to England only pale, corrupted shadows of the classic Greek theatrical models, nearly submerged by coarse amusements. However, stones of the Roman theatres at Gosbeck Farms, St. Albans, and Canterbury remain to the present day as a mute testimony to the first British contact with the advanced stagecraft of the Roman empire. The carriers of the popular, multifaceted Chinese performing arts of the *san-yüe* were peaceful visitors to Japan, hardly conscious of the fragmentary Sanskrit origin of their repertory. However, the sophisticated *gigaku* masks preserved in the ancient capital, Nara, within the precincts of the Tōdaiji temple, and in the National Museum of Tokyo leave no doubt that, as in England, the first imported theatre arts in Japan presented certain features of an advanced, mature craft. Both England and Japan reached the high points of their theatrical achievements only after their assimilation of basic religious and cultural heritages imported from the mainland. In both countries a breakthrough of theatre forms destined to achieve world fame happened in the late Middle Ages and in the seventeenth century: the Cycle and Morality plays, followed by the Elizabethan splendor in England, and the *nō*, followed by the prodigious Genroku achievements of mature *kabuki* and of exquisite puppet plays in Japan.

Theatre presents, in Japan as elsewhere, a synthesis of the idealized past tradition elevated to the function of myth and archetype, as well as the concrete present system of beliefs and moral values determining the decisions which bridge the everyday routine of life and drama. As the English theatre finds its mythical and archetypical roots in the classical Greco-Roman and Christian heritages, so does the Japanese theatre find its roots, its inspiration, and its inexhaustible resources of regeneration in the two main spiritual forces of Japanese tradition, Shinto and Buddhism.

Both Shinto and Buddhist heritages are complex, having assimilated widely different elements of distant origin such as shamanism, Hinduism, Confucianism, Taoism, and, later, Christianity. These were present in the Japanese islands at different stages of development and sophistication during different periods. The fortunes of Shinto and Buddhism alternate in Japanese history. A Shinto-dominated beginning was followed by Buddhism's triumph as a new, fashionable, imported religion in the sixth century A.D.; the compromising medieval fusion of Shinto and Buddhist cults was eventually followed by Shinto revivals in modern times. From the beginning of this process strong shamanistic and magic folk beliefs were present, and, at the popular level, eventually came to the foreground of the daily practice of both religions. Several intellectual and artistic leaders at the same time dedicated themselves to esoteric practices leading to the perfection of special arts, sometimes as a quest for Buddhist enlightenment beyond the high levels of artistic achievement, while others deepened their research for a sophisticated interpretation of the primitive Shinto heritage.

During the fourteenth century, a situation ideal for the birth of a great theatrical epoch developed in Japan, created by the synthesis of a vital popular tradition with the sophisticated input of extraordinary artists. The elements of popular entertainment and primitive shamanistic ritual transmitted through the *kagura* and *sarugaku* traditions blended with the refined performance of poetical texts, and with the profound spiritual insight of such remarkable masters as Kan'ami, Zeami, and Zenchiku to give life to the classical age of the *nō*.

The *nō* masters transformed the popular thrill of experiencing the "other" dimension through primitive shamanistic ritual into a sublime experience unexplainable with words, but referred to in the secret tradition of the *nō* with the vocabulary of Buddhist enlightenment, which the actor and the courtly audience shared at the blossoming of the mysterious flower of a performance of the highest rank.

Before, during, and after the formation of the *nō* a great number of popular entertainments developed throughout Japan, with colorful dances, juggling, acrobatics, and comical sketches; for centuries these were often inserted in the middle of rituals, eventually becoming either an essential part of them, or inspiring new forms of theatrical entertainment. By the seventeenth century the abundant reservoir of folk performances made it possible to build, on the basis of *nō*'s greatness, a popular theatrical tradition of incredible vitality in both *kabuki* and *jōruri*.

Following the reopening of the country in 1868, when the frenzy for modernization swept Japan, the new myths of progress through westernization were translated into the *shimpa* and *shingeki* achievement of creating the modern drama of Japan. After passing through phases of political preachment and social involvement, *shingeki* and its more recent underground and avant-garde theatre offshoots eventually came to reflect the hopeless soul of a world power sharing with the other industrialized nations the malaise of contemporary loneliness and despair. In the meantime, a tenacious love for the beauty of the past and waves of nationalistic pride kept the traditional performing arts alive through periods of crisis and rebirth, making possible the unique pluralistic, multifaceted, colorful spectacle of today's performing arts in Japan.

The present volume offers an outline of the present state of knowledge about the Japanese theatre. It is obviously impossible to do justice to all aspects of this extraordinarily rich field of research within the limits of this book. Hard choices were unavoidable. Proportional priority was given to areas which are less known and in which satisfactory syntheses are either nonexistent in western languages or hard to reach, such as the period of the origins, *kagura*, *gigaku*, and the origins and theories of the *nō*. Other important areas which are covered by excellent and easily accessible studies, such as *kabuki* and *bunraku*, were given a comparatively shorter treatment. For the readers who want to continue the study of the Japanese theatre, the overview of the history of western scholarship in the last chapter and the comprehensive bibliography offer a fairly complete orientation on the field, though limited to studies in western languages. The contents of this book, however, are often based on research in Japanese, which is quoted only when necessary in the notes at the end of each chapter.

I am grateful to the many people who made the writing of this volume possible. First of all I want to thank my wife

Maria, to whom this labor of love is dedicated. Over several decades in a number of countries many teachers and friends generously shared with me their knowledge and dedication to research. They are too many to be individually acknowledged here. I want, however, to pay homage to the memory of the two specialists of Japanese theatre who helped me most during my seven years of studies in Japan, the late Toida Seiichi and Sugino Kitsutarō. Their selfless friendship and assistance during my first explorations into this difficult field remain in my memory as a precious symbol of the noblest virtues of old Japan. Many scholars and artists in Japan made it possible for me to become familiar with the different worlds of the theatrical arts of that country. A very brief list should include the friends of the Zeami Kenkyūkai, especially the late Toida Michizō, Honda Hideo, Nishi Kazuyoshi, and Yamamoto Jirō; moreover, Honda Mitsuhiro, Gotō Hajime, and Matsuda Tamotsu. Important were, in my understanding of *kabuki*, the friendship with Gunji Masakatsu and my meeting with Baiko VI and Utaemon VI, while my many encounters with Fukuda Tsuneari and Mishima Yukio made me aware of the nature and problems of *shingeki*.

I am particularly grateful to Samuel Leiter for his close scrutiny of the text; to Leonard Pronko, Robert Karpen, and Antony Calabro, who read the manuscript and offered several important suggestions; to my daughter Laura-Lee Griffith, for long hours spent at the computer; and to the students who helped me in various capacities, especially Miyagawa Chiori for her assistance in the compilation of the glossary.

Grateful recognition is also due to the generous providers of the illustrations for this book—the late Sugino Kitsutarō and Toida Seiichi, and, recently, Matsuda Tamotsu and Gotō Hajime, with the helpful and generous support of the Tsubouchi Memorial Theatre Museum at Waseda University.

PERIODS IN JAPANESE HISTORY

PRE-HISTORY and PRIMITIVE PERIOD *(Genshi)*

Jōmon		? -	250 B.C.
Yayoi	ca.	250 B.C. -	300 A.D. Beginning of *kagura*
Kofun	ca.	300 -	710

ANCIENT PERIOD *(Kodai)*

Yamato	300	- 710	Beginning of *gigaku*
Nara	710	- 794	Beginning of *bugaku*,
Heian	794	- 1192	*dengaku, sangaku/sarugaku*

MEDIEVAL PERIOD *(Chūsei)*

Kamakura	1192	- 1333	
Muromachi or			
Ashikaga	1333	- 1573	Beginning of *nōgaku*
(Namboku	1336	- 1392)	
(Sengoku	1467	- 1568)	

EARLY MODERN PERIOD *(Kinsei)*

Azuchi-			
Momoyama	1573	- 1600	Beginning of *jōruri*
Edo or			and *kabuki*
Tokugawa	1600	- 1867	

MODERN PERIOD *(Kindai)*

Meiji	1868	- 1912	Beginning of *shimpa*
Taishō	1912	- 1926	and *shingeki*
Shōwa	1926	- 1989	
Heisei	1989	-	

The Japanese Theatre

CHAPTER I

THE BEGINNINGS

Jōmon Period (-ca. 250 B.C.)[1]

The Japanese contribution to theatre, which is one of the richest and most original in the world, had a relatively late start. The inhabitants of the Japanese islands were just awakening from a nomadic pattern of life some three centuries after Greece had reached the peak of her spectacular dramatic creativity, as India was giving birth to the monumental theoretic systematization of Sanskrit drama, and after China, a prosperous unified empire under the Han dynasty (200 B.C.-220 A.D.), had developed sophisticated forms of court dance and ritual, shadow puppets, and a variety of popular entertainments. No evidence of performance in the nomadic communities during the Jōmon period (ending ca. 250 B.C.) is available. Only guesswork is possible about the *dogū*, impressive up to one-foot high figurines handcrafted in clay, and the up to six inch wide earthen masks belonging to the artifacts of this period. These objects were probably used in magic rites of fertility, exorcism, and for the cure of illnesses. The nude female earthen figurines, however, might suggest some connection with trance dances recorded centuries later in the oldest Japanese written sources, in which a ritual disrobing of a female shaman was performed.

Yayoi Period (ca. 250 B.C.-ca. 300 A.D.)[2]

During the Yayoi period the nomadic tribes went through a process of cultural transformation, with long-reaching consequences for the development of the performing arts. They

1

settled and organized agricultural communities, introducing rice culture, the farming family, and the village. The classless society of the wandering groups gave place to a stratified agricultural society based on the ownership of land. Fishing, hunting, and gathering the natural products of the earth no longer constituted the only sources of nourishment. During this time the rituals connected with the phases of the newly introduced planting, transplanting, and harvesting of rice became of fundamental importance in the rhythm of the village celebrations, and began to fuse with ancient beliefs and magic rituals performed to assure a good supply of fish or game.

The first written source is to be found in the Chinese *History of the Kingdom of Wei* (ca. 297 A.D.),[3] where it is related that formerly some hundred organized communities existed in the Japanese islands, each with a king, whose office was hereditary. Several of the ruling houses would bid through envoys for an official recognition of supremacy by the Chinese court, because evidently the Chinese emperor was acknowledged as the legitimate source of authority. The steady contact with China counts among the main reasons for the rapid transformation during the first few centuries A.D., and for the trend towards unification under one supreme ruler, following the ideal of the Chinese emperor. The process of unification furthered a strong concentration of the official court performances within the ruler's palace compound and the few main shrines where he/she worshiped. Chinese influences were also paramount in the development of ritual, ceremonies, and secular performing arts. The route to and from China usually passed through Korea, where shamanism had existed since ancient times. Korea, therefore, probably played a role in the shaping and diffusion of shamanistic practices in old Japan.

The importance of magic and sorcery during this stage of evolution must not be underestimated. *The History of the Latter Han Dynasty*, a Chinese source from ca. 513 A.D.,[4] relates that in the second half of the second century A.D. the country of Wa (Japan) was in a pitiful state of war and great confusion, having been without a ruler for many decades. A woman, the famous queen Himiko, who concerned herself with magic and sorcery and bewitched the populace, succeeded in restoring order and providing unity. Queen Himiko (or Pimiko) was probably a *miko*, a Japanese version of the northeastern Asian tradition of a shaman; that is, a medium who acts as the bridge between the people and the ancestral deities, and performs magical rituals of purification, healing, and divination. In her exalted position of supreme ruler she might well have begun a primitive form of the ceremonies that later became the duty of the emperor as head priest of the Shinto religion.

The Chinese sources give mostly general descriptions of local Japanese customs which could largely apply to many primitive communities. The people of Wa used to dance and sing while the head mourner would wail and lament during funeral rites. They performed divination with baked bones and tortoise shells. Some of the observations, however, reflect habits which became traditional in Japan, and fundamental for positions and movements of dance, such as showing deference to superiors by squatting or kneeling with both hands touching the ground and clapping the hands in worship.

Kofun Period (ca. 300 A.D.-710 A.D.). The Haniwa

The fascinating fired clay images called *haniwa* (*hani* means clay, and *wa* means ring, circle) appear during the Kofun (or Tomb) period in connection with the development of majestic grave sites and more elaborate rituals for the dead. They represent a variety of objects such as huts and boats, animals such as horses and monkeys, and also dancers and musicians. Some scholars suggested that the *haniwa*, found in most cases in tomb-mounds, actually functioned as substitutes for an old custom of burying alive the personal attendants of important personalities, such as emperors and princes, together with their deceased lord. This explanation, however, is today no longer commonly accepted. It is generally assumed that *haniwa* played an important role in funeral rites and probably in magic fertility cults as well. Some *haniwa*, for example an almost two foot tall costumed female shaman, a one-and-a-half foot tall nude dancing girl and a few drummers, probably serve to illustrate the oldest written Japanese sources about dance and shamanistic trance.

Kojiki *and* Nihongi *(Eighth Century)*

The *Records of Ancient Matters* (*Kojiki*) and the *Chronicles of Japan* (*Nihongi*)—the oldest indigenous sources for Japanese history—present an uneven, intricate mixture of myth, native tradition and historical facts, altered and arranged in imitation of Chinese models to comply with the purpose of validating the political and religious demands of the ruling Yamato court. The interpretation of the few texts connected with the performing arts must take into consideration some complex exegetic problems. Ancestral and cosmic concepts of the deities involved (*kami*) are probably present at different levels of meaning. Many contradictory interpretations of the ancient texts have been proposed by Japanese and foreign scholars. Notwithstanding the difficulties, important insights are offered by such texts as the one related to the myth of Ame-no Uzume-no-mikoto's performance in front of the heavenly rock cave, which is a treasure of information because of its projection of contemporary religious rites and dances into the legendary account of the myth.

Uzume's Trance

The sun-goddess Amaterasu, repeatedly offended by her brother Susa-no-wo, took refuge in the heavenly rock-cave, leaving the world in darkness, at the mercy of the evil powers of the night. "Because of this, constant night reigned, and the cries of the myriad deities were everywhere abundant, like summer flies; and all manner of calamities arose."[5] As a consequence myriad deities came together in a divine assembly which met in a dry river bed (a traditional place for theatrical performances to the present time). With the aim of locking the sun goddess out of her heavenly rock dwelling, the deities (*kami*, here the ancestors of the Japanese people) performed rites, some of which apparently based on the principle of sympathetic magic; for instance, they brought together cocks and made them crow as an anticipation of the desired dawn. Then they prepared a mirror of iron and an eight-foot long string of five hundred jewels, and summoned two deities to remove the whole shoulder-bone of a male deer, and to perform a divination, using heavenly papaya wood. They

4

adorned the sacred place with uprooted *sakaki* trees (*cleyera japonica*) on the upper branches of which they hung long strings of beads, with a mirror on the middle branches, and white and blue *nikite* cloth on the lower branches. The *nikite* perhaps symbolized the rice and fruit offerings, and later became the strips of white and colored papers still to be seen in the Shinto shrines. In this setting the goddess Uzume "bound up her sleeves with a cord of heavenly *pi-kagë* vine, tied around her head a headband of the heavenly *ma-saki* vine, bound together bundles of *sasa* leaves to hold in her hands, and overturning a bucket before the heavenly rock-cave, stamped resoundingly upon it. Then she became divinely possessed, exposed her breasts, and pushed her skirt-band down to her genitals." At this point the whole audience laughed together. Some interpreters propose the theory that the thunderous laughter was primarily a ceremonial, ritual response, rather than a natural reaction to a comical "obscene" disrobing; that is, according to the principles of sympathetic magic, the joy of having the sun restored was expressed in advance through laughter as a means of forcing the god to grant the object of the expressed joy. According to other interpreters, the very obscenity of the dance would have provoked a hearty laughter. For these scholars, the playful showing of the genitals for entertainment's sake represents the mythical moment of birth of the theatrical event; that is, the moment when the generative function of the organs of reproduction is purposely set aside, and their "theatrical" use for sole entertainment is discovered and celebrated. Obscenity as such becomes in this theory the core of the element of "show" which gives birth to a theatrical event.[6] Amaterasu, amazed and curious, opened the cave, stepped out attracted by the mirror, and thus gave back to the world the sun, the source of light and heat.

Some scholars see in Uzume's myth influences of rites and ceremonies usual during solar eclipses in the old traditions of Assam, Burma, South China, and minority populations of Southeast Asia, and consequently a testimony for the probability of part of the primitive inhabitants of Japan and their rituals having originated from those ethnic groups. Others stress the connection with shamanistic influences from Korea and North Asia. Uzume's dance would be primarily a projection into timeless myth of the performance of a *miko*, the Japanese version of a female shaman who performed ecstatic and erotic dances until relatively recent times (in fact, the *miko*-medium, although rare, is not yet completely extinct). Another hypothesis presents Uzume's dance as a ritual for the repose of departed souls, or, better, for appeasing the souls of the ancestors (*chinkon-sai*, literally spirit-pacification ceremony). The interpretation of Uzume's dance as an entertainment for a tribal chief has also been proposed.

Probably these interpretations, and several variations on them, contain partial truths. A strong connection with the *kagura* is undeniable, and the interpretation that recognizes in the description of Uzume's dance a projection into ageless myth of shamanistic *kagura* performances during or around the seventh century A.D. seems, in any case, to be valid. The texts describe in detail elements which are still present in the performance of several *kagura*; for example, the branches of the *sakaki* tree, the mirror, the symbols of the offerings (that is, the pendants of white and colored papers trimmed into inch-wide strips), the ropes made of twisted straw suspended around performing areas before Shinto shrines, and the use of objects like a twig or a tuft of grass as the temporary abode of the *kami* by whom the *miko* is possessed in her trance-dance. Moreover, a number of *kagura* are still performed after sunset, because it is during darkness that the *miko* perform their conjurations, when the spirits of the dead appear, and the help of the protector *kami* against the evil influences is most needed. In general, shamanistic activity requires darkness also as a symbol for the journey of the shaman from the limits of normal consciousness into the light of the dimension where the sacred communications take place.

The function of divine possession (*kamigakari*) is extremely important in this context, and fundamental for further developments of the Japanese performing arts. Its meaning is never clearly defined in Japanese tradition, and varies with the times. In early antiquity it was probably understood simply as the dance of the gods; that is, the performers "became" the *kami*. Later, with the development of stronger shamanistic activity and consciousness, *kamigakari* referred to the act of divine presence in the medium; that is, the *kami* would make the shaman, or the object in the hand of the shaman, their temporary abode, and dance and speak through the shaman. This happened in ceremonies or entertainments (*asobi*) which the *kami*, through conjuration, were invited to preside over or take active part in.

Fear of revenge by restless spirits has remained a powerful presence through the centuries in Japanese society, generating an endless tradition of soul-appeasing (*tamashizume*) cere-monies (also called *chinkon-sai*). In general the preoccupation with the *tama*, the substance of which the vital element of both man and *kami* consists, is central in the performance of a *kagura*. Most *kagura* are performed either to appease a revengeful *tama*, or to prevent the *tama* from leaving the body, or to attempt to summon back the departed *tama* into the dead body, or to inject additional new life into a debilitated *tama*.[7] A Japanese scholar proposed the inter-pretation of Uzume's dance as a *chinkon-sai* performed, during the winter, in behalf of the sun, which looked as if it had lost its vitality.[8] The description as related in the *Kojiki* would reflect the form of such a ceremony as it was performed during the sixth or seventh century A.D., when it was a ritual intended to infuse new vital energies combined with shamanistic possession. The women of the Sarume clan were the official performers of the *chinkon* rites, while the *miko* were specialists in shamanistic practices. The two groups of women are supposed to have belonged to different clans, but mutual influences seem eventually to have eliminated the original differences in performance. The description of Uzume's dance would correspond to a time in which the Sarume had been already strongly influenced by the *miko*, but still kept the main function in the festival. Later the *miko* took over the functions of the Sarume, who then disappear from the records.

In the *Nihongi*, Uzume's performance is recorded as *wazaogi*, and the same name is also used for a performer. The Chinese ideograms representing this native word are still used for the common designation of an actor, though they are presently read *haiyū*. The same word *wazaogi* appears again in the *Nihongi* as applied to the myth of the two brothers Po-wori and Po-deri (also named Umi-sati-biko and Yama-sati-biko, or, more commonly, Umisachi and Yamasachi), a myth also common to the populations of the South Sea Islands.

7

Umisachi's Pantomime

Umisachi, the godly fisherman, and Yamasachi, the godly hunter, exchanged their tools for their own amusement. The experiment, however, had no success. Yamasachi lost his brother's hook, and could not find any way to placate Umisachi's anger. The desperate Yamasachi was miraculously taken to the palace of the sea-god, who most kindly regained for him the lost hook, and also gave him his daughter as wife. Later, Yamasachi received as a present the two jewels which command the ebb and the flow of the tide. Whenever Umisachi would abuse his brother, Yamasachi retaliated with sudden changes of ebb and tide. Umisachi had to give in, and became his brother's subordinate *wazaogi* (performer), dancing the pantomime of his desperate struggle against the quickly rising waters:

> Thus the elder brother knew the power of his younger brother and was about to yield his allegiance to him, but the younger brother turned his angry countenance against him and would not speak to him. At this the elder brother put on a waistcloth, rubbed red clay on his palms and on his face, and said to his younger brother: "I have defiled my body thus, I will be your mime for ever." Then he raised up his feet and stamped them in imitation of his drowning painfully. At first, when the tide covered his feet, he did the foot-divination; when it reached his thighs, he ran around; when it reached his waist, he rubbed his waist; when it reached his under-arms, he put his hands on his breast; and when it reached his neck, he raised up his hands and waved them about. From that time until now, this has never ceased.

Umisachi is the first professional actor, as distinguished from the shaman, who is mentioned in any written Japanese document. The account seems to be related, in general, to the period of struggle for supremacy among the different tribes. The Hayato clan from Kyūshū became subject to the victorious court of Yamato, the ancestors of the present imperial family. On the occasion of festivals and banquets the

8

Hayato, smeared with scarlet earth, would perform comic pantomimes of their defeat. This dance, the original *Hayato-mai*, was probably meant as a renewal of the promise of obedience to the conquerors. It may have been accompanied by a public recognition of the Yamato supremacy and by the offering of a tribute in the form of products of the land and hand made crafts.

Utagaki

The oldest Japanese sources of history and poetry testify to the existence of *utagaki* (lit. song-fence) festivals, which took place in summer, spring, and autumn. The nature of these open-air festivities is a subject of controversy, partly because they went through notable changes from the prehistoric days to forms which reveal the later influence of Buddhism. Originally the youth of neighboring villages would assemble on beautiful hillsides (such as the famous Mount Tsukuba in Ibaraki prefecture, and Kishimagatake in Hizen) and spend days and nights in singing, dancing, and sexual promiscuity, which would often end in the choice of a spouse from a different community. Some *utagaki* songs also hint at indiscriminate sexual freedom involving married people, a kind of primitive carnival without masks, such as the Saturnalia in ancient Rome. A page of the *Zoku Nihongi* narrates an *utagaki* which took place at the court of the Emperor Shōmu in 734. More than 240 people participated in a series of songs and dances in the presence of the Emperor. No mention of any sexual promiscuity is to be found in this kind of *utagaki*, which seems already to have gone a long way in the direction of today's *bon-matsuri* (Buddhist festival of the dead). Several scholars consider the present *bon-odori* (a very popular, simple dance performed by most of the people participating in the festival of the dead during the summer nights of the *bon-matsuri*) as a development of group dances common to the *utagaki*.

Several contradictory hypotheses have been advanced about the original nature and meaning of the *utagaki*. Some scholars connect them with fertility rites or with initiation ceremonies, while others stress the independence of the *utagaki* from any religious or magic practice, and consider them as an example of non-religious entertainment or as a smart political move to assimilate recently conquered neighboring tribes through marriage. Whatever the original nature and meaning might have been, there is no doubt that the *utagaki* were an important platform for the development of pre-dramatic types of performing arts.

"Indigenous" versus "Imported"

The types of performances described by the *Kojiki* and the *Nihongi*, including Uzume's magic trance, ancient *kagura*, Umisachi's pantomime of a drowning man, the group dances of the *utagaki*, the occasionally mentioned celebrations for the building of a new house, or for the funerals of a local chieftain, can be dated only approximately, reflecting conditions generally considered to have existed in the first four to five centuries A.D.; that is, during the Yayoi and Kofun periods. A strong influence of Chinese civilization, in most cases through the mediation of Korea, is commonly admitted during this time. It is highly probable that the performances described in those documents, including the shamanistic practices of trance-dances, received an essential contribution for their development from the continent as part of the great impact of the new, imported social and cultural structures.

This consideration is important because it cautions against using a division of performing arts into "indigenous" (*kagura*, *Hayato-mai*, etc.) and "imported" (*gigaku, bugaku, sangaku*, etc.). It is prudent simply to refer to the import of Buddhism as a dividing line, and consider ancient *kagura* as a pre-Buddhistic type of performance, and *gigaku* or *bugaku* as belonging to a later, newer period of Japanese culture, after the impact of the introduction of Buddhism.

The exclusion of continental influence in the *kagura* should be considered unrealistic. On the other hand, it would be a mistake to underestimate the importance of the native heritage and the originality of early developments based on conditions unique to Japan.

The new monarchic organization gave an impetus to celebrations in honor of the ruler, and such celebrations called for secularization of local dances. Many of the best performances from the different tribes were taken to the court of the victorious Yamato monarch, where they eventually lost their primitive magic meaning and went through a process of artistic refinement as an entertainment and sign of submission to the new ruler. The names of these dances are recorded, sometimes with a simple description which allows a conjecture about the type of the dance, such as warrior dance performed with swords, field dances, and hunt dances.

The change from a nomadic type of life to a stable agricultural community had as a consequence the establishment of permanent shrines and the designation of locales where the performances took place, a first step toward the building of permanent stages, out of which the later forms of the physical theatre evolved.

There is no doubt that the surviving documents cover only a small part of the extremely rich heritage of local rituals, folk entertainments, magic dances, and primitive comic sketches, which constitute a unique treasure still partially alive in an immense variety of local festivities spread throughout Japan. This inexhaustible reservoir of inspiration is the hidden stream which has nourished the surprising periodical renewals of the Japanese performing arts throughout their history to the present time.

NOTES

[1]The name Jōmon (rope pattern) is given by archeologists to the Neolithic age of Japan (approximately 8000 until 300 or 250 B.C.) because of the ropelike designs in the pottery of the epoch.

[2]The name Yayoi derives from the site called Yayoi in modern Tokyo where remains of this period were found for the first time.

[3]Tsunoda, *et al. Sources of Japanese Tradition*, 6-9.

[4]*Ibid.*, 9.

[5]Tr. by Philippi, *Kojiki*, 81. Philippi's translation is used throughout for quotations from the *Kojiki*, while the quotations from the *Nihongi* are from the translation by Aston.

[6]Tessari, "Baubo. Frammenti di un mito di fondazione dello spettacolo comico," 3-20.

[7]"*Tama* as understood by the ancient Japanese was essentially an amoral and abstract thing, a sort of life force that controlled only the physical well-being." Webber, *The Essence of Kabuki...*, 16. Origuchi Shinobu, the great scholar of folklore, argues that the difference between *kami* and man was understood by the primitive Japanese in terms of sharing a larger or smaller "quantity" of the original *tama*. ("Tama no hanashi," in *Origuchi Shinobu zenshū*, Tokyo: Chūōkōronsha, 1954, vol. III, 261).

[8]Matsumura Takeo, *Nihon shinwa no kenkyū*. Tokyo: Baifūkan, vol. III, 79-91.

CHAPTER II

KAGURA

The Word Kagura

The obscure origin of the word *kagura* has given rise to a number of theories about its etymology and original meaning. The Chinese characters used for *kagura* since the early documents of the eighth century A.D. indicate *kami* (deities) and music, and convey the meaning of music or entertainment of, or for, the gods. Those Chinese characters, however, were applied to pre-existing indigenous Japanese sounds only after the introduction into Japan of the Chinese way of writing. Evidently, the interpretation of the word cannot start from a later application of convenient Chinese characters, but must have its foundation in its earlier pronunciation. Most attempts to clarify the etymological issue illustrate some aspect of the multifaceted reality of *kagura*.

The proposed derivation of the word *kagura* from the word *kamigakari* (divine inspiration, divine possession, or the person who is possessed by the god) clearly stresses the shamanistic nature of many primitive *kagura*, their connection with trance, communication with the spirits of the dead, and possession by the deity, while the dancer becomes the speaker of the possessing *kami* to the audience.

The proposed derivation from *kamieragi* (entertainment of the gods, very similar in meaning to the already mentioned *kamiasobi*) stresses the elements of joy, laughter, and entertainment which certainly were important in many primitive *kagura*, including the type mirrored in Uzume's dance.

The most probable origin of the word *kagura* is today considered to be a euphonic contraction of *kam(u) kura* (the

13

seat of the deity, the place or abode where the spirit or power is supposed to dwell, while presiding over, or taking part in, the performance). It is speculated that the oldest form of *kagura* might have consisted in setting up a temporary *kamu kura* in the form of a sturdy pillar, invoking or summoning the ancestral deities, having a sumptuous meal with abundant rice wine, singing and dancing, and eventually dismissing the conjured spirits. Later, the pillar disappeared, and the *kami* were believed to reside in the objects held in the hand (*torimono*) of the shaman: *sakaki* tree branches, paper pendants, pine branches, bamboo, sword, halberd, willow, and bow and arrow, among others, which became the standard equipment of many *kagura*. These *torimono* are considered by many today to be the essential element of the *kagura*; that is, as the actual *kamu kura* or seat of the god, the probable origin of the name *kagura*.

Use of the Name Kagura

The name *kagura* is in common use for a variety of radically different performances to be found almost all over Japan. It is important at this point to keep in mind that the name *kagura* designates the total event, which in many cases consists of structurally different parts. The first part of many *kagura* is strictly ritualistic and concerned with the business of preparing the conditions for the presence of the *kami*. To this part belong ceremonies that have as a purpose the purification of the place (*za*) where the gods will temporarily reside (the *kamiza*, which can be a person or an object such as the *torimono*). Once the abode is ready, the *kami* is conjured and invited to take possession of it; in the purified *kamiza* the *kami* is manifested, and through this the prayer for rejuvenation and prolongation of life is supposed to have its desired result. This is the main business of *kagura*. For the performing arts this part is important, but often not the most colorful and intriguing.

Once the *kami* is present, the business of entertaining the illustrious divine guest becomes paramount. Now the *kagura* becomes the environment or occasion of performance for any entertainment the people or priests would consider appropriate to entertain the particular *kami* in attendance, and, of course also the audience. This explains the variety and changing style of *kagura* performances. While the first part has tended to remain the same through the centuries, the entertainment part could, theoretically, present anything.

In fact the entertainment part of the *kagura* has often changed through the centuries to reflect contemporary tastes and fashions. In recent times even music from the west could be found in an event still called *kagura*. In some cases, however, the entertainment part reached a point of stabilization and froze in a form which was eventually considered by the local organizers to be as essential to the festival as the first part.

There are also cases in which the ritualistic part of *kagura* eventually disappeared, and only the traditional entertainment part was left, entering the stream of folk performances in the yearly *matsuri* (festivals) of countless villages. This complex phenomenon is at the root of much confusion and many variations in the use of the name *kagura*, and of the staggering diversity of content of whatever has appeared under that name from antiquity to the present time.

While some elements in the entertainment might still reflect archetypes from the very origins of Japanese civilization, the majority depend in their origin and form on later theatrical genres like *nō*, *kyōgen* or even *kabuki*, and more modern performances, not excluding those of western origin. This capacity of *kagura* to assimilate and present the most varied forms of entertainment has prompted Frank Hoff to propose a description of *kagura* as "an occasion" or "an environment for performance" and "a system which has produced various performance types during its long life-time."[1]

The name *kagura* has been applied almost as a synonym for *minzoku geinō* (usually translated, rather misleadingly, as "folk performances"). However, following the categorizations proposed by the Japanese scholar Honda Yasuji the almost countless performances to be found in the countryside should be divided into three major categories of which *kagura* is but one.[2] Honda's division is based on the function or purpose of the performance. The purpose of *kagura* is to pray for an infusion of life-force, for the prolongation or revitalization of life. The two other categories are *dengaku* and *furyū*, which will be described in the context of the folk performances preceding the birth of *nō* and *kabuki*. The function of *dengaku* is to pray for the abundance and fertility of the fields. *Furyū* are performed to avoid pestilence; i.e., for defense from life-menacing forces.

Adding to the confusion about the use of the term *kagura* is the fact that there are folk performances in the countryside which have been inappropriately called *kagura* although they do not belong to that category. There are also performances which are strictly *kagura* but are not usually called so, and dances within a *nō* play or a sequence of *bugaku* dances that are also called *kagura* probably because their origins are in some way related to *kagura*.

Division of Kagura

The main traditional division is that into *mikagura* and *satokagura*. *Mikagura* are, generally speaking, performances inside the precincts of the imperial palace, by the court musicians (*gakunin*) of the imperial household. *Satokagura* is a term applied to those *kagura* performed outside the compound of the imperial palace. *Sato* means village; during the Heian period (794-1185), however, it also designated the area of the city outside, and in opposition to, the zone occupied by the imperial residence. Occasionally the court musicians would perform in shrines like Ise, Kasuga, and Kitano, and their performance would be called *satokagura*. Later this term became a general, common designation for every type of *kagura* including those following traditions substantially different from that of the court, and excluding only the *mikagura*.

Four fundamental types of *satokagura* can be recognized in the rich treasure of local folklore. The first is the generic *miko kagura*, originally connected with shamanistic dances performed by the maidens at the service of the shrines. The second is the *Izumo kagura*, centered around the yearly rite of changing the straw mat of the inner sanctum (*gozagae no shinji*). The third is the *Ise kagura*, focused around the peculiar rite of *yudate*, the boiling of water in a large kettle and sprinkling the congregation with it as a means of purification. The fourth is the *shishi kagura*, in which wandering priests with lion (*shishi*) masks perform for the purpose of exorcism and for the prevention of sickness; it includes *yamabushi kagura*, *bangaku*, *daikagura* etc.

Mikagura

The oldest records of *kagura* are concerned with performances at the Yamato court. It is assumed that the *mikagura* (*mi* is an honorific) originated primarily from *kagura* performed by visiting groups of neighboring clans, and not from rituals by the court priests and *miko*. The shamans of those clans would impersonate, or would be possessed by, their own gods, and convey divine good wishes to the head of the ruling Yamato clan and his gods. The form of the *mikagura*, however, was influenced by old shrine rituals aiming at either the infusion of fresh vital energy (*tamafuri*, lit. shaking of the spirit) or the appeasement of the *kami* (*tamashizume*).

The rituals for the infusion of vital energy and for the repose of the deceased eventually merged and were called *chinkon-sai*, a name originally used for the ceremony to pacify the soul of the emperor.

The present *mikagura* is traced back to the *Niiname-sai*, a harvest festival during which the *kami* were appeased through the offering of the newly harvested rice, the staple food and the source of alcoholic beverages. The rice wine made from the new crop was believed to contain the very essence of the rice-spirit, an extra dose of which would undoubtedly imbue the participants with new vitality. The extra infusion of energy was particularly needed by the new emperor when elevated to his office. This was probably the reason for a special edition of the annual festival on that occasion. Songs, music, and dances accompanied the event. The songs were related to the agricultural nature of the festival. The popular music and dance were very simple in the beginning, but they became more ceremonial and sophisticated under the influence of Chinese music and Chinese instruments. A fixed ritual, submitted to the strict etiquette and extreme formalism ruling every aspect of life at the palace, took the place of the original shamanistic possession. The original popular entertainment was reduced to a minimum, and songs with instrumental accompaniment took their place.

The first records about the *Niiname-sai* date back to the second half of the ninth century. More detailed descriptions from later documents make it possible to reconstruct with relative precision the program of the *mikagura* as they were performed at the beginning of the eleventh century. The conservatism of the courtly Shinto liturgy has preserved the *mikagura* to the present time in a form which is substantially the same, although shortened. Its parts follow:

A) Niwabi. Within the compound of the imperial palace in front of the shrine dedicated to the goddess Amaterasu (Naishidokoro, presently called Kashikodokoro) where the sacred mirror is kept, a garden fire (*niwabi*) was lit. The director of the performance (*ninjo*) first entered onto the dancing area, which was covered with straw mats and was situated in front of the fire. At the sides sat about seven musicians and fifteen or sixteen singers, divided into *motokata* (leaders, sitting on the left side of the *niwabi*) and *suikata* (followers, on the right side). The singing was performed alternatively by leaders and followers in a way which has been compared to the strophe and antistrophe of an ancient Greek choral ode.

Opposite the fire sat the *ninjo*, the director or main performer. He is considered to be the successor to god Futotama in Uzume's myth, who had the task of organizing and directing the ritual performances, and of speaking the words of conjuration and summoning. The *ninjo* role was performed by a member of the imperial guard, costumed as a noble warrior of the Heian period, with its special court hat (*kammuri*) and feather-like eye protections (*oikake*) at the sides, which had the function of keeping the dust from the warrior's eyes. The movements of the *ninjo* were already probably much as they are nowadays: slow, dignified, ritualistic. He proceeds towards the fire combining semi-circular movements forward and to the sides—a remnant of the purification dance at the beginning of a *tama shizume* ceremony; that is, of the dance which would induce divine possession. The *ninjo* carries in the hand a *sakaki* branch with a metal circlet hanging from it, a symbol of the sacred mirror.

The *kagura* songs are generally considered as having little literary value. Among them, the *niwabi* song is probably the best. It is composition of 31 syllables (*tanka*, five verses following the scheme of 5-7-5-7-7 syllables) found also in the famous collection of ancient poems, *Kokinshū* (compiled in 922):

miyama ni wa	hail seems to be falling
arare fururashi	deep amid the mountains
toyama naru	their slopes
masaki no kazura	garlands of *masaki*-tree leaves
irozuki ni keri	turning brilliant crimson

B) Achime no Waza (art of Achime). This second part is no longer preparatory, it is already the very heart of the ceremony. The leaders and members of the chorus exchange a series of "oh" sounds to summon the deities.

The interpretation of the word Achime is obscure and controversial.[3] Probably it derives from the performers of the *Azumi-kagura*, a group of dancers visiting the Yamato court from the shrine of Iwashimizu, who originated this part of the court celebration. Whatever its origin, the *Achime no waza* represents today, in a highly stylized form, a magic summoning of the gods. The drinking of sake was possibly also connected with the greeting of the divine guests, and was meant to improve the *ninjo*'s capacity for divine possession. After the drink the *ninjo*—originally in a state of trance—danced the role of the summoned *kami*.

C) Torimono *Songs*.[4] The original meaning and function of the object held in the hand of the *ninjo*, the *torimono*, has been differently interpreted: as a symbol of the offerings to the god, as a taboo, as an instrument of shamanistic transmission of messages from the dead, of supernatural manifestations of a god, or as an instrument for appeasing the souls of the dead. As already explained, there is today a consensus that the *torimono* is actually the place where the *kami* takes his temporal abode during the divine possession. The branch of the tree in the hands of the medium stands for the tree itself, which in the primitive belief was the seat of the god, or the place where it would appear. According to this theory all other *torimono*, such as spears, staffs, and the like would be later additions. Another theory worth mentioning considers the *torimono* as symbols identifying the possessing *kami*, just as in Greek mythology the trident would identify Poseidon and the *kerykeion*, or herald's staff, would indicate Hermes.

The *torimono* songs are simple compositions in the form of *tanka*, like the *niwabi*. Their present form is probably a re-elaboration, by court musicians of the eighth or ninth century, of early, sometimes even prehistoric songs. Their content is related to the *torimono* themselves: the *sakaki* or *cleyera japonica*, a glossy-leaved evergreen considered sacred in Shinto ritual; the *mitegura*, a wand laden with strips of white and colored paper, symbol of primitive offerings in nature; the *tsue*, or staff; the *sasa*, or bamboo grass; the *tsurugi* or sword; the *hoko*, or halberd; the *hisago*, or gourd; the *kazura*, or vine; etc.

D) Karakami. After the last *torimono* song came the *Karakami*, a ceremony in honor of Kara, a god of Korean origin, who at the time of the moving of the capital to Kyoto was in charge of protecting the new imperial residence. At the beginning of the Heian period (late eighth century, and probably also during the ninth century), a festival in his honor was celebrated every year. Later the cult became less and less important; the god was simply invited to the *mikagura* and the *Karakami* became practically one more *torimono* song. After the *Karakami* came a repetition of the *Achime no waza* with the magic "oh" sounds. At this point various entertainments were added—an anticipation of what later happened in the *satokagura* with the insertion of *sarugaku* performances.

E) O-saibari *and* Ko-saibari.[5] The previous steps of the *mikagura* correspond to the summoning of the gods and their taking possession of a temporary abode (*kamioroshi*, descent of the deity). The following *saibari*, on the contrary, are the musical entertainment for the gods—or of the gods as active participants in the entertainment (*kamiasobi*, entertainment of the gods).

Several theories have been advanced to explain the origin of the name *saibari*. The *saibari* are often explained as songs of the grooms. The Chinese characters, however, mean "songs to excite horses," which could imply some connections with popular horse-drivers' songs. Probably the name comes from a Chinese model, called in Japanese *saibara*, which might have served as a pattern for the verses of old, regional songs performed at court by visiting groups from subjugated clans. The *saibari* are divided into *ō-saibari* and *ko-saibari* (great and small *saibari*). The *ō-saibari* are structured according to the form of the *tanka*, the same as the *niwabi* and *torimono* songs, but diluted by numerous repetitions. The *ko-saibari* do not follow any fixed scheme and are definitely folk songs. In contrast to the *torimono* songs, which are connected with religious items, the *saibari* often have a more secular and purely entertaining content, and sometimes can even be described as love songs. They are extremely simple and devoid of any literary ambition.

F) Senzai no Hō. The *senzai no hō* is usually considered a part of the *saibari*. It deserves, however, special attention, because it seems to convey a fundamental meaning of the *mikagura*. It consists of the repetition—alternatively by the leader and members of the chorus—of single words, like *senzai* (a thousand years) or *yorozu* (ten thousand generations; i.e., in eternity), expressing good wishes for long and prosperous life. The interpretation is difficult; it seems, however, to mean the well-wishing of the invited gods to the emperor, after they have been made benevolent through the preceding entertainment.

G) Sōka *and* Hoshi. It is not possible to establish a satisfactory interpretation of these last two sections. *Sōka*, read also *haya-uta* (probably meaning quick song) has the form of a simple question-and-answer dialogue which is almost non-translatable, and which is preserved in different versions. Sometimes it reminds one of children's songs, sometimes of *sarugaku* performances. *Hoshi* were the songs which probably accompanied the dismissal of the gods (*kami-age*) in the early morning at the end of the *mikagura*.

In their present form the *mikagura* are performed every year in mid-December within the precincts of the imperial palace, in the small garden facing the sanctuary dedicated to the goddess Amaterasu. The place of the ceremony is enclosed by curtains. The *mikagura* starts at about six p.m. and ends after midnight, with an intermission, the total actual time of performance being about five and a half hours. When it gets dark the emperor arrives, and the director of the performance starts the series of the above-mentioned ceremonies. All but the last *torimono* song are no longer accompanied by dances. At the end the emperor receives from the *ninjo* through an intermediary the branch of *sakaki* empowered, because of the sacred dance, to give a fresh infusion of vital energy. The emperor is not supposed to sleep, because sleeping would make his vital element vulnerable.

Mikagura are not for the general public to see. Their unique blend of remnants of primitive magic and refined, elegant court atmosphere still preserve a character of sacred liturgy, centered in the priestly function of the imperial dynasty.

Satokagura

The term *satokagura* was originally used for the *kagura* performed by the court musicians outside the palace in the main shrines of Shinto worship. In general, such performances have followed the pattern of the *mikagura* to the present time. Later, the term *satokagura* was improperly applied also to a multifaceted, colorful variety of rituals and theatrical performances by *miko*, local Shinto priests, professional entertainers, and amateur lay people, all over the Japanese islands. The generic term *miko kagura* is related in general to *kagura* performed by *miko*, without specific relation to the content or form of the performances themselves. The division into *Ise kagura*, *Izumo kagura*, and *shishi kagura*, on the contrary, is based on traditions which present differences both of content and style of performance.

A) Miko kagura. The word *miko* is used mainly for priestesses, female shamans/mediums, and shrine maidens, but male *miko* are not rare in primitive Japanese tradition. *Miko* were chosen through sacred lot or, in some communities, because of family tradition. Some of the first rulers of primitive Japan were probably *miko*, and the principal *miko* of the great Shinto shrines have enjoyed since their foundation a very prominent social position.

It seems that originally the *miko* were supposed to be virgins, who would abandon their practice when they married. There are, however, many cases of *miko* who continued in their functions after their marriage. Besides the *miko* belonging to the shrines, there were *aruki miko* (wandering *miko*) who also would act as mediums conjuring the souls of the living and the dead, pronounce divine oracles, and pray for the faithful. A relatively high percentage of these wandering *miko* were blind. A number of *miko* became professional entertainers and prostitutes.

The importance of the *miko* for the performing arts of Japan cannot be overestimated. The beginning of several forms of later genres of theatre are connected with *miko*, as it was the case for the *shirabyōshi* and the puppets. The first *kabuki* is attributed to a wandering *miko*, the legendary Okuni.

This type of *miko*-shamaness has not completely disappeared, especially in more remote villages in the mountains. Most of today's *miko* at the service of Shinto shrines, however, are girls belonging to the families of Shinto priests. They take care of menial duties and also perform elegant, slow, dignified *kagura* dances, in which it is often hard to discover even a trace of imitation of the original trance phenomena.

The *miko kagura* had their origin in the fact that the *miko* prepared themselves to become the *kamiza* of the god (i.e., his temporary abode) through dances, as a way to purify themselves and the object in their hand in order to become worthy of divine communication.

Primitive shamanistic rituals were seminal for the origin of dance in Japan, and provide the source of the two oldest terms for dance: *mai* and *odori*. *Mai* is derived from the custom of the shamaness of circling around and around to reach a state of trance (*mau* is a contraction of *mawaru*, to rotate, to move in circular motion). *Odori* is traced back to the fact that male shamans would leap repeatedly up and down to induce the deity to possess them (*odoru* means to leap, to jump). Ancient *miko kagura* might well be the source for such fundamental dance movements as the rythmical stamping of the feet (to pacify the spirits) or lifting both hands into the air (to invite the deity to take possession); they may also be responsible for developing linear, geometrical floor patterns stressing meaningful directions, both linear and circular, from the center to the cardinal points.[6]

The dances of the *miko*, during which she would lose her personality to acquire that of the possessing supernatural power, eventually lost the shamanistic contact and became the choreographed dances still popularly known as *miko kagura*. Today's *miko kagura*, however, often follow a new choreography which, with some western influence, was established less than a century ago by Tomita Makiko, and became popular and standardized in many shrines, replacing the old imitations of trance and destroying local characteristics.

B) *The Ise Tradition.* The basic division of the *satokagura* into three groups each following a set of similar patterns; i.e., the Ise, Izumo, and *shishi* schools or traditions, is due to the life-time research work of Honda Yasuji, which was introduced to the west primarily in the writings and translations of Frank Hoff.[7] Building on the research of pioneers like Kodera Yūkichi, Origuchi Shinobu, and Nishitsunoi Masayoshi, and adding an extensive personal observation of performances in the Japanese countryside, Honda established the classification system accepted today by most scholars. He found in his field research that a group of festivals located in various prefectures all shared a central focus, the *yudate*, or ritual of boiling large cauldrons of water as an act of worship, and sprinkling the audience as a means of purification. The flowers of the boiling water; i.e., the steaming vapor, were highly esteemed because of their magical power. At the Ise shrine the rite of purification, performed by a *miko* using a tuft of grass to sprinkle the faithful during the service, was followed by a variety of performances which had the function of increasing the efficacy of the prayer. The entertainment at Ise consists of short skits played by masked actors who impersonate the half-divine old man *Okina*, the *miko*, the demons, and the comic figure.

The type and number of the performances varied with the change of taste and fashion during the historical eras, both at Ise and in other shrines which followed the same pattern. Another factor in the quality of performance was the availability or non-availability of professional troupes of varied theatrical arts. The financial situation of each shrine played an important role in determining the presence or non-presence of professional artists during the main festival. In most cases, especially in remote parts of the country or in poorer communities, the local people took over the task of presenting the entertainments, which often took the shape of an imitation of whichever type of performance was available at the time. This is the reason why some *kagura* of different traditions look like deteriorated *nō* or *kyōgen* plays—because that is exactly what they are. This is also the reason why in the entertainment part of different *kagura* traditions it is possible to find both elements that precede the *nō*, and others that derive from the *nō*. In reality, many *kagura* present a variety of entertainment forms at different stages of preservation, reflecting the time in which a certain show, or part of a show, froze into a relatively consistent form.

C) *The Izumo Tradition.* The archetype of the Izumo group is held at the Sada shrine (Shimane prefecture) every year on September 25, beginning in the evening and lasting late into the night. As the name of its central rite indicates (*gozagae no shinji*, divine service of changing the straw mat) it is focused on the event of replacing the old mat inside the sanctum of the shrine with a new one. This rite is preceded by a *torimono* dance in which the performer holds the new straw mat—dancing with the mat being a way to invite the god back to the shrine in an annual ritual of renewal. Today a specially prepared smaller mat substitutes in the dance for the actual size mat replacement.

It was probably at the beginning of the sixteenth century that the local shrine officials added performances of special religious *nō* plays to the *kagura*. These *nō* were a dramatization of the story of the shrine and of other mythological subjects. Scholars believe they see in these texts remnants of the *nō* forms which preceded the classical *nō* perfected by Zeami at the end of the fourteenth century. Today five of such remnants called *yakume nō* are performed in one evening. Originally the *nō* plays were presented by the same shrine priests who were in charge of the *kagura*; presently, however, the duty is shared by a local organization of young men.

The Izumo tradition, including both the original rites and the added *nō*, had a remarkable success and spread over most of Japan. The artistically highly demanding *nō*, in the hands of non-professionals, underwent a process of thorough change. As a result, it can be found in different places at different stages of corruption. The long songs (*utai*) of the classical *nō* were first shortened, then simply disappeared to give place to more popular songs (*uta*), or to mute pantomime, or to improvised prose. A number of performances of the Izumo tradition today are based on texts rewritten in the nineteenth century, under the influence of the Meiji effort to revitalize the myths connected with the birth of the Japanese nation and the central position of the emperor in Japanese history. An example of such effort is the *Edo kagura*. Today's repertory of *Edo kagura* consists of mythological subjects drawn in recent date from the *Kojiki* and the *Nihongi*, including victorious struggles against monsters and fabulous visits to the

25

world of the gods and the afterlife—sometimes vaguely reminiscent of the representations of hell in the medieval European mysteries, and of mythological pantomimes in Imperial Rome.

In the *Edo kagura* the influence of the *Mibu kyōgen*, the masked, mute pantomime from Kyoto,[8] determined the fact that, to this day, the performances are predominantly mime, and all the actors wear masks. It is not impossible to witness surprising novelties performed as part of the *Edo kagura*, which can range from a Spanish tango to a piece of contemporary western music.[9]

D) *The* **Shishi** *Tradition. Shishi* means lion. In ancient Japanese, however, the word designated edible wild animals, such as wild boars or deer. As a matter of fact, lions did not exist in Japan, and the "lion" mask was imported from the continent, long before any real lion was seen on Japanese soil. *Shishi* dances of various types—native deer or wild boar dances, imported lion dances, and a combination of them—are among the oldest in recorded history. They found their way into the sophisticated arts of *nō*, *kabuki* and *bunraku*, and still make up a good percentage of the folk celebrations all over Japan. While in the Ise and Izumo traditions the *kami* is temporarily manifested through the performer in a state of possession, in the *shishi* tradition the *kami* is believed to be present in the lion mask, and the function of the performers is to carry around the god present in the mask with the purpose of repelling such evils as sicknesses and fires all around the countryside.

There are two major groups of *shishi kagura*. The *daikagura*, originally from Ise, are mainly acrobatic. A greater importance must be given to the *yamabushi kagura*, which is also called *bangaku*, *gongen mai* (*gongen* is the manifestation of a god and *mai* means dance), *shishi mai* and so on.

The *yamabushi*, now reduced to a very modest number, had an important function in the cultural history of Japan. They are ascetics originally associated with some indigenous mountain worship, who used to spread their faith by moving in groups of fifteen or sixteen through the district assigned to them as a kind of parish. The *yamabushi* would perform at shrines and in the largest room of a farm house—to the delight of local farmers—their own rites of incantation, sword dances, magic with fire, and their masked plays. Some two hundred of these plays still survive. They include about ten pieces in which the *shishi* performs alone, about sixty farces (*kyōgen*), and over one hundred serious plays. Many of the latter are corruptions of *nō*, as was the case in the Ise or Izumo traditions. The plays are divided into: a) *shikimai* (ceremonial dances) including such plays as *Okina*, obviously common to the *nō* tradition; b) *onnamai* (women dances); c) *bangakumai* or *bushimai* (warrior plays—both women and warrior plays contain numerous derivations with the same title as famous *nō*, like *Miidera* and *Funa Benkei*); d) *kamimai* (god dances). As an example of older forms of *yamabushi kagura* the *onnamai nenjū* can be mentioned, it being a simple story about the miraculous rejuvenation through faith of an old couple. In this and other, higher quality plays the paramount importance of storytelling is evident. The whole performance appears more like an illustration, with masks and costumes, of the story told by the narrator, rather than the performance of a play. Even highly climactic moments are often narrated, not by the character involved nor by the chorus, but by the narrator in front of the curtain. This happens, for example, in the suicide scene of the play *Hataori* (The Weaver), in which a woman throws herself into the pond because she falsely believes that her husband has abandoned her. This characteristic position of the narrator might suggest a very old origin of some *yamabushi kagura*, pointing to a state of transition from pure storytelling to a full theatrical performance.

NOTES

[1]Hoff, *Song, Dance, Storytelling: Aspects of the Performing Arts in Japan*, 141.

[2]*Ibid.*, 142.

[3]Lombard believes that Achime derives from Uzume (*An Outline of Japanese Drama*, 38).

[4]*Ibid.*, 40-44.

[5]*Ibid.*, 45-50.

[6]Honda Yasuji, "Reflections on Dance, Its Origins, and the Value of Comparative Studies," 100.

[7]*Ibid.*, 99, and 102-104.

[8]Sieffert, "Mibu-Kyogen," 119-151.

[9]Sadler, "O-Kagura: Field Notes on the Festival Drama in Modern Tokyo," 275-300.

CHAPTER III

GIGAKU

Introduction

During a long and important period of Japanese history between the seventh and the tenth centuries *gigaku* was one of the most developed and popular performing arts in Japan. Despite its predominant position in a time of profound change, the whole phenomenon of *gigaku* would possibly have been forgotten (but for the name and one late record of a performance of the thirteenth century) were it not for the extraordinary testimony of a large number of splendid masks and a few items of costumes and props that survive. These treasures have given occasion to many scholarly speculations. Only few convincing conclusions about the origins and the essence of *gigaku* have been reached to date, and very little hope exists for any substantial improvement of our knowledge in the future.[1]

History

Buddhist religion and culture, which reached the Japanese islands in several waves during the sixth and seventh centuries, and deeply affected many aspects of Japanese life, also changed the process of evolution of the performing arts. The introduction of *gigaku* was the turning point in this process. In 562 an envoy brought back from Korea equipment belonging to *gigaku*—probably musical instruments, masks and costumes. The dance itself, however, was introduced by the first *gigaku* performer who, according to the *Nihongi*, arrived in Japan in 612: "Mimashi, a person of Kudara [in Korea],

29

arrived as an immigrant. He is said to have studied in Wu [China] and learned *gigaku*. He was given permanent residence in Sakurai, where he gathered youths and taught them *gigaku*."[2] Prince Shōtoku, the Regent whose powerful patronage played a decisive role in securing a great diffusion of the newly introduced Buddhist culture, provided for the continuity of the art. He supported Mimashi's school and preserved the imported *gigaku* props in important temples.

Under the patronage of the court, *gigaku* reached a peak of popularity during the first half of the eighth century, but disappeared from the court performances at the beginning of the ninth century, when *bugaku* took over as the official entertainment at the imperial palace. *Gigaku* continued to be performed and taught in temples far from the capital late into the fourteenth century. Serious reservations can be advanced about the conformity of these late performances with the old court *gigaku*, since it appears that in the twelfth century both music and dance rapidly decayed, and the so-called *gigaku*—at least in many cases—had become akin to the processional *gyōdō*, a ritual consisting in carrying around a Buddha statue while Buddhist monks and the faithful chant prayers. Scholars disagree about the conjectured date of *gigaku* extinction. As a matter of fact, some masked processions and primitive pantomimes preserved in remote mountain temples might be considered as a last surviving remnant of rural, deteriorated *gigaku*.

Contents and Style

No description of contents or style from the golden age of court *gigaku* is available. With the exception of a few catalogues of masks, musical instruments, and props from the eighth to the eleventh century, the only detailed document is a late record of a full program as it appears in a book written in 1223; that is, four centuries after *gigaku* had disappeared from the court and five centuries after the peak of its splendor and popularity. Because of lack of better sources, this description from the *Kyōkunshō* (Selections for Instruction and Admonition) is the point of departure for every study and speculation about the structure of a *gigaku* performance. The text itself is often difficult to understand, even in translation, because of the use of very rare names of musical keys and of obscure masked roles. An interpretation of this text, supported by the evidence of the earlier catalogues of masks and props and the knowledge of the extant masks, gives the general idea that a performance of *gigaku* started with a solemn procession, probably from the temple to some kind of stage inside the temple precincts, where the main performance of dances, pantomimes and music took place. At the end the procession would form again and go back to where it started.

A) *The Procession.* The number of people participating in the procession was, at least in the eighth century, more than forty. The leader, *Chidō*, opened the parade—a red headed mask with wide mouth, long nose, widely opened, bulging eyes, dark eyebrows, and sometimes sparse chin whiskers. His function was, like that of similar procession leaders in old India and China, to prepare and purify the air and the route from any possible evil influence. He appeared with spear in hand and sometimes he was accompanied by two assistants, who would dance and help him in purifying the route. The *Chidō* was followed by four people impersonating the lion (*shishi*) and the children who accompanied the lion (*shishi-ko*).

The similarity of a *gigaku* lion mask to a real lion is quite vague. The tiny ears, applied to the large, cylindrical mask which covers the whole head, might better belong to a cat. The jaw is movable, but a study of the structure reveals that it could open and close only through the dance movement of the whole head and not from inside. Tongue and snout are red, the teeth are white, the color of the applied hair varies, brown, red, or green. *Shishi* masks were believed to have the power of healing sicknesses and exorcizing evil spirits—in Japan probably as much as in native ancient Assyria and West Asia. Two persons manned one *shishi*. They were both covered with one large piece of cloth, or with hairy hides. The legs were covered with red trousers, the feet with straw sandals. Children, who accompanied and led the lion, are mentioned in Chinese records, and remained popular in several types of later lion dances, even in *kabuki*. The children's masks have a smiling, friendly face with large ears. The paint is dark vermillion, with white or yellow-grey teeth, and painted eyebrows. The lion with the children was followed by: two *hisashi-mochi*, probably baldachin or fan carriers, without masks; a first group of twelve musicians; a spear carrier; two

31

more *hisashi-mochi*; and eventually a second group of twenty-one musicians, all without masks. The musical instruments were the seven-holed Chinese flute, drums, which probably were carried hanging from the neck or fixed at the hips (*koshitsuzumi*), and cymbals (*dobyōshi*). Before the procession was formed the *netori*, a formal tuning of the orchestra, gave the signal for the beginning. A simple musical accompaniment in all likelihood continued through the procession and the performance.

B) *The Performance.* It is not possible to reconstruct the passage from the procession to the actual performance, or the type of stage used. Probably a provisional, elevated platform was sometimes built for the occasion; there is no proof, however, of its existence. On the contrary, there seems to be evidence that at least part of the pantomimes were performed on the flat ground in front of temple buildings.

The first number was a lion dance (*shishi-mai*). The second was a solo dance of the Kuregimi (or Go-kō, a king or nobleman from Kure; that is, from the province of Wu, around Nanking). Some authors conjecture that it parodied the demeanor of young Chinese princes. However, the documents make it uncertain whether it was a serious or comical dance. No better known is the performance of the third mentioned dancer, Kongō, who is, with Rikishi, a very popular and beloved god of the Buddhist pantheon. These are the two guardian deities who inspired numberless pieces of sculpture admired at the entrance of Buddhist temples all over Japan. It is not known whether Kongō performed alone at first, perhaps with an assistant, or whether he performed together with Rikishi. Next was Karura; that is, the ugly snake-eater Garuda, a powerful bird-god venerated in India, who performed an unidentified dance—possibly a parodistic imitation of killing and devouring a worm. This was followed by Baramon, representing a member of the highest priestly caste among the Hindus, the Brahmans. Again only conjectures are possible. His dance has been imagined as a typically Japanese parody of the holiness expected from a priest, a motive destined for great popularity in later *sarugaku, kyōgen, kabuki*, and so on.

The description of the next number, involving several roles and a certain dramatic plot, is worth reading in a text from the *Kyōkunshō*:

Next, "Konron":...In the beginning, five women
are standing in front of a lantern; two of them are
holding percussive rings, and two others are
carrying bags. Then two dancers [the Konron]
make their entrance and dance. Finally, manip-
ulating their fans and casting suggestive glances,
they simulate making love to two of the five
women. Next comes Rikishi: he makes his
entrance, clapping his hands; Kongō opens the
gate....This is called the phallus-swinging dance.
There is a representation of the five women being
made love to, and of the infidel Konron being
subjugated. They are pulled about by ropes tied to
their phalli. Rikishi tears off the phalli and swings
them about as he dances.[3]

The text presents many difficulties and there are
differences of interpretation. It is not possible to decide
whether there were really five women (*gojo*) or whether *gojo*
means simply *Kure-otome*; i.e., women from Wu, without any
specific number. Also unknown is whether the phallic dance
was performed with wooden phalli, or with symbolic phalli,
like the spear of the Rikishi. Some scholars think that the
dance of the Rikishi was originally an exorcism performed
with the spear, which subsequently fused with Buddhistic and
phallic elements. Whatever the origin, there is no doubt that
the intention of the pantomime was not at all obscene; on the
contrary, it was full of religious meaning. It is possible that
the Rikishi's victory over the lascivious non-Buddhistic
Konron had the meaning of a victory of Buddhism over non-
Buddhistic magic—the penis being the place of magic powers.
It is certainly worth considering the possible parallel with the
procession of the *phallophoroi* (phallus-carriers) in the Greek
komos and the birth of the Attic comedy, both connected with
fertility cults. For Japan *gigaku* was the cradle of a full-
fledged theatrical performance, just as the *komos* was, at least
partially, the cradle of comedy for Greece.

The masks of the women present a round face painted in
white with red cheeks and red mouth; they are probably the
most realistic among the *gigaku* masks. The Konron masks on
the contrary are very dark or black. The big bulging eyes and
the enormous mouth with jutting teeth convey a demonic

expression. Konron are interpreted as dark complectioned persons from the South Seas (*K'un-lun*). The masks for Rikishi and Kongō are very similar. Mistaken identifications are to be found even in specialized catalogues. Their rather frightening expression is meant to deter evil spirits, and not to scare the faithful. Kongō appears younger than Rikishi. He is more relaxed and less aggressive than Rikishi, as seen in the expression of their mouths.

Only speculation is possible in the following number, performed by Taikofu and the Taikoji. The only evident facts are that the masks of Taikofu generally represent an old man with a restrained, half-painful smile, and the Taikoji are, like the *shishi-ko*, children. Scholars have imagined that the two children were step-children, or orphans; that the Taikofu was actually a female role; that a visit to the temple was involved in the pantomime; that the two children would comically mock the uncertain steps of the old man, and so on.

After Taikofu follows the dance of the *Drunken King from the Land of the Western Barbarians* (*Suiko-ō*). This dance from Central Asia (the land of Hu) had plenty of movement and comic variations, and included about eight drunken retainers (*Suiko-ju*) on the stage. The mask of the king is particularly elaborate, with a very long nose and a beautiful headdress. The masks of the retainers present a much greater variety of expression—though always with the long nose of the barbarians from Hu—and there is evidence that their costumes were particularly rich and colorful.

The last number was a *bugaku* dance, the *Butokuraku*, about which almost nothing is known. It is not strange that a *bugaku* dance would end a *gigaku* performance; the same happened in China, where at the end of a *san-yüe* performance a *cheng-yüe* or a *tsu-yüe* dance would conclude the entertainment.[4]

This reconstruction of a whole program shows that *gigaku* was a compilation of several disconnected numbers, different in origin and content, without a dramatic unity. The lists of masks and equipment from the eighth to the eleventh centuries suggest a great flexibility in the number of performers and in the order of appearance—therefore also a lack of fixed rules and of any developed dramatic structure. The occasionally proposed comparison of the looser *gigaku* with the structure of Aristophanes' Old Comedy (consisting of prologue, *parodos* or entrance song of the chorus, dramatized debate between two actors and the supporting semi-choruses, *parabasis* or address of the chorus to the audience, histrionic scenes separated by brief choral odes and final exodus; that is, more or less processional exit of the chorus) does not seem to do justice to the more advanced, fixed dramatic structure of the plays, and the variety of content and invention of the great Greek comedian. On the contrary, it seems more appropriate to entertain the possibility of a comparison of the *gigaku* with the older, already mentioned processions of the *phallophoroi* (phallus-carriers), which gave birth to the chorus and the *parabasis* of the Old Comedy. Consideration of the central pantomime alone, without connection to the rest, has led some scholars to surprising, not always well documented hypotheses, to be briefly considered below in connection with the controversy about the origin of *gigaku*.

Controversy about the Origins

There is a large variety of scholarly opinions about the origin of *gigaku*. The hypothesis of a Korean origin seems to be excluded by the fact that the Korean performances showing some similarity to *gigaku*, like the mask drama called in Japanese sources *sandai-geki*, developed under the influence of the T'ang culture (A.D. 618-907), while *gigaku* belongs to the pre-T'ang era. Also, the theory that Mimashi, the person responsible for the introduction of *gigaku* into Japan, might be an Indian who brought *gigaku* directly from India or Tibet, does not seem to have any serious foundation. Recent studies prefer to locate the immediate origin in pre-T'ang China, without excluding a more remote origin in western regions.

The form of Chinese musical entertainment considered as the immediate source of *gigaku* is probably the same which gave birth, at a later time, to *sangaku* and *sarugaku*; that is, the *san-yüe*. This Chinese word designates in contemporary Chinese documents both a wide variety of "numbers" and the popular music accompanying them. The *san-yüe* included over one hundred numbers described in the sources—a parade of juggling, acrobatics, dances, songs, magical tricks, comical pantomimes, farcical sketches, parodies, clowning, wrestling, dexterity games, and the like, most of which nowadays would be found in a carnival, a circus or a night club.

According to this hypothesis, the essence of *gigaku* was not religious. In Japan the contact and association with the Buddhist temples, which eventually became its exclusive place of performance, gave *gigaku* the character of a religious procession. The wave of Chinese culture which brought *gigaku* to Japan selected out of the several elements of the original *san-yüe* only dances, music and some pantomimes, which were the elements that probably prevailed in China at the time as well. Later, when the acrobatic, magic, and juggling elements fully developed and became dominant in China, successive waves introduced them to Japan, giving birth to *sangaku*. According to this theory, therefore, *sangaku* did not develop directly from *gigaku* in Japan; rather both *gigaku* and *sangaku* had a common origin from the same *san-yüe* tradition, but at different times of contact, and from different elements of it.[5]

Whichever might be the immediate origin of *gigaku* masks and performances, several questions about their remote origin remain open. A study of the characteristics of the *gigaku* masks reveals that they represent myths and types which are certainly not Chinese. The face masks seem to be connected with the carving art of the Scythians. The head masks have occasioned many attempts to prove the existence of a bridge between the theatre of China and Japan, and the theatre of Greece and Rome, across the Near East and India. As a matter of fact, a close comparison of some *gigaku* masks with late Roman comic masks presents some striking similarities. One hypothesis sees in the episode of Konron, the women of Wu and Rikishi a transformation of a Greek myth. Hera and Iris would be the models for the women of Wu, satyrs for Konron, Heracles for Rikishi. The possibility of a long arch stretching from the Near East to Japan—traveled by nomadic populations who combined the western art of carving masks with Indian mythology and Buddhist faith—remains as intriguing and fascinating as the surprising presence of a Greek modeling of a pillar in the Hōryūji temple of Nara, or the discovery in Japan of the winged horse, possibly a Pegasus-motif, in decorative patterns contemporary to *gigaku*.[6]

Survival of Gigaku

Some of the dances and face masks which were introduced with *gigaku* were probably assimilated into the court performances and remained as part of *bugaku*, after the latter replaced *gigaku* as the official court entertainment. Some of the big head masks became in a modified form standard equipment of the *gyōdō*, the still performed and rather popular Buddhist processions. There is no doubt that the extraordinary success of the lion dance (*shishi-mai*) is a proof of the lasting influence of *gigaku* on later performing arts. The musical instruments of *gigaku* are to be found again in later *dengaku*. Moreover, it seems highly probable that the sophisticated *gigaku* masks had some influence on the *nō* masks, either directly, or indirectly, through the *gyōdō* masks and the many intermediate mask forms which were recently studied and catalogued, pertaining to pre-*nō* *sarugaku* and *dengaku*.[7]

NOTES

[1]Blau, *Sarugaku und shushi*, 68-71. See also Kleinschmidt, *Die Masken der Gigaku*, and Lucas, *Japanische Kultmasken.*

[2]Tr. Araki, *The Ballad-Drama of Medieval Japan*, 36.

[3]Tr. Araki, *ibid.*, 38. Very few minor modifications were introduced into Araki's translation to facilitate its being understood in the present context. The reading "Kuron" instead of "Konron" is preferred by some scholars.

[4]*Tsu-yüe* were Chinese folk music and folk entertainments which eventually found their way into *bugaku*. See Blau, 106. *Cheng-yüe* were originally Chinese popular songs (Blau, 101).

[5]*Ibid.*, 116.

[6]Niizeki Ryōzō, *Gekibungaku no hikaku kenkyū* (Comparative studies in dramatic literature), Tokyo: Tōkyōdō, 1964, 13 and 15.

[7]Gotō Hajime, *Nōmenshi kenkyū josetsu* (Introduction to the study of *nō* mask history), Tokyo: Meizendō Shoten.

CHAPTER IV

BUGAKU

Introduction

Theatre historians generally emphasize as extraordinary and unique features of *bugaku* both its uninterrupted survival from the eighth century to the present day, and the fact that in these court dances, aspects of performing arts from ancient India, Tibet, and China, which long ago disappeared in their native countries, can still be experienced in a meaningful way. However, if we consider the historical meaning and position of *bugaku* within the frame of development of the Japanese theatre, the often disregarded fact that *bugaku* was substantially different in its beginning from its present form seems to be of greater importance than its survival and its function as a showcase for long extinct continental performances.

During the period of introduction from T'ang China and of adaptation to Japanese taste (that is, from the eighth to the eleventh century) *bugaku* was much more theatrical, creative, and influential on later performance forms than its present frozen state or thirteenth century source materials might suggest. A high degree of freedom was characteristic of the Japanese court arts until the eleventh century, and *bugaku* was no exception. Slowly, the impulse towards change declined, giving way to the lofty forms of stylized elegance dictated by the taste of a highly ceremonial court etiquette which still exists today. This phenomenon has a parallel in poetry, where the realistic style of the *Manyōshū* from the middle of the eighth century is in sharp contrast with the formalistic elegance of the *uta-awase* poetry of the twelfth century.

39

The Words Bugaku *and* Gagaku

The Chinese character *gaku* in the composition of many Japanese entertainment terms is often translated into English as "music" (e.g., *bugaku*, dance-music; *dengaku*, field-music; *sarugaku*, monkey-music; etc.). This concept of music is not restricted to our present technical meaning of the word "music," which is rendered in Japanese as *ongaku* (lit. sound-music). It appears rather to be used in a broader sense, similar to the classical Greek concept of *mousiké*, which includes a number of performing arts. The translation "entertainment" seems therefore to be more appropriate.[1]

Bugaku is often referred to as *gagaku*, or included in *gagaku*. A clarification of terms is therefore necessary. *Gagaku* is often used as a generic term which includes both purely orchestral music (specifically designated as *kangengaku*) and music accompanied by dance (*bugaku*). For clarity, the term *gagaku* will be used in this book in referring to music, and *bugaku* in referring to dance. *Gagaku* is the classic court music which was brought to Japan from China during the eighth century. It attained its greatest popularity between the ninth and the eleventh centuries, during the Heian period. The corresponding Chinese term was pronounced *ya-yüe* ("correct" or "elegant" music) and was reserved only for the ceremonial music of official Confucian rites, as opposed to folk music (*tsu-yüe*) or barbarian music (*hu-yüe*). However, the Chinese *ya-yüe* does not correspond to the Japanese *gagaku* artistically. What was introduced to Japan by Chinese and Korean musicians, and by Japanese students coming back from Chinese centers of learning, was primarily banquet music (*engaku*) and not the "correct" music of Confucian ceremonies. Some "correct" ceremonial music did reach Japan, either directly or through the Korean court; but the repertory of *gagaku* consisted largely of pieces that would have been classified as "informal" or "barbarian," and considered ethically "perverse" according to traditional Chinese standards. The Japanese do not seem to have been seriously preoccupied with the moral implications of music, at least not as much as the Chinese. Esthetic beauty seems to have been the Japanese focal point. Consequently, the real meaning of *gagaku* in the minds of the Japanese was probably "elegant" rather than "correct" music.

A popular, though incorrect, name for *gagaku* is *shō-hichiriki* (i.e., the name of two instruments of the *gagaku* orchestra). This still seems to be the best description for making oneself understood among uneducated Japanese who are not familiar with the specialized term *gagaku*.

All the *gagaku* pieces originating before the T'ang dynasty (618-906) are called *kogaku* (ancient music). Those composed during and after the T'ang dynasty are called *shingaku* (new music). The latter include the pieces that were created in Japan according to the imported pattern. In the over twelve hundred years of *gagaku* history, a strong conservativism regarding the classical pieces has been observed. The court musicians, however, over the epochs have contributed new compositions, or arrangements of old motives, which are actually performed along with the well known pieces in *gagaku* concerts.

History of Gagaku *and* Bugaku

The arrival of Korean music in Japan is recorded as early as 453 A.D. under the names of the Korean kingdoms of origin (Shiragi, Kudara, Sankan, Koma, etc.). The music from Koma (*Komagaku*) prevailed and eventually lent its name to all music of Korean origin. The importation of Chinese music began under the Sui dynasty (589-618) and reached its peak during the early T'ang dynasty (618-906) from which it took the name *Tōgaku* (T'ang music). Tradition holds that in 736 two priests, one from India and one from Indo-China, came to Japan and introduced dances and music from their countries. *Tenjikugaku* is the music from India, *Rinyūgaku* is that from Indo-China.

The first time the word *gagaku* appeared in official Japanese documents was in 701, when the Gagakuryō was instituted. The Gagakuryō was Japan's first imperial academy of music, comprised of over 400 members, teachers and students. Many of the teachers came from China and Korea, a situation comparable to nineteenth century America, when Italians and Germans dominated the field of music. At this time, native Japanese music was not included in the Gagakuryō, but was relegated to the Outadokoro, the court school located also within the precints of the imperial palace.

During the first half of the ninth century, the retired emperor Soga and his officers reorganized the structure of the *gagaku* orchestra and its repertory. This reorganization created the bipartite division of "music of the left" (*sahō-no-gaku*) and "music of the right" (*uhō-no-gaku*). The term Tōgaku, T'ang music, prevailed for all musical compositions included in the "music of the left;" i.e., Chinese, Indian, and Japanese. The term Komagaku prevailed for all musical compositions of Korean and Manchurian origin, and the elements assimilated from *gigaku*; i.e., it became equivalent to "music of the right." In a similar way, *bugaku* is divided into "dances of the left" (*sahō-no-mai*) and "dances of right" (*uhō-no-mai*).

The origin of the division into "left" and "right" dance and music is not known. Some connection with Confucian ideals has been suggested. It probably originated in the practice of alternating the entrance to the stage from two *gakuya* (dressing rooms or tents), one situated at the right and the other at the left of the stage. "Dances of the right" are accompanied by "music of the right," and "dances of the left" by "music of the left."

The dances usually follow each other in pairs (*tsugaimai*); that is, a dance of the left follows a dance of the right, the latter being an "answer dance" (*kotaemai*). As a rule, a major piece of the left is "answered" by a major piece of the right. However, when a piece of the left is followed by another composition of the left, the music of the second work is performed in the style of the right. Probably because of this alternate rhythm, the western terms "strophic" and "antistrophic" have been used for the dances of the left and of the right, respectively.

Gagaku reached a peak of popularity at court, as an official performance and as a private pursuit of the noblemen, during the tenth century. A complicated system allowing for the co-existence of a retired and a reigning emperor provided Kyoto, the capital, with a number of smaller courts in addition to the Imperial Court. These lesser courts were filled with entertainments in the form of poetry, dance, and music. Chinese poems (*rōei*) were chanted; *gagaku* patterned folk songs (*saibara*, not to be confused with the already described *saibari* of the *kagura*) became very popular—not to mention the more lively and less *gagaku*-like banquet music (*enkyoku*) and banquet poems.

After the splendor of the aristocratic culture in Kyoto during the Heian period (794-1185), the Kamakura period

(1185-1333) followed, during which the prestige and effective power of the court aristocracy were sharply reduced. In this era, the power of the new military class, the samurai, became the decisive factor in Japanese political, social, and cultural life. Consequently, *gagaku* and *bugaku*, the musical and theatrical expression of the vanishing aristocratic supremacy, followed their patrons into the shadows of an uncertain survival. The *gagaku* orchestras were disbanded in moments of crisis, and at times it was difficult to find enough musicians for a single court performance.

It was only in the sixteenth century, during the process of reunification of the country under the great generals Toyotomi Hideyoshi and Tokugawa Ieyasu, that the samurai started to show some interest in *gagaku* and *bugaku*. Ieyasu reorganized the remaining artists into two main groups: one continuing at the imperial court in Kyoto, the other in Edo, the Shogun's headquarters. Contemporary documents show a sharp reduction in numbers; only about one-tenth of the hundreds of musicians and dancers of the Heian period remained. This situation obtained during the Tokugawa period (1600-1867).

The Meiji Restoration (1868) with its fervor for modernization and westernization, had even less interest in the traditional court music and dance. Only a few musicians and dancers have continued the tradition up to the present time. After the Second World War, the Japanese government recognized *gagaku* and *bugaku* as an important national treasure (1955). In 1960, *gagaku* and *bugaku* were performed for the first time in America, and in 1970 in Europe, leaving a deep impression abroad and thereby enhancing the relevance of such artistic forms in Japan.

Public performances in big theatres (often televised) made a first hand knowledge of these traditional arts available to millions of Japanese. *Gagaku* and *bugaku*, for some fourteen hundred years the exclusive domain of families of artists who handed down their virtuosity from father to son, have recently become objects of study and practice in Japanese universities such as the Tōkyō Geijutsu Daigaku and the Kunitachi Ongaku Daigaku. The national and international interest in *gagaku* and *bugaku*, both at the level of scholarly research and of performance, seems to be increasing, allaying any fears of the extinction of these art forms.[2]

Division of Bugaku

There are major, medium, and short *bugaku* pieces (*tai-*, *chū-*, *shō-kyoku*: literally great, medium, small compositions). The number of dancers (six for major pieces, four for medium, two or one for small) was sometimes considered as a criterion for this division. Because of the constant change since the ninth century in the number of dancers for the same piece, this criterion is no longer considered as decisive as the length and wholeness of the piece; i.e., whether it has preserved the original, entire, tripartite structure of *jo*, *ha*, *kyū*, or not. A piece still preserving its original three parts is considered major; if it has two, medium; if only one, short.

Because it became a structural pattern of every *nō* play, and of most *nō* programs, and later reappeared in *nagauta*, the heart of *kabuki* music, the importance of *jo*, *ha*, *kyū* in the history of the Japanese theatre must not be underestimated. In *gagaku*, *jo*, *ha*, *kyū* are the standard musical movements, often translated as exposition, development, and climax. Harich-Schneider defines: "*Jo* is the obligatory prelude in tempo rubato, *ha* the central movement of orchestral court music. *Kyū*, 'allegro', is the last movement."[3] This tripartite structure has to do with the tempo of *gagaku* music, which is much slower than most western music. Even the so-called "climax" or final phase is hardly quicker than the rest. A parallel with western musical movements should not be exaggerated. The three *gagaku* movements of a major piece are independent compositions, linked loosely, in a way which can be better compared to a musical suite than to the three movements of one western composition. The central part, *ha*, consists of three sections (*ha-sanjō*), a feature carried over to the *nō* (a full program of *nō* consists of one play for the *jo*, three plays for the *ha*, and one play for the *kyū*).

There are several types of *bugaku* dance:

a) *Bubu* (or *bu-no-mai*, military dances) have some connection with war, and often celebrate mythical or historical victories. Swords, spears, and shields are used as props. The dancers' costumes follow the patterns of ancient warriors' garments. The dance movements are broad and strong, and there are slow, solemn simulations of battle movements (e.g. in *Bairo*).

b) *Bunbu* (or *bun-no-mai*, "literary" or court dances) represent the majority of all *bugaku* pieces. They are not related to war; on the contrary, they illustrate the values of a peaceful culture. A typical example is *Shundeika* (Flowers in the Spring Garden), which represents four noblemen of the Heian period dancing under the cherry blossoms.

c) *Warawamai* (children dances) are performed by elaborately costumed children. A typical example is the dance *Karyōbin*, usually performed by four ten-year-old boys in female attire, wearing magnificent feathered headgear and wings on their shoulders, and carrying copper cymbals.

d) *Onnamai* (women's dances) were performed during the Heian period by women. Nowadays, insofar as they are still preserved, they are performed by masked male dancers. Examples of once-famous *onnamai* are *Shunnōten* and *Ryūkaen*. The original style of dance can hardly be reconstructed, but what is preserved seems to add a touch of feminine grace and smoothness to the otherwise manly movements.

e) *Hashirimono* (running dances) were originally full of quick movements. With their special running technique they gave birth to stylized dance movements. Examples are *Genjōraku*, *Kitoku*, *Nasori* etc. In *Genjōraku* the dance describes one of the "barbarian" people hunting snakes in the woods, and eating symbolically the killed reptile.

Historical Outline of Bugaku *Dances*

The following scheme divides the *bugaku* dances according to their origin and their corresponding musical accompaniment:
A) "Native," or more precisely, from pre-Buddhistic and pre-historic times:
1) Music: a) *kagura-uta*, b) *azuma-asobi*, c) *yamato-uta*, d) *kume-uta*, e) *ōuta*, f) *ruika*.
   With the exception of the *ruika*, which are only music without dance, the corresponding dances are:
2) Dance: a) *ninjomai*, b) *saruga-mai* and *motomego-mai*, c) *yamato-mai*, d) *kume-mai*, e) *gosechi no mai*.

B) "Imported" with Buddhist culture: from the sixth century
   A.D.:
   1) Music and dance of the left (*sahō-no-mai*, or strophic
      dances): a) from China: *Tōgaku*, b) from India:
      Tenjikugaku, c) from Indo-China: *Rin-yūgaku*.
   2) Music and dance of the right (*uhō-no-mai*, or
      antistrophic dances): a) from Korea: *Komagaku*,
      b) from Manchuria: *Bokkaigaku*.
C) Development during the Heian period:
   1) Chanted Chinese poems: *rōei*.
   2) *Gagaku*-patterned folk songs: *saibara*.
D) Later, new compositions and adaptations of old musical
   and dance patterns, e.g., for special occasions in the
   imperial house up to the present time.

Bugaku *Costumes*

The history of *bugaku* costumes is worthy of note because
it illustrates in a dramatic way the change of the visual picture
brought to the stage of Japan by the influence of imported
Chinese culture. The process started by *gigaku* was brought to
a climax by *bugaku*. The exquisite, brightly-dyed silk brocades
associated with the common image of costumes for the
Japanese theatre are not originally from Japan. The favorite
color for clothing in old, pre-Buddhist Japan seems to have
been white (mostly hemp or mulberry bark fiber, sometimes
silk). The robes of Shinto priests (*kannushi*) and of the *miko*
who performed *kagura* were, and often still are, white, or, at
least, predominantly white. No wonder, therefore, that the
silk robe of the *ninjo* (principal male dancer) in the *bugaku*
piece *Sonokoma*—an adaptation from a *kagura* dance—is
basically white, though in the stylized fashion of a dress
uniform for a Heian period warrior.

Bugaku dances of Japanese origin were generally
performed in the official uniform of the dancer's court rank,
e.g. for the *Azuma asobi*, the basic white court uniform of the
imperial guard of the Konoe (*Konoe no bukan*).[4] The
introduction of Buddhism with its colorful ceremonies and, in
general, the strong influence of continental culture during the
seventh century were responsible for the new court fashion of
vividly colored silk attire. However, these never completely

replaced the preference for white in the ritual Shinto robes. *Gigaku* already presented a magnificent display of brilliant colors which were quite a marvel for the Japanese at the time of their introduction. For example, the children who accompanied and led the lion in the lion dance, are described as costumed with a bright purple robe over a light brown, wide *hakama* (a divided skirt for man's formal wear) and a red *obi* (sash). The robe of Kongō is described as yellow, his *hakama* as indigo blue; the *obi*, as well as the stockings, red. There is no doubt that the novelty of the colorful pageantry of precious, brightly dyed, imported silk costumes, and of impressive, also very brightly painted masks and props like fans and portable canopies was one of the major reasons of the enormous success of *gigaku*.

When weaving and dyeing techniques reached a highly sophisticated level; that is, starting from the beginning of the tenth century, the complex patterns woven into the rich silk brocades of many *bugaku* costumes became fashionable at court performances. For all the dances imported from the mainland, the ordinary costumes (*tsune-shōzoku*, as distinguished from the rarely-used *betsu-shōzoku*, or "special costumes") are red for those of the left, and green for those of the right.

Most of the dances require white footgear of thickly-knitted silk, with a thin deerskin sole, and black-lacquered silk court hats.

An explanation of details of individual costumes is often problematic and open to interpretation. Original Indian, Tibetan, and Indo-Chinese motifs were first adapted to the Chinese taste of the T'ang court, and then to the Japanese taste of the Heian court. The transformation of the dances contributed to some changes in the design of the costumes, since there is evidently a strong relationship between them and the dance movements. In the military dances, because of the need to remove impediments so as to permit free use of swords, lances, and shields, sleeves were closely bound to the arms. However, in the "cultural dances" the sleeves hung loosely.

The replacement of old *bugaku* costumes is a routine duty of the Imperial Household Office. However, the extraordinary natural dyes and the exquisite brocades of the old days can hardly be matched by any new products today. As a consequence, the average quality of the *bugaku* costumes is slowly deteriorating, though some superb pieces dating back three hundred years are still in use.

Bugaku *Masks*

The characteristics distinguishing *gigaku* from *bugaku* masks are usually obvious—only a few hybrid cases are known. *Bugaku* masks are generally smaller than their *gigaku* counterparts. Most *gigaku* masks cover the whole head, while most *bugaku* masks cover only the face. A characteristic of some *bugaku* masks, which is not to be found in *gigaku*, is the separate chin, tied with strings to the jaw. This feature is also characteristic of the *Okina* masks still used in *nō*.

Both *gigaku* and *bugaku* masks were imported. They do not reflect any specifically Japanese mythological heritage. Replacements for broken, damaged, or worn out masks, or even additions in an epoch of expansion, were carved in Japan. However, according to the opinion of specialists, this highly skilled local reproduction of the continental models did not grow into the creation of new types of *bugaku* masks. Clear confirmation of this ritual sense of respect for fixed typology is provided by the fact that the *bugaku* pieces of Japanese origin never use masks. The *bugaku* masks were usually carved by professional sculptors of Buddha images (*busshi*). These sculptors signed their names on the back of the masks they made and on those they repaired. This custom was also adopted by the carvers of *nō* masks. We know the names of some famous carvers of *bugaku* masks which have been catalogued as national treasures. Most of these artists lived in the twelfth century, like Gyōmen, or in the thirteenth century, like Seiyōten and Jōkei. The art of carving *bugaku* masks is not extinct. New masks are sometimes commissioned for special occasions, although they are only replicas of fixed types.

There are two different types of masks in *bugaku*: *zōmen* and *kamen*. *Zōmen* are white rectangles (originally paper, now usually silk) with highly stylized, abstract features painted in black. Most *bugaku* masks are called *kamen* or *bugakumen*. They are traditionally divided according to their size (large, medium, and small; *tai-*, *chū-*, and *shō-men*). This division, however, is without a clear standard of measure. *Tai-men*, or large masks, cover not only the face, but also the sides of the head. They are probably the oldest *bugaku* masks, and the closest to the Chinese *gigaku*. They are used, for example, in *Senju* and *Ni-no-mai*. Examples of medium sized masks are those for *Genjōraku*, and of small masks, those used in *Kotokuraku*.

Bugaku masks usually represent supernatural beings, often animal gods from the fantastic worlds of Indian and Chinese mythology, or faces of different peoples from the Asian continent.[5] A characteristic of *bugaku* masks is that, with one or two exceptions, each mask is used for only one piece. *Nō* masks, to the contrary, are often used for several different plays.

Bugaku masks are carved in paulownia wood, covered with hemp cloth, and coated several times until the cloth hardens. The masks are eventually painted, although eyebrows, eyelashes, and beards are glued on, not painted. The old masks have lost their original hair and now only show the many holes where hair was imbedded.

Bugaku *Props*

The list of props used in *bugaku* consists mainly of the following items: spears—*ho*, some of which are about nine feet long, and *sao*, some of which are over ten feet long; swords—*tachi*, which include swords and spears of full size and weight, with elaborately ornamented scabbards and hilts; maces—*shaku*; drumsticks—*bachi, gosanbachi*; a serpent—*hebi*, about eight inches long, made in the shape of a coil; an oversized jewel—*tama*, almost four inches in diameter, painted in five colors: one type was built of earthenware, and was broken during the dance, scattering shredded paper; wings—*hane*, attached to the shoulders; stools, used by the dancers before starting some of the dances; a pitcher and an earthenware vessel—*heishi*, the pitcher of sake, a little over one foot high, and *doki*, a sake cup about six inches in diameter; cherry blossoms—*sakura no hana*, a branch of artificial flowers, about seven inches long: other artificial flowers are also used; a branch of the *sakaki* tree, in the *ninjomai* originated from the *kagura*; a straw coat and a bamboo hat—*mino* and *kasa*.

Musical Instruments

The *gagaku* orchestra featured percussion instruments, strings and winds all playing together for the first time in the history of Japanese music. The visual effect of the *gagaku* musical instruments is striking. The most decorative instruments are the two *dadaiko*, gigantic drums usually placed on separate platforms at the sides of the stage. They almost look like elaborate decorative wings framing the open stage, or sometimes, in older pictures, like a sort of backdrop.

There is no standard size for the *dadaiko*. The brightly painted, flame-like carvings, which surround the drum itself, and the sun-shaped ornaments can reach a height of over twenty feet. The total effect of the *dadaiko*, with their powerful tone, is more theatrical than musical.

The other instruments are also very colorful, especially in combination with the costumes of the musicians. There are several types of drums, including the *tsuri-daiko* (a drum suspended on a stand in front of the player), the *san-no-tsuzumi* (used for *Komagaku*), and the *kakko* (used for *Tōgaku*). These last two are horizontal drums with two deerskin heads tied by ropes. There is also a bronze gong, the *shoko*. The wooden clappers, *shakubyōshi*, are used by the chorus leader during the *gagaku* vocal pieces.

The string instruments include the *wagon* (a six-stringed zither) and the *gaku-so* (a thirteen-stringed zither), the direct predecessor of the very popular *koto*. The third string instrument is a four-stringed, pear-shaped lute with four frets, called the *biwa* or, more precisely, the *gaku-biwa*, as differentiated from the later types of *biwa*. It is played with a *bachi*, a small plectrum. The function of the *gaku-biwa* is primarily rhythmical, while the wind instruments carry the melody. The *hichiriki* is a double-reed wind instrument made of specially prepared bamboo. It has nine holes, seven on the top part and two underneath. Its sound is comparable to that of an oboe—at the time of its introduction it was the subject of controversy and sharp criticism. There are also different types of flutes, the *kagura-bue* (inherited from the *kagura*) and the *ryūteki* or *yokobue* (a seven-holed Korean flute used for *Komagaku*). The most interesting wind instrument is a mouth pipe organ, the *shō*, derived from the Chinese *sheng*, with seventeen reed pipes which are rooted in a round wind chest.

Gagaku music provides a solemn, archaic musical background for the *bugaku* dances. Its essential composition consists of one melody played simultaneously on a number of different instruments, with the effect of several voices, each individually discernible in the total sound, singing as one. A musical theme is repeated with slight variations to suggest the evolution of the universe in the limitless, cyclical flow of time.

Beneath the ancient sounds of *gagaku* music and the forceful, symmetrical movements of *bugaku* dance lies the principle of perception of and conformity to "the harmonies of the spheres." Impersonally beautiful sound and emotionally detached dance were the means through which the Japanese Imperial Court of the seventh, eighth and ninth centuries expressed its comprehension of the vast, solemn force which gives birth to all cosmic and earthly movement. *Bugaku* became a celebration of this spiritual principle and of the way in which human behavior can conform to the order and rhythm of this force.

The Bugaku *Stage*

There are several types of *bugaku* stages. The *shikibutai* (*shiku* means to spread, lay, and *butai* means stage) is a temporary stage built of Japanese cypress (*hinoki*), usually consisting of two platforms connected in the middle. It stands between seven and ten inches high on the floor of a hall, or in a garden, or on the stage of a modern theatre. The shape of the *shikibutai* is square: each side measures about eighteen feet. The two tents (*gakuya*) for the actors are set up about eighteen feet from the stage. When the *shikibutai* is built on the stage of a modern theatre, for example in the National Theatre of Tokyo, an effect as close as possible to the standard high stage (*takabutai*) of the Imperial Household is achieved through the borrowing of features actually belonging to the *takabutai*: the dance platform is covered by heavy green damask with a flower pattern, surrounded by a three foot wide strip covered with white cloth and framed by the brightly painted two foot high rail.

The standard open-air high stage (*takabutai*) is about three feet high, also square; each side measures about twenty-four feet. When it is not permanently built, it is made of four parts that can be assembled. Important features of the *takabutai* are the two stairs (each about six feet wide), one stage left for the dances of the right, the other stage right for the dances of the left. A rail, usually about two feet high, painted in bright Chinese cinnabar, beautifully frames the stage and the stairs. On top of the *takabutai*, in its central part, the already described *shikibutai* is spread, with all the features described above.

Besides the standard wooden stages, other types of *bugaku* stages are used. In Osaka, at the Shitennōji temple, there is a permanent *bugaku* stage built in stone (*ishi no butai*). When it is prepared for performances, a wooden *shikibutai* with rails is temporarily set up on top of the stone stage. In the great Kasuga shrine of Nara, during the yearly Wakamiya festival, *bugaku* is performed on a permanent turf stage (*shiba no butai*). Within the compounds of the same great shrine, *bugaku* is also performed on a surface of white sand in the *ringo no niwa*, a garden covered with carefully raked white sand. There are in addition stages on the water, and stages on boats, which were originally built for the entertainment of noble guests during pleasure excursions outside the grounds of the imperial palace.

NOTES

[1]Some sections of this chapter follow closely Ortolani, *Bugaku: The Traditional Dance of the Japanese Imperial Court.*

[2]According to Wolz, "Bugaku Today" (1983), p. 116, there are in Japan twenty-two groups that are involved in the performance of *bugaku* dance, without counting the groups dedicated only to *gagaku* music. The most important group is the Imperial Household Music Department, with a permanent staff od twenty-five members. Fifteen groups belong to such religious organizations as the Meiji shrine and the Zōjōji temple in Tokyo, the Kasuga shrine in Nara, the Itsukushima shrine on the island of Miyajima, and the Tenrikyō church in Tenri. There are also six amateur clubs located in Tokyo, Kyoto, Nara, and Osaka, the most prosperous among which employs five instructors for a total of over fifty students. Some of these clubs, and a few shrines, admit also women, who find there the only access to the practice of an art traditionally reserved for men.

[3]Harich-Schneider, *A History of Japanese Music*, 77.

[4]Blau, *Sarugaku und shushi*, 129-131, explains the origin of the Konoe-fu as an important unit of imperial guards, about four hundred men strong during the eighth century. The Konoe guards fulfilled specific functions such as escorting the emperor and serving as bodyguards. The added function of performing music and dances, and supervising their performances, became soon important. The Konoe appear often in the records concerning *gagaku* and *sangaku*.

[5]Eckardt, "Konron, Reste kontinentaler Mythologie in der japanischen Bugaku," 17-30.

CHAPTER V

THEATRICAL ARTS IN THE NINTH TO THIRTEENTH CENTURY

The Words Nō, Kyōgen, Nōgaku

The word *nō* means skill, craft, or the talent of the artist and his ability to perform. In this book it is used alone, together with other words (for example *dengaku nō*, *shugen nō*), or in combination with *gaku* to form the word *nōgaku*.

When used alone, *nō* indicates the classical form of theatre which developed within the *sarugaku* tradition starting from the second half of the fourteenth century, reached its full maturity with Zeami and Zenchiku during the fifteenth century, and continued without interruption to the present time.

The words *dengaku nō*, *sarugaku nō*, *ennen nō*, and so on, all refer to performances during the period of about two centuries preceding the appearance of the *nō* in the second half of the fourteenth century. A wide variety of shows are therefore included, from first attempts toward the formation of rather primitive plays, to fully developed, important traditions such as the *dengaku nō*, which reached heights comparable to the classical *nō* in the mid-fourteenth century.

The word *kyōgen* is usually translated "wild words" because the Chinese character for *kyō* is the same as for *kuruu*, "to go crazy," while *gen* stands for "words." There are those, however, who prefer to define *kuruu* in this case as "being totally concentrated in something." They stress the importance of the dialogue and propose the meaning of "being soaked in words." Whichever the interpretation, the word *kyōgen* has a very wide use, alone and in association with other words, and belongs to several traditions, including the *kabuki*. In the present context, *kyōgen* indicates the comical form of traditional Japanese theatre which developed parallel with the *nō* and is still performed mainly between the plays on a typical *nō* program.

Nōgaku is an increasingly accepted word which conveniently indicates both the classical *nō* and the *kyōgen* as two facets of one tradition.

This book's use of these terms is largely arbitrary, because in the original texts and in the various scholarly studies there is a wide variety of confusing usages. For example, in the texts of the secret tradition of the *nō* Zeami refers to his art as simply *sarugaku*, and it was common to hear the word *sarugaku* used by *nō* artists to refer to their art until recently.[1]

The Sangaku *and* Sarugaku *Traditions*

When dealing with the wide variety of folk performing arts of the *sangaku* and *sarugaku* traditions during the centuries that precede the formation of the classical *nō* and *kyōgen*, many historians stress their unassuming characteristics as folk entertainment and their primary importance as theatrical traditions that gave birth to *nōgaku*. There is a danger, however, of forgetting that the multifaceted *sangaku* and *sarugaku* entertainments probably represented what was the most vigorous, colorful, and creative theatrical activity during the era of the highest courtly splendor in Japanese history, the Heian period (794-1192),[2] and during the Kamakura period (1192-1333) when there was a surge of new artistic vitality in the provinces.

Sangaku and *sarugaku* certainly deserve a close look in themselves, independently from those forms to which they eventually gave rise. Moreover, *sangaku* and *sarugaku* should not be considered merely as folk entertainment. During the Heian period, variety acts of the *sangaku* and *sarugaku* folk tradition were viewed at the imperial court as a standard part of a program of formal entertainment (*shikigaku*) performed by the same court musicians and dancers who regularly performed *gagaku* and *bugaku* as their main occupation. The

Shinzei-kogaku-zu (Shinzei's Illustrations of Ancient Music, the oldest main source of illustrations for courtly entertainments—mainly of the early Heian period—contains fascinating sketches of both *bugaku* and *sarugaku* numbers.

The Words Sangaku *and* Sarugaku

Several translations have been proposed for the term *sangaku*: "scattered music," "unofficial entertainment," "miscellaneous performances," and so on. *Sarugaku*, on the contrary, is usually translated as "monkey music" or "monkey entertainment."

The word *sangaku* is a Japanese pronunciation of the ideograms for the Chinese *san-yüe* (also transliterated as *san-yüo*), from which it derived both contents and name. *San-yüe*, as already briefly mentioned in the passage on the origin of *gigaku*, was a generic designation for all popular entertainments which did not belong to the canon of the "officially" recognized state entertainments. The Chinese character *san* was widely used in several instances to designate anything unofficial, non-ritualized, and belonging to the villages rather than to the capital and/or court. Combined with the character *yüe* (for "entertainment," "music," or "performance") it became the current name for all non-official shows, which comprised four major groups. The first group, based on physical dexterity, included a variety of acrobatics, juggling, wrestling, games with balls, racing, and dextrous acts of all kinds—a tradition which is still alive, at least partially, in much admired contemporary Chinese companies of gymnasts and acrobats. The second group was based on magic, and comprised a rich repertory of conjurations, adaptations of rituals which promised eternity or long life, illusionists' tricks, miracle cures, imitations of shamanistic possessions, adaptations of Taoist magic, and demonstrations of the wonders of Buddhist miracles; these last primitive demonstrations might well have been an important element for a later development of dramatic pieces similar to the medieval European miracle plays. The third group was based on dance and music, and included a great variety of folk dances, songs, and music accompanied or unaccompanied by some kind of performance: almost any piece of dance or music that did not have the seal of approval as officially recognized state music was automatically classified under *san-yüe*. The fourth group included a number of comical performances based on pantomime, disguise, farcical exaggeration, and short dialogue; it contained therefore the seed of simple dramatic sketches.

The history of Chinese *san-yüe* is long and complex. Influences from various regions of the empire and from the outside "barbarians" played an important role in the changes of fashion and prevalence of different types of entertainments during many centuries. What we must keep in mind is that this enormously rich popular tradition did find its way to Japan in different waves, giving birth to and periodically influencing the development of its Japanized version; i.e., *sangaku*.

Concerning the word *sarugaku*, which appears to have taken over the functions of the word *sangaku* around the end of the tenth and the beginning of the eleventh centuries, many interpretations about its origin and meaning exist.

The sound of the word is commonly explained as a change in pronounciation from *san(u)* to *saru*. More controversial are the interpretations of why the character for monkey was used to write the new word. Some Japanese scholars interpret it as a recognition of a profound change in the contents of the art: the comical-pantomimic, monkey-like Japanese element of imitation (exemplified by the myth of Umisachi and embodied by the concept of *monomane*) had become so important by the end of the tenth century that it justified the use of the character for monkey in writing the word. Some scholars have seen the source of the pronunciation of *saru* in *zaregoto* (joke). Others find plausible its derivation from a *sangaku* number that became so popular that it gave its name to the genre. In this number, either a real monkey, or an actor disguised as a monkey, would jump through a ring with music accompaniment. Others have noticed that some *sangaku* numbers involving monkeys and frogs (or actors disguised as such) were absorbed into *bugaku* at an early stage of the adaptation of that form to Japanese taste; a rejection of the primitive pantomime of monkeys occurred in *bugaku*, where these pieces remained only as music, while the popular monkey entertainment, called *sarugaku*, moved from *bugaku* to *sangaku*, becoming very successful and probably influencing the change in the genre's name.

Relation between Sangaku *and* Sarugaku

An important breakthrough in the complex problem of the relationship between *sangaku* and *sarugaku* is to be found in the research by Gotō Hajime.[3] Gotō has compiled extensive data providing a new insight into the real meaning assigned to performance terms at different times and under different circumstances, thereby clarifying the rather confused understanding of the relationship of *sangaku* to *sarugaku*. He noticed that most conclusions drawn by his predecessors were based on data collected primarily in the capital and the major centers of worship, where the records were better kept and more available; such conclusions had been simply and arbitrarily extended to the general condition of the arts in the provinces as well. Gotō decided to search for data in the provinces and spent decades in field research, collecting every possible clue concerning popular entertainment in minor temples and shrines all over Japan. His work is aimed primarily at establishing the origins of the *nō*, but of course his research goes over the sources of *sangaku* and *sarugaku*, their relationship, and the general state of the performing arts in Japan before the *nō*.

According to Gotō, the two major antecedents of the *nō* are the traditions of *sangaku* and that of *wazaogi*, or comic pantomime. Gotō finds that during the Heian period, a shift occurred in *sangaku* from a concentration on circus-like spectacle to a focus on the art of *monomane* (mimesis, imitation). This meant a shift from physical to mimetic skills, from acrobatics to what at the time was perceived as "realistic" acting. In Japanese terms, it was a triumph of the "indigenous" genius for *wazaogi* over the "imported" skills. *Sangaku* of the Heian epoch was performed in two very different sets of circumstances. As a popular, informal entertainment, it was presented primarily in small shrines and temples. As part of the courtly, formal *shikigaku* (ceremonial music, consisting mainly of *gagaku* music and *bugaku* dances), it was performed at court and in a few major centers of worship. A differentiation in name was therefore felt to be needed for record-keeping purposes. While the term *sangaku* was retained to designate the popular entertainment, the new term *sarugaku* was frequently applied to the ceremonial performances. This distinction primarily indicated a difference of place and circumstances, rather than of content, for the latter remained basically the same. This record-keeping differentiation of terms was not always carried out with uniformity, and there is understandable confusion between the two terms *sangaku* and *sarugaku* in many sources of the Heian period.

The ceremonial *sarugaku*, performed by the conservative court musicians who also performed *bugaku*, was more formal and reflected the imported Chinese contents. On the other hand, the informal *sangaku* of the countryside freely displayed the native comic elements, and developed original Japanese realistic contents in the style of *monomane*.

With the collapse of the political hegemony of the Heian court nobility at the start of the Kamakura period (1192-1333), the ceremonial *sarugaku* eventually ceased to be performed. In the meantime, under the new *samurai* administration centered in the capital city of Kamakura, festivals and services at smaller shrines and temples—and with them, *sangaku*—became very popular in all provinces. Gotō shows that *sarugaku* performers, who had lost the protection of the court and still wanted to avoid the hard labor in the fields and high taxes, formed groups of professional performers called *hōshibara* who donned the habit and wore the haircut of monks, but in reality did not belong to any monastery or temple; the habit and the exterior religious appearance were their way to escape high taxes and conscripted labor in the fields. They became responsible for the enormous increase in popularity of *sangaku* outside the capital and the main, official places of worship. For money, the *hōshibara* would perform anything, including religious services for the dead. Real monks did not have a family, but the gypsy-like *hōshibara* did have wives and children. Their deceit was not unknown to the authorities, who kept a suspicious attitude towards these vagrants. The *hōshibara* specialized in tricks, acrobatics, magic, and comic *monomane*. They performed for popular religious services and festivals held primarily at minor shrines and temples in all parts of the country. Court officials of the Konoe imperial guard, which was in charge of ceremonial music, had always looked condescendingly at performances of *sangaku* and *sarugaku*, even at court and major religious institutions. They considered them merely peripheral, miscellaneous entertainment, added but not really belonging to what they considered to be the real thing. Their interest and esteem remained concentrated in *gagaku* music and *bugaku* dance. Thus, the spectacular development of *sangaku* in the Kamakura period was surely an accomplishment of the low-class *sangaku* performers in the provinces, and not of court officials in the capital. For these reasons, Gotō greatly emphasizes the previously neglected records from the provinces and smaller centers of worship.

Concurrent with the remarkable growth in popularity of *sangaku* outside the capital, the outcaste performers sought to improve gradually their social position by linking their art with the life of the populace—the obvious purpose being to increase and strengthen their hold on the patronage of provincial audiences. They found that link in popular religious beliefs. Gotō is convinced, on the base of his findings, that in this endeavior *sangaku* performers greatly developed their special *monomane* acting skill. The introduction of masks, a means for the concrete representation of gods and various spirits, is adequately explained through this theory. *Sangaku* gradually changed into a masked drama during the thirteenth and fourteenth centuries; that is, during the Kamakura period (1192-1333) and the period of the Northern and Southern Dynasties (1333-1392).

During the Kamakura period, the term *sangaku* slowly disappeared from written records, perhaps because the term *sarugaku* seemed more dignified, especially when *saru* was written with the divine, rather than the animal character for monkey. The name change was part of a complex pattern of social climbing by the outcaste *hōshibara*. They began actively to pursue the acquisition of rights and rank, to glorify their presumed ancestors and "discover" family connections with illustrious priestly performers, to call their occupation a divine service, and to consider themselves Shinto priests and their art a form of *kagura* (which traditionally had been performed by Shinto clergy). Gotō thinks that this long-range effort eventually won them acceptance by the populace, who previously would have objected to outcastes daring to assume the status of Shinto priests and *yamabushi* (mountain ascetics), or to assume in masked performances the features of the actual objects of worship, local gods and spirits. Gotō favors the opinion that the very term *hōshibara* might be related not only to their exemption from taxes and conscripted labor, but also to some religious meaning. In conclusion, the gradual disappearance of the term *sangaku* would be a result of the success of the performers, who would have sought to make the public forget their outcaste origin. The use of the term *sarugaku* would be part of the successful change of public image eventually achieved by the *sarugaku* actors on their way toward becoming the lofty performers of *nō* at the court of the Shogun.[4]

An important confirmation of Gotō's interpretation of the process of social climbing through the claim of divine origin and direct descendance from illustrious ancestors is to be found in the writings of Zeami, the founder of the *nō*. In the fourth chapter of the *Fūshi-kaden* he writes that the origin of *sarugaku* should be found in the dance of Uzume and in *kagura*. Besides claiming an origin from the Shinto goddess Uzume he also establishes a sacred connection with the Buddha himself, stating that the Indian dances that evolved into *sarugaku* were performed at the suggestion of Gautama Buddha during his lifetime. A very illustrious, less remote ancestor is also claimed, Hata no Kōkatsu. During the reign of Emperor Kimmei (540-571), Kōkatsu, an infant of gentle features and "gem-like" appearance, was found floating in a vase on the river Hatsuse. Kōkatsu appeared in a dream to the Emperor, announcing his supernatural origin and mission. During his life at the imperial court he achieved the highest accomplishments in the art of *sarugaku*. Eventually, his transformation into a divine being completed his process of deification as the sacred person who "handed over to his descendants this art of *sarugaku*."[5] An even higher and more metaphysical root of the *nō* is claimed in the later scripts of Zeami; that is, the very sacred reality of the Buddha-nature, or *a priori* pure essence (*shō*)—in opposition to the deceptive superficiality of the illusory world.[6]

Zeami's testimony was not directed to the wide public, because his treatises were jealously kept within an extremely restricted family circle. It shows, however, the continuous effort to claim ties with the highly respected religious past of the Japanese performing arts, and to build up the personal pride of the future generations of *nō* actors. Zeami's treatises prove that already at his time a near-abyss separates his proud, priest-like consciousness from the low reality of the despised *sarugaku* oucastes of a few generations before his time. It is reasonable therefore to accept Gotō's theory, that such transformation was the result of a successful effort of social climbing through persistent promotion of religious claims on the part of the *sarugaku* performers over several generations.

Heian Shin Sarugaku *in Performance*

The standard Japanese source for the content of *sarugaku* in the Heian period is the work *Shin sarugaku ki* (Account of the New Sarugaku) by the famous scholar Fujiwara no Akihira, who died at seventy-eight in 1066. Akihira's testimony is especially remarkable if we consider that he had been the tutor of two crown princes and head of higher education at court in a time of courtly splendor. His high praise for the *sarugaku* performers demonstrates that the actors involved had reached a sophisticated degree of skill, and that the total set-up of the festival was of excellent quality.

Akihira left a number of important writings encompassing poetry, prose, history, and correspondence. His interest in events and people outside the court environment distinguishes his contribution from that of other scholars of the time who concentrated on recording the events inside the imperial palace. The *Shin sarugaku ki* reflects Akihira's interest in the common man, as it describes performances in the outskirts of Kyoto during a festival geared to the entertainment of a general audience. Akihira provides a list of about twenty-eight numbers which made up the entertainment for the event—the best he had seen in twenty years. The twenty-eight pieces can be divided into four groups.[7]

The first group comprises pieces that do not belong exclusively to the *sangaku-sarugaku* tradition, but are shared with other traditions such as *dengaku* and the puppets. Four pieces are assigned to this group, one based on witchcraft, a dance of a dwarf, a *dengaku* dance and song connected with rice-planting rituals, and a *kugutsu* dance involving puppets.

The second group comprises acrobatics and conjuring arts belonging to the old *sangaku* tradition, also four in number: unspecified tricks from the China of the T'ang dynasty, a ball and pebbles dexterity game similar to the children's game of jacks, diabolo, and juggling with eight balls.

The third group comprises one-man pieces of mimicry and lion dances: a solo imitation of a wrestling match, a solo imitation of a backgammon game, and two different lion dances.

The fourth group comprises pieces which better illustrate the transformation of *sarugaku* in the direction of drama; that is, the increasing importance given to the dramatic elements and, in general, to the mimetic process. The main subjects of the sixteen numbers listed by Akihira and grouped by Inoura under the description of "dramatic sketches" are as follows:[8] four are concerned with parodying petty civil servants or important local magistrates, in such ways as by exaggerating their gait and posture, exposing humorous or grotesque movements, revealing unexpected and therefore funny traits, or performing an impersonation of an old man in a dance; five have to do with a parody of people of a religious or quasi-religious status, such as Buddhist monks, a nun, and a professional wisher of good fortune. They are caught in moments that are incongruous with their vocation, such as the supposedly chaste, but actually pregnant, nun seeking a gift of swaddling clothes for her soon-to-be-born baby, a young shrine maiden (*miko*) behaving coquettishly like a prostitute, a revered monk coveting a beautiful stole, and, in another sketch, tucking up his trousers and running away in consternation because of a fright; two are parodies of the behavior of women, such as an older woman blushing like a young girl, and a high-ranking court-lady absentmindedly exposing her face which was supposed to be covered by a veil; four are related to the humorous imitation of men in various situations, such as a glutton who has overeaten and strikes his belly thereby moving his breast bones, a city fellow who enjoys off-color jokes, and the typical hick from the country who does not know how to behave in the big city.

Many of the above mentioned dramatic sketches were enriched with a variety of prologues, dialogues, songs, and dances—probably to the point where they resembled short, mostly farcical, plays. Such "plays" are considered by scholars as important steps in the process of transition to such sophisticated art forms as the *kyōgen* and the *nō*, which developed about three centuries later.

The transition from the eleventh century *shin sarugaku* to the fully developed plays of the *nōgaku* tradition of the fourteenth and fifteenth centuries remains, however, a rather obscure and poorly documented process. It developed during the period of almost three centuries that divide the activities of the type described by Akihira from the mature *nōgaku* masterpieces of Zeami and Zenchiku's time. At this point, historians of the Japanese theatre introduce inconclusive evidence about theatrical activities which cannot be properly identified, including few documents about plays developed at court, in the temples and shrines, and among the common people. Such evidence is meant to fill in some measure the gap, or, at least, to illustrate the theatrical culture medium out of which the unique masterpieces of *nōgaku* were born.

The Shushi Sarugaku

An important form of activity of many Buddhist temples was the practice of exorcism, which also provided one of the major sources of income. It is therefore no wonder that a number of illustrative plays about the content of the incantations and about the stories connected with the sacred places of worship should develop. It is recognized by recent authors that the Buddhist temples, and, to a lesser degree, the Shinto shrines, took the place of the imperial court as the primary centers of performing arts development during the second half of the Heian period—a function that also continued through the Kamakura period. It is also generally admitted that at those places of worship various forms of popular art were performed, not only on the occasion of festivals, but also as rituals that were repeated at the request of the faithful. The exorcisms and the simple plays representing the effects of the rituals were actually performed by clergy or other employees of the temple belonging to various levels of the complex hierarchy in the religious community. It is very difficult to determine clearly who was responsible for what, and what performance actually corresponded to the various names mentioned in the records, because of the changing hierarchical organization of the great temples and shrines and the fluctuating functions of each category of people at the service of temples and shrines.

A typical example of the above difficulty is the case of the *shushi* (or *jushi*, or *noronji*, or *zushi*, or *sushi*). Scholarly opinions on the value of their art and the importance of their contribution are at considerable variance. They range from a totally negative judgment to enthusiastic praise for their originality and greatness and their essential importance as the missing link between *shin sarugaku* and *nōgaku*.[9] The very fact that scholars cannot establish the correct reading of their name is indicative of the uncertainty surrounding the *shushi*.[10]

The name *shushi* means magician, master of conjuration and exorcism, and there is no doubt that *shushi* were involved, at least at the beginning of their existence, in the practice of sorcery, exorcism and incantation at temples and shrines. Some scholars see a relation of derivation or identification between *shushi* and *jukonshi*, who were very popular in the Nara period, especially in the eighth century, as practioners of geomancy and magic imported from the continent. According to these scholars, the *jukonshi* slowly lost their popularity and influence, and tried to gain back the favor of the people by becoming performers of *sarugaku*. Others see in the *shushi* the descendants of the practitioners of that part of *san-yüe* which specialized in divination and magical acts.

Most scholars today accept the theory of Nose, which considers the *shushi* as deriving from temple servants, the *hō-shushi*, who had the task of performing a number of ceremonies of exorcism, divination, and magic popular at the time among the faithful of the major Buddhist sects. Later on, the *sarugaku* actors who resided in special villages close to the temple substituted, according to this theory, for the *shushi* in many of their functions, adding a theatrical professionalism to the performance of their practices. These scholars give the name of *shushi sarugaku* to the fusion of *shushi* exorcism practices and *sarugaku* theatrical imagination.[11]

In general, the contribution of the *shushi* is singled out by many scholars in their effort to find a source for the serious nature of the *nō* plays, which reached their high point with the great masters of the *sarugaku* tradition in the second half of the fourteenth century.

The comical element of *sarugaku* represents no problem, because there is a tradition of continuity in the comical *sarugaku*. The always serious, lofty, sometimes tragic *nō* plays, on the contrary, do not seem to find in the *sarugaku* tradition a sufficient background. Hence the effort to assign the position of "the missing link" to the tradition of the *shushi*, and therefore to stress their importance as illustrators of solemn, mysterious practices of exorcism and of sacred legends related to the temples.

Some documents, however, seem to contradict the above hypothesis that the *shushi* shows were mysterious and solemn (i.e., a suitable antecedent of the *nō*) in contrast to the comical, acrobatic *sarugaku* performances (that is, the suitable antecedent of *kyōgen*). In the twelfth century *shushi* performances were forbidden in time of official mourning, when other comical and profane shows were suspended, while sacred and solemn performances were especially prescribed.[12] It seems therefore that *shushi* performances were considered as non-sacred by the authorities.

The debate does not reach, unfortunately, any final conclusion. We are left with a few definite elements of the *shushi* theatrical presence, such as their splendid costumes, the favor they enjoyed with a very sophisticated court audience, the use of a chorus and the same stage as the *sarugaku* performers, and, in general, a close relationship with the *sarugaku* performers. To a more or less justified speculation belong the theories that the *shushi* actually developed plays illustrating religious traditions, such as the effects of the exorcisms they practiced, and that their performances reached high degrees of skill, thus preparing the way for both the religious content of the *nō* plays and the sophistication of their performance. It also seems probable that some *shushi* actually joined *sarugaku* troupes.

Whatever might have been the contribution of the *shushi* and their relationship to the *sarugaku* professionals, it is safe to acknowledge that a vigorous tradition of performances of various kinds developed under the patronage of temples and shrines. Among these performances the representation of some form of plays based on Buddhist traditions certainly occurred, not only in the simple form of puppet-shows, but also in live performances by people in the service of the temples. These performances can be safely considered as one of the logical antecedents of the great development of *sarugaku nō* which led to the formation of the *nōgaku* tradition.

The Okina Sarugaku

The historical period which precedes the appearance of *nōgaku*, especially the thirteenth century and the first half of the fourteenth, has been the object of research by several Japanese scholars; unfortunately, there has been thus far no satisfactory conclusion proving continuity between the performances by the *shushi*, the various forms of *sarugaku* and *dengaku*, and the birth of *nō* and *kyōgen*.

Many historians introduce at this point the performances of *Okina sarugaku* as a possible bridge between the shows by the *shushi* and the *nō*. Okina has a long history in the performing arts of Japan, and belongs to several traditions, from *kagura* to *dengaku*, *sarugaku*, *kabuki*, and the puppets. It is still performed as an important ceremony in the *nōgaku* tradition and in many *minzoku geinō* (popular performing arts), at the beginning of the year and at the opening of important events. Depending on the connection with popular performances in the rice-fields, or at shrine festivals, or in temple celebrations, the interpretation of the meaning of roles in the *Okina* play varies from Shinto *kami* to sophisticated Buddhist personifications. In the Shinto tradition the roles of Senzai, Okina, and Samba are interpreted as *kami* bestowing long life, fertility to the fields and animals, and peace and prosperity to the land. Some scholars explain Okina as a derivation from the *ta-aruji*, the local *kami* of the field who would be invited as principal guest to the celebrations of rice-field dances. The three principal roles, which in the popular tradition assume the meaning of the *kami* of longevity, fertility of the fields, and of the womb, also have been identified with three powerful gods of the Japanese pantheon, Hachiman, Amaterasu, and Kasuga.

In the case of the *Okina sarugaku*, according to the oldest source (dated by some scholars around 1280), the intent of the *Okina* play would be that of illustrating the depth of the Buddha's law. Senzai would represent the Buddha, Okina would stand for Monju (Manjusri, the Bodhisattva of wisdom) and Samba for Miroku (Maitreya, the Bodhisattva of mercy). Should this document and its interpretation be authentic, the *Okina sarugaku* would have been born in a completely Buddhistic tradition, as an invention of Buddhist monks of the Kōfukuji temple in Nara. According to Honda's speculation, the *shushi* were chosen from among the temple servants to be the performers of this new ceremonial show. A strict connection between *shushi* and *Okina sarugaku* seems beyond any doubt to have existed, since the Okina dance was still described as *shushi hashiri* (*shushi* dances) in the fourteenth and fifteenth centuries. Scholars argue that the surviving *shushi* who eventually joined groups of *sarugaku* actors brought with them the tradition of representing *Okina* and that therefore the *sarugaku* actors became the legitimate heirs as performers of the *Okina*.

The characteristic Okina masks featuring an enigmatic, timeless smile, in the three variations of *chichi no jo* for the Senzai role, *Okina* for the Okina role, and *kokushiki* for the Samba role have survived with almost no important variations at least seven centuries, and are still used all over Japan for countless Okina performances in the *nōgaku* and *minzoku geinō* traditions.

A feature of the Okina performances has struck the curiosity of scholars. Words are sung which apparently have no meaning, at least in their present form, and resist any definitive explanation. Some scholars believe they are a corruption of ancient ritual formulae spoken in a language—perhaps Tibetan—which, being unknown to the users, gradually lost even a resemblance to the original pronunciation. Other scholars suppose that the magic formulae for exorcism might have been meaningless from the very beginning, or that they were just sounds which became part of the instrumentation; that is, something like the *kakegoe* of the *nō*.

Some important influences of *bugaku* on the *Okina sarugaku* are the *jo, ha, kyū* structure, which became essential also to the *nō*, and the fact that the *Okina* masks are closer to some *bugaku* masks in the method of construction and type represented than to the later *nō* masks. This influence might have been direct, or filtered through the *shushi*, or through *dengaku*.

The historical importance of *Okina sarugaku* is certainly great. For the first time in the history of Japanese theatre we encounter a type of performance which unites a dramatic structure of a religious nature accompanied by a mimetic illustrative dance with a chorus and instrumental music—the whole a result of the direct evolution of the theatrical forms of the Heian period—preserved in its essentials to the present time and actively alive in the repertory of the *nō*.

The Furyū *Tradition*

Echoes of the deep transformation that was happening outside the court in the *sarugaku* and other traditions are reflected in records and diaries of courtiers. The occasion is often the detailed description of poetical competitions and other entertainments in which the nobility used to spend a large amount of time. The losers' punishment consisted in their having to entertain the winners by the performance of miscellaneous arts. The description by noblemen of such punishments therefore becomes an important source of learning what was then so generally well known that it could be expected to be performed impromptu by anybody participating in the competitions. From the sources it is clear that scenes from the then developing *sarugaku nō* were among the penances inflicted on the losers, along with favorite songs and dances from various folk traditions such as *furyū* and *dengaku*. Imitations by noblemen of the fashionable popular performing arts were also usual as informal entertainment during relaxed drinking parties and during rehearsals for the formal entertainments of the important yearly court festivities.

The twelfth-century play *Honjo no monjaku* (Inquest in the court of the local governor), performed for an official messenger of the Emperor on his visit to Nara, has reached us in a detailed description, which allows a reconstruction of its remarkably developed technique of suspense and social satire. The six-character play was elegantly performed by professional *bugaku* dancers with the suprise element of the participation also of the real local magistrate in the role of himself. The locale of the play is the police station and the whole action happens there, in one act, during which the magistrate and the chief of police enter, introduce themselves, take their place; they are followed by the thief who is brought in by the two assistants to the chief of police; an interrogatory follows, during which the thief pleads not guilty; the wife is brought in to testify, but she pleads ignorance and refers the judges to her husband; eventually the thief is submitted to torture, and he reveals the amazing fact that both the former governor and the magistrate know very well where the stolen property is.

The play belongs to the *furyū* tradition,[13] which, during its long history, has given to Japan a number of entertainments, especially those in the form of colorful group dancing and parades in luxurious costumes.

The *furyū* tradition as it is still practiced in the guise of *minzoku geinō* is characterized by performances whose purpose is to avert pestilence (as distinguished from the *dengaku* performances, which function as prayers for the abundance of the grain crop, and from *kagura*, which seek to prolong and revitalize man's life). The wild dancing and the bright costume colors are used to attract the harmful spirits of disease, and the gaudily decorated poles, umbrellas and hats are believed to become the place were the spirits are collected and drawn out of the village.

In general, the term *furyū* was applied to spectacular parades and group dancing in fancy-dress processions that became very popular at the end of the Heian and during the Kamakura period. This tradition also developed plays such as the one described above, in fancy dress, accompanied by music, which were remarkable for their dramatic nature with a relatively long dialogue and a variety of contents.

The Ennen *Tradition*

The development of plays presenting some characteristics of the *nō* structure first took place, according to some scholars, within the tradition of the *ennen* performances. The name *ennen*, originally indicating prayers for longevity, came to be used for banquets honoring the guests of the temple or the shrine after the services. It became customary to add some elements of entertainment to the banquet. In time, the banquets disappeared, while the performance element grew with the addition of numbers borrowed from the then popular *geinō* (folk performing arts). It is therefore no wonder to find in the programs of *ennen* celebrations the mention of performing arts as varied as children's dances (*warabemai*), *gagaku* music, songs of the *imayō*, *rōei*, and *ko-uta* type, *shirabyōshi* dances, *dengaku*, *sarugaku*, and the like.

When scholars refer to *ennen nō* they refer to a

development within the performances of *ennen* parallel or, in some cases, similar to that of the *dengaku nō* and *sarugaku nō*. In effect it is a phenomenon that evolves within the various traditions at approximately the same time; that is, the development of the mimetic element in the introduction of a more complicated plot. We may view this as beginning what might be considered the formation of "plays" in opposition to the usual ancient "sketches." As a matter of fact, some of the most important documents of this phenomenon that have reached us belong to the *ennen* tradition, and testify to a lively creativity of the performers in the service of the temples. Some scholars think that the *sarugaku* and *dengaku* professionals learned from the *ennen* performers how to employ treasures of Indian and Chinese legends in order to develop dramatic content.

Because of the connection with the temple activities, it became traditional in the *ennen* to introduce the performances with a prologue (*kaikō*) which consisted of praises and explanations of the ritual services. Long spoken dialogues and the dramatization of legends related to the Buddhist tradition seem to have been the major contributions of the *ennen nō* performances.

Scholarly opinion holds that the *ennen* originally were performed by the temple clergy. It is a matter of controversy, however, whether professional *sarugaku*, *dengaku*, and *shirabyōshi* performers eventually took over, at least partially, the more and more complicated and sophisticated *ennen* of the period of splendor, which corresponds to the time of the *nō*'s development (the second half of the fourteenth century).

Magnificently produced *ennen* performances continued with extreme luxury and splendor under the patronage of the Ashikaga shogunate through the fifteenth and the beginning of the sixteenth centuries at the major Buddhist temples in the capital and in Nara—at a time in which also the *nō* had similarly reached its peak of development and the favor of the shogunate. The main plays of the *ennen* repertory are preserved in a book compiled at the Myōraku-ji temple, which was spared the ravages of war bacause of its isolation in the mountains. This book, *Tenmon-bon* (*Book of the Tenmon Era*), contains the texts of fifty-two pieces, and remains the most important source for the study of *ennen*.

A study of the plays that go under the heading *ennen nō* reveals a similarity to the structure and elements of the classical *nō* plays of the *sarugaku* tradition. The question of priority and originality has not been, and probably never will be, solved. Such a question, however, does not seem to have vital importance in the context of a process that saw a continuous give and take among the many performers of the different performing arts. They all would have been together at the same festival sponsored by the same public religious institutions where these arts were actually presented—often on the very same day, or as different attractions of the same celebrations divided over several days. Temples and shrines actually functioned as sponsors of a variety of entertainments; the festivals were like a showcase of all the best available talent; and the cross-fertilization of different traditions was a matter of fact, mutual imitation being limited only by the personal skill of the artists involved.

The long spoken passages of the *ennen* had different names and structures. One of the most important, the *tōben*, or *tō-no-ben*, considered as one among the possible origins of *kyōgen* because of the comic nature of its dialogue, probably was not developed to the point of presenting true dramatic roles.

An analysis of *ennen* plays shows elements of dramatic structure and of content which are the same as in the *nō*. In plays of the *renji* (first part of an *ennen nō*) there is a *michiyuki* or journey of the main character (the monk of the temple), an incantation to conjure up ghosts, and the appearance of ghosts. In plays of the second part of an *ennen* (*shōfuryū*) the main characters are travelers or Confucian scholars on the way to a remote destination, and the main emphasis is on the dances at the end. In plays of the third part, *daifuryū*, the characters represent kings and nobles; they also travel to some place, and invoke the god of that place, or a ghost who eventually appears and performs something extraordinary.

Masks were used, sometimes borrowed from other traditions. Elaborate costumes, typical of the *furyū* tradition and proportional in their splendor to the means available to the sponsoring temple, sometimes gave to the performances a characteristic of extravagance. The approximately six by eight meter stage for the *ennen nō* was located in the garden of the temple, with the greenroom behind it and, at the sides, two small artificial mounds which symbolized the abode of the ghosts, and also provided the place for the musicians.

The Dengaku *Tradition*

The *dengaku* (rice-field entertainment) tradition developed from folk rituals performed in connection with the rice-culture among the common people, not at first in temples and shrines, but in the fields themselves. The primitive *ta-asobi* (rice-field entertainment) and *tamai* (rice-field dances) were both a prayer for a good harvest and entertainment for the farmers. As was the case with the *kagura*, the beginnings of the rice-field dances were connected with magic religious beliefs. The songs were originally meant as a conjuration of the spirits of the fields, and the dances as an entertainment for the conjured spirits, to receive their protection and obtain a good harvest.

The festival would also take the shape of a performance of the struggle between good and bad spirits for the control of the fields. The bad spirits would conceal their faces behind white cloth and cover their heads under large straw hats. Spirits would come from far away and confront the main spirit of the local fields (the *ta-aruji*, a name later used for the owner of the field).

The songs and dances of the field festivals (*ta-matsuri*) became very popular and gave birth to a tradition of folk performing arts in which the element of entertainment, often exclusive of ritualistic religious meaning, became prevalent. *Dengaku* is the direct heir to this rich and colorful tradition. The professionalization of the performers and the fashion among the town and court people of performing both the colorful dances and the acrobatics that became typical of *dengaku* made it extremely popular during the late Heian and Kamakura periods—at times even more popular than *sarugaku*. The group dances in colorful costumes, the acts performed on stilts (*taka-ashi* and *hitotsu-ashi*), and the development of the prototype of Okina are typical of this tradition.

During the Heian and Kamakura periods a number of entertainments from the *sarugaku* tradition were taken over by *dengaku* professionals, while the *sarugaku* professionals

73

assimilated elements from the *dengaku* tradition. This situation accounts for a number of uncertainties in the definition of which arts belonged to which tradition, and for the fact that the evolution of drama also occurred in both traditions. In general it can be stated that while the *sarugaku* professionals found their major sponsorship in the Buddhist centers of worship, the *dengaku* troupes had their base of operation in the Shinto shrines.

While the *dengaku* performed by professionals developed into a serious competition for the *sarugaku* troupes, a simpler form of *dengaku* continued to survive in the many farming communities, performed by local talent. The case of community *dengaku* learning from the professional *dengaku* was not rare, because it was common practice, when economically feasible, to invite professional *dengaku* troupes to the major village festival. Eventually the local, community *dengaku* survived, even to the present time, while the professional *dengaku nō* troupes disappeared, their function being eliminated by the triumph, in the Muromachi period, of the *nō* troupes of the *sarugaku* tradition.

The Shugen *Tradition*

The *shugen* tradition that gave birth to a peculiar form of *nō* called *shugen nō* was an entertainment developed by the *yamabushi*, the mountain ascetics already discussed in connection with the *shishi* tradition of *kagura*.[14] As a matter of fact, a number of performances that today are catalogued as part of the *shishi kagura*, such as *bangaku*, *yamabushi kagura*, *kumanomai*, etc. are the remnants of a tradition of *shugen nō* that developed during the thirteenth century and reached a peak during the fifteenth century.

As part of their missionary endeavor the *yamabushi* developed their own performances, probably on the basis of what they had seen presented at temples and shrines by professional *sarugaku* and *dengaku* actors. The *yamabushi* shows had the specific task of illustrating their faith. They included a ritual part consisting of incantations and purification through boiling water (*yudate*) and fire (*hibuse*), and a form of lion dance, the *gongenmai*, during which the god was supposed to take residence in a lion mask. A form of

Okina dance also was used. Other numbers included dances illustrating the extraordinary powers of the *yamabushi*, and the stories connected with the *kami* of the mountain or other deities.

The shows were presented in a space approximately three by two meters, usually in the worship hall of the shrine or in a large private house. No decor was used, and the text was sung; the dancers seldom spoke or chanted. The masks were borrowed from other traditions such as *dengaku* or *kyōgen* and, besides the usual musical instruments (flute, cymbals, big drum), the *sasara*, a clapper, sometimes was used.

Characteristic of the *shugen* tradition is the fact that the performers were the *yamabushi* themselves, some of whom became well known for their talent. In the course of the centuries, however, after a period in which their shows were enriched through the assimilation of plays and techniques from other traditions, the *shugen nō* deteriorated to the level of rather primitive folk entertainment—especially after the governmental decree of 1868 which ordered the separation of Shinto and Buddhism. What is left today is more appropriately classified under the *shishi* tradition of *kagura*.

Kusemai, Shirabyōshi, Ko-uta *and* Rambu

The fact that the oldest *nō* plays are primarily composed of dance and music with very little drama has led many scholars to posit an early connection between the *nō* and forms of dance and music popular in the centuries preceding its birth. Therefore, before introducing some of the theories about the origins of the *nō* it will be convenient to give some basic information about forms of dance and music that are often mentioned in the theories themselves.

Kusemai dances had, without doubt, some degree of influence on Zeami's father, Kan'ami. Zeami writes in his *Go-on* that his father had learned the art of *kusemai* from Otozuru, an experienced teacher from Nara, who probably belonged to a school well known for a kind of *kusemai* music and dance which was not as extreme as the term suggests.[15] At the time when Kan'ami introduced *kusemai* into the early *nō*, such dances and their music had a reputation, in the eyes of conservative courtiers, similar to that of jazz in conservative society during the early decades of our century. It is also sure that *kusemai*, just like jazz, did become very popular, despite highbrow opposition and adverse criticism.

Whatever the role of *kusemai*, we know unfortunately very little about their music and dance. Many documents relative to them deal only with the reaction they caused, such as the feelings of disapproval on the part of Emperor Gokomatsu (1392-1412), who did not want to have anything to do with them, because he thought *kusemai* was a music of a time of disorder. It seems that rhythm was the principal characteristic of this kind of music, and that the dances were similar to the *shirabyōshi*, from which they probably derived.[16]

The *shirabyōshi* received similarly adverse criticism, for instance from Fujiwara Moronaga, a court nobleman of the twelfth century, who defined the music of the *shirabyōshi* dances as that of a "nation close to ruin." The dancers pirouetted with the head erect, looking towards the sky: "a painful sight, they are disgusting dances, both in their music and movements." Time and success brought fame and respectability to some *shirabyōshi* dancers. Among them were famous wives or mistresses of very important persons at the top of Japanese society. Just as Justinian I in ancient Constantinople married Theodora, the famous ex-mime, so did the Emperor Gotoba (1183-1198) marry an ex-*shirabyōshi*. Moreover, every Japanese knows the love story of the legendary hero Minamoto Yoshitsune and the beautiful, unfortunate *shirabyōshi* dancer, Shizuka Gozen, subject of famous *nō*, *kabuki* and puppet plays.

A number of explanations have been given for the origin of the term *shirabyōshi*, which eventually was used for both the dances and the dancers. Often, the term is derived from the traditional costume of the dancers; that is, the ample white (*shiroi*) blouse (*suikan*) which covered the large trousers (*hakama*). Literally, the name means "white rhythm." The most probable derivation is from a type of rhythm called *shirabyōshi* which was very simple and plain, and was found within the Buddhist *shōmyō*, a chant that roughly corresponded in its religious functions to the Gregorian chant in the liturgy of the western Middle-Ages.

It seems sure that the *shirabyōshi* used a fan during their dance, and that the drum was the principal accompanying instrument—which seems to confirm that the rhythm and not the melody was essential in the original music. Later on there is mention of cymbals and, starting from the mid-fifteenth century, of a flute, a sign of a melodic element. It also seems that the structure of the show remained basically the same during the four or five centuries that preceded the *nō*. It consisted of an introductory song, followed by a number of other songs and dances. The program lasted one hour or more, and was divided into two parts, of which the second was danced at a quick rhythm marked by stamping.

Although some *shirabyōshi* dancers were lucky enough to engage the love interest of high-ranking courtiers and samurai, in general both the rare male and the more numerous female *shirabyōshi* dancers occupied a very low social status. Both *shirabyōshi* and *kusemai* women were considered, and, in most cases, were, prostitutes. Their actual social standing fluctuated, depending on their success and who was protecting them. The *shirabyōshi* who married the emperor, of course, reached the highest rank of social respectability. Most *shirabyōshi*, however, were ranked with the group of outcastes which included prostitutes and entertainers, and were supposed to live in the special villages where the outcastes resided.

While the male *shirabyōshi* appear always to have been a small minority as compared to the female, the contrary was true of the origins of the *kusemai* performers; in time, however, female *kusemai* dancers also became prevalent, and by the fifteenth century they had eliminated males almost completely.

The structure of the *kusemai* dances was similar to that of the *shirabyōshi*: short songs and long dances, divided into two parts, of which the second had an accelerated rhythm. *Kusemai* subject matter was originally mainly religious and connected with Buddhism.[17]

Zeami in his writings shows interest especially in the musical part of the *kusemai* and not in its dance. The insertion of the *kusemai* into the *nō* happened in the beginning as an addition, like an intermezzo or a variety show number, and not as a part of the *nō* piece itself. Until the fifteenth century there are records of *nō* actors who composed *kusemai* independently from the *nō*. The process of assimilation resulted in a musical revolution and in a new textual structure, with the *kuse* becoming a key part, a kind of spine of *nō* dramaturgy.

Zeami says that, before the assimilation of the *kusemai* as an integral part of the *nō*, the normal style of the *sarugaku nō* was that of the *ko-uta*. Unfortunately, we do not know much about the *ko-uta* music either.

The word *ko-uta* (small songs) has a long history probably dating back to the end of the tenth century, when, according to some scholars, it may have been used for popular songs accompanied by the *wagon*, an instrument with six strings, similar to the modern *koto*. The term *ko-uta* would have been created to distinguish those songs from the *ō-uta*, the court songs performed under the auspices of the court school, Outadokoro.[18] For our purposes it is important to notice that the *ko-uta* were not religious in their contents. As can be read in the *Kanginshū*, a collection of *ko-uta* put together in 1518, the subject matter of *ko-uta* is prevalently amorous or reflective of personal feelings.[19] Their music was considered by contemporaries as splendid. Unfortunately, the only *ko-uta* music which survived as such to the present time is that which accompanies simple *ko-uta* in the *kyōgen*, which are performed in an unpretentious rhythm with simple hand-clapping, or with a flute called *hitogiri*. Because of the sparse documentation on the subject scholars speak rather vaguely about *ko-uta* music. The only certainty is that the *ko-uta* music was considered as something traditional and accepted, providing an agreeable melody, while *kusemai* music probably brought the rhythmical element into pre-eminence.

Another term which is found in connection with the theories of the origin of the *nō* is *rambu*, which is mentioned together with the various arts performed at court, and is given an important role in the formation of the *nō* by some scholars. The ideograms indicate that *rambu* was used for non-classical, "disorderly" dances. Honda describes its characteristic as complete freedom of movement, without any fixed rules, in the frame of diverse music, both instrumental and vocal.[20] In the Middle Ages *rambu* was also used as synonym for the *sarugaku* of the professional *sarugaku hōshi*. The term *rambu* is also found, however, in the same program with numbers called *sarugaku*, which implies a differentiation. In such cases scholars believe that *rambu* indicates comical dances, costumed and with mimicry, performed by non-professional members of the court, such as employees and dignitaries—in contrast with the numbers performed by the professional *shushi*, *shirabyōshi*, *sarugaku hōshi* and other artists hired for the occasion.

Social Position of the Performers

The problem of the social status of the performing artists in Japanese society is rather complex, and is barely touched upon in most studies about the Japanese theatre in western languages. This problem becomes extremely important in the consideration of the origins of the *nō*, because it was recently proposed as a key point of discussion in the explanation of the rise of the *nō* actors to pre-eminence in the artistic world of Japan.

A historical perspective is necessary to understand the changing social status of several categories of artists, within and outside such main sponsoring structures of the performing arts as the court, temples, and shrines. Everywhere in the world those who have a definite social rank, and also happen to perform, receive their status from their position in society regardless of whether or not they perform. This basic rule applies in Japan, too, and the social status of a noble courtier or a member of the imperial guard within the hierarchy of the imperial household did not change because of an occasional performance. The same was true of several categories of temple and shrine officers, who received their official social status from their position within the hierarchy of the temple or shrine.

The problem of social status for the performers begins with the development of professionalism, in Japan as elsewhere. A great difficulty in the study of this problem is due to the fact that contemporary sources are preoccupied with conveying the chronicles of court life or of the high clergy, but systematically neglect to inform about the lower classes of society; even less do they bother to describe anything connected with the outcastes, unless indirectly and on the occasion of events that also touched the upper social strata. There is no doubt that, in general, the social standing of the professional performers, even inside the formal organization of a shrine or a temple, was very low. Most professionals of *sangaku*, *sarugaku*, *dengaku*, and even some of *bugaku* and of the puppets, belonged to the outcastes of Japanese society.

Japanese scholars have entered this field of research since the thirties, notwithstanding the understandable reluctance of today's performers to collaborate in the research because they do not like to be reminded of the social status of their ancestors.[21] The results of such research draw a rather dismal picture of the life of these performers in special villages called *sanjo*, where the privilege of exemption from taxes and forced labor was paid for at the price of being cut off from the social life of any other category of Japanese society, being despised as outcastes, and deprived of what nowadays would be called basic "civil rights." Even when professional *sarugaku* performers belonged to a powerful temple, and were thereby probably entitled to wear the uniform of that temple and be called *sarugaku hōshi* (or monks of the *sarugaku*), they still were obliged to reside in *sanjo*.

During the Kamakura period, the four categories of people who belonged to the outcastes and therefore were likely to be found in the *sanjo* were: first, butchers, tanners, and makers of leather goods; that is, those who were "impure" because connected with the slaughtering of animals; second, dyers and manufacturers of bamboo articles; third, performers of many kinds, including the professionals connected with such entertainments as the *shirabyōshi*, the *biwa* minstrels, puppeteers, and others: to this category also belonged prostitutes and diviners; fourth, undertakers and caretakers of tombs.

The restrictions imposed on the outcastes varied in different periods, but in general they were denied any social intercourse with the rest of the population and could hardly expect any protection of the law. The humiliations implied in the state of being an outcaste were many, and ranged from strict limitation of occupation, prohibition to circulate in public except at specific hours of the day, to strict regulations concerning clothing and place of residence, severe punishments for minor violations of the rules, and so on. The entertainers would obtain exemptions from some of these rules so that they could travel under the protection of the temple they belonged to and use on the stage types of clothing otherwise forbidden to outcastes. Their position was, however, always dependent on the favor of those in power, and favorable circumstances were precarious.[22]

In the *sanjo* the *za* or schools of *sarugaku* were formed in imitation of the *za* of *dengaku*, which appear to be the first organized troupes of professional performers. Japanese *za* share similarities with the medieval guilds organizing the various professions in Europe. The *za* of actors were jealous of their monopolistic privileges in the areas near their places of origin—a protectionism which has provided an occasion for scholars to argue the existence of a strong and fierce competition. The privilege of belonging to a *za* was expensive for new members, and the number of members was strictly limited. It seems that the traditional number of members for a *za* of *dengaku* was limited to thirteen, while no such constant number limitation is known for the *sarugaku* troupes. The strong contrast between their despicable condition as outcastes on the one hand, and, on the other, the possibility of receiving favor not only from the masses but also from the highest authorities (which could imply living at court and sharing the "heavenly" elegance of the imperial compound or the court of the Shogun) established a dynamic basis for the upward mobility of the most gifted artists; it also predicted the systematic campaign to establish a lineage which would eventually cancel the brand of outcaste established at birth.

NOTES

[1]The terminology here followed is basically the same as in Inoura, *A History of the Japanese Theatre I.*

[2]Blau, *Sarugaku und shushi*, is the most detailed western language work about the popular performing arts during the Heian period.

[3]Gotō Hajime, *Nōgaku no kigen* (The Origin of *Nōgaku*), Tokyo: Mokujisha, 1975.

[4]Parts of this chapter follow closely Ortolani, "Shamanism in the Origins of the *Nō* Theatre."

[5]Ortolani, "Spirituality for the Dancer-Actor in Zeami's and Zenchiku's writings on the Nō," 148.

[6]*Ibid.*

[7]Inoura, *A History of Japanese Theatre, I*, 42-45.

[8]*Ibid.*, 43-44.

[9]Blau, *Sarugaku und shushi*, 427.

[10]The authoritative *Engeki hyakka daijiten* (*Encyclopedia of Theatre Arts*, 6 vols, Tokyo 1960), in an article written by the *nō* scholar Nose Asaji, prefers the reading *jushi*, condemning as a later mistake the reading *noronji*. Another authoritative scholar, Takano Tatsuyuki, on the contrary, believes that the reading *noronji* is correct, because supposedly older. The reading *shushi*, however, preferred by Blau in his already mentioned volume, *Sarugaku und shushi*, has found more acceptance in recent years, especially in publications in western languages (Keene, O'Neill, Araki, Ortolani; Sieffert on the contrary prefers *noronji*).

[11]Many other theories were proposed, among which the possible connection of the *shushi* with Korean shamans (H. Eckardt).

[12]Blau, *Sarugaku und shushi*, 281.

[13]*Furyū* as a form of performing art is to be distinguished from the related word *furyū*—pronounced in older times *fūryū*—which was used as an adjective with the basic meaning of urbane and elegant, suggesting the spirit of ancient poems and legends, and was applied to objects such as beautiful robes.

[14]*Shugendō*, or "the way to achieve supernatural powers through training," was a religion that combined a pre-Shinto mountain cult with elements of Shinto, Buddhism, and Taoism, and stressed a severe training of its itinerant monks, the *yamabushi*.

[15]The ideogram presently read *kuse* was used in the *Genji monogatari* to describe a non-conformist type of dance and music which belonged to the *bugaku* repertory: it does not seem, however, that that *kuse* dance and music had any connection with the *kuse* of the period we are now contemplating, nor it is sure whether the ideograms used later for the term *kusemai* were read *kusemai* or *kyokubu* at the time of the *Genji monogatari*.

[16]O'Neill, "The Structure of Kusemai," 100-110.

[17]The differences between *kusemai* and *shirabyōshi* are difficult to establish, because both dances are very little known to us. O'Neill suggests that the music was different, and that the *shirabyōshi* performed songs without a connection in the subject matter, while the *kusemai* probably presented more sustained and more unified pieces. In reality so little is known that some scholars even denied to the *kusemai* any significant proportion of dance, giving primary importance to the music and the songs. See O'Neill, *Ibid*.

[18]A more recent theory attributes the origin of the *ko-uta* to court ladies who would have performed such songs before the *gosechi no mai*, a dance by five young girls in the presence of the emperor at the *Gosechi chōdaishiki* ceremony, celebrated every year in November.

[19]An English translation of the *Kanginshū* by Hoff is available in his *Song, Dance, Storytelling: Aspects of the Performing Arts in Japan*, 1-72.

[20]Honda Yasuji, "Rambu," in *Engeki hyakka daijiten* V, 567.

[21]The history and problems of the outcastes within the Japanese social structure are studied in *Japan's Invisible Race* edited by De Vos and Wagatsuma; unfortunately the volume does not include any research about outcaste performing artists.

[22]Some of the flavor of the social status of the entertainers is brought to life in the semi-historical novel *The House of Kanze* by Albery, and the play *Zeami* by Yamazaki, translated by Rimer, *Mask and Sword: Two Plays for the Contemporary Japanese Theatre by Yamazaki Masakazu*.

CHAPTER VI

NOGAKU

Theories on the Origins of Nō

The scarcity of factual information about the many types of performances that existed in Japan between the eighth and the thirteenth centuries has led to the development of several theories about the origin of *nōgaku*. In some cases the interpretation of the available documents is suggested by the social sciences and reveals ideological trends in the historical evaluation of cultural events.[1]

Theories about the origins of *nō* can be divided into two major groups according to their basic approach. The first group includes interpretations that concentrate on the study of the performers—individuals or groups—as members of families traditionally dedicated to one genre of performance. Such theories are based on sociological research, and they establish genealogical lines of succession. Presumably, each succeeding generation of performers corresponds in some measure to developments in the performance itself. Theories in the second group proceed from the analysis of play texts, records of actual performances, and written chronicles describing festivals, dances, music, singing, and other details related to such events. Available artifacts like masks, costumes, stages, and illustrations of all kinds are also investigated. These theories rely heavily on historical interpretation of the above mentioned data. Of course, the two groups do overlap, but the basic division seems valid and helpful.[2]

The theories of such scholars as Nose Asaji, Hayashiya Tatsusaburō, Morisue Yoshiaki, and Hattori Yukio belong to the "sociological" group. Their patient research has established beyond any doubt a lineal connection between fourteenth-century *nō* actors and many previous generations of *sarugaku*, *dengaku*, and *sangaku* performers. One instance of this method of investigation is Hattori's tracing the personal line of descent of the Komparu School, probably the oldest and most conservative of the five remaining schools of *nō*. Hattori connects the Komparu line to Mimashi, the performer who introduced *gigaku* into Japan from the Korean kingdom of Paekche in 612. According to Hattori, the mysterious god Okina as portrayed in *nō* is actually a deification of a popular hero of seventh century A.D., Hata no Kawakatsu (or Hata no Kōkatsu). Hata learned the art of *gigaku* from Mimashi and subsequently founded the Enmai troupe, a family of Yamato *sarugaku* performers acknowledged as the ancestors of the Komparu School.[3]

This type of research has also disclosed important facts about the organization of the *za* (companies) of *sarugaku* and *dengaku*. It has provided invaluable insights into the low social status of *za* members, and has revealed details of *za* relationships with sponsoring shrines and temples and with the civil authorities in general. Such research has shown, for example, that while performers were exempt from conscripted labor and taxes, they were also obliged to endure the humiliation of residing in *sanjo*, the villages where outcastes lived. Unfortunately, the mere knowledge that *nō* performers were descendants of *sarugaku* performers tells little about how the development of the art itself took place; it only establishes that "it happened in the family."

Another recent study of this type suggests a possible source for the content of several *nō* plays. According to Akima Toshio the family of Kan'ami and Zeami, the founders of *nō*, belonged to a group of outcastes, the Asobi-be, who specialized in funeral rites. This family specialization provides a plausible origin for Zeami's frequent use of ghosts as protagonists in his *nō* plays.[4]

Also of a sociological nature is the theory proposed in 1948, and later modified in 1957, by Matsumoto Shinhachirō.[5] Matsumoto's initial theory is based on the Marxist concept that the birth and development of new art forms depend strictly on social and economic conditions of the time. He insists that *sarugaku* of the Heian period (794-1192) was a product which ended with the society that generated it (i.e., the nobility of that period's imperial court). The new *samurai* aristocracy, he maintains, produced *nō* as something completely different, without any connection to previous art forms. Matsumoto makes the significant assertion that *nō* cannot be regarded as having simply arisen from the integration of preexisting traditional forms, but must be recognized as something really new and unique. Critics have argued against this theory that it is not possible to imagine something, no matter how new, without strong roots in the traditions of the past. Marxist critics have hailed Matsumoto's theories as revolutionary and discerning; other critics have not failed to expose his various factual errors.

In response to many suggestions and observations, Matsumoto qualified his position in 1957. He described *nō* as the art of outcastes, who sought with all their might to obtain the favor of the new ruling *samurai* class by catering to their tastes. Success in art was the only hope for these outcastes to move out of the lowest social condition to a position of privilege. The example of Zeami, who became the favorite and lover of Shogun Ashikaga Yoshimitsu, shows just how decisive patronage by the powerful could be to artists and their art.

The above and other similar theories seek the origins of *nō* in socioeconomic and political factors, and focus primarily upon the people with whom the art originated: the earliest families of *nō* performers, the social classes from which *nō* performers arose, and the patrons of the art. Alternatively, the second group of theories seeks the origins of *nō* in texts and records of actual performances, very often those of earlier forms of performing arts which were popular at the time of Kan'ami and Zeami. This method of analysis has revealed, among other things, a connection between *nō* and shamanistic rituals of possession.

Famous pioneers of historical research into *nō* sources, such as Nogami Toyoichirō and Nonomura Kaizō, believed the roots of *nō*, which generally excludes comic elements, to be different from those of *kyōgen*, which is essentially comic. This, however, proved to be a more or less arbitrary distinction. Such researchers had assumed that, during the centuries for which extant documentation is extremely scarce, there were two basically different types of *sarugaku*. They believed that one type, remaining in close contact with Buddhist ceremonies and temples, evolved into *sarugaku nō* and was performed by actors who gave birth to the schools of *nō*. The other type of *sarugaku*, *shin* (new) *sarugaku* was a popular comical kind of entertainment. For decades many specialists believed that the farcical elements of *shin sarugaku* had been gradually assimilated into *dengaku*, which then developed into the more refined *dengaku nō* that in turn gave birth to *kyōgen*.[6]

Further research into the performing arts of the centuries in question has shown that, after the Heian period ended, there was in fact no such assimilation of *shin sarugaku*'s farcical elements into *dengaku*, and that *dengaku* remained a predominantly religious performance, notwithstanding the assimilation of acrobatic techniques. In more fundamental opposition to this theory is the fact that, at the time of the genesis of *nō* in the second half of the fourteenth century, both *sarugaku nō* and *dengaku nō* appear to have had a strong affinity in both content and style. Zeami himself considered the great masters of *dengaku nō*, including his contemporaries Itchū, Kiami, and Zōami, to be at the same level as the great masters of *sarugaku nō*, Kan'ami and Dōami. At the same time, Zeami never could have considered *kyōgen* masters at the same level as the masters of *nō*, because *kyōgen* was itself regarded as inferior to *nō*. Therefore, the theory that *kyōgen* evolved from *dengaku nō* is unpersuasive. Moreover, the texts do not indicate whether *sarugaku nō* or *dengaku nō* was the first to develop those dramatic elements that constitute the structure of surviving *nō* texts. In the thirteenth and fourteenth centuries, the titles of *sarugaku* and *dengaku* plays and the content of the texts were, as far as is known, very similar, showing no great difference between the two forms.

A similar theory—proposed in recent decades by important theatre historians, among whom Kawatake Shigetoshi is the best known—connects the origins of *nō* with the Buddhist temple performances by the *shushi* and the origins of *kyōgen* again with *shin sarugaku*. This theory, in several variations, assumes a parallel between the supposed religious content and elaborate costumes of the *shushi* and the religious content and beautiful costumes of *nō*; it also assumes a parallel between the comic-farcical characters of *shin sarugaku* and those of *kyōgen*. The difficulty with this theory is again that historic continuity cannot be documented, neither between *shushi* performances and *nō* nor between *shin sarugaku* and *kyōgen*.

Kawatake, in view of this difficulty, presents the theory more as a pattern of relationships between the serious element—the representations by *shushi*—and the comic parody (*modoki*) of that seriousness found in the performance of *shin sarugaku*. According to him, this pattern was established by *shushi* and *shin sarugaku* and kept through the following centuries as a model for the relationship between *nō* and *kyōgen*. As Blau correctly notes, this hypothesis says nothing about the origins of *nō*; it merely reiterates that there is a standard pattern to all Japanese festivals since time immemorial—the combination of serious ritual with comic amusement.[7]

Hayashiya Tatsusaburō traces the origins of *nō*—through the dances of *shirabyōshi* and the free type of dance called *rambu*—back to ancient *kagura*. He believes that *kyōgen*, on the other hand, derived from parts of old court *sarugaku* and parts of *ennen*.[8]

Among other theories, it seems important to mention again Honda Yasuji's study on the importance of the *Okina sarugaku* as a possible link between the gradual disappearance of performances by *shushi* (from the end of the twelfth century) and the emergence of *sarugaku nō* (in the middle of the fourteenth century).[9] Also important are those theories (e.g. by Takano) stressing the importance of *bugaku* court dance elements—such as the *jo*, *ha*, *kyū* principle of its *gagaku* music, the stage, and the masks—in the formation of *nō* play structure, music, and mask shapes. Umehara Takeshi also claims a decisive role for *bugaku* in determining the origin of *nō*. He notes that the initial purpose of performing the *bugaku* dance *Somakusha* (or *Somakusa*) at the Hōryūji temple during the annual Shōryōe festival was to appease the soul of the late Prince Shōtoku (ruled 593-621, or 622), which was restless and vengeful over the extermination of his descendants. Umehara theorizes that Zeami may have been a professional *chinkonsha* (performer of rites for the repose of departed souls) and that he used *Somakusha* as a model for his ghost plays. Indeed, in both that *bugaku* dance and in Zeami's numerous ghost *nō*, the supporting actor (*waki*) plays the role of a monk appeasing a distraught and vengeful ghost played by the *shite* (main actor), and leads him eventually to a state of peace and repose.[10] O'Neill makes two additional important points. First, he notes that the earlier *kusemai* dance was an important structural element incorporated by *nō*; second, O'Neill maintains that

Chinese Yuan drama (Yuan *zaju*) exerted an appreciable influence on the formation of *nō*.[11]

It is very important in this context to mention again Gotō Hajime's contribution, which was explained at length in the previous chapter, in the discussion on the relation between *sangaku* and *sarugaku*. Gotō's summary of new data from the provinces seems to sustain his claim that *nōgaku*, a tradition comprising the two facets of *nō* and *kyōgen*, developed primarily within the realm of the religious and popular *sarugaku* outside the capital, because of the need to please provincial audiences which strongly favored the "native" inclination toward dramatic *monomane* over the "imported" taste for circus-like skills. The serious, at times tragic *nō*, so profoundly different from *kyōgen*, is explained by Gotō as a creation of the outcaste provincial performers, the *hōshibara*. In their long-range effort, over several generations, to change their despised social image into a respectable one, they switched to the performance of serious, dignified, religious subject matters. At the same time they invented family ties with illustrious, legendary performers of religious dances. Because they were outcastes, no records existed of their real ancestors. This circumstance made it easier for them to claim family ties with the most respected priestly performers of religious rites of the past, all the way back to Uzume and Buddha's disciples, and justify their impersonation of sacred roles through the use of masks, a task traditionally reserved to real monks and priests. The spectacular development of *sarugaku* into *nōgaku* was strongly supported by Shogun Yoshimitsu and his court in Kyoto, and was therefore eventually influenced by their aristocratic taste. The final result, in Gotō's view, is that *nō* and *kyōgen* form an astonishing temporal and spatial synthesis, a harmonization of city and country, of entertainment and religion, of the comic and the serious, and of popular and elite tastes. In a word, *nōgaku* is a uniquely fascinating mirror of the colorful and multifaceted medieval Japanese culture.[12]

Recently, a question has arisen about the influence of primitive *kagura* shamanistic rituals on the formation of the *nō*. A number of scholars have analyzed the movements and functions of *nō* actors as derived from the ceremonies and functions of shamans in *kagura* ritual. Ikeda Saburō traces the origins of the travel scene (*michiyuki*) at the beginning of *nō* plays to the self-introduction of the visiting god in *kagura* performed by the *ninjo* (a Shinto priest). Ikeda also traces the origin of the *waki*'s role in *nō* to the role of the god-assistant to the principal god in the *hanamatsuri* (festival of flowers, celebrating the birthday of Buddha at the time of the cherry blossoms). He explains the *shite* role in *nō* as having originated from the role of the main god in that festival, performed by a religious leader.[13]

Honda Yasuji is the scholar who has contributed most to a systematic analysis of shamanistic possession in *kagura* and its influence on *nō* origins. He traces the development of the principal role, the *shite*, back to *kamigakari*, the divine possession which is typical of Japanese shamanism: the spirit takes possession of the shaman-medium, usually the *miko*, and uses her tongue to communicate directly with the faithful. It is also the basic structural device of ancient *kagura* performances. It can take one of three forms: *kamikuchi* (mouth of the god), in which the spirit speaking is a *kami*; *ikikuchi* (mouth of a living human being), in which a live human spirit leaves its body in a faraway place, takes possession of a medium, and speaks; and *shinikuchi* (mouth of a dead person), in which the ghost of a deceased person speaks through the shaman. Honda remarks that in the type of *nō* play in which the *shite* impersonates a supernatural being, god, ghost, or even a faraway soul, his role derives from that of the *miko* in *kagura* who, while in a state of *kamigakari*, is overtaken by a spirit and utters the *takusen* (divine utterance). As a corollary, the *waki* role is often that of a monk because it derives from the role of the ascetic who, in many shamanistic rituals, induces the *miko*'s divine possession. Honda notes also that the *waki* was originally a flute player, the flute being the instrument used to bring about the descent of the god (*kamioroshi*). The two parts of the classical ghost plays are modeled on the incantation/conjuration and the actual possession of a medium resulting from the incantation —corresponding to the first act—and the apparition of the god, ghost, or demon in true form in the second act.

Honda also has argued that one further crucial structural characteristic of *nō* derives from shamanistic ritual. Many *nō* plays are structured very much like an illustrated, acted-out narration of a past event—more like a narrated reenactment than like the apparent presentation of the actual event itself, as is the common practice in *kabuki* and western drama.[14] Hoff compares Honda's theory to that of Gerald Else who postulates that Attic tragedy originated in the performances of *rhapsoidoi* (ancient Greek storytellers). For Honda, *nō* structure reveals its origin in the telling of the story (*katari*) by the shaman.[15]

At this point, several other important analogies that show the connection between *kagura* and *nō* should briefly be mentioned. The *nō* stage and the *kagura* performing area both create a sacred space, set apart for the projection into our dimension of the "other dimension" outside our time—a space within the ritual frame of the *illud tempus*. The importance of the journey that occurs in both shamanism and *nō* has been also underlined. In some cases the shaman travels in spirit to the other world and there meets gods and departed souls from whom he later relays messages to the faithful. More often, the shaman projects the "other world" into the sacred space and accomplishes there in a symbolic way his journey to the "other dimension." Such a journey also takes place at the beginning of *nō* plays: an ascetic (the *waki*) reaches a special place where he makes contact with a spirit belonging to the other world, or reaches the other world itself and finds a ghost.

Carmen Blacker has remarked that shamanism operates in the gray area between Shinto and Buddhism.[16] The same can be said of many *nō* plays, in which the nebulous sphere of mixed beliefs—and popular awe of shamanistic practices—can much better justify ghostly apparitions and the possession of living men by gods, spirits, and faraway souls than can any official Buddhist or Shinto doctrine. In fact, *nō* music and *kakegoe* (the strange, guttural sound of the drummers' voices) have been traced to shamanistic rituals. The drums are traditional Japanese trance-inducing instruments; the flute, as mentioned before, is an instrument for conjuring the descent of the spirits; and the *kakegoe* are part of the invitation to the gods to manifest themselves. Thus, the gliding movement of the *nō* actor in performance imitates the midair locomotion of a ghost or supernatural being. The stamping of the feet derives from movements for the pacification of the souls of the dead in the *tamashizume* (spirit-quelling) ritual of ancient *kagura*. In addition, the fact that the *shite* in *nō* almost always carries either a fan or some other object is derived from the *kamigakari* ritual in *kagura*. The possessing spirit was believed

92

to reside temporarily in the *torimono* (held object) in the hand of the main *kagura* performer, the *miko*, or the *ninjo*. The constant use by the *shite* of a *torimono*—such as a fan, spear, bow, or *sakaki* branch—is well explained by the deeply rooted belief in possession and consequent veneration for the temporary abode of the possessing spirit. This prevented the performers from abandoning the sacred prop even after the conscious influence of its original function had faded away.

History of Nōgaku

A) *Kan'ami*. The history of *nōgaku* has its starting point in the middle of the fourteenth century, when Kan'ami began his professional activity. Kan'ami was born in 1333, the year of the transferral of the shogunate from Kamakura to Kyoto, an event decisive for the transformation of the provincial *sarugaku nō* into the lofty classical *nō* so successful at the shogunal court. Kan'ami (the name is also often romanized as Kannami or Kanami) was known in his youth as Miyomaru and Kiyotsugu, and, according to an inscription on the portrait of his grandson (the actor Kanze Kojirō Nobumitsu), received the name Kanze from a priest on the road to the Hase temple in Yamato.[17]

Important in Kan'ami's official genealogical tree is the samurai/priestly descent, and the identification of Kan'ami's mother with the sister of Kusunoki Masashige, a strong supporter of the southern court in exile against the Ashikaga Shoguns (who supported the northern court in Kyoto). The real or claimed family connection with an enemy of the Ashikaga was most probably unknown to the young Yoshimitsu when he started favoring Kan'ami and Zeami. At a later time, however, it might have played a role in the fall from favor of Zeami and in determining his exile during the last years of his life. Why the child Kan'ami, born in a samurai family, was entrusted to an outcast *sarugaku* master for the purpose of training as a professional performer—an unlikely or at least very unusual case—is explained as supposedly being a direct order of the *kami*, Kasuga Myōjin, who wanted the gifted youth in his service as a performer at his shrine.

When Kan'ami began his activity as an apprentice, a number of *sarugaku nō* companies were active in the Yamato province. They performed mostly in the service of shrines and temples, but they were also trying to gain a general audience outside the places of worship. While still a young man Kan'ami founded a *za* of his own in Yūzaki, hence the name Yūzaki *za* given to his company until it became the Kanze *za*, the name since used to the present time by the most powerful school of *nō*.

Kan'ami is credited with the inspired creation of a new synthesis between *monomane* and *yūgen*; i.e., between the popular dramatic mimetic element and the elegant, sophisticated spectacle attuned to the aristocratic taste of the Shogun's court. His teachers were Inuō, a master of the Omi *sarugaku*, famous for his elaboration of *monomane*, and Itchū, a master of *dengaku nō*, who had preceded Kan'ami in a successful attempt at a synthesis of *monomane* and *yūgen*, and similarly achieved a great success at the Shogun's court. Kan'ami's fame was so well established by 1374, that the young Shogun Ashikaga Yoshimitsu decided to witness one of his performances at Imagumano in Kyoto. Yoshimitsu was at the time only seventeen, but had already developed the esthetic judgement which made him one of the most enlighted patrons of the arts Japan has ever had.

Kan'ami's performance at Imagumano was of great historical importance because it decided both his and his son Zeami's destiny. Zeami was at the time a beautiful twelve-year old apprentice who appeared as a *kokata* (child actor's role) in his father's shows. The admiration of the Shogun for Kanami's art and for Zeami's beauty resulted in a new life for Kan'ami's troupe, which became a frequent performer at the court of the Shogun, and marked the beginning of a long-lasting love and friendship between the most powerful man in Japan and the outcaste Zeami. Kan'ami's extraordinary talent and versatility as an actor was widely recognized by the audiences at large, and deeply admired by the Shogun himself and by Zeami, who hardly missed an occasion in his writings to celebrate the greatness of his father as an ideal performer. Kan'ami is described by his son as a big man who could play the role of a woman with extreme grace or imitate very successfully a young boy of twelve, while entrancing the audience with a most flexible and beautiful voice. While performing for the Shogun, Kan'ami began the process of refinement of his art which was brought to full accomplishment by Zeami. In the treatises on the secret tradition of the *nō*, such basic ideas as the concepts of *monomane*, *yūgen*, and *hana* are reported as taught by Kan'ami to his son, who claims for himself only the role of writing down the teaching of his master.

Kan'ami is also well known as a very important playwright, who probably wrote the first texts that can qualify fully as classical *nō*. He authored dozens of plays, some of which appear to be original, while others are certainly re-writings of pieces from various traditions. A number of his plays are still extant, either in the original form or as rewritten by Zeami—as, for example, the famous *Kayoi Komachi* and *Hyakuman*. His contribution to the formation of performance elements in the classical *nō* is also essential. He introduced changes in the dramatic structure of the plays and in the music and patterns of dance. He is responsible for the utilization of his training in *kusemai* to combine traditional *ko-uta* modes with *kusemai* techniques, and to establish the *kuse*—either sung while dancing, or sung while sitting—as a key structural element of the play.

In the opinion of several modern historians Kan'ami appears as a brilliant innovative artist who should be credited with the creation of the *nō*, and who thus prepared the way for the unique accomplishments of the greatest theatre genius Japan ever produced, his son Zeami.

During this first and the following early periods of *nōgaku* history the *kyōgen* plays did not reach a fixed literary form. Instead, the actors improvised, as in the *commedia dell'arte*, following the broad lines of an agreed-upon scenario. The lack of written texts makes difficult a meaningful reconstruction of the plays themselves. Historians generally believe that the plays were pretty much the same as they are today, although the acting at that time might have been much cruder, and without much stylization. Gen'e, the founder of the Okura School of *kyōgen*, is usually mentioned by the historians of this period as having created a great number of *kyōgen* plays. It is also obvious that from the beginning there was a clear separation between the *nō* and the *kyōgen* actors. The *kyōgen* actors were always considered as inferior to those of the *nō*. With few exceptions the level of artistry was generally low among the *kyōgen* players.

B) *Zeami.* Little is known about Zeami's life. The controversy about the date of his birth has subsided, and at present most scholars agree that he was born in 1363.[18] According to the document known as the Kanze-Fukuda Genealogy, he was born at the Kamijima residence in Nagaoka of the daughter of the priest Takehara Daikaku, lord of the fief of Obata, and his childhood name was Kiyomoto. According to the same document, he was entrusted for his earliest childhood training to a member of the Komparu *za*—a fact which would explain better Zeami's close, life-long connections with the Komparu School and his later choice of Zenchiku as son-in-law and successor in the artistic leadership of the *nō*. His encounter with the Shogun Yoshimitsu in 1374 placed Zeami in a unique position of favor at the court, but also made him the target of both envy and contempt by the courtiers who saw a disgrace for the nation in the homosexual relationship of the Shogun with the "beggar" actor. Yoshimitsu was at the time seventeen, and Zeami twelve. The famous poet Nijō Yoshimoto wrote a long letter in which he praises the extraordinary talents of Fujiwaka (Zeami) in his art, in poetry writing, and in playing court kickball (*kemari*). It is clear that the position of favor at court also meant a unique chance for Zeami to converse with the most erudite men of the time and learn, while still very young, a great deal about poetry and classical culture in general. He could also witness the performances of the best contemporary artists and study with eager attention the taste, moods, and expectations of the court audience. It is reported that Zeami received many valuable gifts from wealthy feudal lords and others who were trying to gain through him favorable attention from the Shogun. Zeami's position of favor, however, does not seem to have been without its ups and downs, nor was he always the first among the *nō* artists Yoshimitsu called to perform on important occasions.

Kan'ami's death at age fifty-two in 1384 left the twenty-two-year-old Zeami with the responsibilities and the leadership of the *za*. His life at the court of Yoshimitsu is highlighted by some important performances which were recorded as particularly solemn and/or successful. He also began to write his treatises on the secret tradition of the *nō*; these are today considered one of the major contributions to the study of the essence of acting and the problem of training.

Under Zeami's leadership the house of Kanze became very powerful, absorbed several other *za*, and succeeded in almost overwhelming the domineering *dengaku nō*. Zeami's patron Yoshimitsu died in 1408, and his successor, Yoshimochi, showed a preference for the art of the *dengaku* actor Zōami. Although now in a secondary position, Zeami's troupe continued to perform at major festivals and other events, and Zeami himself seems to have kept a very respectable place in the artistic world. The years between 1418 and 1424 were, however, less occupied with performance activities; Zeami used the change of pace to dedicate more time to the writing of his experiences and his reflections about *nō* art. The treatises of the secret tradition of this period—evidently influenced by the author's age—reveal a deep transformation of Zeami's ideals and views of the artistic mission of the performer. They also illustrate his deepened familiarity with Buddhist thought, probably of the Zen sect.

Yoshimochi's death in 1428 marks the beginning of a period of unpleasant setbacks for Zeami. The new Shogun Yoshinori not only did not show favor, but also was clearly antagonistic towards both Zeami and his son, Motomasa. In the opinion of some, the reason of his harsh treament stemmed from Zeami's and Motomasa's alleged support of the cause of the southern dynasty against the policy of the Shogun. Whatever the motives, it is a fact that in 1429 Yoshinori forbade Zeami and Motomasa to perform for the cloistered Emperor Gokomatsu at the Sentō Imperial Palace. In 1430 came Zeami's removal from the prestigious position of music director at the Kiyotaki shrine. In the same year Zeami's second son, Motoyoshi, decided to abandon his acting career and became a monk. In 1432 Zeami's favorite son, Motomasa, his great hope for the continuity of the genuine *nō*, died—and to the present time the suspicion persists that he was murdered, possibly for the same political reason that brought about Zeami's exile two years later.

In 1434 the seventy-two-year-old Zeami was banished to the island of Sado. A few circumstances seem to indicate that his political connection with the southern dynasty, or the suspicion thereof, might well have been the major cause of Zeami's disgrace. Some scholars, however, do not exclude the possibility that the eccentric and perverse ruler might have exiled the famous old master only because of a difference in taste, or rather because of artistic dislike combined with Zeami's opposition to the succession of On'ami—Zeami's nephew and the great favorite of the Shogun Yoshinori—to the leadership of the Kanze school, after Motomasa's death.

The last years of Zeami's life were very productive for his writing. Tradition has it that he was eventually pardoned by the emperor himself and came back from exile to live with his son-in-law, Zenchiku. There is speculation that in the late years of his life Zeami was a priest of the Ji sect of Buddhism; some of his writings of the late period show a preoccupation with Buddhist terminology and profound religious thought, which seems to give credibility to that speculation. We know that he died in 1443 at about eighty.[19] His burial place is recorded to be in the Fuganji temple in Yamato, where also his wife, Juchin, was buried shortly afterwards.

Although Zeami is known all over the world by this name, he never actually used it when signing a document or speaking of himself. According to the usage of the time one's name was an important sign of different phases of an artistic career. Zeami was therefore given several names during his long life, and was referred to in different ways after his death. As a young performer he was called Fujiwaka (or Tōwaka), Motokiyo, Kiyomoto, and then renamed Zea by Yoshimitsu (his full, honorific name being Zeamidabutsu). He signed his letters or treatises mostly with the name Zea, or Zeshi,[20] and later in life Shiō.

Zeami's extraordinary accomplishments encompassed many different areas. He was the best actor of his time, the foremost playwright of the *nō* tradition, the first—and to the present time—most important theoretician of theatre esthetics in the intellectual history of Japan, a powerful and innovative theatre manager and artistic director, and an acclaimed musician and choreographer responsible for making the *nō* a continuing success for centuries. All these achievements give him a unique place as one of the very few great geniuses in the history of world theatre.

C) *On'ami and Zenchiku.* Zeami had shown the way of the *nō* in its splendor and its depth. His heritage was continued by two almost opposite artists, Zeami's nephew, On'ami, and Zeami's son-in-law, Zenchiku. The former developed the splendor of the performance, the latter the depth of the artistic inspiration and of the theoretical speculation.

On'ami (1398–1467), originally known as Kanze Motoshige, received his prestigious name from his protector, the Shogun Yoshinori. He was the son of Zeami's younger brother, Shirō, about whom very little is known. The relationship of the young On'ami with Zeami and Motomasa remains uncertain. When Zeami was still childless, he probably adopted the recently born nephew to insure an officially recognized heir to the house of Kanze. It seems unquestionable that On'ami was a very imaginative and gifted performer, because he attracted the attention and the favor of Yoshinori several years before the latter's succession to the shogunate.

There is no doubt that there was a discrepancy in the style of *nō* between On'ami on the one hand, and Zeami/Motomasa on the other. On'ami excelled in the interpretation of demon roles, which Yoshinori loved and Zeami diligently removed from his repertory towards the end of his life. Zeami, who moved in his later life more and more towards a style of quiet depth, openly disapproved of On'ami's brilliant and glossy style, favored, however, by Yoshinori.

Zeami's and Motomasa's setbacks became On'ami's gains: On'ami was sent in their place to perform for the retired Emperor Gokomatsu at the Sentō palace, and he became the director of music at the Kiyotaki shrine. After Motomasa's death, in spite of Zeami's opposition, On'ami became the fourth head of the Kanze school (Kan'ami being the first, Zeami the second, and Motomasa the third). It is not known how much On'ami was involved in Zeami's downfall and in his exile. It is sure that Zeami tried to resist the pressures of Yoshinori in favor of On'ami's succession as head of the House of Kanze, although, after Motomasa's death, On'ami was the legitimate successor to the office. Zeami showed his displeasure towards his nephew in not yelding to the pressures of the Shogun and in entrusting the precious manuscripts of the secret tradition to his favorite son-in-law, Zenchiku, completely by-passing On'ami.

On'ami's merit consists primarily in his brilliant and youthful injection of new life into the *nō*, in his melodic improvements, and in his system for recording accurately even the most detailed changes of tone. Although opposed to the profound and simple interpretation of the great masters who preceded him, and of his contemporary Zenchiku, On'ami's style paved the way for the trends which were to dominate the following period.

During On'ami's time the number of plays performed on one occasion increased rapidly, especially in the case of the so-called *kanjin-nō*, or performances to raise funds for such pious purposes as the construction of a new temple. There were events in which the number of plays presented in one day reached the extraordinary number of fifteen or even sixteen. On'ami performed in anywhere from six to nine of them. The time for the performance of one play was shorter then by at least one third compared to today's standards.

Very few documents are available about Komparu Ujinobu Zenchiku's life.[21] The year 1405 is generally acknowledged as his year of birth. No precise record is available about his death, which occurred some time between 1468 and 1471. Although he is always referred to as Zenchiku, he actually used this Buddhist name only after age sixty-one. As a child he was called Kanshi, and, at the time of his succession as head of the Komparu troupe in his early twenties, he was known as Ujinobu. Zenchiku's introverted character was repelled by publicity. He was definitely more interested in high-level friendships with cultural leaders than in stardom, and was therefore probably responsible for the scarcity of information about his public performances. That he was a superb actor, however, we know for certain from the severest and most competent contemporary critics, Zeami himself and his son Motomasa, who shared secret writings about the *nō* with the young Zenchiku. In the spirit of the time this was a gesture of the highest esteem and friendship. After Motomasa's death Zeami chose his on-in-law Zenchiku as his spiritual successor, entrusting him with the precious manuscripts of the secret teachings—the supreme proof of recognition by the old master of Zenchiku's artistic achievements. Zeami's affection for Zenchiku also appears in two personal letters, extant in the original handwriting, sent to the beloved son-in-law from exile on the island of Sado. While

Zeami was in exile, Zeami's aged wife was taken care of in Zenchiku's house. According to tradition, when Zeami eventually was allowed to return from exile, it was Zenchiku who received him in his home.

An insight into Zenchiku's complex spiritual world is gained by noting who his friends were. They were among the most intelligent and significant personalities of his time. It was an epoch of decadence in the shogunate, gradual erosion in the feudal system, political restlessness, and social distress—a sharp contrast to the splendor of Yoshimitsu's firm rule during Zeami's youth and early maturity. Zenchiku's friend Ikkyū (1394-1481) was the most popular and influential Zen master of his time; Shigyoku (c. 1383-1463) was reknowned as a prominent teacher of Kegon Buddhism; Ichijō Kanera (or Kaneyoshi, 1402-1481) was very famous as a poet and as the greatest scholar of his time, well versed in Chinese philosophy, especially in the Confucian point of view. Zenchiku looked for and found in their company competent and sophisticated criticism of his art and speculations on aesthetics, an occasion to deepen his knowledge of Zen and Kegon Buddhism, and of poetry and Chinese classical philosophy.

As a playwright Zenchiku was credited with many famous *nō* plays. A typical list compiled by Bohner includes 39 titles.[22] The change of attitude of the most authoritative Japanese specialists in the attribution of *nō* plays has fluctuated in recent years from one extreme to another, leaving beyond serious doubt, however, Zenchiku's authorship of such classics as *Bashō*, *Teika*, *Yōkihi*, and *Ugetsu*.

Zenchiku is usually considered a conservative as far as his style of performance is concerned, and a developer of Zeami's spirit of depth and elegance. His writings about the essence of the *nō* are based on a metaphysical insight that makes him one of the few profound theoreticians of aesthetics among the finest performers of any epoch and country.

Zenchiku belonged to the Komparu school, based in the Yamato province, and was attached to the ancient Kōfukuji temple in Nara, as its main center of activity. During his time the few major companies (*za*) overwhelmed the other smaller *za* and absorbed most of them. The Komparu *za* was, with the Kanze *za*, the Hōshō *za*, and the Kongo *za*, one of the few survivors that succeeded in prospering to the present time. The troupes of *dengaku nō* and *ennen nō* were rapidly decaying, while *shugen nō* had retreated to small shrines in remote provinces. Amateur *nō*—a phenomenon that has continued to the present time in different forms and with several shifts in popularity in the course of the centuries—started to grow in popularity as *nyōbō sarugaku* and *nyōbō kyōgen* (performed by amateur women), as *chigo sarugaku* (performed by boys), and as *te sarugaku* (performed by amateurs who in some cases became semi-professionals). By the end of this period *nōgaku* had reached a position of undisputed preeminence in the world of quality entertainment both at the court of the Shogun and at the major temples and shrines.

D) *Nobumitsu*. The direction given by On'ami to the *nō*, suitable to the needs of an art which had to please an increasingly wide audience, became the official style of *nō* in the following period when Japan was ravaged by continuous civil wars, until the peace imposed by the the Tokugawa rule at the beginning of the seventeenth century. *Nōgaku* experienced the growth crises of an art that was becoming increasingly established as a tradition. Theoretical developments were nil, but the need for innovations in the dance and music patterns was felt and there was a development of individualistic characteristics and differentiations within the schools. More dramatic effects were introduced into new pieces no longer stressing Zeami's vision of the quiet, profound beauty of *yūgen*, but concentrating on the creation of earthly conflicts—a step in the direction of more realistic drama.

In this last creative period of *nōgaku* an artist who gave form to the spirit of the time was a son of On'ami, Nobumitsu, who inherited his father's style and conception of the art, and was the last important *nō* playwright. Kanze Kojirō Nobumitsu (1453-1518) was not a *shite* (principal actor) like Kan'ami, Zeami, Motomasa, and On'ami. He was a *waki* of the House of Kanze; i.e., he performed the secondary role as a partner of the *shite*, thus having a special incentive to increase the importance of his role through a greater concentration on human conflicts between the *shite* and the *waki*—rather than on the usual solo exploration of conflict within the *shite*'s soul.

Among Nobumitsu's plays the most famous are *Funa Benkei*, *Ataka*, and *Momijigari* which are still very frequently performed. Other notable playwrights of this period are Kanze Yajirō Nagatoshi, a son of On'ami, and Komparu Zempō Motoyasu, a grandchild of Zenchiku, who authored a number of important plays, among which *Ikkaku sennin* is especially well known abroad, also because of its successful *kabuki* adaptation.[23]

The popularity of *nōgaku* in the Japanese society of this period grew widely. It was common even among the populace to hear the chanting of *nō* and *kyōgen* texts, while court aristocrats did not try to hide their involvement in the study and practice of the *nō*. *Nō* texts were collected and commented on. In essence, *nōgaku* had become the undisputed principal entertainment not only at court and at events organized by temples and shrines, but also as a theatrical form independently produced and performed for the public at large.

Kyōgen profited from the epoch of great confusion because of the civil wars, which furthered the previously impossible mixing of the classes and brought to the surface vigorous new forces and long suppressed feelings. Criticism by the commoners became more open and sarcastic, and found in *kyōgen* an eloquent expression. The three major schools, Okura, Sagi, and Izumi—mostly originated from performers related to *sarugaku* and *dengaku* of the Omi province—consolidated their position of preeminence and were in a healthy competition for the highest achievements. The formative process of today's "traditional" *kyōgen* was almost completed by the end of this period; it was, however, still open and had not yet reached the frozen form which became traditional during the Tokugawa regime.

E) *The Tokugawa Period.* During the Tokugawa period *nōgaku* achieved the form that has remained substantially unchanged to the present. While *kabuki* and *jōruri* were gaining the enthusiastic support of the new middle class and the populace in the big cities, *nōgaku* completed its process of artistic stabilization under the patronage of the Shogun, the feudal lords (*daimyō*), a great majority of the *samurai*, and a growing number of sophisticated commoners. Whereas dynamic theatrical experimentation had a spectacular outlet in the popular new forms of theatre geared to the taste of the upcoming middle class, *nōgaku*, on the contrary, began to chrystalize as efforts to preserve its high esthetic standards prevailed over sporadic attempts at renewal. Importance was given to the detailed preservation of the sequence of dance movements and positions, to the faithful reproduction of interpretations by the great masters, and, in general, to a slow, interpretations by the great masters, and, in general, to a slow, ceremonial tempo which favored the creation of an aura of loftiness aimed more at the approval of upper class initiates and connoisseurs than at the pleasure of the general public.

The hierarchical and bureaucratic Tokugawa regime did not fail to acknowledge the value of a ceremonial and traditional entertainment such as the *nō*, and contributed to strengthening the process of stabilization. The shogunal government (Bakufu) issued an official recognition of the four long established *za* (Kanze, Hōshō, Komparu, and Kongō) and of the newly formed Kita—placing the Kanze school at the top of the five. Each *za* had a great number of artists belonging to the "family" and access to it was reserved to the natural or adopted "sons"—thus preventing any take-over or innovation by strangers. The official heir to the tradition of each *za* was, and still is, the head of the main family (*sōke*), a very important office which continued to be hereditary. The smaller *za* either affiliated themselves with one of the five major *za*, ceased to exist, or, in a few cases, joined their fortunes to the popular new forms of entertainment. In the latter case they made important contribution to the professionalization of acting and singing skills of *kabuki* and *jōruri*, and furthered the adaptation of *nō* plays to the new dramaturgy.

The rigid and sometimes constricting organization of the *za* during the Tokugawa period had a decisive influence on furthering strict control of the quality of the performances and promoting a constant effort of painstaking fidelity to the tradition. It also developed a very special world detached from the reality of the present life, devoted to the cult of the past, and to the re-creation from the inside of the process that once had been a splendid discovery. The fact that many members of the higher social strata belonged to this special world as devoted spectators or, very often, as amateur practitioners placed the *nō* masters in the position of revered teachers for the new Japanese aristocracy; the latter consisted of some survivors of the old court nobility, the *samurai* families, and some wealthy upstarts who had begun to mix with previously inaccessible social classes. The phenomenon of members of the new cultured middle-class joining the elite in large numbers began around the middle of the Tokugawa period.

The heads of the major schools of *nō* were called also *iemoto*, a name which was first applied to the arts in the *Sadō shinkōō* (1718) by Seki Chikusen, where it is used to describe the head of a school of tea ceremony.[24] The institution of the *iemoto* in the arts was of course much older, and can be traced back to the Heian period in relation to *bugaku* and *kadō* (the art of *tanka* poetry; that is, of short poems consisting of five verses following the 5:7:5:7:7 syllable pattern). It was, however, only during the Tokugawa epoch that the *iemoto* system became a general pattern of social organization within the world of most traditional arts; it bore a unique cultural function encompassing the preservation and transmission of almost every kind of art and craft not only among professionals, but also among amateur *samurai*, merchants, farmers, nobles, and priests. The enormous increase in the number of disciples due to the long years of peace and to the prosperity of many merchants made necessary intermediate masters who received from the *iemoto* the rank and the right to teach. An often complicated hierarchy was thus created within the school, and its secrets, training and written tradition were gradually revealed by a pyramid of teachers culminating in the *iemoto* himself. The *iemoto* had the exclusive right of interpreting and preserving the orthodox, traditional form of the art of his school as transmitted, through blood relations or adopted descendants, since the school's foundation. In the *iemoto* system, a personal teacher-disciple relationship is essential, and disciples do not communicate the artistic secrets to the outside world. The teaching method is not theoretical or abstract; instead, it proceeds as the secret transmission from person to person of a private spiritual heritage through practical, experimental, and concrete training.

The *iemoto* of the powerful houses of *nō* became a kind of teacher/king, immensely respected and faithfully served by his disciples, with the right of allowing or prohibiting a performance, deciding who would be the main performer among the many artists of the school, interpreting the correctness of a certain dance pattern, punishing and expelling individuals from the school, determining the use of the costumes, masks, and theatrical equipment, handling the finances, awarding rank and diplomas, and, since the Meiji era, also holding the copyright for all textbooks and material published by the school. It is no wonder that the *iemoto* began to feel as if they belonged to the highest strata of society, since, in fact, they had the means to associate with the rich and the powerful—thus becoming oblivious to their outcaste beginnings.

During the second half of the Tokugawa period the number of supporters and amateur *nō* performers (in the form of *utai* singing or of *shimai* dancing) among the commoners grew greatly. Scholars cannot provide accurate figures but think that their number became considerable. The opportunity to learn—through the participation in the *iemoto* system—the traditions embodied in the world of *nōgaku* was certainly a factor in the formation of a cultured middle-class that became the heart of the new social mobility in the apparently static structure of the late Tokugawa society. The *iemoto* system thus contributed not only to the preservation of ancient patterns of *nō* art and to keeping alive precious moments of beauty discovered by a master, but also, paradoxically, to that social transformation that created the need for change and the opening of Japan to the modern world.

During the Tokugawa period *kyōgen* achieved a state of stabilization—from the practice of improvising from a scenario, which continued into the first decades of the Tokugawa era, to the practice of using a fixed text. Following the fixed text, a fixed choreography of movements and patterns of action also prevailed. There was, however, more flexibility than in the *nō*, because of the more realistic nature of the dialogue and the need—amid the fierce competition of the schools—to keep a fresh and original sense of humor.

About 150 plays were in the repertory of the *kyōgen* schools. The most important book of *kyōgen* theories, the *Warambe gusa*, was written in 1651 by Okura Toraaki. The major collection of plays, the *Kyōgen ki*, was published around the same time. These two publications sanctioned the stabilization of *kyōgen* in a form that was transmitted with few changes to the present time.

F) *After the Meiji Restoration.* The fall of the shogunate was a tremendous blow to the *nō*, an art traditionally identified with the Shogun's court and finacially supported by the shogunal government. The actors, including famous *iemoto* who just a few years before reigned almost like kings, had to face hard choices to survive in a time of great confusion and uncertainty. A great number of *nō* performers had to abandon their art, many *nō* stages were destroyed during the upheaval or converted to other uses, and invaluable *nō* masks and costumes were sold.

The constant efforts of a few *nō* artists who withstood the storm and worked hard to revive the tradition, the protection of a few influential personalities of the new regime, and the interest shown by members of the imperial family supported by the appreciation of foreign diplomats and visiting artists, created a new atmosphere which made possible a slow reopening of stages and reorganization of companies, audiences, and amateur practitioners. Particularly important among the *nō* actors was the contribution of Umewaka Minoru (1828-1909) and Hōshō Kurō (1837-1917); also significant was the Japanese ambassador and politician Iwakura Tomomi (1825-1883), who was the first—spurred by his experiences abroad of presentations of classical opera on official occasions—to organize a few *nō* performances for the emperor in his private residence in 1876, thus beginning for the *nō* a new era of patronage by members of the imperial family. When former American President Ulysses S. Grant visited Japan in 1879, Iwakura had *nō* performed for the illustrious guest in his house, and the praises of the foreign dignitary had a considerable repercussion during the period's very sensitive atmosphere of modernization. The formation in 1881 of an organization, the Nōgakusha (Nō Society), to support a *nō* theatre with a regular schedule of performances, brought about the successful opening of the first *nō* theatre built after the Meiji Restoration in the new capital, Tokyo. In the meantime the schools of *nō* began to get organized again and to re-open their own stages. The activities of the Nōgakusha, later renamed Nōgakudō, the official organization backed by the Imperial Household, were useful in providing some modest financial contribution and badly needed prestige: its limited membership, however, did not provide a wide enough basis for a healthy development. Of greater importance was its reorganization under the new name of Nōgakkai in 1896. The new association had as its president Hijikata Hashimoto, then Minister of the Imperial Household, and was open to the general public, a fact that provided a broader basis for its activities as producer of *nō* performances.

The schools of *nō* have since continued in their recruitment of disciples among the upper classes, and in their cult of fidelity to the traditions stabilized during the Tokugawa period. The *nō* world again produced an uninterrupted series of great performers. It also has attracted the attention of scholars and artists both in and outside Japan, acquiring a reputation as a unique living treasure of traditional beauty and inspiring a number of experimental endeavors in the world of theatre and dance. During World War II the *nō* was favored by the government because of its pure national character. New plays stressing patriotic themes enjoyed a brief period of popularity. The destruction of almost all theatres forced the schools to share one stage right after the defeat. The new prosperity after the war, however, provided new buildings and the luxury of more confortable seating arrangements for the audiences.

Economic prosperity also opened the way to several tours of *nō* troupes in Europe, America, and a number of Asian countries. The teaching by experts in several western universities of regular courses and workshops in the history, theories, and practice of *nōgaku* made the direct contact of numerous westerners with *nōgaku* possible. *Nōgaku* is no longer considered an esoteric, mysterious, and strange phenomenon, but, on the contrary, has become one of the world's recognized and familiar forms of theatre. Japan's great economic boom, especially during the last decade of the Shōwa era (1980-1989) has been at least partially responsible for a steady growth in the number of new *nō* theatres (including the splendid National Theatre), the multiplication of performances, the increase of amateur practitioners, and the expansion of audiences to include territories previously incapable of sustaining a regular program of shows. Although the recent death of great masters such as Kanze Hisao and Umewaka Rokurō has deprived the *nō* world of some of its brightest stars, in general it can be said that the *nō* at the end of the twentieth century enjoys a healthy and broad base of support, which promises artistic continuity for the future.

Zeami's Secret Tradition of the Nō

The treatises written by Zeami and Zenchiku contain a wealth of insights into the art of the actor, the methods and timing of training, the way to write a play, the nature of the theatrical experience, and the ranking of the performances. It is important to keep in mind that Zeami's treatises were not meant for the average reader, but were directed to the one person who would inherit the leadership and the responsibility of the school. The transmission of the tradition of many arts was entrusted from *iemoto* to *iemoto*, one generation after the other. The treatises presupposed a thorough knowledge of the art itself and of the terminology commonly used, plus an oral transmission (*kuden*) which was equally or even more important, especially because it was connected with the actual training "from body to body." Secrecy in the transmission was a common practice in the various arts, and not a peculiarity of the *nō* tradition.

Among Zeami's treatises, some of which are very technical and hardly relevant for the non-performer, the most important, in order of completion, are the following.[25]

A) *The* Fūshi-kaden. The first treatise is the *Fūshi-kaden*, also commonly called *Kadensho* (Teachings on Style, and the Flower, or, The Book of the Transmission of the Flower), the main part of which was written about 1402, and then completed (the sixth and seventh section) by 1418. The first chapter of this treatise is often quoted in connection with a tentative reconstruction of Zeami's life, because the sequence of training steps suggested is interpreted by some as autobiographical in substance. The introduction to the *Fūshi-kaden* presents some important statements about the Indian origin of the *nō*, as handed down since the age of the gods, and developed in Japan since the reign of Empress Suiko, when the Prince-Regent Shōtoku commanded the legendary Hata no Kōkatsu to create public entertainments for the sake of national peace. The origin and the illustrious transmitters of the *sarugaku* claimed by Zeami place this art completely in the religious tradition of the main temples of the country, and by implication place the *sarugaku* actors in a position as respected religious members of the staffs of such temples or shrines—a great contradiction to the harsh reality of Zeami's outcaste youth. The introduction also states the need of total dedication to the *nō* to the exclusion of any other art, with the exception of poetry, and prescribes basic prohibitions of sensual pleasures, gambling, and heavy drinking.

Seven chapters follow. The first traces the practice of the *nō* in relation to the age of the actor; that is, the phases of training from childhood to maturity (about age six to fifty and older).

The second chapter explains some basic elements of *monomane* (imitation, mimesis) and examines the roles of women, old men, mad persons, Buddhist priests, *shura* (dead warriors), gods, demons, and Chinese roles. Zeami gives advice for a successful interpretation, suggesting the appropriate age of the *shite*, the attitude demanded by each role, a wise choice of mask and costume, and other practical tips.

In the third chapter a series of questions and answers are dealt with, which include how to foresee the success of a performance and harmonize its *ying* and *yang*, the strategies to adopt during a competition of *nō*, the vital importance of *hana* (flower), and the distinction between the passing flower of youth and the true flower.

The fourth chapter, entitled "Matters Pertaining to the Gods," reiterates the teaching about the sacred roots of *nō*. Zeami has no hesitation in transmitting the tradition that the first instance of a performance of *sarugaku* in the age of the gods was the dance by the goddess Uzume in front of the heavenly cave where the Sun Goddess Amaterasu had hidden herself. Further Zeami establishes an even more sacred root of the *nō* in India. The Indian dances that evolved into *sarugaku* are said to have been performed at the suggestion of Gautama Buddha himself during his lifetime and, assisted by his powers, the dances resulted in pacifying a riot and in making possible the continuation of the Buddha's preaching. *Sarugaku* is then said to have been originated in Japan by a divine being, Hata no Kōkatsu, who is claimed to be the founder of the family (Zeami at times used as his signature the name Hata no Motokiyo, presuming his lineage as descending directly from Kōkatsu). Zeami then traces the lineage of the main *sarugaku* companies who were at work during his time, and describes the important religious functions performed by the *sarugaku* troupes for the achievement of peace in the country.

In the fifth chapter Zeami addresses "The Most Profound Principles of the Art of the *Nō*." First he explains that the reason why he writes his account is for fear that the genuine art of the *nō*, already in decline, will otherwise disappear, because the real flower (*hana*) can only occur by the mastery of the principles handed down from his predecessors. He then explains the difference in style between the two major branches of *sarugaku*, the Omi, which emphasizes the style of *yūgen*, and Yamato, which on the contrary gives precedence to *monomane*, concluding that the true great artist must master both possibilities. The problem of the audience's response to different skills is then examined. The true, great master who has achieved his flower will be able to move even an undiscriminating audience, using at his discretion any style, Omi, Yamato, or even that of *dengaku*—the purpose of *nō* being, after all, to bring happiness and prosperity and to promote long life for everybody, from the nobility to audiences in mountain temples or in the far-off provinces. Zeami then examines the causes of the *nō*'s decline, which include the involvement of the actors in worldly attitudes and vulgar desires, the making of prosperity into an ultimate goal, or an end in itself, instead of making the art the end of the endeavor and remaining honest and open.

The sixth chapter, "Training in the Flower" deals with the playwright's techniques in composing a play. Zeami is aware of the importance of the plays and declares that writing texts is the very life of the *nō*. He gives advice on the choice of the subject matter, how to start and develop the theme in order to achieve certain effects, and how to keep a sense of balance and symmetry, which is essential for success in *sarugaku*.

In the seventh chapter Zeami deals in depth with the nature of *hana*, the flower. Pressing the parallel between the flowers in nature and the *hana* he is talking about, he stresses the importance of the variety of flowers, and the element of novelty, fruit of technical mastery, and thorough practice. He also stresses the importance of reaching the point at which imitation is no longer imitation, because the actor becomes his role and therefore no longer needs to imitate any more. The total transformation into the role will also avoid the risk of a superficial imitation of the qualities of a role, which would result in poor acting. The real flower will bloom only when the actor identifies himself with the true essence of the whole role, reaching thus the exterior expression of the role through interior identification, and not through a direct attempt at imitating it. Other important advice concerns the importance of secrecy to preserve the sense of novelty (a decisive element of success) and the keen awareness of the Law of Cause and Effect: the cause of success being the skills the actor acquired after years of relentless training. Thus becomes clear that negligence in training results in failure.

Contemporary readers who equate *nō* with static and painstakingly faithful repetition of fixed patterns might be surprised to discover that the final pages of Zeami's fundamental treatise are a hymn to flexibility, adaptability, and readiness to change even during the same performance. Always, at all costs, the sense of novelty must be preserved through a constantly aware intuition of the changing wishes of the audience—an awareness which becomes second nature to the great master. Zeami closes his treatise by stating that the secret tradition is meant only for one person in each generation, who must be chosen not only because of lineage, but also because of real insight into the art.

B) *The* **Shikadō.** The *True Path to the Flower* (*Shikadō*) was written by Zeami when he was 58, in 1420. It is a relatively short treatise which reiterates some of the items already taught about the basics of *nō* dancing and chanting. It also begins the system of ranking the levels of accomplishment, a process that will be developed in later treatises.

Zeami states in this treatise that in *nō* there are two basic arts; i.e., dancing and chanting, and three role types to which all other roles can be reduced; i.e., an old person, a woman, a warrior. The young actor, between ten and seventeen, does not need to study the three roles nor the use of the mask, which is accomplished when he comes of age. Zeami specifies how all subsequent roles are derived from these three: the style of a quiet and solemn god is adapted from the style of the old man, several roles which require great taste and elegance come naturally from the style of women's roles, and roles requiring powerful body movements and foot stamping derive from the warrior role.

Zeami teaches that an art that remains external is to be despised. The real master must achieve internalization through constant practice and rehearsal until he understands quickly how to put himself totally into the object of his imitation.

The young actor should not directly imitate the peak performances of the great master who has reached the state of perfect freedom, but follow the teacher step by step in learning the two basic arts and the three roles.

Zeami discusses the three basic elements in the performance of *nō*; i.e., skin, flesh, and bone. Of these, bone represents the actor's naturally inherited talent, flesh represents his acquired skills in chant and dance, and skin the elegance of his outward appearance on stage. The master must fuse all three elements. When he reaches a perfect fusion, he will involve the audience in an enraptured forgetfulness of itself. The art of the performance will then have the quality of being inexhaustible in its depth and constantly elegant.

The last question Zeami deals with is related to the distinction between "substance" and "function" in the *nō*. Only the artist who looks at the *nō* with the spirit grasps its substance; those who look at the *nō* with just the eyes remain on the outside of the substance and see only something that derives from it, but is not the substance. An effort to imitate this outside function is doomed to failure. The master, however, who succeeds in fully manifesting the substance identified with its exterior function will achieve an art which is beyond description.

C) *The* **Kakyō.** The *Kakyō* (A Mirror Held to the Flower, 1424) is especially important for its extensive discussion of the concepts of *yūgen* and *myō*, besides a variety of topics which include very technical instructions about: pitch and voice production; the secrets of body movement to achieve effects of gentleness and power; the actor's aural and physical timing; the actor's ability to see himself with his spiritual eyes as the spectators do, from left and right, in front and behind (which makes it possible for the actor and audience to share the same image, and for the actor to master the right and the left, the front and the rear); the principle of matching the moment of the actual beginning of the chanting with the exact instant in which the audience expects the actor to start (this is something that must be grasped instinctively); the application of the principle of *jo, ha, kyū* to the various combinations of programs, depending on the type of event and the atmosphere created in the audience; the need of proper practice to get to the point at which the disciple can reach the spirit of the teacher, and not only the external appearance, because "what is felt by the heart is ten, what happens in movement only seven."

The part that deals with *yūgen* is particularly important. (The reader will find further discussion of *monomane, yūgen, kokoro,* and *hana* in the following section, "The Basic Concepts of Zeami's Esthetics"). Zeami begins by stating that *yūgen* should be considered as the highest and most comprehensive principle in the art of the *nō. Yūgen* should be learned by observing the behavior of the nobility, whose refined, dignified, mild, and elegant deportment represents its essence. Their way of speaking, their words and habitual means of expression, are a paragon of *yūgen* in speech. When the melody flows smoothly and naturally and the sounds are suitably mild and calm, *yūgen* of chant and music exists. In dance, *yūgen* must be manifested through fluent and unostentatious grace. Even when playing demon roles the performer should not forget to preserve a graceful and elegant stage appearance.

Zeami then explains the importance of moments of non-action, when nothing seems to happen on the stage. This is one of the great secrets of the tradition. It is based on the continuous, profound concentration of the actor, who is supposed never to relax his inner tension. The actor's concentration unites him with the deepest self, which is a metaphysical reality identical for all things. The moments of non-action, as well as those before and after, are all rooted in the same deep reality, the *kokoro* of all things, which provides the profound continuity to the apparent non-continuity of action. Thus the actor, through his concentration transcending his own consciousness, ties together the moments before and after the instant in which nothing happens, while the audience perceives the profound inner link and deeply enjoys the moment of non-action. His interior intensity gives life to the illusion of performances that otherwise fall flat—like puppets to which the supporting strings have been cut. The great master should live in a state of continuous concentration, even off the stage, day and night.

The practice of this special continuous concentration will have a very special result, the moments of *myō* (peerless charm, or the marvellous, or the sublime). *Myō* takes the meaning of exquisite and delicate, and is achieved when the actor truly has learned his craft and attained perfect fluency, when he has transcended all stages of his art to the point where he performs everything with ease and exhibits every skill without effort, thus achieving a selfless art that rises above any artifice. In the discussion about the *myō* Zeami includes Buddhist principles that support the need for the actor's union in spirit with the world of nature and for the achievement of an ease of spirit comparable to the boundlessness of that nature itself.

D) *The* **Kyūi.** The treatise *Kyūi* (also read *Ku-i* by some Japanese scholars, The Nine Levels), has received the special attention of several western scholars because of its enigmatic characteristics and the fascination of its attempt to establish a hierarchy of achievement in performance. A whole theory of acting is outlined implicitly in the dense and sometimes elliptic description of the nine levels or ranks. They divide all actors into categories according to their progress in the art, and also describe different levels at which the master who has reached the top can operate.

An interpretation which over-stresses the esthetic-metaphysical aspect of the treatise runs the risk of missing Zeami's intent to provide a guide for how to discern and classify levels of performances; on the other hand, an interpretation that neglects the basic implications of thought behind the rankings is inadequate.[26]

The text of this treatise is undated, but was probably written when Zeami was about sixty-five years old. The heavy use of Buddhist terminology indicates that the treatise was probably written after he became a monk.

Zeami divides the treatise into two parts. The first describes, from the highest to the lowest, the nine levels at which an actor can operate. The second then relates the nine levels to the sequence of training and to the function of guiding an experienced actor in the use of different performance levels throughout his professional career. The practical function of offering exclusive guidance for his successors was certainly the reason for Zeami's writing this treatise, as it was with the others. The way he wrote it, however, is very revealing of the profound involvement of the aging Zeami with metaphysical and religious concepts from various sources, of which Zen Buddhism, although important, is only one.

In the *Kyūi* the level or rank of operation is called *kurai*, and to each *kurai* corresponds a certain characteristic appearance (*fū*, translated as "art" or "style" or "marks") which can be perceived externally, and which is the clue by which the master can classify his disciples. Zeami starts his treatise from the description of the highest level and then descends one by one to the last. For clarity's sake the lower levels are explained here first, ascending then progressively to the top.

In the description of each level Zeami follows a pattern. He gives a name to the level which is related to the characteristic of the "marks" involved, then quotes a famous saying, mostly Zen or Confucian, followed by a brief description based on an explanation of the saying.

The nine levels are divided into three groups of three each. The three lowest levels classify performances limited to surface acting, which reveals a complete lack of formal training and of *yūgen*. The three middle levels classify performances that reveal different degrees of training and the appearance of *yūgen*. The three highest levels classify performances that go beyond whatever can be taught through formal training, thus reaching the highest quality of *myō* (translated as "peerless charm" by Rimer-Yamazaki, "miraculous" by Keene and Nearman, "sublimity" by Ueda, "merveilleux" by Sieffert, "wundersam" by Benl). Of these three highest levels, only the top one reveals the fullness of the quality of *myō*—making such level indescribable, and transparent to a deeper reality.

The lowest, or ninth level, presents the marks of coarseness and leadenness; that is, it describes a completely untrained, blunt, heavy performance; the actor appears incapable of differentiating between natural and performance behavior. The eighth level presents the marks of strength and crudeness; that is, a performance in which an actor displays a vigorous energy and some sense of direction of the energy: he lacks, however, control over his performance, like the tiger cub to which he is compared. The seventh level presents the marks of strength and delicacy; that is, it describes a performance in which a sense of restraint, the fruit of the actor's natural discernment, is added to the untrained energy. The intervention of the actor's mind is symbolized by the cold gleam of a precious sword. Some sporadic success is possible at this level, which is, however, achieved without formal training, and therefore not under the control of the performer and not sufficient for professional theatrical use.

The three middle levels have in common the profound changes introduced by formal training through the transmission of the craft of acting from master to disciple. Level six presents the mark of early beauty, or "surface design;" that is, the beginning, still superficial result of a technical proficiency acquired through imitation of the teacher. It is not yet the real path, but the gate to it, implying that the way to the interior is through the study of its exterior manifestations. The fifth level presents the marks of versatility and precision; that is, a great achievement in mastering the craft, without, however, achieving creativity. This is the decisive point which divides the artist from the craftsman. An actor either succeeds in entering the upper levels and becoming a creative artist, or will return forever, with his improved craft, to the lower ones. In this level, the mountain peak of the true art of creativity is still concealed by the clouds. It is only in level four that the mark of the true flower appears. The clouds are now dissipated, genuine creativity has blossomed, and the actor begins to enter the realm of the flower. This is the completion of the process of formal training. The discipline of the craft empowers the new artist to sustain his genuine creativity and control repeatedly the effects of his art.

The upper three levels describe the realm of the accomplished artist, in the process of deepening and simplification that leads to the supreme peak of performance. The description is a guide for the head master in order to recognize the phases of this development in the great artist, and to advise accordingly, since the master-disciple relationship does not cease even after the achievement of the highest levels.

The third level presents the mark of the flower of tranquillity, as symbolized by a mound of snow in a silver bowl. The first explosion of creativity in a myriad of colors of the previous level is now filtered through the snow-crystals and simplified to the whiteness of the snow: pure whiteness is the sum of all colors, yet cancels all colors—a symbol for the process of simplification leading to a sense of tranquillity. The breakthrough to simplicity seems to indicate the opening of a first glimpse into the realm of permanence in contrast to the multiplicity of sensory illusion.

The second level presents the mark of the profoundly brilliant flower. Scholars usually stress the element of profundity on this level, following Zeami's indication of the limitless depth of the highest mountain. The scale is immensely more impressive here than on the previous level. Thousands of mountains are covered with snow; why is there one peak unwhitened among them? The Zen saying has prompted many explanations, from Nose's interpretation that the master reaching this level represents an exception among the exceptions symbolized by the thousand whitened peaks, to the interpretation that the unwhitened peak represents a sudden lack of *yūgen* in an otherwise flawless performance. The calm of the previous flower would be enriched through the addition of an element of surprise. The non-*yūgen* proceeding from the master becomes an ornament to his art when suggested by intuition. This special touch in the art of the master is referred to as *ran-i*, or rank of the sublime. Ueda's explanation is worth quoting: the irrational element of a black peak among all white mountains would represent the other world beginning to invade the world of ordinary senses. "Natural beauty is not enough: there must be the beauty of the supernatural, a strange kind of beauty perceptible to only those supreme artists who are endowed with extraordinary sensitivity. A Nō actor able to perform the Style of Profound Flower leads his spectators to a state of trance, in which they can appreciate the beauty of the strange and wondrous."[27]

The supreme level presents the mark of the miraculous flower (or the flower of peerless charm, or the mysterious flower, etc.). Zeami proposes a dictum that appears in several Buddhist texts in connection with the experience of the enlightenment, in which the apparent contradiction is resolved in terms of transcending limitations of space and time through the interior eye: "In Silla, the sun shines brightly at midnight." The enlightened eye, moreover, would recognize the above paradox to be as senseless—or as meaningful—as any logical affirmation based on the uncertain fragility of the human illusion. Nearman writes: "For the actor on the first level, within every action and at every instant, the Absolute is ever-shining, and although not seen by the eye, can be perceived directly by the perceiving Mind. Actor, art, technique, beauty, meaning are no longer discernible because they are no longer separable....The integration of actor, acting and what is acted is complete...At such a performance, the spectator is moved but can no longer identify what it is that moves him. Indeed, that level of rapport is reached where actor and audience are as one, and the functioning of analytical and critical faculties is held in abeyance."[28] The aging Zeami seems to have presented here a concentrated summary of his meditations, in Buddhist terms and conception, of the supreme achievement of a lifetime of dedication to the *nō*. The sublime flower seems to reveal, to visualize, to make present the transcendental world of Truth beyond the senses, the world of Permanence beyond impermanence; for a moment the audience is enraptured to touch in unison with the artist, the Ultimate; that is, the amazing austerity of the last indescribable Reality. The primitive function of a medium seems here to be restored to the actor, but at a higher level. His mediation is not, as in the case of the shaman of primitive Japan, between the living and the dead: the actor becomes a medium between the temporal individual in the audience and eternal, universal Permanence.

In the second part of the *Kyūi* Zeami gives intructions about the order in which to train. The apprentice should first study the middle three levels, next the upper three, and then the lower three. The technical training therefore comes first, and remains for Zeami the *conditio sine qua non* for the blossoming of the true flower. Only the mastery of technical skills makes possible the opening of the interior intuitive feeling which remains the key for the inner development and perfection of the art—the realm of the three superior levels. The final degree of achievement is not only a total removal of all duality (the actor is now his art) beyond critical acclaim and beyond success in society: it appears to have been conceived as the final spiritual result of the actor's total dedicction to the way of the *nō*; i.e., a kind of almost religious union with the Absolute through artistic accomplishment.

From the heights of the superior levels the master can eventually enter the realm of the three lower levels and use them for effects that can be worked out in harmony with the total performance. This is not, however, always necessary. Some masters choose not to use those lower levels, and this is, for Zeami, also acceptable.

Basic Concepts of Zeami's Aesthetics

Zeami did not define the concepts he uses throughout his many treatises. The writings were directed to one successor in the leadership of the school who evidently was already familiar with the terms. Moreover, the meaning given to his terminology did change over the years, so that, for example, the nuances of the concept of *yūgen* vary considerably from the early to the late treatises. It therefore seems useful to analyze the fundamental terms used throughout the treatises. These are *monomane, hana, kokoro, yūgen,* and *rōjaku.*

A) Monomane. For Zeami *monomane* was a working concept that certainly did not need any explanation: it was the specialty of the Yamato *sarugaku* tradition he belonged to, that stressed mimesis (then corresponding to what we would today call realistic acting) as opposed to the tradition of the competition, the Omi *sarugaku,* that stressed the elegance of dance and singing over the drama. An analysis of *monomane* reveals five elements or principles (imitation, truthfulness, identification, essentialization, and limitation, or choice).[29]

The first principle of imitation includes the realistic imitation of anything, which allows for an unlimited number of types of *monomane.* Zeami insists that the actor must study his object of imitation with the greatest care. When the performer must imitate persons to whom he can hardly have access, such as court ladies, he must seek advice, as he has not had an opportunity to observe their behavior. Zeami insists on accuracy of realistic imitation, on hard study to achieve it, on humility in asking advice from experts, and in asking for criticism after the performance.

The second principle of truthfulness stresses the idea that every falsehood in imitation weakens the performance. Zeami warns in the *Kakyō* that in all acts of imitation, if there is a false element, the performance will become rough and weak. It is therefore a great mistake to concentrate on creating an emotional impact upon the spectators by forcing the true nature of the imitated object. The mistake often originates from the actor's false perception that a quality like elegance or forcefulness exists independently of the object. Actually, it lies within the object itself. Thus, the quality of elegance in a performance is the result of a truthful imitation of an elegant object, not of an effort directed to the quality of elegance itself.

The third principle of identification is a deepening of the very idea of *monomane*. Zeami says that the performer should identify with the character, and should grow into the object of his imitation. Imitation leads to identification; that is, to a point where the actor should no longer be imitating the object that was external to him, because he has fused with it and the object is no longer external. At the point of supreme identification, imitation is replaced by the realm of "non-imitation."

Identification is achieved not with the total object of imitation, but with its *hon-i*, variously translated as "true intent," "interior essence," or "inmost nature." This implies the principle of "essentialization;" i.e., the process by the actor of reducing to the *hon-i* each character or object of imitation. An imitation that fails to catch the *hon-i* becomes an external, superficial imitation; it might look similar, but does not look right. The inmost essence of any object is not the whole object because the process of abstraction presupposes setting apart non-essential and individual details. The performer is not supposed to seek a naturalistic re-creation of an individual person or object in its entirety. He seeks, rather, an identification with the interior, essential traits of a universalized character or type, such as the old man, the warrior, the beautiful court lady, or the monk.

The fifth principle of limitation (or choice) is dictated by the preoccupation with audience approval and is related to avoiding anything that could break the spell of beauty in the performance and avert the favor of the powerful sophisticates. *Monomame*, theoretically open to everything, is limited in the *nō* through the exclusion of people whose menial occupation or unsightly appearance might be considered unpleasant by the noble audience. The exclusion of horror and vulgarity, and the use of unrealistically neat and beautiful costumes for pilgrims at the end of a long, fatiguing journey, or for humble gardeners, is a consequence of this principle.

B) Hana. For Zeami the flower (*hana*) is a most crucial concept in understanding the relationship between the actor and his audience. Konishi calls the flower "the key term and conception in Zeami's theory," and defines it as follows: "In Zeami's sense the Flower is an effect resulting from an excellent performance. When the audience is caught up in the actor's performance, we can say that there is Flower. Thus, the Flower is everything for the actor, because if he has failed to create it his audience will sooner or later desert him."[30]

The achievement of the flower is the goal of *nō* training. It is a purely theatrical value, based on a successful interaction between the actor and the audience. This is the reason why so many commentators, who care more for literature and esthetics than for theatre, write profusely about *yūgen* (a term derived from literary criticism and from philosophical sources) while almost ignoring *hana*. The flower has little to do with literature and everything to do with successful audience involvement in the miracle of communication achieved when actors and spectators unite in a spiritual community to experience the celebration of *nō*.

Zeami first distinguishes two basic types of flower: the temporary flower (*jibun no hana*) and the true flower (*makoto no hana*); then, within the true flower, he describes the various degrees of flower, as seen in the *Kyūi*.

The temporary flower is the result of the natural beauty and fascination of youth: it is not yet the fruit of training, but rather depends on the passing physical attraction of youthful charm. The temporary flower dies a natural death as soon as youth disappears.

The true flower is the result of long years of rigorous training; it blossoms from the mastering of technique and is clearly superior to the temporary flower. It manifests itself in a number of nuances and degrees of perfection, reaching the peak in the mysterious flower of the miraculous that sublimely unites actor and audience in a unique experience of the Absolute.

The question: what creates the flower? is answered by Zeami indirectly in a series of reflections on the subject. The first condition for the flower's appearance is the capacity in the actor of bewitching the audience, moving it deeply, fascinating it; that is, the performance must be *omoshiroki*. The second is the capacity of surprising the audience with novelty, with something unique, unexpected, original, and fresh; that is, the performance must be *mezurashiki*. The great artist is in some measure unpredictable, surprisingly new and fresh—he has the newness and freshness of creating a performance as if it were the first time every time.

Timing, in order to surprise the audience, becomes an essential element in creating the flower. The great actor must find the right moment to catch the public off guard, and sometimes it need be only a little movement, an almost invisible gesture that makes the flower blossom. The concept of mind or intuition (*shin* or *kokoro*, further explained below) is used by Zeami to describe the imponderable interior power of discernment which instinctively chooses the right play and the right style of acting for a particular audience; intuition is the interior eye which is always alert and ultimately decides timing, when to start and when to pause, whether to create a lively atmosphere or insist on quiet elegance, or even to sit down in contemplation.

A flower needs a seed to blossom. Zeami speaks in different contexts of the seed of the flower, sometimes assigning this important function to the mastering of the technique (*waza*), sometimes to *yūgen*. In conclusion, the true flower is the result of perfect technique, plus the personal talent and fascinating depth of the actor, plus surprise in the audience at the novelty and freshness of the acting, plus the adaptability provided by intuition, plus *yūgen*. The variety and degree of perfection of components and possible combinations explains the multiplicity of flowers.

C) Kokoro. The concept *kokoro* is probably the most metaphysical among those used by Zeami, and therefore mostly avoided by critics interested either in literary and esthetic criticism, or in theatrical practical values for the concrete problems of actor training. It is, however, indispensable in tying the poetical descriptions of the highest levels of performance to their root according to Zeami's thought. *Kokoro* is used by Zeami to indicate the ultimate foundation of the art of the *nō*, the source of the greatest impact upon audiences, the ultimate source of genuine *yūgen* performances, and the explanation of the secret of the unique fascination of the moment of "no-action." According to Pilgrim, *kokoro* in Zeami's use "encompasses such things as feeling and emotion, soul and spirit, mind and the objective knowing process, consciousness and self, intent and will, a pure and non-conscious mind, and a spiritual state representing the deepest levels of the total self."[31]

Pilgrim finds four major levels of *kokoro*. The first is that of emotion and feeling, giving birth to *yūgen*. The second is that of a self-conscious, knowing, object-centered, distinction-making mind (*yōjin*) which is aware of good and bad in the performance. The third is the heart of the unconscious, spontaneous void: the performer is no longer aware of himself, of the good and the bad, of the art itself. The distinction-making, self-conscious mind (*yōjin*) has disappeared; the art becomes *mushin* (literally, nothingness-heart). All division is overcome in the unity with the Source; the performance becomes *myō*; i.e., sublime, mysterious, numinous, indescribable. In this type of *kokoro* performance, the artist is not aware of performing *myō*. In the *myō* of the flower of the miraculous, it is no longer the individual, self-conscious, distinction-and judgement-making mind, but the instinctive, spontaneous, free-flowing mind of the master actor that has reached unity with *mu* (nothingness) and *kū* (emptiness).

The fourth level of *kokoro* is the all-encompassing, deep, and spiritual heart. This is the real *kokoro*, while the mentioned stratification in four levels is only a fiction of the mind, a western device for clarification. Zeami sees only the totality. When he uses the term *kokoro* in one of the partial meanings, he does not lose the perspective of the total *kokoro*, which is the root of the ultimate art that includes all the above.

The reality of *kokoro* is therefore rooted in the true essence of all things, or the all-encompassing, unchanging, pure Buddha-nature. The various facets of *kokoro* appear and work in the artist at different levels: emotional, rational, pre-rational-intuitive-spontaneous-sublime. The reality remains the same; it is the artist who passes through phases or stages of skills and realizations, eventually becoming one with the heart of everything, unconsciously and spontaneously following the rhythms of the One, the Absolute, the primordial Energy. The One is the entire process and includes everything, beginning to end. In a similar way, the art rooted in *kokoro* also includes everything, from the emotional to the rational to the pre-rational intuitiveness, *yūgen* and non-*yūgen*, sublime and non-sublime, to the comprehension of all and the insertion into the One-All. The great master, in synchronization with the *kokoro* of the Buddha-nature, in a real sense becomes its appearance on the stage, moving the *kokoro* of the audience deeply in an indescribable way. *Kokoro* is therefore the supreme secret, above all other secrets. No other secret has more consequence for the ultimate aim of the *nō* tradition and its future perpetuation.

Zeami uses the image of puppets and strings. Puppets are not self-moved; the strings effect the movement. So it is for the supreme master. He is not self-moved; he is governed in each step by the invisible heart (*kokoro*) that holds all forms and techniques of the *nō* together, and unites all powers in his masterful performance, in his life, and in his audience.

D) Yūgen. The roots of the word *yūgen* extend into Buddhist terminology of the later Han period in China (22-220 A.D.). Originally *yūgen* referred to the hidden meaning behind the surface of the sutras. In the tenth century in Japan, probably for the first time, it was used in poetic criticism with the meaning of "profound." In Zeami's time it was a fashionable term in judging the beauty of poems at the court of the Shogun, and it seems that it was used primarily to express refined elegance. Zeami's innovation consisted in applying a literary concept not only to judge the quality of *nō* texts, but also to express an elegant, refined quality in its performance.

Scholars have noticed the difference in meaning Zeami gives to *yūgen* between his early and later writings.[32] The elegant beauty stressed at the beginning of his career gives place later to a combination of elegance with depth and a touch of cosmic truth. Ueda writes: "If the term *yūgen* is etymologically analyzed, it will be found that *yū* means deep, dim, or difficult to see, and that *gen*, originally describing the dark, profound, tranquil color of the universe, refers to the Taoist concept of truth. Zeami's idea of *yūgen* seems to combine its conventional meaning of elegant beauty with its original meaning of profound, mysterious truth of the universe. Zeami perceived mysterious beauty in cosmic truth: beauty was the color of truth, so to speak."[33]

With age and the ravages of destiny, cosmic truth grew more and more to mean for Zeami the reflection of the truthful essence of humanity, a sad beauty. Zeami seems to find towards the end of his career a greater *yūgen* when his heroes and heroines become the representatives of humanity, suffering from causes beyond human control, for which, like Oedipus, they have no personal responsibility. "*Yūgen* is the beauty of seeing such an ideal person go through an intense suffering as a result of being human" writes Ueda.[34] The progression in depth does not stop at the level of human and cosmic sadness. Beyond the painful impermanence of the illusory world of the senses the highest forms of *yūgen* become a revelation of their roots in *kokoro* and therefore in the mystery of Permanence. At the supreme level *yūgen*, *hana*, *mushin*, *kokoro* make no more sense; they are all one in an experience that defies any logical explanation.

E) **Rōjaku.** The characters used for the term *rōjaku* indicate old age and tranquility, and a proper translation seems therefore to be the quiet beauty of old age. In his theoretical writings, Zeami seems to be especially fascinated by the thorough process of reduction to the very essence of the *nō* that is involved in the portrayal of an old person by a great master. The glamour of refined elegance of a court lady is gone, the strength of a warrior also is no longer there. The great challenge for the real master is to cause the flower to bloom while portraying old age. The interpretation of an old person is for Zeami the true mystery of the way of the *nō*, and is symbolized by a lonely flower blossoming on a withered branch of a cherry tree.[35]

Zenchiku's Theories on the Nō

Until very recently Zenchiku's theoretical writings had not been available in translation except for bits and pieces. In 1993 Thornhill's English translation of Zenchiku 's basic treatises, *Rokurin ichiro no ki* and *Rokurin ichiro no ki chū*, was published with scholarly commentary, thus providing western readers with a wealth of information about Zenchiku's religio-aesthetic world.[36] Yet, this deep, quiet, fascinating *nō* master still remains a most intriguing, and sometimes difficult-to-penetrate thinker. He elaborated the theory of the unity of poetry and dance (*ka-bu-isshin*), and explained the cycle of birth, development, and perfection of the *nō* in a fascinating series of reflections accompanied by beautiful illustrations for his theory of the six circles and one dew-drop (*rokurin ichiro*).

A) Ka-bu-isshin. The same urge to establish social respectability for the outcaste *nō* actor, so evident in Zeami's writings and life efforts, might well be at least partially responsible for Zenchiku's speculations about the connections between the highly esteemed "way" of the *waka*, then the most important form of poetry, and *nō* dance. Zeami tried to provide a basis for social respectability for the *nō* actors through the dubious connection of family descent from the performers of the sacred *kagura* at the imperial court. Zenchiku, on the contrary, seems to rely on an objective basis: the origin of the art of the *nō* from the very same source that also gave birth to *waka* poetry, the art practiced by emperors and nobility. Zenchiku formulated his theory of the unity of poetry and dance with a Japanese expression, *ka-bu-isshin*, which literally means "song-dance-one-heart." From the same source, (*kokoro*, as explained above) are born both the song (here synonymous with *waka* poetry) and the dance (here synonymous with *nō*). For Zenchiku, *waka* and *nō* build a living unity, sharing the one essence. *Nō* acting, singing, and dancing are as much a creative artistic activity as the composition of a *waka* poem: both are born from the same source of inspiration in the same soul, the *kokoro* of the artist. *Waka* and *nō* fulfill therefore the one goal of communicating, though through different means of expression, the same creative inspiration of the artist. The task of the *nō* actor accordingly is to create a theatrical expression for the poetical text of the plays, in which several *waka* and other classical poems are often actually quoted. The deepest possible understanding of the plays and their interior inspiration become the object of painstaking research for the actor. Zenchiku is often engaged in elucidating, explaining, and interpreting. He even adds poems to convey the special atmosphere, the mood he feels to be the key for the actor's penetration into the *kokoro* of the play.

Zenchiku gave poetical expression to his theory in his play *Ugetsu*, which is described at length in the section *The Nō Plays* of this chapter.

B) Rokurin ichiro (Six Circles and One Dewdrop). Zenchiku develops his theoretical speculation about the very nature of the *nō* art primarily in his *Rokurin ichiro no ki* (A Record of Six Circles and One Dewdrop, 1456) and in the later *Rokurin ichiro ki chū* (Commentary to "A Record of Six Circles

127

and One Dewdrop," 1465). Zenchiku's basic purpose in writing these treatises is to transmit to posterity the essence of Zeami's teachings about the *nō*. Zenchiku has a constant recourse to Buddhist ideas, mixed with Shinto and Confucian attitudes, in trying to explain esthetic experiences.[37] His concept of the six wheels or circles is based on an inspiration he had from the Bodhisattva Kannon while meditating at the Hase Kannon temple. It would be a great mistake not to take into account that Zenchiku was a deeply religious man, familiar with the Mahayana Buddhist view of life and its formulations, therefore taking for granted that *satori* (enlightenment) is the most important experience/purpose of human life. Although the enlightened experience of the Absolute Truth is beyond description, and therefore futile to talk about, the standard teaching of the Buddhism familiar to Zenchiku aknowledges a multiple and relative world, and a partial truth which should be explained to help disciples to enter the domain of the One Absolute Truth. According to Pilgrim, the key to the explanation of the six circles lies in a short writing by Zenchiku, the *Nika ichirin* (Two Flowers, One Circle), where the first three circles appear as "pointing to enlightenment or Buddha-mind, the one aspect of true performance upon which everything else is based. The fourth, fifth, and sixth circles emphasize the functioning of this enlightenment or Buddha Mind in performance."[38]

The very beginning of the *Rokurin ichiro no ki* states Zenchiku's belief that at the foundation of every performance, as well as of all art, all life, and all existence, is the fundamental Buddha nature. He describes this first foundation with a drawing of an empty circle, an illustration of the primordial *mu* (nothingness), and with the word *utsuwamono* which means receptacle, vessel, and also capacity or ability. This first circle is called *jurin*, the wheel of life, or, as Thornhill translates, the Circle of Longevity. At the level of performance, this round, empty "vessel" is related to proper breathing which smoothly joins together one's singing in an uninterrupted, round form (without a beginning or an end) and is experienced by the actor as an inexhaustible life-force.

The second circle is called *ryūrin*, read also *shurin*, the wheel of the vertex, or the wheel of arising, or, according to Thornhill, the Circle of Height—the ideogram indicating the vertical position. The first appearance of the spirit, of consciousness, of individuality is there symbolized through a vertical shaft that divides the primordial unity. It is the place where *yūgen* appears as the primary esthetic manifestation on stage. At the level of performance this second circle mirrors a style of high and clear singing that emerges from the primordial vessel, "the plain ground of the tranquil Circle of Longevity," (Thornhill) with an effect of chill beauty and deep emotion.

The third circle, *jūrin* (the wheel of settlement, or the wheel of dwelling, or, according to Thornhill, the Circle of Abiding) presents a very short vertical line, rather thickly drawn by Zenchiku at the bottom of an otherwise empty circle, symbolic of achieved settlement. The meaning seems to be connected with the manifestation of enlightenment in every single action that has settled, that has its dwelling, its beginning and end, in the One Supreme Reality: each and every moment of the *nō* must dwell in the spirit of *yūgen*—the spirit of *yūgen* being a different name in this context for the Supreme Reality. In the realm of performance this circle probably emphasizes the awareness of the performer that each of his movements and each of his sung phrases smoothly and without effort arise from and disappear into settled *yūgen* patterns.

The first three circles indicate the essence of the art of the *nō*. Zenchiku's meditation begins in the realm of the highest level of performance as described by Zeami in the *Kyū-i*; that is, in the sublime realm of *myō*, and analyzes it in its metaphysical essence: first in its ineffable Unity, which is like a womb out of which the *nō* is born; then in the birth of the song out of that unity; that is, the birth of *nō* like a golden wave of consciousness and impermanent existence from the ocean of formless emptiness; eventually in the settlement of that wave, of each wave in the spirit of *yūgen* that is again the Supreme, the Absolute: "In the performance of *nō* all that takes place moves [in circular fashion] out of and back to this dwelling place."

The fourth circle, the wheel of phenomena, or, according to Thornhill, the Circle of Forms (*zōrin*) illustrates the workings of the above three circles in the practical performance of the *nō*. Zenchiku lovingly painted inside this circle the moon and the sun, mountains and ricefields, woods, birds in the sky, a little hut, a domestic animal lying in the grass, and a man: in a word, a symbol of all existing things, a compendium of the universe; i.e., *yūgen* reaching all creation. This circle is about the performer learning every aspect of the *nō* and extending his knowledge to all phenomena, reaching a perfect combination of *yūgen* with mimetic acting (*monomane*) extended to every variety of role. "It speaks of the accomplished actor," writes Pilgrim, "who not only stands in the roundness and circularity of the first three circles, but effectively functions within a particular world—both the world of life in general and the world of Noh specifically."[39] According to Thornhill this circle "represents the art of *monomane*, the ability to portray an individual character convincingly....This mimetic style must be mastered before the more advanced style represented by the next two circles can be attempted."

The fifth circle, *harin* (the wheel of breaking) continues the description of the functioning of the first three wheels in the concrete world of the *nō* performance. It warns us to break through the images, forms, and so on, to reach in everything the enlightened view of the Supreme Reality. At the same time the harsh lines that break the circles into spikes refer to the breaks in style that the consummate master uses in his performances, and that not only preserve the unity with *yūgen*, but add a special beauty to it. This circle represents the aging master who performs "a forceful, inelegant demon role without displayng the vulgarity that a younger peformer might reveal" (Thornhill). In such cases, the conventional, smooth, external beauty symbolized by the circle is broken, only to reveal the higher skill of the old master. This special skill had been designated by Zeami as *ran-i*, which can be translated as rank of the sublime.

The sixth circle is again empty: the wheel or circle of emptiness, *kūrin*, looks exacly the same as the first, *jurin*. Zenchiku writes that when the master reaches the highest, he goes back to the beginning, *jurin*. This paradox is an echo of the Zen paradox that states: "Full enlightenment looks just like non-enlightenment." "The accomplished, aged actor returns to the young, untutored style of the child actor, expressing a most profound beauty through the performance of naive, child-like dance and singing styles" (Thornhill). Although the appearance of the consummated master is that of an old man, his heart is that of a child. The superfluous and the artificial are completely eliminated; the beauty of the essential is perfectly purified. Zenchiku is probably thinking of this highest, indescribable experience, echoing Zeami's praises for the rank of the sublime (*myō* and *ran-i*) and for *rōjaku*, when he writes about the music of a light rain on the few left-over branches of the famous old cherry trees in Yoshino, Ohara, and Oshio—covered with moss, a few cherry flowers scattered here and there....

   Ichiro is written with the characters *ro* for "dew," and *ichi* for "one." One Dew-Drop is here the symbol of the Spirit, and Zenchiku draws it with loving care in the form of a beautiful sword. Zenchiku writes: "This drop of dew has nothing in common with either emptiness or form. It exists completely independent. Not a single grain of dust is touched by it. It has the form of a sword." The sword is a symbol of the Mind that cuts through the many objects, through all obstacles and all distinctions, and returns everything to the One Mind of origin. Because it cuts through all theorizing, it also means the immediate revelation of truth, the comprehensiveness of the Absolute where the cycle begins and ends. Zenchiku develops this final thought more clearly in the one circle he drew for the *Nika ichirin*, which includes the six circles clockwise along the circumference and the sword in the middle. This all-unifying picture represents the total cycle, which for Zenchiku is supposed to be ever present in each action of the *nō* performer. He writes: "These seven items are all present in each melody, each word, and each style of performance."[40] In conclusion, Zenchiku is convinced that the performance of the miraculous flower is the product of an artist who operates psychologically and metaphysically in perfect union with the Buddha-nature, and who is driven by the One Supreme Energy and the One Supreme Truth, of which he becomes unconsciously a transparent revelation.

   Zenchiku's abstract speculation has a very practical, soteriological message for the would-be *nō* master and any would-be great performer: sublime beauty blossoms only as the mysterious flower of a deep personal spirituality that leads the artist to a humble dispersal of the ego into a unity with the Principle of all energies and truth, and sustains him in a lifetime dedication to the art.[41]

The Nō *Plays*

A) *Classification.* Today only about 240 plays make up the repertory of the five *nō* schools. They are a selection from an estimated 2000 texts (to which at least an additional 1000 titles should be added) that are known to scholars. The plays surviving in the canon were chosen in fact according to the taste of the Tokugawa period, which did not follow the criterion of popularity and success with wider audiences, but rather the sophisticated taste of the ruling class. Some of Zeami's best known masterpieces, such as *Matsukaze*, *Nonomiya* and *Kinuta*, evidently composed to please the elite at court, do not seem to have been particularly welcome to the larger mixed audiences of the big festivals in Zeami's time. These, on the contrary, loved plays of no literary value, now vanished from the stage.

Nō plays are classified according to different criteria. A first broad division groups all *nō* plays into two categories: *mugen nō* (plays about dreams and phantasms, featuring in the *shite* role a being from the "other" dimension, such as gods, ghosts, demons, or spirits of plants appearing in a dream or dreamlike experience) and *genzai nō* (plays featuring in the main *shite* role a protagonist belonging to the world of the living). Another criterion for broad classification is based on whether a piece has a dramatic plot (*geki nō*; i.e., drama-*nō*) or is little more than a dance-piece (*furyū nō*; i.e., dance-*nō*).[42]

The classical division into five groups according to the content of each play is probably the most practical, and is still commonly used, along with the others, in the *nō* world. It is also important because the construction of a formal program of *nō* is traditionally based on a selection and sequence of plays from each of the groups.

The first group is called *waki nō* (from the *waki*; i.e., the supporting role) and it contains plays in which the main role represents a deity, hence the alternate name of *kami mono* (plays about gods) for the works in this group. The purpose of these plays is usually to narrate the story of the origin of a shrine, or simply to praise a *kami*. In performance, plays about gods require great dignity and a ceremonial mood. A number of them are structured in two acts. In the first, the deity appears in disguise, and in the second reveals, with a mask and costume change, the real self. About thirty-nine plays belong to this group: famous among them are *Takasago* and *Chikubushima*.

The second group contains about sixteen plays called *Asura nō*, or *shura mono* from the name of the Buddhist underworld, where warriors killed in battle were believed to wander without peace. The protagonist usually impersonates the ghost of a famous *samurai* who appears to a monk and implores him for prayers and special rites that might assure salvation. Especially dramatic are the second act scene when the warrior re-appears in splendid *samurai* war costume as his true self, and the danced narrations of the final battle which cost the life of the conjured hero. Famous in this group are, among many others, *Tamura* and *Atsumori*.

The third group contains the *katsura mono* or wig plays, which feature women in the *shite* role; they are also called *onna mono* (women pieces). Some of the greatest *yūgen*-filled masterpieces of text and dance are among the thirty-eight pieces belonging to this category. Pieces in which the spirits of plants appear in feminine form also are frequently counted in this category. Famous plays in this category are *Bashō* and *Matsukaze*.

The fourth group contains about ninety-four plays that are traditionally performed in the fourth place in a five-*nō* program. In the *nō* jargon they are simply called "fourth group pieces," and comprise a number of sub-groups: important are the *kyōran mono* or madness pieces, a number of *genzai mono* (plays about the present time), and a group of plays about revengeful ghosts (*onryō mono*). The fourth group provides some of the most dramatic and most frequently performed plays, such as *Aya no tsuzumi*, the cycle of the Ono no Komachi plays, and *Kinuta*.

The fifty-three plays of the fifth group are called *kiri nō* (final *nō*) because they are performed at the end of a program and feature in the *shite* role non-humans from the mythological world, such as demons, monsters, goblins, and the like. They are utilized for a quick finale full of movement and color.

B) *Dramatic Structure.* The first division of a play is into *ba*, somehow corresponding to our concept of "act." Although there are one-act plays, most *nō* are in two acts. The break between acts becomes apparent when the protagonist leaves the stage for a mask and costume change, and the *ai*, or short interlude between the two *ba*, is performed by the *kyōgen* actor. There are cases in which the *shite*'s change of identity is accomplished through a costume change on the stage. The first act is usually called *mae-ba*, and the second *nochi-ba.*[43]

Each *ba* is made out of five *dan*. A *dan* corresponds more or less to what today would be called a "scene;" i.e., a breakdown of the play's action into phases of a certain completeness in themselves. The basic scenes of each first act are the following: first, the entrance of the supporting actor; second the entrance of the protagonist; third, the dialogue between supporting actor and protagonist; fourth, a performance (*shigoto*; i.e., what the *shite* "does") as centerpiece of the action of the play, which in most cases is the narration by the protagonist of the story (*monogatari*) upon which the play is based, and might contain the revelation of the *shite*'s true self; fifth, the withdrawal of the protagonist. In the second act the sequence is less regular, but sometimes it is faithfully repeated with the following differences: the *waki* waits on the stage, instead of entering; and the *shigoto* of the fourth *dan* is usually an introduction to the climax of the final dance in the fifth *dan*.

The further divisions of a *dan* into *shōdan*, *setsu*, and *ku* are based on differences in rhythm, language, pitch, and so on in smaller divisions of the text and corresponding performance. For instance, the *shōdan* can be divided into seven categories, to which belong parts where the rhythm follows a beat and others where it does not; where the text follows the seven and five syllable line principle, or does not; where a rhythm is spoken as recitativo, and so forth.

The division into five *dan* follows the rule of *jo, ha, kyū* (introduction, development, finale), that had been taken over by Zeami from the tradition of *bugaku* and faithfully and consistently applied to all phases of *nō*. To the introduction (*jo*) corresponds the first *dan*; i.e., the appearance or the waiting of the supporting actor (*waki*). To the development (*ha*) corresponds the second, third, and fourth *dan*; i.e., the entrance of the protagonist (*shite*), the dialogue between protagonist and supporting actor, and the narration of the story (*monogatari*) by the protagonist. To the fifth *dan* corresponds the final *kyū*.

The application of the *jo, ha, kyū* rhythm is also respected in the choice of *nō* plays to form a program. Of the five *nō* chosen the first represents the *jo* or overture, the second, third, and fourth form the *ha* or "break" from the overture; and the fifth represents the final, climactic *kyū*. This three-phase rhythm is also to be found within the subdivisions of each act and scene; it exercises the function of a universal organizational principle in each part of both text and performance of dance and music.

The above outlined structure changed with the development of later *nō* drama, especially under the influence of Kanze Kojirō Nobumitsu. He composed a number of plays about the present time (*genzai nō*), such as *Ataka*, in which the supporting role became a partner in the development of the conflict of the play, and no longer was in a secondary position relative to the protagonist. This change from conflict concentrated in the soul of the *shite* and expressed through re-enactment of past events, to a dramaturgy of conflict between living beings in many ways similar to western traditional models, represents a transition to what will later be inherited by the *kabuki* and *jōruri* traditions.

C) *Authorship and Criticism.* The attribution of authorship of a large number of *nō* plays presents many difficulties. There is a remarkable variety of opinions among the major experts in Japan—the authorship of even famous plays such as *Dōjōji* being in doubt.

No date for the composition of any play is ever given. In many cases the texts are, in their present stage version, known to be the result of many rewritings over several generations. The process of transformation and adaptation seems to have continued even in the case of revered masterpieces definitely attributed to Zeami or other masters, if we are justified in drawing a general conclusion from Zeami's few handwritten manuscripts compared with today's official stage versions of the same plays. To the lack of sufficient historical documentation must also in most cases be added the scarcity of serious critical analysis which could indicate convincing internal stylistic evidence. Furthermore, a widespread disinterest among literary scholars in the study of theatrical texts, coupled with the difficulty of access to major collections of *nō* texts owned by the major schools, is responsible for the infant stage in which textual criticism still finds itself.[44]

Another characteristic of the most sophisticated *nō* plays is that of using many quotations of poems—in part or in their entirety—from both the Chinese and the older Japanese collections of classics. This is particularly true of the plays written for the court of the Shogun at the time of Yoshimitsu, who was fond of the sophistication and elegance of numberless allusions. The abundance of quotations at times makes it even more difficult to attribute a play to an author, whose skill was not so much in creating exquisite poetry, but in selecting the appropriate poems to evoke a related mood and in weaving them, in their entirety or in chosen verses, into a thick, rich brocade of concentrated poetic text. For western readers not familiar with the poetic classics from ancient China and Japan, it is common to attribute to the playwright the astonishing beauty of some parts of the plays, although these parts probably are just quotations from some of the most beautiful treasures of Chinese and Japanese poetry.

In the case of the greatest among the *nō* playwrights, Zeami, the abundance and appropriateness of his quotations do succeed in their function of establishing highly poetic moods on the stage. Such exquisite accomplishment is beautifully harmonized with the original creation of immortal characters, who are poetically outlined and justly famous for their theatrical effectiveness.

A large number of plays have been tied to Zeami's name. Among them, about twenty are definitely considered as his, while a much larger number are catalogued among works that may be considered Zeami's, and a dozen are thought to have been revised by him. The list of plays of uncertain attribution to Zeami is also long, being nearly thirty.[45] Similar uncertainty exists about the authorship of Zenchiku's plays—very few are attributed to him without doubt. The shift from acceptance of long lists of plays as definitely by a certain author, to a systematic doubt arguing the lack of sufficient evidence to attribute authorship except for a very few plays, has settled down to a reasonable compromise. In the meantime, a few Japanese literary scholars, such as Yokomichi Mario, Omote Akira, and Katō Shūichi, have dedicated serious critical attention to the problems connected with the transmission of the texts, and the changes and the integrity of the original; unfortunately they have limited most of their efforts to the better known among the plays in the canon.

136

There is no doubt that some *nō* plays rank among the acknowledged masterpieces of the world's dramatic literature. On the other hand it is also true that, like the majority of plays in other genres, most *nō* plays do not possess high literary value. Many texts were conceived merely as simple, short, unpretentious librettos—a necessary but secondary accessory to performance.

The loss of a large number of texts, and the lack of access in translation to a substantial number of existing *nō* plays (many pieces belonging to the canon are not yet available in translation, and practically no non-canonical *nō* has been published in any non-Japanese language) is, of course a drawback to the western critic, but probably does not deprive him of the best examples, which were carefully preserved, and dutifully translated. The situation is not much different from that of the classic Greek dramatic heritage. It seems correct to assume that in both cases probably the best masterpieces were saved—or at least that the saved examples are among those that were worth saving and among the best and most representative of the genres.

A great difference is to be found in the amount of international scholarship generated. The few surviving classic Greek plays have been the object of a vigorous and self-confident critical tradition of scholarly research in many languages. The work of literary analysis done by non-Japanese scholars on the comparatively numerous preserved *nō* plays is still in a phase of infancy. The difficulties of rendering in translation the beauty of the original range from the extreme abundance of allusions and quotations, to the almost impossible task of handling the numerous plays on words.[46] The rich, topical imagery, the creation of the very special feeling of a precious fabric of ancient poetry, and the sophisticated narration and re-experiencing of ancient tales, might not come through with their full impact; still, in spite of the imperfect translations, they hardly ever fail to fascinate western readers of the finest *nō*.

D) *Zenchiku's* **Nō** *Plays.* While Zeami's plays are always translated and commented on in every western publication about the *nō*, Zenchiku's work as a playwright is less well known in the West. Zenchiku's plays are rich in a poetic atmosphere of elusive beauty—a brand of *yūgen* that is deep, delicate, exclusive, nostalgic.[47] His *Yōkihi* (Japanese for Yang

Kuei-fei, the favorite mistress of the Chinese Emperor Hsüan Tsung, r. 713-756) is a dramatization of the last part of the *Song of Everlasting Sorrow* by the Chinese poet Po Chü-i (772-846). In the play Yōkihi is already in the mythical Land of Immortality, the legendary island of P'eng-lai, after the cruel separation from her beloved Emperor and premature death in exile—now a musing ghost totally immersed in sorrow and nostalgia. There she is visited by a Taoist sorcerer sent by the Emperor, who will carry her message of love to the world of the living. Poetry flows from the repository of the heart, where memory works like a powerful filter to distill from any debris of actuality and triviality the past experiences of enchanting, fleeting moments. Memory magnifies and intensifies the interior image which appears to occupy Yōkihi's entire soul—a process out of which tragic madness is born. Reality in the world is spread over a long period. Memory, on the contrary, is compacted, concentrated, overwhelming in the "now" of reminiscing, without the actual presence, about the beauty of a lost human love in the context of a cosmic feeling for nature. "Even the reflections of the moon I am staring at, all alone, weep for me and soak my sleeve." The cosmic dimension of sorrow is only hinted at in *Yōkihi*.

In *Bashō* the unity of the universe constitutes the very theme of the play. Plants, as well as every living being, will attain salvation, because "even non-sentient herbs and trees share the one absolute reality." The plantain tree appears as a beautiful woman to a hermit. The text, a delicate sequence of images from the world of nature accompanied by elegant dance, expresses the joy at the prospect of salvation, and the flimsiness of everything mortal in the final description of the gale, "racing downwards, bending the pines, tearing up flowers and grasses." At the end, "Alone stands the plantain tree, its leaves all torn to shreds."

Ugetsu is a baffling, elusive masterpiece in the genre of poetic drama. Its dramatic structure is loose and vague, it is not clear who is who in the principal roles, and the connection between the first and the second part of the play is weak. The nebulous contours, however, enhance the poet's main purpose of concentrating in a highly specialized area of the human spirit, the seat of pure aesthetic pleasure. The unity of inspiration of the play comes from there, the first part being a contest of astonishing refinement in the art of contemplation, fruition, and poetical expression of beauty, and the second a supernatural confirmation and definition of Zenchiku's *ka-bu-isshin* theory. It seems that more precisely drawn characters and more logical connection between the two parts of the play were the least concerns of the author, having hardly any bearing on the main issue, the penetration into the interior sanctuary of beauty worship.

The characters are, in the first part, the poet Saigyō (1118-1190) in the supporting role; i.e., the *waki*; an old man, probably an incarnation of Sumiyoshi Myōjin, the patron god of poetry, as the main role; i.e., the *shite* (more precisely, *maejite*); an old woman, probably a companion to the *shite*; i.e., the *tsure* or *shitezure*. In the interlude between the two parts of the play, the *kyōgen* actor, called *ai*, plays the role of a guardian god of a subsidiary shrine appearing in a dream to Saigyō. In the second part the main role; i.e., the *shite* (more precisely, *nochijite*) is an old keeper of the shrine, who is possessed by the god of Sumiyoshi, a Bodhisattva patron of poetry called Kōkitokuō bosatsu; the old woman, who left the stage with the old man, does not reappear; Saigyō, the *waki*, remains on stage to the end.

At the beginning of the performance, after the musicians and the chorus enter as usual, a symbolic hut (a bamboo frame with a light wooden roof) is placed in front of the musicians, upstage center. The frame is closed by a curtain facing the audience—the old man and the old woman enter the stage walking behind it, invisible to the audience. The old man sits stage left, under the part of the roof that is still whole, the old woman on the contrary sits at his right, under a broken roof; both are still invisible to the audience.

The time of the play is the 12th century, during a crystal-clear autumn night. The place is the vicinity of the Sumiyoshi shrine, in the Settsu province, near modern Osaka. The poet-priest Saigyō (*waki*) enters and sings about his pilgrimage with no destination but to seek the beauty of nature. He comes from visiting the Sumiyoshi shrine, where the god patron of *waka* poetry is honored. In the meantime night falls; the poet sees a faint light from a little hut built on pilings over the pond and decides to ask for a night's shelter there. While Saigyō approaches the hut, the curtain is removed by an assistant, and the old man, sitting motionless, sings of the beauty of the moon and of the music of the wind sounding like drizzling rain. The old man at first refuses Saigyō's request—the hut is too small and poor; he will find a better place in the neighborhood. The old woman, however, has recognized in the pilgrim a wandering priest and wants to have him as a guest. The old man explains the unusual state of the roof. There is a difference in taste and a long-lasting dispute between himself and the old woman. She loves the moonlight immensely; she does not want to repair the broken roof, in order to enjoy fully the beauty of the moon penetrating into the hut during the moonlit nights. He loves the music of the rain immensely, therefore he does want to repair the roof in order to enhance his pleasure in the rustling of the rain. They cannot come to an agreement. As a result the roof is whole on the side where the old man lives, while it is partly missing and falling apart on the old woman's side.

Saigyō is astonished at the unique argument—the priority in beauty between the silvery moonlight and the music of the rain with the rustle of the falling leaves. While the old man proceeds to describe his point of view he pronounces inadvertently two seven-syllable verses which can become the conclusion of a *waka* poem (a *waka* has five verses with 5-7-5-7-7 syllables). They express the concern about repairing or not repairing the roof of the humble hut. Saigyō fulfills with joy the task:

tsuki wa more	may the moon penetrate
ame wa tamare to	may the rain accumulate
tonikaku ni	according to either desire
shizu ga nokiba o	the humble roof
fuki zo wazuroo	should or should not be repaired?

The poem is now complete and they sing it together. The chorus proceeds with praise and the invitation to enter the hut. While the three actors sit motionless in front of the symbolic frame, the chorus sings and meditates on a poem by Po Chü-i (772-846) about the pain of a man who, at the sight of the moon, realizes how the same moon gives himself happiness, and the far away friend nostalgia.

The quiet atmosphere is broken by the old woman who hears an approaching shower. The old man has noticed the familiar music of the rain too. How can that be, however, since the crystal-clear sky, purified by the evening breeze, is radiant with moonlight? No, it is not the rain. The autumn wind has visited the pine tree nearby the roof, and made it

140

1. The main performer (*ninjo*) in the *mikagura*, holding a branch of *sakaki*, and wearing the uniform of an officer of the imperial guard.

2. The *niwabi*, the garden fire lit in front of the shrine of the *kami* at the beginning of an ancient *mikagura*.

3. A performance of Bichū Shinden Kagura, a type of *satokagura* in the district of Kawakami, Okayama-ken.

4. A contemporary phenomenon of divine possession (*kamigakari*) during the Bichū Kagura.

5. *Gigaku* mask of Konron, the lascivious molester.

6. *Gigaku* mask of a lion (*shishi*).

7. *Gigaku* mask, often interpreted as Chidō, National Museum, Tokyo.

8. *Gigaku* mask of the guardian god Kongō, who defends the maiden Gojo, molested by Konron.

9. *Gigaku* mask of Gokō, the noble man or king from Kure.

10. *Gigaku* mask of Gojo, the maiden who is molested by the lascivious Konron, preserved in the Hōryūji temple.

11. *Gigaku* mask of the bird-demon Karura.

12. *Embu* dance on the *bugaku* stage, as it appears in the *Bugaku emaki*.
Notice the tall *dadaiko* on the right-hand side, and the musicians on the right.

13. *Bugaku* stage of the Imperial Palace in Tokyo for a performance in the
1960s.

14. An ancient *bugaku* performance of *warabemai* (children's dance).

15. *Bugaku* greenroom, for the same performance.

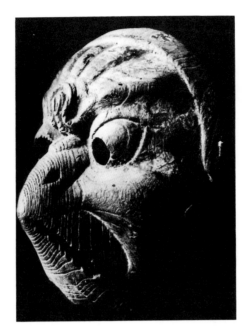

16. *Bugaku* mask of Kuron Hassen, from *Gigaku men taikan*.

17. *Bugaku* mask of Ninomai.

18. *Bugaku* mask of Nasori,
Horyūji Temple.

19. The "abstract" *bugaku* mask
for *Anma*. It is painted in black on
white silk.

20. Musical instruments used for *gagaku* music.

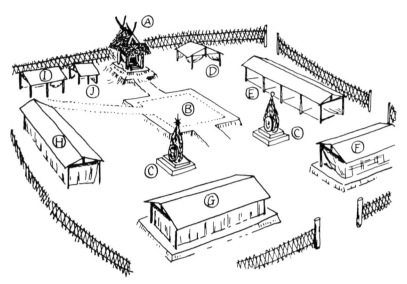

21. At the center (B) the *tsuchibutai* (earth-stage) of the Kasuga Wakamiya shrine in Nara used for *bugaku* and other performances. Notice the large *dadaiko* (C) for the *gagaku* orchestra, and the little shrine (A) where the *goshintai* (object representing the presence of the patron god) is processionally carried to preside over the performances. The other buildings are used as greenrooms and to shelter important guests.

22. *Tsuna watari* (rope crossing), a *sangaku* entertainment; from the *Shinzei kogaku zu* (twelfth century). The shrine maidens balancing on their wooden clogs are juggling ten and twelve fire gems respectively, while the priestess at the right carries the fire out of which the balls are made.

23. *Rōgyoku sangaku,* a juggling act with balls, from the *sangaku* tradition. From the *Shinzei kogaku zu*.

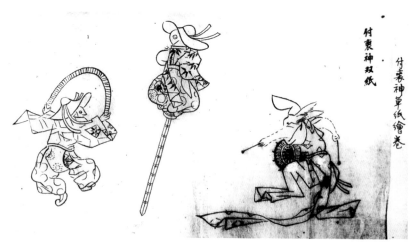

24. *Binzasara* (left), *issoku* (center), and *kakko* (right), from the *dengaku* tradition.

25. *Rōken to sanjūdachi,* juggling act with seven swords and balancing three people.

26. *Ennen mai,* from the *Enko taishi den.*

27. The stage for an *ennen* performance.

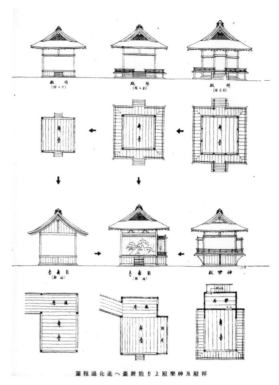

殿拝及神樂殿り上能舞臺へ進化過程圖

28. Development of the *nō* stage from the *haiden* (shrine building in front of which the worship ceremonies are performed) and the *kaguraden* (stage for *kagura* performances) according to the *Kokuhō nōbutai*.

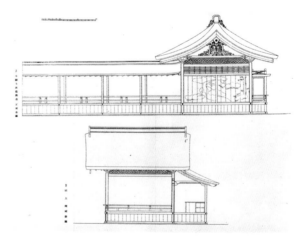

29. Front view of the *nō* stage according to the *Kokuhō nōbutai*.

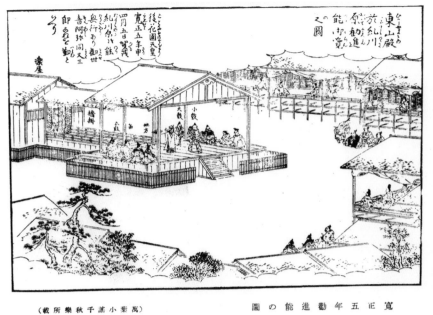

（茂葉小諸千秋樂所載）　　　　　寛正五年勸進能の圖

30. A *kanjin nō* (benefit performance of *nō*) at Higashiyama in 1465. Notice that the *hashigakari* is directly behind the main stage.

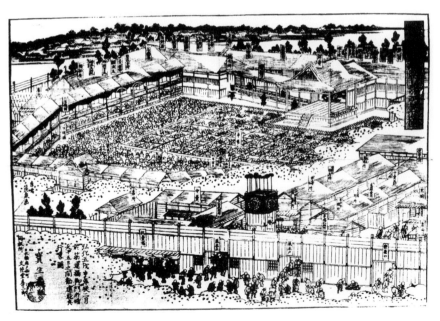

31. The stage for a *kanjin nō* in 1848. The large crowd testifies to the popularity of special benefit performances.

32. A performance of *chōnin nō* during which the townspeople (*chōnin*) had access to the palace.

33. The stage at the recently built Kokuritsu Nōgakudō (National Nō Theatre).

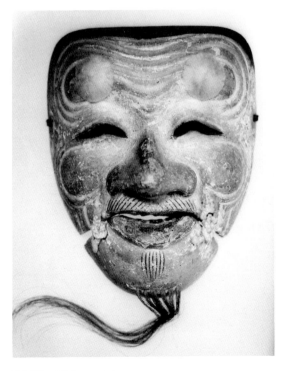

34. The Okina mask.

35. A scene from the *nō* play *Kinuta*, interpreted by Honda Hideo, December 1963. It illustrates the dance of the ghost of a wife who died because she believed that her husband had abandoned her.

36. A scene from the *nō* play *Sotoba Komachi*, interpreted by Sakurama Michio, November 1958. The old poetess Komachi sits on the stupa.

37. From the *nō* play *Kikujidō* (Chrisanthemum Jidō), performed in September 1961: the child who makes an elixir of eternal youth dances in front of the flowers.

38. From the *nō* play *Tsuchigumo* (The Ground-spider), (performed in August 1960): the spider disguised as a priest throws its webs on Yorimitsu.

39. From the *nō* play *Funa Benkei*, the ghost of general Tomomori attacks Yoshitsune who sits on the boat (December 1963).

40. In the *kagami no ma*, just before the beginning of the performance, the *nō* musicians and the *shite* prepare for their entrance on the stage.

41. The four instruments used in *nō*: from the left, the *daiko* (stick-drum), the two hand-drums *ōtsuzumi* and *kotsuzumi*, and the flute, *fue,* in the front.

1. *Jurin*, the Wheel of Life. The writing inside the picture does not belong to the wheel, which is supposed to be a completely empty circle, like the sixth wheel, *kūrin*.

4. *Zōrin*, the Wheel of Phenomena

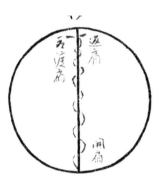

2. *Ryūrin*, the Wheel of Vertex

5. *Harin*, the Wheel of the Break

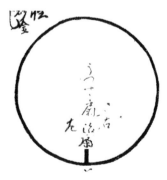

3. *Jūrin*, the Wheel of Settlement

6. *Kūrin*, the Wheel of Emptiness

7. Ichiro, one drop of dew, symbolized by the sword

8. The Picture of Perfect Wisdom. The characters in the circles read, from the top right, clockwise: *ju* (for *jurin*); *ryū* (for *ryūrin*); *jū* (for *jūrin*); *zō* (for *zōrin*); *ha* (for *harin*); *kū* (for *kūrin*).

42–49. Drawings from the *Rokurin ichiro no ki*, photographed by Benito Ortolani from the original manuscript by Zenchiku, which is in the possession of the Iemoto of the Komparu School. (Captions are printed under each picture.)

50. The stage of *Okuni kabuki*. Notice the orchestra, still basically the same as in the *nō*, and the draping instead of the *matsubame* as background.

51. Okuni conjures the ghost of Nagoya Sanza (from the *Kunijo kabuki ekotoba*).

52. An *onna kabuki* dance. Notice the *shamisen* and the outlandish tiger fur on the centre of the stage.

53. Stage of the *onna kabuki*. Painting from the Tokugawa collection.

54. The old *kabuki* theatre Nakamura-za, at the time of the *wakashu kabuki* (mid-seventeenth century).

55. The Ichimura-za *kabuki* theatre in Edo (1764) during a *kaomise* performance. Hanging scroll (Tsubouchi Memorial Theatre Museum).

56. Interior of a *kabuki* theatre of the Temmei period (1781–1788). From a wood-block print by Utagawa Toyoharu.

57. The stage of *kabuki* about 1802. Notice the revolving stage, the traps, and the entrance of the *hanamichi* at stage left, almost at the center. From *Shibai gakuya zue shūi*.

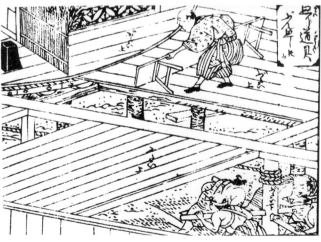

58. The hand-operated mechanism of the revolving stage (*mawaributai*) at the beginning of the nineteenth century.

59. Portrait of Ukon Genzaemon, a famous *onnagata* during the time of the *wakashu kabuki*, said to have founded the *kabuki* art of female impersonation (mid-seventeenth century). After the ban of *wakashu kabuki*, Genzaemon devised the cloth covering the shaved part of the head.

60. Portrait of Mizuki Tatsunosuke (1673–1745), from the *Furyū Shihō byōbu* (1700). Chikamatsu wrote for him several plays.

61. Danjūrō II (1689–1758) in *Ya no ne*. A wood-block print illustrating the characteristics of the *aragoto* style, with oversize arrows and typical *kumadori* make-up.

62. Portrait of Nakamura Utaemon I (1719–1786), a wood-block print by Toyokuni.

63. A scene from the *kabuki* play *Yotsuya kaidan* by Tsuruya Namboku IV (1755–1829) with Onoe Kikugorō V (1844–1903) in the role of Oiwa, performed in Tokyo in 1886.

64. The actor Ichikawa Ennosuke III (born 1939) in *Michiyuki hatsune no tabi* at the Kabuki-za theatre in Tokyo.

65. The present stage of the Kabuki-za theatre in Tokyo, during a performance of *Miyajima danmari*. A *danmari* is a highly stylized pantomime in which the characters perform a battle as they grope for one another in the dark.

66. *Kairaishi* or *Kugutsumawashi*, the oldest form of hand puppets, from the *Jinrin kimmō zui*, 1690.

67. Early puppeteer performing *nō plays*. Illustration by Hishikawa Moronobu from the *Konogorogusa* (1682).

68. Mural painting of early puppeteers from Miidera no Emman-in.

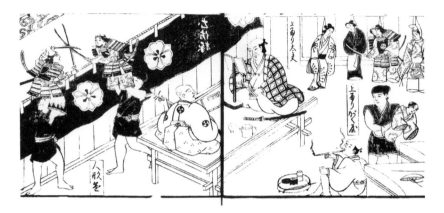

69. From behind the curtain of the puppet theatre of Yamamoto Tosa-no-jō. Both the puppeteers and the chanter are not visible to the audience. Illustration by Makieshi Genzaburō from *Jirin Kimmō Zui*, 1690.

70. A scene from the *bunraku* play *Yoshitsune senbonzakura*, with Yoshida Bungorō as main puppeteer, in the 1960s.

71. A head dated 1738, used in the Kimpira *jōruri*. The puppet was handled by three puppeteers. Head found and photographed by Sugino Kitsutarō in 1967.

72. A contemporary head of a *bunraku* female character.

73. A contemporary head of the *bunraku* character Bunshichi.

74. A scene from the *shimpa* play *Igai* (1894), as performed by Kawakami Otojirō in the role of Itakura Sōzō, and by Fujisawa Asajirō in the role of the *geisha* Umeji.

75. An early (1911) *shingeki* performance by Tsubouchi's Bungei Kyōkai of Ibsen's *A Doll's House*, with the actress Matsui Sumako as Nora, and Doi Shunshō as Torvald.

76. A 1913 performance of Gorky's *The Lower Depths* by the *shingeki* troupe *Jiyū gekijo*, directed by Osanai Kaoru (1881–1928) at the Imperial Theatre.

rustle and tremble. This would be an urgent warning for an ordinary housewife to begin immediate preparations for the coming winter. The old couple on the contrary will enjoy in tranquillity to the last the beautiful loneliness of the autumn night. While the *shite* performs a quiet dance, a famous sentence is sung, "*shigure senu, yo mo shigure suru.*" It says, in a complicated play of words, how also in a night, in which no rain falls, the music of the rain can be heard, because the leaves fall like drops of rain. The atmosphere is colored with the sadness of old age. The *shite* sings and laments how the falling leaves force him to think of his old age, and cause him to cry. Drops of dew lie on the fallen leaves. Are they really drops of dew? Are they not rather tears? Moonlight shines on the wet leaves. Again and again red maple leaves fall. They are also wet with drops of dew—or maybe it is not dew; it is the blood-stained tears of the old man. With a peaceful movement of the fan, the *shite* collects the imaginary leaves. He will soothe his sadness with the echoes of the beloved music of the rain.

The first part of the play ends with an incipient revelation of the true nature of the old man. Now a change in tone of voice and behavior must show his divine dignity. The text says little, and there are differences in the actual interpretation of this change. The actor is faced with a difficult and vague task, and it might well be that Zenchiku meant that Saigyō is now asleep, and the rest of the play happens in a dream.

The same god, who probably appears in the first part as the old man, will manifest himself, it seems, in the second part through a Shinto priest of whom he takes possession.

Before the second entrance of the protagonist (i.e., the *shite*, this time no longer an old man, but in the costume of a Shinto priest, possessed by the god of Sumiyoshi), there is an interlude in which, always in a dream, Saigyō receives the visit of a guardian-god who explains the divine possession: the words of the Shinto priest are actually words by the god of Sumiyoshi, and therefore to be accepted with great respect. At this time the stage assistant removes the hut from the stage.

The second part is as usual mostly dance. In this case, however, the text serves also the purpose of extolling the excellence of the *waka* poetry and consequently of the nō dance. A *waka*, the *shite* sings, consists of five verses, which are symbols of the five primary elements, wood, fire, earth, gold, and water. The initial verses of the *waka* symbolize heaven, the final verses earth. A *waka* is therefore a symbol of the universe and its original principles. The god of Sumiyoshi, patron of *waka* poetry, speaking through the Shinto priest, states that only very few are real masters of this art, and therefore he has really appreciated the beautiful, perfect poem improvised by Saigyō. At the end of the play—comes a poetical insertion of Zenchiku's *ka-bu-isshin* theory. The text says: "the recitation of the *waka* and the sleeves of the dance are the same". In other words, poetry and dance; i.e., *waka* and *nō*, are one in essence ("the sleeves of the dance" is apparently a synecdoche: it indicates the dance of the *nō* which does use movements of the sleeves). After the delicate, sophisticated dispute of the first part, the divine word itself confirms at the end the extolled, basically equal value and dignity of *waka* and *nō* performance.

The Performance of Nō

In general it can be said that the *nō* dance consists of basic postures (*kamae*) and dance patterns (*kata*) which do not stress acrobatic complexity but rather require a deep concentration on an interior process resulting in the projection of intense but relaxed energy.[48] The performer in the basic standing position is supposed to keep the torso "in one piece," slightly bent forward, with the back forming a straight line; his head must be held erect with the chin pulled back; the arms are curved downwards and kept slightly toward the front of the body, with the elbows lifted and the hands at the sides; the knees are slightly bent, the feet kept parallel to each other. The image projected by this position, enhanced by the long and wide sleeves of the costume, is that of a powerful flow of energy.

Systematic effort and training is required to acquire the habit of gathering the energy necessary to unify body and spirit in the control of the "center point" in the lower abdomen, supposedly corresponding to the body's center of gravity. This process is supposed to strengthen the pull of gravity in this central place and to reinforce the performer's projection of an appearance of weight and power. The projection of energy is also helped through the imaginary lines of force emanating from the center of the body in all directions. The performer also moves as if drawn forward by this force. The master is supposed to reach a point in which he can perform all the above without tension or rigidity, breathing evenly and feeling a deep relaxation together with the highest concentration. The simple starting position thus becomes a powerful instrument to project the "spirit of the *nō*" from the very beginning.

The basic movement of walking (*hakobi*) requires the performer to keep the beginning position unchanged from the hips up while he glides on his heels—making sure that no up-and-down vibration might confuse the impression of a non-earthly being gliding on air. The dance patterns in the *nō* are relatively few; they have gone through a thorough process of stylization and simplification, leaving a few semantic remnants only in some of them. The majority are presently deprived of specific descriptive meaning and fulfill the function of abstract dance. Probably the most common semantic pattern preserving the primitive function of illustrating the meaning of the dance is the *shiori*; i.e., when the *shite* lifts his hands (or one hand) close to the eyes in sign of weeping.

Nō music is conceived completely in terms of its function in the theatrical performance and gives to the total performance a unique, solemn, and haunting atmosphere.[49] The *nō* chant derives from *shōmyō*, the sophisticated and rich tradition of Buddhist chanting that traces its roots to India. The basic instrumental accompaniment and the patterns of song and dance derive from *gagaku*. Moreover, the instruments are adaptations of *gagaku* instruments. For example, the two types of hand drum used in *nō*, the *ōtsuzumi* and the *kotsuzumi* resemble the *san-no-tsuzumi* used in *gagaku*. In most plays, only the two hand drums and a flute (the *nōkan*) constitute the *nō* orchestra, which, in a limited number of plays, also includes a stick drum, the *taiko*. To the four instruments some authors add a fifth, the human voice, which is used in the form of *kakegoe* (attached calls), perceived by the audience as strange guttural shouting or moaning of special syllables, without meaning as words, but, as part of the official score, indicating the beat at established moments.

The Nō *Stage*

The shape and the size of the main stage (*honbutai*) and of the temple-like roof on top of it are derived from the shrine worship pavillion and the *kagura* pavillion of ancient Japanese architecture; its measurements were determined by the traditional Japanese modular system of building, which is based on standardized units.[50] This explains the constant square footage of the main stage (three square *ken*, equivalent to about 320 square feet) under the main roof, sustained by four square pillars. With the exception of the few remaining old stages preserved in shrines and temples, which sometimes present differences in various details, existing *nō* stages follow the strict prescriptions of the code established by the Tokugawa government in the eighteenth century, which is quite specific in all details of measurements, materials, ornamentations, orientation, and so on.

The standard stage is built of Japanese cypress (*hinoki*). The floor is about three feet above the ground, and is polished for use by the dancers who glide over it wearing special white socks (*tabi*). Under the stage floor are buried giant pots (nowadays sometimes substituted for by bowl-shaped concrete hollows), whose purpose is to provide resonance, thus making the stage an additional percussion instrument when stamped upon by the actor. The *hashigakari*—a bridge connecting the stage with the mirror room—that historically has fluctuated in position (center back, upstage left, or upstage right), settled upstage right during the past few centuries. The many details of understated ornamentation in the building of the stage are meant to give a sophisticated sense of deceptive simplicity: there is hardly any stage in the world that is the object of so much care in its details—from the trimmings of the roof to the painting of the pine tree on the wooden backdrop, the finishing of the pillars with fluted or beveled corners, the painstakingly combed pebbles around the stage area, and so forth.

The *matsubame* (pine tree painted as the only permanent decor of a *nō* performance) represents for some commentators the famous Yōgō pine at the Kasuga shrine in Nara beneath which, according to tradition, the god of the shrine was seen dancing in the shape of an old man. On the occasion of the annual Kasuga Wakamiya festival the *iemoto* of the Komparu

School still stands under that pine with the understanding that he will become a kind of *kamigakari* or receptacle of the local god in the traditional opening performance of *Okina*. According to others, the painted tree is a remembrance of the time in which *sarugaku* was performed outdoors against the background of pines, just as the painted bamboo at the sides bring to mind the actual bamboo canes which were used to mark the entrance to the stage.

The use of the stage is strictly prescribed, and no space is left for improvisation or unauthorized changes. Each pillar has a name related to the positions of the *waki* (*wakibashira*, where the supporting actor usually sits), the *shite* (*shitebashira*, at the entrance of the main stage where the protagonist usually stays), and the flute player (*fuebashira*, near the seat where he performs); the fourth pillar, the *metsukebashira*, takes its name from its function of orientation for the masked performer. The main stage itself is referred to by the performers as if divided into nine square spatial units, each with a name which the actors can use to explain the movements and the locations of the dramatic action.

To the visible complex of the *nō* stage also belong, besides the main stage and the bridge, the rear stage (*ato-za*), onto which the bridgeway opens and where the orchestra sits, and the side-stage (*waki-za*), where the chorus sits. The bridgeway begins in the mirror-room (*kagami no ma*) where the *shite* pauses before his entrance to put on his mask and accomplish his tranformation into the role. The members of the chorus (*ji-utai*) enter the stage through a small and low entrance, the *kiritoguchi*, which is a lateral opening in the rear stage, opposite the bridgeway. The stairs in the center of the front of the stage (*shirasu hashigo*) are never used in performance.

Several authors have remarked on the special function of the *nō* stage as a sacred space where the meeting of our world with the other dimension is represented. The bridge becomes the passage through which gods become visible, restless or angry ghosts appear to haunt, or to implore the prayers that can give them salvation, dreams concretize, and sad tales of the past are relived—if only for the fleeting and concentrated re-enactment of the high points in a dance born out of memory. On the other hand, in the *genzai nō* which feature living human beings in the roles of both *waki* and *shite*, and also in the performance of *kyōgen*, the *nō* stage becomes the place for the realistic performance of present human conflicts, thus opening the way for developments which will lead in the early Tokugawa period to the birth of the new *kabuki* stage.

Costumes, Props, and Masks

Among the striking elements of visual beauty in a *nō* performance are the costumes and the masks. The best *nō* masks are considered as national treasures and are admired as masterpieces of world rank. The sumptuous costumes, however, are not the heritage of primitive *sarugaku*, which stressed simplicity in contrast to the luxurious display of the competing *dengaku* tradition. The habit of donating precious garments to the actors as a sign of appreciation for excellent performances provided the *sarugaku* actors, once established at the Shogun's court, with costly gold brocades and silk damasks which, from the time of Yoshinori's protégé On'ami, gradually became their habitual costumes. The casual use of donated garments evolved into a sophisticated and strictly regulated use of patterns, colors, and types of garments for each role and each occasion. During the Tokugawa period the process of standardization reached its completion. The result was a style of costume which does not specifically represent the dress of any period, but rather synthesizes several centuries of courtly fashion. Many of the best costumes in use today were made during the Tokugawa era, and the few new costumes generally repeat the patterns established at that time.

The very name used for the *nō* costumes, *shozoku*, instead of the more common *ishō*, indicates a sense of respect for the precious, often old and frail garments. Under the costume the *shite* wears a padded white undergarment which contributes to the sense of solidity in the final statuesque appearance. The visible garments are called, in general, *kitsuke*, and are divided into several kinds. The most important are the heavy silk kimono for male characters called *atsuita* (literally "heavy board") and the counterpart for female characters, the *surihaku*, which are subdivided into several groups depending on the woven patterns and the colors. *Surihaku* can be made of plain white silk, or painted and embroidered (*nuihaku*). A number of outer garments made of precious brocade are used, such as the *karaori*. *Eri* (collars) of various colors are worn beneath the basic kimono along the neckline—white indicating a lady of important status, while red would be used for a woman of lower rank. For the male roles different kinds of the wide divided skirt (*hakama*) are worn with complementary *kariginu* (hunting robes, or robes for daily use by courtiers), *nōshi* (a more refined robe), or *happi*, a precious brocade robe that reaches only the hip and is usually richly decorated with gold.

Two basic kinds of gowns for women are the *chōken*, loose and unlined, and the *maiginu*, the dancing robe that is tightly gathered around the waist.

For commoners the costumes basically are made of hempen cloth and the colors are somber. Such are also the costumes for most *kyōgen* roles.

A variety of wigs (*kazura*) are used, although there are plays in which the actors appear without them. Headdresses are also important to complete the exterior appearance of the actor. They range from a variety of caps indicating the status of a courtier, a warrior, and the like, to a variety of crowns, hoods, and head cloths.

Contrasting with the sumptuousness of the costumes are those props that are notable for the reduction of the object represented to its barest essentials. Stage properties (*tsukurimono*) represent such objects as boats, carts and huts, and are mostly built for each performance, using bamboo wrapped in white cloth. Their construction is such that they can be handled by one or, at most, two stagehands without any trouble—with the exception of the bell in *Dōjōji*. The props used by the actors, such as a fishing net on a pole, small water buckets, fans, brooms, halberds, lances, lutes, and so on, are often very elaborate and realistic, and are preserved from performance to performance.

Some can have several purposes. The most used is the fan, which can signify a sword, a writing brush, a flute, a water scoop, and many other things. The lidded and lacquered bucket is used as a seat for the *shite*, while the lid frequently serves as a gigantic *sake* cup in *kyōgen* plays. A one-mat platform (*ichijo-dai*, about three by six feet) is used for the purpose of establishing a separate place on the stage, such as a height on a mountain or in the clouds, or simply as a base for other stage props.

One of the most characteristic and impressive achievements of *nō* are the masks, which have become a familiar symbol of Japanese theatre as a whole. Their artistic beauty, complex craftmanship, and deep symbolism have been celebrated by several authors as probably the highest artistic achievement in the history of masks anywhere in the world. Although the work of masters that deserve the highest recognition in the history of Japanese sculpture, the best exemplars of *nō* masks are not to be seen in museums, but usually belong either to collections of *nō* schools—and, therefore, are in the possession of the respective *iemoto*—or to private collections which often are not catalogued and are not available to the general public for research or enjoyment. Such treasures are reserved for the private, rare viewing of a small group of insiders, collectors, and investors: they rarely surface in special performances, and remain, for the most part, preserved in special silk envelopes, and kept in wooden boxes that naturally adapt to the changes in humidity and preserve the precious contents from the otherwise devastating effects of excessive dryness, dampness, and prolonged exposure to light. Because the basic types of *nō* masks are limited, and at least some exemplars for each of the types are known, limited access does not affect the fundamental study of the masks, although it limits our knowledge about particularly beautiful examples, and sometimes about variations which would contribute to a deeper and more complete knowledge of the field.

In a discussion of *Okina* Zenchiku explains the source of the healing power of the mask in the creative force that is transfused through the artist into it.[51] Since the source of the sculptor's creative act for Zenchiku is the very same Absolute, the divine source of all creativity, the mask becomes something more than a simple wooden representation of a type; it contains within itself—almost like an independent soul—an active participation in the divine power it received, thus becoming a source of healing and spiritual inspiration both for the actor and the audience. Certain special feelings are therefore considered as generated by the mask itself—as a product of the *kokoro* or "mind, spirit" of the mask—and not by the actor. Whatever the metaphysical explanation of the reason for the mask's sacredness and effectiveness, it is a fact that the sense of special respect for the mask as something sacred is still alive among the performers of the *nōgaku* tradition, who dutifully bow to the mask before putting it on for the performance—even in the case of a monkey mask for a child actor in a *kyōgen* play. The case of an *Okina* mask kept in the tabernacle of a shrine and venerated as a sign of the presence of the divinity (*gongen*) is not exceptional. The mask, therefore, more than other phases of the *nō*, appears to show remnants of the connection between art and folk religion, which has still not completely disappeared, but was much more explicit at the time of Zeami and Zenchiku.

The history of the *nō* masks is strictly intertwined with the development of the *nō* itself. The legendary Hata no Kōkatsu, considered by Zeami as the founder of *sarugaku* in Japan under the Empress Suiko in the sixth century, is reported to have used a mask carved by Prince Shōtoku himself. From that epoch an *Okina* mask is preserved, thus giving evidence that masks were used since the beginning of *sarugaku*, at least in the performance of some non-human roles. The alliance between *sarugaku* troupes and powerful temples and shrines after the dispersal of the imperial court company and school of *sarugaku* towards the end of the eighth century resulted in all-male performances, requiring masks for the female roles. The assumption of quasi-priestly functions also furthered the development of masks for roles connected with exorcisms and ghostly apparitions. To the unassuming exterior appearance of primitive *sarugaku* corresponded rather simple masks. It was the splendid-looking *dengaku* of Zōami that introduced the sophisticated look of the *zō-onna* (Zōami's woman), which was inherited by *sarugaku* and became a symbol of the *nō* itself. A great flexibility and a variety of new types flourished in Zeami's time, although he himself did not seem to give the mask a very important role in the training of the actor. With the stabilization of *nō* during the Tokugawa period eventually came also the standardization of the mask types and the rigidity in their use.

Scholars have counted up to over 450 different types, many of which, however, are only slight variations from basic prototypes. The division into twelve groups of masks, six belonging to *nō*, and six to *kyōgen*, gives a basic idea of the variety of masks currently used.

A first group includes the "unique" (*tokushu*) masks; i.e., those that in most cases are used only for one specific play. To this group belong the *Okina* masks, which present the three variations of *Okina, chichi-no-jo* and *emmei-kaja*; the "blindman" (*mōmoku*) type with variations named after the plays *Yoroboshi, Semimaru,* and *Kagekiyo*; and a few "exclusive" (*sen'yō*) masks, such as those used only for *Yorimasa, Shunkan,* and *Shōjō.* The second group comprises a variety of demons and gods, both male and female, among which is included the famous horned demoness of jealousy, *hannya*; typical for this group are the masks inspired by the sculptures of the guardian gods at the gates of Buddhist temples of the Kamakura epoch, with bulging eyes and wide-open mouth, like the *ōbeshimi.* The third group includes a number of "old man" (*jō*) varieties, both for roles of living and dead personages. The fourth group includes both *otoko* (man) and *onna* (woman) masks; the *otoko* type covers roles from youth to maturity, while the *onna* type includes all ages, from very young to very old age including the deranged type. The fifth group of *ryō* (spirit) masks includes both divine beings and ghosts, male and female.

The six *kyōgen* types include *Okina, shimbutsu* (deities), *ningen* (human), *bōrei* (ghosts), *oni* (demons), and *dōbutsu* (animals).

Kyōgen: *A New Perspective*

Kyōgen has developed in close relationship to the *nō*, and since the beginning has been considered as a necessary comic relief between the performances of the always serious, often tragic, *nō* plays. While on one hand the historical interdependence of origin has been stressed in recent years by the gradual use of the term *nōgaku* to include both *nō* and *kyōgen*, on the other a new awareness of the importance of *kyōgen* as an independent form of classical comical theatre has developed. For centuries, Japanese scholars not only had considered *kyōgen* as unworthy of mention but also as an irrelevant appendix to the *nō*. Their low esteem was echoed by the first western historians of Japanese literature. For example, Karl Florenz judged that *kyōgen* plays cannot be considered as comedy but only as simple-minded comical intermezzo, and Michel Revon reduced all *kyōgen* to worthless infantile buffooneries. Similar negative criticism of the genre was repeated until recently, when a new interest was generated in the field of theatre research, as distinguished from literary criticism, by the extraordinary theatrical values of gestural stylization and popular language—the latter, ironically, one of the major causes of previous neglect.

Although pioneer scholarly work was begun already in the 1920s by Ikenouchi Nobuyoshi, and later by Nose Asaji, only after World War II did a new attitude develop in Japanese scholarship, which now was eager to propose a prototype of a Japanese comical theatre comparable to its western counterpart. New studies and experiments with performances independent from *nō* resulted from this recent trend—including presentations abroad of all-*kyōgen* programs, and the teaching of the art in both Japanese and foreign schools independently from the *nō*.

Kyōgen is the oldest and most important living Japanese theatrical tradition based on conversational comic dialogue; it has existed without interruption since at least the fourteenth century. Being close to the popular vein of humor from the very beginning, and for centuries committed to an oral tradition and to improvisation, *kyōgen* was much more open to continuous change than *nō*, and was stabilized only in the Tokugawa period with the standardization of texts, a standardized special *recitativo* with interspersed songs, and standardized patterns of movement and dance.

The world of *kyōgen* includes not only the short comical plays that are relatively well known in the west, but also the less well-known participation of *kyōgen* actors in ceremonial roles in *Okina*, or in important roles in regular *nō* plays, such as the boatman in *Funa Benkei*.

Critical study of *kyōgen* texts in recent years has revealed implications of changing attitudes and social criticism, e.g., in the rapport of Tarō-kaja (the smart servant) with the often embarrassingly awkward feudal lord, interesting aspects of "black comedy" and sentimental poetry, and important insights into popular language and expressions. The critical edition of the texts has also revealed the differences in content and style in the various epochs of *kyōgen* history, making obsolete the usual generic, non-differentiated, and superficial judgements. The value of stylized performance and of the theory behind it also has captured the attention of western scholars, who now rank the theories of Okura Toraaki (1597-1662) on *kyōgen* as an important contribution to the understanding of the essence of the comic.[52]

The Theories of Okura Toraaki

Toraaki became the head of the Okura school in 1646; in his new responsibility he felt that he was invested with the mission of preserving the orthodox tradition, in open polemic with the new Sagi school which indulged in novelties of which he deeply disapproved. His crusade was of the greatest importance; he committed to writing for the first time all the *kyōgen* texts, and also compiled a guide for young *kyōgen* actors, the *Warambe gusa*, which remains the fundamental treatise for the study of the spirit and techniques of *kyōgen*.[53] Toraaki takes as a starting point the consideration of the *nō/kyōgen* unity and the consequent acceptance for *kyōgen* of Zeami's aesthetic parameters. Following Zeami, Toraaki recognizes *monomane* as the primary element of *kyōgen*. The difference betweeen *monomane* in *nō* and in *kyōgen* is that in the former the imitation concerns mostly illustrious or even divine roles, while the *monomane* of *kyōgen* aims at the ordinary—even reducing to an ordinary level people belonging to the aristocracy, or to the supernatural world. Toraaki establishes clear limits to the imitation, since the function of *kyōgen* is to provide relief from the tragic atmosphere of the *nō*, but not to destroy the dignified and refined *nō* atmosphere of *yūgen*. Vulgar and coarse laughter and a tasteless realism must be therefore banished. Even when imitating a drunk or a crazy person the *kyōgen* actor should never offend the good taste of a noble and educated audience. Respect for the fundamental atmosphere of *yūgen* remains as the norm to distinguish what is acceptable on the *nō* stage.

Toraaki also analyzes the differences between *nō* and *kyōgen*. While the *nō* brings on stage a world that usually escapes our senses; that is, the world of the other dimension where gods, ghosts, and other invisible beings operate, *kyōgen* brings on stage a very concrete world comprised of clever servants, foolish feudal lords, husbands in search of amorous adventures, and shrewish wives, as well as gods reduced to the level of non-heroic humanity. The *nō* therefore makes visible and concrete the invisible and the abstract; the *kyōgen* on the contrary makes "unreal" the most concrete and real world; that is, it transforms it into a humorous, stylized, theatrical representation which becomes like a world of fantasy and fairy tale.

Toraaki does not think that *kyōgen* should accomplish the function of satirizing vice and teaching a moral lesson. It contains very little ethical indignation nor is there a heroic sense of life. Rather, at the core of *kyōgen* should be a sense of human equality, and a search for truth under the veil of the joke—practical and unpretentious truths of common sense. What is essential is to use the old and well-known and to transform it into something that is perceived as new and freshly discovered. This search for the truth eliminates the coarse, low, indecent comicality which elicits an easy but sick and superficial laughter, deprived of profound compassion and understanding for the human situation. For Toraaki the final purpose of *kyōgen* is not to provoke laughter at any cost; it is better to be pleasant than comical; to be sublime and moving is even better. The category of pathos is therefore the final and highest for Toraaki. When, beyond humorous situations, the insight touches the essential limitations of the human condition in the cosmos, *kyōgen*, like *nō*, provides a way to reach the truth beneath the surface of the object; that is, the invisible essence of the object—a sobering truth that echoes the meaning of Zeami's later interpretation of *yūgen*, implying the cosmic sadness of being human.

Classification of Plays

The present repertory of *kyōgen* includes the plays performed by the two surviving schools, and counts 254 plays in the Izumi School against 180 in the Okura tradition—out of which 177 are common to both, with more or less relevant variations. The Sagi school ceased to exist over a century ago.

The criteria of classification vary. In the Okura school, plays are divided according to the role of the main character, who is called *shite*, as in *nō*. The first group contains the *waki kyōgen*, which usually follow a *waki nō* at the beginning of a program; in such plays the *shite* sometimes performs the role of a god, and the content is usually congratulatory. The second group, *daimyō-kyōgen*, includes plays in which the *shite* enacts a caricature of a feudal lord (*daimyō*). The third group contains the *shōmyō* (minor feudal lord) *kyōgen*, also called *Tarō-kaja mono* from the astute servant type called Tarō-kaja, as famous in *nōgaku* as Harlequin in the *commedia dell'arte*. In the fourth group, *muko onna kyōgen*, the *shite* either plays the role of the *muko* (bridegroom, usually inexperienced and getting into trouble) or of *onna* (woman, usually plain but aggressive and married to a weak husband). The fifth group, *oni yamabushi kyōgen*, contains plays in which the *shite* humorously plays the role of an *oni* (demon or ogre) or of a *yamabushi*, both supposedly gifted with extraordinary powers but in reality making a rather poor showing. In the sixth group, *shukke zatō kyōgen*, the *shite* performs as either a monk (*shukke*) who behaves against others' expectations, or a blind or otherwise handicapped protagonist (*zatō*). A final group, *atsume kyōgen*, includes a miscellaneous collection (*atsume*) of pieces which do not fit in the other five categories.

Other divisions are based on the three essential elements of any *kyōgen*, the dialog (*serifu*), the singing (*ko-uta*), and the dance (*mai*); or according to the degree of difficulty in performance, starting from the simplest that require little training (*ko narai*); much training (*ō narai*); heavy training (*omo narai*); or very heavy training (*goku omo narai*).

The Performance of Kyōgen

In *kyōgen*, as in *nō*, a great importance is given to training and to complete dedication to the art. The tradition is transmitted within the family, from generation to generation, and great care is given to the fidelity to patterns (*kata*) of dance and movement typical of the school. The impression given is one of controlled and stylized elegance even when the imitation is that of servants and drunks. Neither obscenity nor vulgarity is shown, and the costumes are accordingly orderly, always perfectly clean, neat, and well pressed. Actors perform pure pantomime with no props at all, as in the case of miming the opening of an imaginary sliding door. However, they also use such fanciful props as an extra large lacquered lid for a cup to drink gallons of imaginary *sake*, real ropes to tie Tarō-kaja's arms to a real pole, or a fan for many expressive purposes as in the *nō*. The many changes in facial expression are very important in the numerous *kyōgen* plays which do not require a mask; in the *nō*, however, the very few plays without masks are performed with a constantly serious expression. Furthermore, a greater acrobatic skill is exhibited in *kyōgen* than in *nō*, especially in the performance of animal roles requiring non-human agility and extraordinary dexterity and mimetic ability.

Mystery Plays and School Theatre of the Jesuits

A previously neglected chapter of the history of the theatre in Japan has been that of the performances promoted by the Jesuits in the second half of the sixteenth century and the beginning of the seventeenth and covering the period from the beginning of Christian missionary activities in the Japanese islands to the time of the bloody persecutions that officially abolished Christianity in Japan. The recently published research by Thomas Leims provides a fascinatingly rich documentation of a lively and far-reaching theatrical activity in several Japanese mission centers, not only limited to far-away Kyūshū, as it was assumed by Japanese scholars, but also in the very heart of the theatrical life of the country, in the capital city of Kyoto itself.[54] Leims provides for the first time a thorough documentation taken from the vast treasure of contemporary letters written by the missionaries (especially Portuguese Jesuits), from published and unpublished reports by European travelers, and from dictionaries and grammars of the Japanese language compiled by the missionaries for use in the training of their European recruits. The resulting picture shows that the Jesuits did show the same eagerness in the use of plays and theatrical illustrations of the Christian truths as a method of educating their students and their faithful in Japan as they did in Europe. As part of their effort of communicating with their converts they became very well versed in the contemporary forms of Japanese theatre, especially the *nō* and *kyōgen*, and adopted in their educational shows some of the indigenous techniques and dances. Leims reaches the conclusion that the influence of the missionary dramatic

155

activity on the development of Japanese performing arts, in an extremely sensitive period that saw the formation of the first *kabuki odori* and of more "realistic" forms of Japanese entertainment than the *nō* and *kyōgen*, should be considered as much more important than it has been until now by both Japanese and non-Japanese theatre scholars. The influence, however, is for Leims not one of imitation but of inspiration and incentive to original creativity; that is, a phenomenon of transculturation, something of the same nature as the influence of the Japanese wood-block prints on Van Gogh and Degas: without the Japanese inspiration those nineteenth century European painters would have probably produced different works, but still they would have given to the world their own unique masterpieces. Likewise here, concludes Leims, the formation of the new genre *kabuki odori* would have been different without the contact with the Christian dramaturgy and the Christian spectacular forms of processions and liturgy introduced by the Jesuits. The new important genre(s), however, would have anyhow found their own way to be born and to enrich further the already rich indigenous theatrical tradition.

NOTES

[1]The section on the origins of the *nō* partially reproduces, with few adaptations, Ortolani, "Shamanism in the Origins of the *Nō* Theatre," 166-173.

[2]Blau, *Sarugaku und Shushi*, 325-331.

[3]Ortolani, "Shamanism in the Origins," 168.

[4]Akima, "The Songs of the Dead: Poetry, Drama and Ancient Death Rituals of Japan," 501-507.

[5]Matsumoto Shinhachirō, "Nō no hassei" (Origins of *nō*), *Bungaku* 25/9 (1957), 13-30.

[6]Nonomura Kaizō, "Nōgaku no hassei to hatten" (Origins and development of *nōgaku*), in vol.2 of *Nōgaku zensho*, ed. by Nogami Toyoichirō, Tokyo: Sōgensha 1942, 71-167.

[7]Blau, *Sarugaku und Shushi*, 326.

[8]Hayashiya Tatsusaburō, *Chūsei geinōshi no kenkyū* (A study of the history of the performing arts in the medieval era), Tokyo: Iwanami 1960, 355-389.

[9]Honda Yasuji, *Okina sono hoka* (Okina and other matters), Tokyo: Meizendō 1958.

[10]Umehara Takeshi, *Kakusareta jūjika: Hōryūjiron* (The concealed cross: a treatise on the Hōryūji temple), Tokyo: Shinchōbunko, 1972.

[11]O'Neill, *Early Nō Drama*, 42-52.

[12]Gotō Hajime, *Nōgaku no kigen* (The origins of *nōgaku*), Tokyo: Mokujisha 1975, 575.

[13]Ikeda Saburō, "Nō to sengyō geinō to" (Nō and previous performing arts), *Bungaku*, 25/9: 31-42.

[14]Honda Yasuji, *Okina sono hoka*, 191-230.

[15]Hoff, "*Heteron ti Gignomenon: Katarimono no Butaika* in Japan and Greece; A Comparative Study." Typescript, 1975.

[16]Blacker, *The Catalpa Bow: A Study of Shamanistic Practices in Japan*, 33.

[17]Hare, *Zeami's Style: The Noh Plays of Zeami Motokiyo*, 12-16 summarizes the problems connected with the credibility and accuracy of the genealogical tree of Kan'ami's ancestors.

[18]See Ortolani and Nishi, "The Year of Zeami's Birth. With a Translation of the Museki isshi," and O'Neill, "The Year of Zeami's Birth: A New Interpretation of Museki Isshi."

[19]Zeami's age is given here according to the western reckoning. According to the Japanese way of reckoning age he was eighty-one at the time of his death.

[20]Recently Matsuda Tamotsu wrote a book arguing that ther name Zeshi should be used instead of Zeami (*Zeshi: Sarugakunō no kenkyū* Tokyo: Shindokushosha, 1991).

[21]Thornhill, *Six Circles, One Dewdrop*, 15-20. Parts of the following paragraphs reproduce, with few modifications, Ortolani, *Zenchiku's Aesthetics of the Nō Theatre*, 1-3.

[22]Bohner, *Nō: Einführung*, 299-305.

[23]See Inoura, *A History of Japanese Theatre I*, 123-124, for a brief list of the major *nō* playwrights and the most important *nō* plays.

[24]Ortolani, "Iemoto," 297-306.

[25]The translation of the titles of the treatises is given according to Rimer and Yamazaki.

[26]See Nearman, "Zeami's *Kyū-i*: A Pedagogical Guide for Teachers of Acting," for a recent commentary on this treatise.

[27]Ueda, *Literary and Art Theories in Japan*, 67.

[28]Nearman, "Zeami's *Kyū-i*," 324-325.

[29]Ortolani, "Zeami's Aesthetics of the No and Audience Participation," 110-112.

[30]Konishi, "New Approaches to the Study of the Nō Drama," 24.

[31]Pilgrim, "Some Aspects of *Kokoro* in Zeami," 394.

[32]Tsubaki, "Zeami and the Transition of the Concept of Yūgen: A Note on Japanese Aesthetics," 55-67.

[33]Ueda, *Literary and Art Theories in Japan*, 60-61.

[34]*Ibid.*, 61.

[35]Komparu Kunio, *The Noh Theatre: Principles and Perspectives*, 14-15.

[36]Thornhill, *Six Circles, One Dewdrop: The Religio-Arsthetic World of Komparu Zenchiku* includes, besides the mentioned translations, also a scholarly discussion of the commentaries by Shigyoku and Kaneyoshi, an important comparison between Zeami's nine ranks and Zenchiku's six-circles-and-one-dewdrop scheme, and useful considerations on the soteriology of performance. The following paragraphs reproduce, with a few modifications, Ortolani, *Zenchiku's Aesthetics of the Nō Theatre*, 3-7.

[37]Thornhill, *Six Circles, One Dewdrop*, 7.

[38]Pilgrim, "Six Circles, One Dewdrop: The Religio-Aesthetic of Komparu Zenchiku," 8.

[39]*Ibid.*, 16.

[40]*Ibid.*, 22.

[41]See Ortolani, "Spirituality for the Dancer-Actor in Zeami's and Zenchiku's Writings on the Nō." For an extensive explanation of the commentaries by Shigyoku and Kaneyoshi to Zenchiku's *rokurin ichirō* treatises see the often quoted work by Thornhill.

[42]Hare follows Zeami's criterion of the three basic roles (*santai*; that is, the old man, the woman, and the warrior) to classify Zeami's plays in his *Zeami's Style: The Noh Plays of Zeami Motokiyo.*

[43]This analysis follows Hoff and Flindt, trs. *The Life Structure of Nō. An English Version of Yokomichi Mario's Analysis of the Structure of Nō.*

[44]Konishi, "New Approaches to the Study of the Nō Drama," 1-2.

[45]Hare, *Zeami's Style*, 44-46.

[46]Keene, ed. *Twenty Plays of the Nō Theatre*, 2-4.

[47]The analysis of Zenchiku's plays follows closely Ortolani, *Zenchiku's Aesthetics of the Nō Theatre*, 2-7.

[48]See Ortolani, "Il teatro occidentale alla ricerca dell'energia profonda, «rilassata e composita» dell'Oriente." The various aspects of dance in the performance of the *nō* are described thoroughly in the three-volume *Dance in the Nō Theatre* by Bethe and Brazell.

[49]The music of the *nō* has been studied by Tamba, *The Musical Structure of Nō*, and summarized by Harich-Schneider, *A History of Japanese Music*, 432-442.

[50]Komparu, *The Noh Theatre: Principles and Perspectives*, 109-149, probably gives the most comprehensive explanation available in English of the *nō* stage, its history, and symbolism.

[51]Nearman, "Behind the Mask of Nō," 20-64.

[52]Ortolani, "Il Ruzante e la teoria del kyōgen di Okura Toraaki," 117-128.

[53]The *Warambe gusa* was published in Japan for the first time only in 1944, and no complete translation is available in western languages. In English the best study on Toraaki is the chapter "Toraaki: The Making of the Comic," in Ueda, *Literary and Art Theories in Japan*, 101-113.

[54]*The Entstehung des Kabuki: Transkulturation Europa-Japan im 16. und 17. Jahrhundert*, Leiden/New York: Brill, 1990, is a revised edition of his 1986 doctoral dissertation with the same title.

CHAPTER VII

KABUKI

Background of Kabuki *and* Jōruri

The history of Edo's theatrical splendor under the Tokugawa regime (1603-1868) has been the subject of several studies by Japanese and western authors, especially since World War II. The wealth of information available makes it possible to reconstruct a rather accurate picture of the complex and fascinating *kabuki* and *jōruri* worlds. Especially important are those studies that relate these genres to the phenomenal development of the new middle class in Edo and Osaka, the big Japanese cities that shared with Kyoto, and eventually took over from it, the leadership of theatrical fashion.

All authors agree that *kabuki* and *jōruri* are the typical theatrical expressions of the Tokugawa culture as it developed in the urban milieu, where the merchants played the main role in their fluctuating and ambiguous position of energetic economic leadership in the face of socio-political oppression. The large theatres supplied the townspeople with the only places for regular gatherings where "their" world could be collectively celebrated—a showplace for their economic success, their licentious fantasies, and daring fashions, as well as for the venting of their veiled criticism of forbidden topics and of their masked aspirations for social recognition.

When the Tokugawa world collapsed, *kabuki* and *jōruri* kept alive a memory and nostalgia for a past that was rapidly disappearing and dissolving into a new westernized society. Just as *bugaku* remained alive at the price of crystallizing into a theatrical monument to the aristocratic court society of the Nara and Heian periods; just as the *nō* paid the same price of crystallization to preserve the taste and refinement of the

162

Ashikaga *samurai* society; just so did *kabuki* and *jōruri* become a frozen monument to the tastes and moods of the Tokugawa merchant middle-class.

A) *Political Background.* *Kabuki* was born as an explosion of lust for life and extravagance celebrating the end of over a century of political chaos, interminable civil wars among ever-changing alliances of feudal lords, ever-recurring devastations, reprisals, and death, under an all-pervading feeling of fear, instability, and insecurity. Peace resulted from the successful leadership of three generals who managed to bring the divided country under a unified, iron-handed, military rule. The two leaders who had started this unifying process, Oda Nobunaga and Toyotomi Hideyoshi, did not achieve a lasting peace: it was only Tokugawa Ieyasu who stopped the bloodbath and quieted social unrest. He is the creator of the system that succeeded in maintaining peace and stability for two and a half centuries—and at the same time determined the parameters of development of the unique Tokugawa society, thoroughly isolated from the rest of the world, and extraordinarily punctilious in its control of a hierarchical organization of each aspect of public and private life.

The theatre was no exception. Probably in no other epoch or place in the world has the theatre been the object of so many decrees of the supreme authority, of abolitions, restrictions, and regulations affecting every detail: regulations prescribed sites of theatre construction, the materials permissible for constructing the roofs of theatre buildings, the areas in which actors were allowed to live and move freely, access by the actors to the theatre's boxes, the kind of clothes the actors were allowed to wear and the precise type of hat they were ordered to wear whenever outside their territory, permission regarding the performance of certain types of dances within *kabuki* presentations, permission for theatres to operate following major scandals, including minutiae which may appear embarrassing to a modern reader, such as prohibiting female impersonators from using public facilities reserved for ladies.

The Tokugawa castle in Edo became the nucleus of the largest metropolis of Japan. Edo, the present day Tokyo, functioned as the actual capital of the empire. In the grounds now occupied by the imperial palace in Tokyo, the Tokugawa rulers set up their court, completely independent from that of the emperor, who was left undisturbed and powerless—a nominal ruler in a nominal capital, Kyoto. The fortress of Tokugawa power was surrounded by the quarters of a permanent army of hundreds of thousands of *samurai* and their families—a continuous austere and oppressive reminder of the military dictatorship that dominated every aspect of Japanese life. It was outside the gloomy atmosphere of those barracks-lined quarters, and precisely in the colorful and lively off-limits red light districts, that Edo was to become the new theatre capital of Japan. As far as theatrical life is concerned for Japan, Edo eventually became, and Tokyo still is, the counterpart of Paris for France, London for England, and New York for the United States.

The establishment of the Tokugawa order did not happen without protest among the *samurai* themselves and without the appearance of opposition groups, among which the *kabuki mono* provide a most interesting occurrence—very much like the British "punk" phenomenon of the seventies and early eighties. They acquire a special meaning in the context of the study of *kabuki*'s background, because they explain the general association that both audiences and government had with the word *kabuki* at the beginning of the Tokugawa era. The verb *kabuku*, used since the middle ages with the meaning of "to slant," or "to tilt," had acquired, by the beginning of the Tokugawa era, a slang usage for any anti-establishment action that defied the conventions and the proper rules of behavior. The *kabuki mono* were therefore people who expressed their anti-conformism through a series of protests against the established order, which ranged from highly unusual ways of dressing to shocking hairdos and extravagantly decorated, enormous swords, and up to four-foot-long tobacco pipes. Like today's motorcycle gangs they would roam the streets and oftentimes engage in acts of violence and riots, flaunting their revolt against all conventions and decency, by performing such acts as playing the flute with one's anus.[1]

The bulk of *kabuki mono* was formed of masterless *samurai*, but youngsters of important *samurai* families, even of *daimyō*, had joined the gangs, in some cases giving a definite political color to violent actions with potential revolutionary implications, and warnings of allegiance to traditional Tokugawa enemies. The execution of a *kabuki mono* in 1612 by a Tokugawa officer provoked the assassination of the officer by the *kabuki* "brothers" of the executed youth. The ensuing search by the authorities led to the discovery of a secret document with 500 signatures of *kabuki mono* which included sons of important *daimyō*. It is no wonder that Ieyasu acted swiftly and executed a large number of the dangerous rebels who were trying to subvert the very foundation of his new order. The fashion of rebellion against convention was adopted, in addition, by a group of court nobles in 1607 who then also received the name of *kabuki mono*: in women's clothing they entered the innermost quarters of the residence where the ladies of the imperial court lived and violated the sacred taboo of a place where men were strictly forbidden, right in the heart of the imperial palace. The scandal ended with the execution of the culprits and the exile of the complacent ladies.

To the Tokugawa regime *kabuki* meant subversion and heresy, something immoral and dangerous, but in the folk mentality the daring and sometimes heroic behavior of a few major *kabuki mono* leaders became the stuff of legend which was celebrated in songs, tales, and on the stages of the very first *kabuki* shows, while their eccentric fashions became popular all over Japan, even in the remotest villages.

In their obsession for providing political stability and avoiding at all costs a return to chaos, Ieyasu and his immediate successors enforced a strict policy of social stability, which in many ways affected the very life and development of the theatre. The new social order and the ethical values upon which it was built became the reference frame for all plays, making it necessary for western readers to study this frame of reference to understand the plays. Of course, many elements belonged to already widely accepted principles and to an already existing social *status quo*; new, however, were the enormous stress placed on the unconditional loyalty to superior authority, the thoroughness of the indoctrination, and the rigidity of the application of the principles at all costs and at all levels of society.

The Tokugawa took over from the old Chinese Confucian theories—adapted for their purposes of imposing a *samurai* dominated structure—the division of society into four classes: warrior-administrators (*samurai*), peasants (*nōmin*), artisans (*kōjin*) and merchants (*shōmin*).[2] The hierarchy was not based on intelligence, preparation, wealth, or capacity, but determined by the interests of the dominating *samurai* class. The farmers provided the bushels of rice, that is, the income of the *samurai*; the artisans made swords and other weapons, the vital companions of the military class. Principles that may be considered unrealistic and reactionary even for seventeenth-century Japan were made to prevail—such as the absolute predominance of a military aristocracy that was useless and ill-prepared for peace purposes and the idea that, at the bottom of the social pyramid, below the farmers and the artisans, were the merchants, deemed a non-productive class making profits on already finished products without producing any themselves. Outside the four classes that made up the quasi-totality of the population remained the small but rather important groups of the old court nobility (*kuge*) around the emperor in Kyoto, which now was reduced to purely ceremonial functions; the *shaji*, that is, the clerical officials of Buddhism and Shinto; and, at the bottom of the social pyramid, the outcastes (*semmin*) among whom were such despised categories of people as prostitutes and *kabuki* actors.

B) Samurai *and* Kabuki. The social classes were far from constituting homogeneous groups. Many *kabuki* and *jōruri* plays present the distress of *samurai* fallen in disgrace and living among merchants, often concealing their true identity. To the *samurai* belonged such different people as the most powerful man in the country, the Shogun himself, powerful and rich feudal lords, high state employees and poor foot soldiers, who hardly had anything more than their pride and their swords. There was a complicated hierarchical ranking among the feudal lords, the government employees, and so forth. Hierarchy pervaded all classes, including the outcastes and the underworld. It was impossible to escape from it, as much as it was impossible not to belong to some group which would be held responsible for the actions of each of its members; thus were created the premises for such frequently seen extreme dramatic situations as where individuals are torn between contrasting allegiances, and are painfully conscious of the consequences of their actions for the whole family or group. The highpoint of this system of "collective responsibility" was introduced by the Tokugawa governor in Kyoto with a 1603 law which divided all citizens into groups of ten, and made all ten responsible for any crime committed by any member of that group.

From the very beginning the government of the Shogun adopted a policy of suspicion and restrictions against *kabuki*.[3] The same characteristics that had given the name *kabuki* to the *kabuki mono* must have influenced both audiences and government to identify the new show by the same term. In the eyes of the shogunate early *kabuki* was another form of rebellious non-conformism, perverse in its eroticism, transvestism, outrageous costumes, and hybrid mixture of religious elements with licentious contents. Moreover, in its initial phases, *kabuki* became a source of frequent riots involving outcastes, townspeople, and, to the dismay of government officials, also *samurai*. The petty *samurai*, deprived in the peaceful society of any meaningful military function, were among the first to fill their idle time by constant attendance at both *kabuki* and puppet shows, although in disguise because of the off-limits locales at which such entertainments took place.

Besides the several ranks of *samurai* in the active service of either the Shogun or of about two hundred *daimyō* existing at the beginning of the seventeenth century, hundreds of thousands of *rōnin* (masterless *samurai*) became an unexpected element of social mobility within the apparently unshakeable stability of the system. The long wars had multiplied the number of *samurai* deprived of a lord, and therefore of an official position and a steady income. Many *rōnin* were forced by necessity to take jobs considered unworthy of a *samurai*, and concealed their shame under a false name—a popular situation in *kabuki* and *jōruri* plays. Among such *rōnin* were the famous forty-seven *samurai* who dared to challenge the authority of the Shogun in order to revenge the death of their master, and who became national heroes of a sort, inspiring the most famous play in the puppet and *kabuki* repertoire, the *Chūshingura*. An unproven but persistent tradition presents a *rōnin*, Nagoya Sanza (previously a *samurai* in the service of the Christian *daimyō* Gamo Ujisato) as the lover and main collaborator of the famous dancer Okuni, the legendary founder of *kabuki*. The historical truth about Nagoya Sanza will probably never be established, but if not Sanza, certainly other masterless *samurai* joined the outcastes in the despised occupation of *kabuki* actor. This explains the origin of illustrious *samurai* family names (such as Nakamura,

Ichikawa, or Onoe) for dynasties of *kabuki* actors, in spite of the official laws that deprived outcastes of the right to a family name.

C) *Peasants and* Kabuki. In the official hierarchy of the Tokugawa society the peasants were ranked after the *samurai*, a tribute to their economic importance in an agricultural society which still recognized a bushel of rice as the measure of wealth. The peasants constituted about 80% of the total population, alone carried the burden of taxation, and, in the great majority of cases, lived in a state of quasi-servitude to the land and the feudal lord, without the right to move away from their fields or choose a different occupation in the cities. Peasants in general did not occupy a position of importance in *kabuki* plays and had very little to do with the organization of the *kabuki* world. However, the reality of a lively amateur *kabuki* in several rural centers, and, even more, of the puppet theatre in numerous villages has been underestimated and almost completely neglected by non-Japanese scholars, who obviously have been more impressed by the rich historical materials about the major performers and the large theatres of the major cities. In general, the heroes of the *kabuki* world are chosen from among the *samurai* and merchants, and the lowly peasants are presented as narrow-minded, petty, cowardly, and comically foolish.

D) *Merchants and* Kabuki. The Tokugawa peace favored an enormous increase in trade and the development of organized production of large quantities of goods required by cities that ranged among the world's most populous of the time. Wealth accumulated in the hands of merchants. They created a tight capitalistic system, favored by the traditional idea that only land could be taxed, leaving the enormous profits of trade tax-free. Some merchants, especially those who secured monopolies of vital products, could compete in wealth with the most powerful *daimyō*. Many *samurai* ended up owing money to the bankers of the new economy, which was rapidly shifting from its agricultural foundation to money and credit transactions. Socially inferior in the official society, the merchants found in the "floating world" of the red light districts—glittering with tea-houses, *kabuki* theatres, and every type of entertainment—an island where social distinction did not count and only cash decided the issues. No wonder then that rich merchants spent enormous amounts of money as generous patrons of that world. Wealth attracted all kinds of artists, who transformed the red light districts into the very centers of a new, colorful, highly original culture, evidently much more worldly than the one which gave birth to the *nō*. The greatest novelist of the Tokugawa period, Ihara Saikaku (1642-1693, who also wrote the *jōruri* play *Koyomi*, The Calendar) made life in the red light districts the main theme of his masterpieces. The masters of *ukiyo-e* wood-block prints multiplied the images of celebrated *kabuki* actors and women of pleasure. In no other nation's dramatic literature—nor in that of Japan in other periods—do brothels and courtesans appear in so great a number of plays, obviously mirroring the new cultural importance of the red light districts in which actors and theatre buildings were confined by law. Success in the arts depended now no longer on the *samurai*, but on the favor of the rich merchants and the ticket-buying townspeople who frequently visited the red light districts. Accordingly, playwrights, actors, musicians, puppeteers, painters, and all other providers of entertainment created a world of fantasy to please the taste of the new patrons. Even the *samurai* world was projected on the stage in the light of that fantasy, and appeared quite different from the somber reality of daily military life and from the sophisticated understatement of Zen-inspired simplicity that had characterized the *nō*; a gaudy, colorful immediacy of overstatement became typical of *kabuki* and *jōruri*.

Both *nō* and *kabuki* are unique and genuine expressions of the Japanese spirit and culture. They mirror, however, taste and ideals of different social classes, in profoundly different environments and epochs.

E) *Outcastes and* **Kabuki**. The word *geijutsu* today has the meaning of "art" with all its metaphysical and "dignified" implications. During the Tokugawa period, however, it was used—without any aura of dignity or respect—to indicate the performances of professional entertainers, sometimes with a meaning equivalent to "tricks." Actors formed a special group among the outcastes, and are referred to in several Japanese sources together with the other groups of outcastes such as *eta*, *semmin*, and *hinin*. This sociological bias is extremely important to understand the history of *kabuki*. The actors were called *kawaramono* (people of the riverbed) or, with a sense of contempt, beggars of the riverbed (*kawara kojiki*). They were submitted to humiliating restrictions of movement and places where they were allowed to live, of people they could mix with, and were even forced to wear a wicker hat as a sign of their despised profession whenever they left their territory. The habit of naming actors and prostitutes together in all official documents originated in the real connection between the two professions at the beginning of *kabuki*. Wealth, success, and fame, connected with a respectable moral life, did not change the social stigma of one's being a "beggar from the river bed" even when "squatting on brocaded mats," but these attributes did establish the premises for changes which slowly took place after the Tokugawa period. A stigma kept hanging over *kabuki* actors for a long time, even after they were officially "emancipated" at the beginning of the Meiji period.

With great popularity a few successful performers reached yearly incomes comparable to the astronomical figures paid to movie stars nowadays. They could afford an extremely luxurious life, and were the object almost of a cult, comparable to the delirium of rock fans for superstars like Elvis Presley or, more recently, Madonna. *Kabuki* fans would fight for a sign of their idols' friendship, send expensive presents, and mourn their deaths with incredible manifestations of public grief. The process of advanced westernization eventually swept away most of the social stigma. Famous *kabuki* actors are now in a position comparable to stars of other show business genres. The Japanese government has bestowed upon a few *kabuki* actors the official recognition as "living cultural treasure," a great honor reserved for the best masters of the major traditional arts.

F) *The Official Morality.* The Tokugawa rulers did not challenge the position of Buddhism as the dominant religion of the masses. As a matter of fact they themselves were mostly pious followers of the Buddha. *Kabuki* and *jōruri* heroes usually take for granted one or another of the Buddhist beliefs, though they often express a rather superficial and diluted faith, comparable to the nominal Christianity of many characters in nineteenth century western melodrama or opera librettos. The sources and standards of morality became ever more definitely separated and independent from the declining religious spirit, both in real life and on the stage.

Worldly preoccupation with political and social stability convinced Ieyasu and his successors to adapt and constantly inculcate doctrines of Confucian origin; these were not only those regarding the division into four social classes, but also those concerning the hierarchy of values in the five fundamental human relationships. Traditional *samurai* ethical principles, such as individualistic integrity and honor (*ichibun*) and "pride" (*iji*), which allowed and even imposed a change of allegiance or rebellion when the sovereign went against "the will of heaven" (*ten-mei*), were thoroughly suppressed in favor of unconditional loyalty and blind obedience to the superior authority. This exaltation of loyalty to the sovereign above all was fostered as contributing to intellectual stability, a necessary foundation of social and political stability. The "official" morality became Confucian, based on the obligations between sovereign and subject, father and child, husband and wife, elder and younger brother, and friend and friend—in the given order of importance. Over and over again loyalty to the constituted authority, that is, the Shogun, was stressed as the supreme virtue, superior even to filial piety. The authority of a husband over his wife was subordinated to parental authority over a daughter, even after marriage. Innumerable situations, complications, and climaxes of *kabuki* and *jōruri* plots can be understood only from this perspective and hierarchy of moral values which praised as virtuous such actions as the killing of one's own son to save the life of a feudal lord's son; the selling of a wife to a brothel to raise the money necessary to prove the husband's loyalty to the lord; parental intervention in separating husband and wife against their will for any reason thought sufficient by the wife's father; and suicide for any one of a number of reasons related to the service of the feudal lord and his interests.

The long peace threatened to soften the traditionally strict military discipline of the *samurai*. Many Tokugawa scholars and teachers expressed their concerns in writings which codified for the first time the long-practiced unwritten code of the ruling class. While the crisis menaced the purity of the *samurai* tradition, the once exclusive *samurai* values gradually became the values of the new elite of merchants and, surprisingly, also of the outcastes and the underworld. Commoner heroes of the stage like the *otokodate* observed the *samurai* code more faithfully than the *samurai* themselves, as exemplified in the famous confrontation between the legendary *otokodate* Sukeroku and the *samurai* Ikyū in the play which takes the name from the former. The world of the stage did not at all challenge the ethical code. On the contrary, it measured everything according to the code, praising its triumph and demonstrating the inevitable ruin of those who did not behave according to it. The situation in which the hero must choose between painfully conflicting duties is not presented as a criticism of the ethical system, but as a tragic climax in which the sacrifice of life is often expected.

G) *Popular Beliefs and the Supernatural.* The importance of the ritualistic substructure in the beginning *kabuki* has been largely neglected by the scholarship.[4] What the common people believed and were concerned with was very different from the purity and depth associated with the western image of Buddhism (especially Zen), and from the stately elegance and dignity associated with the official Shinto ritual at major shrines. Whether or not expressed in Buddhist terminology, seventeenth-century Japanese people were still very seriously concerned—like their fourteenth-century counterparts—with the mysterious and nebulous "other dimension" surrounding the realm of their experience and inaccessible to human beings. The populace was in real fear of the inhabitants of that world, who could willfully cross the barrier into our space at any moment and suddenly cause any kind of change in the course of human life. Shinto *kami* and Buddhist holy "saviors" (the bodhisattva) as well as the benevolent souls (*tama*) of the departed—either already successfully absorbed into an anonymous "corporate Ancestor" or still in the process of reaching that eventual state of peace—were supposed to live in that "other dimension." More directly menacing inhabitants of the "other dimension" were the dangerous *onryō*, the revengeful ghosts of people who met violent death, generally at the height of obstinate unfullfilled passions, and countless spirits of animals and lesser 'powers'. In one word, this "other dimension" was the same realm that had nourished the world of *kagura* and those *nō* plays with ghosts and supernatural beings, and that had given shamans such an important role in both Shinto and Buddhist rituals. The very first documented example of *kabuki*, the performance of Okuni as related in the *Kunijo Kabuki Ekotoba*,[5] ca. 1614, is to be interpreted according to the scheme of a shamanistic ritual of *tama-shizume*, that is, of appeasing a dangerous revengeful *onryō*. The shamaness is the *miko* Okuni herself, who has traveled from her home shrine of Izumo to the capital, and now performs her specialty on the *nō* stage of Kyoto's Kitano shrine, famous for the *tama-shizume* rituals. The *onryō* is the spirit of the recently deceased Nagoya Sanzaburō (often abbreviated as Sanza), who lived from ca. 1575 to 1604, the eccentric, anti-conformist *rōnin* who, because of his outlandish behavior in defiance of the Tokugawa regime, had become a legendary *kabuki mono*, and who also had been Okuni's lover. The important *kami* of Izumo is the divine power operating through Okuni's appearance to liberate the faithful from the dangerous *onryō*. The scheme of the ritual consists in an opening conjuration of the *onryō* by the shamaness; the establishment of communication between shaman and *onryō* when the ghost responds to the conjuration and appears from the middle of the audience to enter on stage; the discovery of those grudges which motivate his vindictive anger (in Sanza's case, his untimely death in a brawl); and finally the pacification and eventual removal of such grudges, thereby allowing for the transformation of the *onryō* into an appeased *tama* ready for its absorption into the "Corporate Ancestor." From the *Kunijo kabuki ekotoba* we might well conclude that Okuni, the founder of *kabuki*, was basically a professional shamaness, and that the very first *kabuki* performances were, in their essential content and dramatic structure, very similar to typical shamanic rituals to appease revengeful ghosts.

The importance of the basic scheme of folk ritual for *kabuki* continues in a number of later plays during the Genroku period *kabuki*, in plays adapted from the *nō*, and in a remarkable group of early nineteenth century plays, the *kaidanmono*, which revived audience interest in seeing revengeful ghosts enacted, and preying on popular shamanic beliefs still very much alive among *kabuki* audiences. In general, the bridging of the gap between the world of our experience and the "other dimension"—where divine powers, friendly and revengeful ghosts, and strange animal spirits influence the human condition—is essential to the determination of the course of events in numerous *kabuki* plays from the very beginnings of the form to the present repertory.

Supernatural powers are believed to have been decisive in the formation of *kabuki* super-heroes such as Yoshitsune, who performed astonishing deeds in a state of *kamigakari* or possession by a divine power. The super-hero is no longer just a valiant man, but becomes a *hito-kami*, or "man-god," who has the power of defeating legions of villains and appeasing powerful *onryō*. In some cases at least the actors who performed the role of such super-heroes were perceived by the audiences as possibly possessed by a god or a spirit: a famous example is the case of Ichikawa Danjūrō I playing the role of the god Fudō Daimyōjin in the play *Tsuwamoto Kongen Soga*, when the audience threw coins on stage. These were actually offerings to the deity who was deemed present on the stage and capable of bestowing blessings in return. This belief seems to be at the root of the special religious cult formed by Danjūrō's fans, and the continuing unique position of the Ichikawa Danjūrō line in the *kabuki* world. Also, the *aragoto* style started by and associated with the line has been considered by such scholars as Gunji Masakatsu and others to derive from the representation of the divinely possessed super-hero capable of "liberating" the innocent oppressed from the clutches of villains or evil spirits. The costume of such *hito-kami* or man-gods has details that are traced back to shamanistic paraphernalia rather than to the armour of warriors.[6]

In conclusion, it would be difficult to understand many of *kabuki*'s more idiosyncratic components if its connections with the worlds of the supernatural and shamanism were to be forgotten by audiences and scholars.

History of Kabuki: *An Overview*

The history of *kabuki* is usually divided into five major periods which span the years from the very first performances around the beginning of the seventeenth century to the present time.

A) *Period of the Origins.* Although the first documented mention of *kabuki odori* (*kabuki* dance) appears in 1603, it is clear that the dance had been around since at least the last years of the sixteenth century. All authors agree that this entertainment developed from the *furyū* tradition, especially from a *furyū* adaptation of the *nembutsu odori*. The word *nembutsu* stands for the repetition of the prayer *Namu Amidabutsu* (often translated as "Homage to Amida Buddha") which was very popular in the Amidistic sects of Mahayana Buddhism. A dance to propagate the use of this prayer was developed by a number of famous Buddhist missionaries at least as early as the tenth century. By the end of the sixteenth century the *nembutsu* dances had become a popular entertainment with all sorts of embellishments, fancy dresses, and use of props. Okuni's *nembutsu* went far enough in the direction of an outrageous mixture of sacred and outlandish elements that it deserved the name *kabuki*. She dressed in Portuguese pants, with a foreign style hat, or used men's clothes, even sometimes wearing a cross hanging from her neck. She mixed the *nembutsu* with profane popular dances and did not refrain from mimicking the daring looks and actions of the *kabuki mono* of her days.

Borrowing from the *nō* the idea of having ghosts appear on the stage, Okuni substituted for the ghosts of famous historical heroes that of a recent folk idol, the *kabuki mono* Nagoya Sanza, who had been her lover and been killed in a brawl a short time before. Sanza's ghost would appear on the stage from the audience and dance with Okuni, re-living the eccentric *kabuki*-like exploits of his lifetime. These also included scenes of sexual innuendo with the lady of the tea-house and of explicit voyeurism in a bathhouse, notorious for employing sexy young girls to attract young customers.

The great success of this first form of *kabuki* (usually called *Okuni kabuki*) inspired groups of prostitutes to expand in imitation of Okuni's *kabuki odori*, making out of the sensual dances an instrument to advertise their services. The exotic three stringed instrument called the *shamisen*, which was to become identified with *kabuki* and *jōruri* music, was introduced at this time. Comical scenes featuring the clowning antics known as *saruwaka*, and comical soliloquies with pantomimes, became very popular, as did the use of women playing men's roles and vice-versa. The costumes were extremely elegant and, especially in the bathhouse scenes (*furoagari no asobi*), very revealing. Exoticism was also evident in the props, such as the long pipes loved by the *kabuki mono* and the tobacco-box (smoking was a novelty imported from the "foreign barbarians"), the rare imported tiger or leopard furs, and so on. This type of performances was called *onna kabuki* (women *kabuki*) or *yūjo kabuki* (prostitute *kabuki*).

Success was enormous with the city audiences, and a number of *daimyō* even invited famous courtesans and their troupes to their castles, sometimes in very distant regions of Japan, to celebrate special occasions. The shogunate, from the very beginning highly suspicious of this entertainment form, at least as early as 1608 began to issue decrees against *kabuki*, calling it a "national disturbance" of morality. The final decrees of 1629 are considered to have ended the *onna kabuki*, and were occasioned by the scandal of important *daimyō* indulging in playing the host in their castles to entire troupes and by a riot in Kyoto during which *samurai* from rival groups stormed the *onna kabuki* stage, leaving many people dead and the stage completely destroyed.

The prohibition against the courtesans appearing on the stage left the field free for troupes of young boys, the *wakashu*, who already had performed either as part of *onna kabuki* or in their own *wakashu kabuki* shows before the prohibition. The *wakashu* were boys between eleven and fifteen; that is, before the *gempuku* ceremony in which the forehead was shaven as a sign of coming of age. Their business was no different from that of the female prostitutes.[7] The *wakashu* shows brought into *kabuki* some new elements, such as the juggling and acrobatics known as *hōka*, and the tight-rope walking called *kumo mai*. Under the influence of a number of *nō* and *kyōgen* masters, who had lost the possibility of working in their field because of political reasons and had joined the *wakashu kabuki* troupe led by Kanzaburō, the *wakashu* developed *kyōgen*-like scenarios for relatively well developed comical plays. Under the protection of the Shogun Iemitsu, who often summoned Kanzaburō and his boys to the castle for his pleasure, *wakashu kabuki* prospered and was widely diffused, but caused the same problems as the *onna kabuki*. As soon as the protector Iemitsu died, his successor prohibited the *wakashu kabuki* in a definitive way in 1652, taking occasion from a series of scandals involving the *wakashu*, such as a double suicide of the wife of a *daimyō* with a *wakashu*, and a serious riot between two *daimyō* over the favors of *wakashu* in Osaka.

The prohibition of the *wakashu kabuki* was overcome through the shaving of the *maegami* (front hair), which made the boys officially *yarō* (adult men), but deprived them of what was considered one of the most enticing features of their sex-appeal. Moreover, the prohibition of the most blatantly erotic scenes, songs, and dances forced the actors to develop the dramatic element of their shows, a development re-enforced by the contributions of the *nōgaku* actors. Although remaining in popular use, the now suspicious name *kabuki* was officially dropped in favor of *monomane kyōgen zukushi*. This phase marks the beginning of *yarō kabuki* as at least partly spoken drama in the realistic manner of *kyōgen*.

As a consequence of the tremendous fire in Edo in 1657, entire sections of the city, including its seven large theatres, were destroyed. Only four theatres were rebuilt, this time following criteria to serve the new dramatic requirements, with wider stages which incorporated the old *hashigakari*; by 1668, the first *hanamichi* had been built, and became a feature which was to become typical and essential to every *kabuki* stage. Around the same time, in 1664, the first plays in two parts, and soon afterwards in three, four, and more parts (*tsuzuki-kyōgen*), appeared, and programs were extended to a whole day of performance. For the first time the draw curtain (*hikimaku*) was introduced and large elements of décor (*ōdōgu*), which at the time appeared very realistic, became usual. The development of the dramatic element, combined with the prohibition against the appearance on the stage of women and with the realism that had characterized *kabuki* from its beginning were conditions that created the phenomenon of the *onnagata*, or female impersonators. They were, of course, necessary to perform such favorite plays as those set in the tea-houses of the red light districts, and to execute the dance element in the performances, which was never completely abolished; the latter soon flourished again, building on the dance traditions of the *wakashu* who had in the meantime grown into *yarō*.

The shaving of the front hair had marked the end of the acting career of the *wakashu* when they turned fifteen. The new regulation requiring every actor to shave his front hair regardless of age made possible a life-long career as a performer. This new situation allowed the time necessary to develop mature talent and truly professional skills, unthinkable in young boys. A system of role-type specialization was established, and became more and more specific and complex as required by the growth and diversification of the plays. Actors became known by the name of their specialty, as *wakaoyama* for the roles of beautiful young woman, *tachiyaku* for the main male roles, *yakkogata* for the servant roles, *dōkeyaku* for such comical roles as the master of the brothel, and *katakiyaku* for villains.

B) *Genroku* Kabuki. Strictly speaking, the Genroku period covers only 16 years (1688-1703). The great fame of this highpoint of Tokugawa culture in the arts, literature, and theatre gave the name of Genroku to an undetermined, but much longer, period of time extending into the 1740s. To the Genroku culture belong such famous poets as the master of *haikai* poetry, Matsuo Bashō; the greatest among Japan's novelists, Ihara Saikaku; a score of the most admired *ukiyo-e* painters, and Japan's most celebrated dramatist, Chikamatsu Monzaemon. During this time the "floating world"[8] achieved those characteristics that made it a symbol of the townspeople culture. *Kabuki* and *jōruri* were so deeply a part of this period that, to the present time, they essentially reflect its glories and its limitations, and are often considered as its synthesis.

The dramatists of the early Genroku period, although still apprentices in the craft of putting long plays together, already faced the difficult task of providing enough materials for day-long performances in at least ten major theatres in the three largest Japanese cities. They coped with an ingenuity that at times betrays their inexperience, finding subjects from every source they could: traditional myths, folk legends, episodes of Japanese history, and the scandal of the day such as the latest amorous adventures of celebrities among the courtesans, and vendettas and the double suicides that had stunned the gossipy red light districts. We know the contents of many of these plays because of the exhaustive outlines contained in the two volumes of the *Collection of Genroku Kabuki Masterpieces* (*Genroku kabuki kessaku shū*). The general impression is that of rather complicated, melodramatic plots hastily and arbitrarily put together, with the generous use of fantastic interventions by spirits and gods mixed with realistic scenes. Horie Webber finds in "this jumble of ill-conceived fantastical melodrama" five "primary plot patterns, namely the house-strife pattern, the revenge pattern, the *onryō* pattern, the *keisei* pattern and the *hito-kami* pattern."[9]

The *keisei* (courtesan) pattern expands on the favorite *yūjo-kai* (whore-buying) scenes, a favorite since the *onna kabuki* time, and adds the many unhappy consequences of ill-fated love affairs in the red light districts. The house-strife (*oie-sōdō*) pattern makes free use in a frequently historically inexact way of the conflicts regarding succession to power in a feudal house: the rightful heir is usually in distress at the beginning of the play but eventually succeeds in achieving his inheritance despite the usurpations of the villain. The revenge-pattern had its most famous example in the later *Chūshingura*. The *onryō* pattern, however, which gave the structure to the first known Okuni play, can be considered in some cases a variation of the revenge pattern on a surreal or suprareal level, when the angry ghost takes the vendetta into his own hands and torments the object of his revenge, appearing in his own terrifying shape or as an animal or an insect.[10] Both the *onryō* and *hito-kami* patterns open *kabuki* plays to the sphere of the "other dimension," the superhuman and the spectacular: in the *hito-kami* (man-god) pattern either a man is elevated to the sphere of a half-god, thus suddenly displaying superhuman and invincible powers, or a god appears disguised as a man, with the same result of deciding in a spectacular way issues that no human could solve.

Beginning from this time, most *kabuki* plays present a multi-part structure, in which each part (*tate*) does not correspond to an "act" or a "scene" of a western play, but is built as a complete drama in itself and is usually performed independently from the rest of the play. These multi-part plays (*tsuzuki-kyōgen*) therefore are like a conglomerate of one-part plays (*hanare-kyōgen*) and are comparable to independent episodes of a mini-series which develops one or several actions. The number of parts varies considerably, in many plays between three and five, but sometimes reaching much higher numbers, e.g., eleven in the extraordinarily long *Kanadehon Chūshingura*— which by the way is one of the few plays sometimes still receiving (almost) full-length productions.

At the center of the formation of this *kabuki* dramatic structure was the process represented by the interaction of *sekai*, or vertical plot, and *shukō*, or horizontal plot. The function of *sekai* (literally meaning "world" and representing the familiar, traditional framework) was to provide the already known background and course of events. The function of *shukō* on the contrary was that of introducing the element of adaptation of the familiar to new circumstances, providing innovation and surprise. The vertical *sekai* represented to the audiences of the Edo period the past, which was identified with the established, old samurai world as mirrored in the *jidaimono*. The vertical *shukō*, on the contrary, was viewed as the process of bringing a work out of the past into the present, which at the time was identified with the new order of the commoners, as mirrored in the *sewamono* plays. The logic conclusion was eventually to mix both *jidai* and *sewa*; i.e., tradition and novelty in the same play, as it was to happen soon in many plays, including the most famous masterpiece, *Kanadehon Chūshingura.*

The preference for an apparently religious resolution featuring divine intervention is evident. Although almost buried in secular materials geared solely to entertain, this *deus ex machina* resolution fulfills the important function of providing a reassuring ending, which was a must for the Genroku audience. The obligatory optimism of the early Genroku was soon to end: in Chikamatsu's later plays a highly poetical, complex outlook on the variety of possibilities in interpreting the human tragedy marked a much deeper and more mature dramaturgy which, however, belongs primarily to the realm of the *jōruri* world.

The importance of the actor in *kabuki* has been recognized by most theatre historians, who do not hesitate to attribute a high priority to the contributions of the great performers. Genroku *kabuki* saw the flourishing of strong personalities, who established the main roles and styles which became standard in the *kabuki* world. Sakata Tōjūrō (1647–1709), a legendary star of the Kyoto-Osaka area, became the paragon of the *wagoto* style, that is, the gentle, soft (*wa*), romantic hero, as opposed to Ichikawa Danjūrō (1660-1704), the legendary champion of the *aragoto* style, the oversize, supernatural, rough (*arai*) hero, especially loved in the Edo area. Both artists are the subject of much Japanese literature, with many episodes illustrating their unique artistic contributions to the establishment of the highest standards in the art of *kabuki* performance, their exceptional popularity and eccentric way of life, and the incredible manifestations of grief by fans at their death. The *kumadori* make-up created by Danjūrō for his *aragoto* roles has remained a symbol of *kabuki* to the present time.

Also belonging to Genroku *kabuki* is Yoshizawa Ayame (1673-1719), the most famous *onnagata*, whose principles and sayings were summarized by the actor/playwright Fukuoka Yagoshirō in the often quoted *Ayamegusa* (Words of Ayame).[11] From Ayame derive the codification of the teaching and the practice of extending the impersonation of a woman to the actor's private life, in an effort to achieve true realism on the stage. This tradition was followed to the extremes of wearing female clothes all the time, carefully concealing the fact of being married and having fathered children, and even tacitly being allowed to bathe in the women's section of the public bathhouse, a practice which was prohibited in 1842.

The *onnagata* excelled in dance plays, developing high skills such as the quick change of costumes later called *shichi-henge* (seven transformations) which made out of the *onnagata* art a complex and unique achievement in theatre history; the actor achieves and sustains the feminine grace and sensuality of a lightly flowing rhythm in spite of the extraordinary requirements of resilience and strength to perform in incredibly heavy costumes and wigs. The *onnagata* became the wonder of even the professional female entertainers who were influenced by the actors regarding the latest fashions and sophisticated manners for use in their own profession.

During the Genroku period the present distinction between "historical plays" (*jidaimono* or period pieces) and "domestic plays" (*sewamono*) began, as well as the practice of merging the characteristics of both genres in one.

In 1699 began the publication of the yearly *Yakusha kuchi jamisen*, which contains a critical evaluation of the plays and actors of the year. It was in three volumes, one for each of the three major centers of theatre activity, Edo, Kyoto, and Osaka. This unique example in the history of theatre criticism continued for almost three hundred years, providing a treasury of information having no parallel in the West.

The first two decades of the eighteenth century were marred by unfortunate events for *kabuki*: the tragic death in Edo of the barely forty-four year old Danjūrō at the hand of a fellow actor in 1704, and the death of Tōjūrō in Kyoto two years later deprived the two *kabuki* capitals of their greatest stars. The scandalous affair in 1714 involving the handsome *kabuki* actor Ikushima Shingorō and Lady Ejima, a lady-in-waiting to the mother of Shogun Ietsugi led to the closing and dismantling of the Yamamura-za (thereby reducing to three Edo's functioning *kabuki* theatres) and a stiffening of censorship of the content of the plays, with the elimination of the popular themes based on events from real life. The 1722 ban on the *shinjūmono*, the double suicide plays, further limited *kabuki* from capitalizing on the sensational contemporary scandals which had been among its chief box-office attractions. Moreover, succeeding to the great generation of giant star-actors was a generation of imitators, who were concerned with repeating the patterns originated by their famous predecessors, thus starting a trend of standardization that greatly dampened the spontaneous vitality of early *kabuki*.

All these elements together made *kabuki* especially vulnerable to the competition of the triumphant puppets. The best playwrights had been alienated from *kabuki* by the arrogance of the actors, and *jōruri* had succeeded in securing the collaboration not only of Chikamatsu, but also of Takeda Izumo (1691-1759) and Namiki Sōsuke (1695-1751), who were probably the two best craftmen in the dramaturgic structuring of plays Japan ever had. The puppets scored enormous success with plays which ranged from Chikamatsu's masterwork *Kokusenya kassen* (The Battles of Coxinga) in 1716, to the two great mid-century works, *Sugawara denju tenarai kagami* (The Secret of Sugawara Calligraphy, 1746) and *Yoshitsune sembonzakura* (The Thousand Cherry Trees, 1747), and, in 1748, the all-time greatest box-office success, the *Kanadehon chūshingura* (The Treasury of Loyal Retainers). The *kabuki* had no choice but to adapt these plays, and in so doing absorb from the puppets, along with their dramaturgy, a number of important scenic and technical elements, as well as the use of the *jōruri* chanter and music, and the imitation of certain stylized dance movements.

C) *Golden Age of* Kabuki *in Edo.* The revitalization of *kabuki* drama through the adaptation of *jōruri* masterpieces opened the way to a complete victory of *kabuki* over the puppets, to the point that by 1780 there was no theatre left in Japan presenting daily *jōruri* performances.

During this time Edo reached a high point of cultural activity, in which even the *samurai* began to participate in the development of *kabuki* music. The increased wealth of powerful merchants meant generous patronage and effective leadership in developing the culture of a city that had become the largest in the world. A long period of peace and the transformation of *kabuki* into a recognized art form had softened the hostility of the authorities. It was known to everybody that some *samurai* indulged in *shamisen* music and were playing with the *kabuki* orchestra concealed behind the box at the side of the stage. While vocal and *shamisen* music had become the object of serious study, dance reached a highpoint of sophistication with the development of the *shosagoto*, dance plays which not only involved the performance of *onnagata* but also involved male roles.

With the flourishing of great plays, of new and more sophisticated music and singing, and with great progress in the quality of dance Edo *kabuki* developed into a mature form of total theatre. Famous actors again gave splendor to the stage: in Edo Ichikawa Danjūrō II (1689-1758) and Danjūrō IV (1712-1778), Nakamura Nakazō I (1736-1790) and Matsumoto Kōshirō IV (1737-1802) brought the acting skill to a new plateau. Theatre architecture and stage decor made great progress with the introduction of an underroof that improved acoustics, and the building of traps that made possible the lifting and lowering of an entire stage set, while the first revolving stage as a permanent feature of the theatre was built in the Nakamura-za in Edo; the date, declare several related sources, was 1793, at least a century before its counterpart was "invented" by Karl Lautenschläger for the Residenztheater in Munich (1896).[12] The roofed, *nō*-like stage was now replaced, at least in some theatres, with a frontal stage occupying the whole width of the theatre.

D) *The Decadence to the End of the Edo Period.* With the nineteenth century begins a period of growing tension and serious menace to the political stability of the country, under the influence of the new ideas and movements that eventually led to the overthrow of the shogunate and the Meiji Restoration (1867/68). The economic crisis led to a series of prohibitions of every kind of luxury for people outside the *samurai* class, and to a serious consideration of the miseries of the masses, thus establishing the premises for the new genre of *kabuki* plays called *kizewamono* (straight *sewamono*) or *masewamono*, dedicated to the depiction of the poor, the wretched, and the underworld. One of the greatest playwrights *kabuki* ever produced, Tsuruya Namboku (1755-1829), was the acknowledged master of this genre. In his best-known play *Tōkaidō Yotsuya kaidan* (The Ghost of Yotsuya), a world of frightful ghosts, thefts, murders, and hallucinations worthy of Edgar Allan Poe brought strikingly modern themes of despair and horror, and an atmosphere of torture, killings, grotesque and supernatural apparitions to the Japanese stage.

The last great *kabuki* playwright was Kawatake Mokuami (1816-1893) who authored some 360 plays. He is especially remembered because of his *shiranamimono*, pieces about Robin Hood-like petty thieves, who use blackmail or other crooked means to extort money from the rich for distribution to the poor. Mokuami stands as a bridge between the *kabuki* at the end of the shogunate, and the difficult times of experimentation with modernized forms of *kabuki* after the Meiji Restoration.

The Tempō reforms of 1841-1843 were an attempt to rediscover the austerity of the old feudal regime in order to salvage a system that was evidently disintegrating. The reforms intended also the abolition of *kabuki*. They were never carried out, but the three *kabuki* theatres were removed from the center of Edo and relocated to the outskirts of the city, where they were rebuilt with minor variations.

E) Kabuki *from the Meiji Period to the Present.* The events leading to the transformation of Japan profoundly changed the atmosphere of the new imperial capital of Tokyo, including the theatre districts, always especially sensitive to social trends. Edo culture was rapidly giving way to a frantic process of modernization which tried to introduce western ways in all fields, including those affecting both the appearance of the stage and its actors (such as clothing fashions, home and public furnishings, hair styles, and make-up), as well as the very spirit of the plays themselves.

Kabuki was one of the first objects of concern to the new breed of educators, who were prompt in summoning the responsible *kabuki* actors and informing them of the "Imperial view; " that is, the order to limit their shows to subjects that could be seen by foreign visitors as well as by parents and children together without scandal. At the same time the names of the historical characters, traditionally disguised in *kabuki*, had to be returned to their exact originals, in order to serve as instruction, and no longer mislead the audience. A number of "modern" modifications were introduced almost immediately by actors who capitalized on such novelties as western clocks, western clothes, and western subject matter. The *zangirimono*, plays in which actors adopted short-cropped western style hair fashion (*zangiri*), were an example of such a trend. The main author of *zangirimono* was the actor Onoe Kikugorō V (1844-1903), who made out of the genre a variation on the old domestic plays (*sewamono*) reflecting a few new exterior aspects of contemporary life, but still adhering to the spirit and the structure of the older works.

The producer Morita Kanya (1846-1897), owner of the Morita-za, was one of the true pioneers in the effort to modernize *kabuki*. He built a new theatre, the Shintomi-za (1872), in the respectable location of Shintomi-chō, far away from the traditional theatre street (Saruwaka-machi); the new building appeared substantially different from its predecessors, both outside, with its metal roof, painted walls, and copper-plated tower, and inside, with rows of chairs in the orchestra for the convenience of foreigners and Japanese now wearing western clothes. His 1878 production of the dramatization of the Satsuma Rebellion, *Okige no kumo harau asagochi* (The Morning East Wind Clearing the Clouds of the Southwest), was an enormous success, partly because of the stunning effect of using western fireworks in the battle scene in which the hero is killed falling from a horse amidst a rain of shells. This hit encouraged Kanya to rebuild the Shintomi-za in direct imitation of western theatres including sparkling gas-lit chandeliers. Opening night was celebrated with a pomp that had never been seen before, with all the city authorities and important personalities in western formal clothes; this event betrayed Kanya's ambition to change *kabuki*'s image from red light district entertainment to one of a dignified "national theatre" fitting for the new capital of the Japanese empire.

While Kanya continued his experiments in modernizing *kabuki*, even to the extent of importing foreign actors and foreign music for a play with scenes located abroad, the actor and playwright Danjūrō IX (1839-1903) tried a reform based on his interest in historical exactness, not only with the names of the historical personalities, but also with the reconstruction

185

of their costumes and behavior. In essence Danjūrō's attempt was actually a Japanese version of the worldwide trend of realism, which required from the actor a new realistic attitude and style of acting (*haragei*, "art from the inner soul") quite in contrast with the "degenerated and external" stylization of *kabuki* tradition. The new plays, called *katsurekimono* (historically accurate pieces), unfortunately found no great playwright to give them life, and the experiment failed. In 1886 Danjūrō gave up performances of *katsurekimono* and went back to the traditional fare of Edo plays. By that time the *shimpa* groups began their movement towards the modern theatre and left *kabuki* with its basic repertory of famous plays from an epoch that was becoming more distant every day.

Kabuki lost many of its characteristics of immediacy and responsiveness to the daily life of the big cities, but acquired a new respectability officially sanctioned by the visits of important dignitaries, including the Emperor and the imperial family in 1887, and foreign chiefs of state.

To counteract an already evident process of crystallization, men of letters for the first time began to write new plays for the *kabuki* in an effort to revitalize the stagnating repertory. This movement was called *shin kabuki* or new *kabuki*. The major dramatists who contributed plays of some importance were Tsubouchi Shōyō (1859-1935), the translator of Shakespeare and one of the founders of theatre research in Japan; the novelist Mayama Seika (1879-1948); and the most gifted among them, Okamoto Kidō (1872-1939), who, from writing newspaper criticism about *kabuki*, became the most successful among the *shin kabuki* writers, with plays like *Shūzenji monogatari* (The Story of Temple Shūzenji) and *Banchō sarayashiki*.

New western style theatres were built, the Yūraku-za in 1908, and the Imperial Theatre (Teikoku gekijō) in 1911. In the latter even actresses—instead of *onnagata*—were employed to perform *kabuki*. The Shōchiku brothers moved from the Kyoto-Osaka area to Tokyo in 1912, and formed the Shōchiku Company, soon to take over the role of sole producing company in the *kabuki* world. Shōchiku gained control of the leading *kabuki* theatre, the Kabuki-za, and dictated the policies that regulated both the commercial and artistic life of *kabuki*, challenged only in 1932 by the Tōhō Company, which for a short time succeeded in breaking the Shōchiku monopoly.

After World War II *kabuki* was regarded as dangerous by the occupying authorities because of feudal ideas contrary to the establishment of a new democracy. Soon, however, every form of censorship was lifted, and *kabuki* for the first time in its history was free of exterior control.[13]

The most important events of the postwar period were the building of the new National Theatre (Kokuritsu gekijō, 1967) a long cherished dream which consacrated *kabuki* as "the" national theatre of Japan; and the several tours of splendid *kabuki* companies to Europe and America, where foreign audiences in their best opera houses acclaimed the traditional Japanese performing art as a world-class theatrical form.

The history of *kabuki*'s survival to the present day shows fascinating aspects of nostalgia for a romantic world of fantasy that had nourished the city population for over three centuries, a strong *iemoto*-like show-business organization, and a treasure of theatrical traditions made out of ever-appealing dramatic masterpieces, spectacular scenery, sophisticated choreography, and very high levels of dancing, acting, and acrobatic skills.

Although the recurring lamentations of the experts—that *kabuki* has lost its soul and lives mostly as a business for tourist attraction—seems from time to time to be justified, the sudden blooming of extraordinary talent and the surprising bursts of amazing vitality defy any prophecy of doom; they promise instead the continuing presence of traditional *kabuki* among the pluralistic offerings of classical Japanese theatre.

Kabuki *in Performance*

Since its beginnings *kabuki* has been appreciated as an "actors' theatre" in which performance has traditionally overridden in importance considerations of literary value or scenic effect. Everything in *kabuki* is centered on the bravura of the star, in the service of whom text, costumes, scenery, and music are orchestrated for maximum effect. The *kabuki* star is as much in the spotlight as the solo dancer in ballet and the principal singer in opera would be. It is therefore important to analyze some of the natural gifts and the demanding skills required to sustain such extraordinary effort.

According to a saying often repeated in this context, the *kabuki* actor must bring to the performance of a play three things: voice, movement, and physical attractiveness. A better understanding of the strenuous demands on the voice of *kabuki* actors is beginning to appear in some writings in western languages, especially under the influence of scholars involved in experimentation with *kabuki* training in Japan and abroad, such as Gunji Masakatsu and James Brandon.[14] The vocal difficulties for the major roles of many *kabuki* plays are enormous. Although problems connected with voice are better demonstrated than written about, it is worth mentioning a few illustrative examples. The mastering of the *ippon chōshi*—the "continuous pattern" used in speeches building up to an explosive climax in the *aragoto* style—requires an extraordinary breath-control that only few experts succeed in achieving. The technique called *nori*, adapted from the chanting of *jōruri*, implies a very sensitive capacity of "riding" (*noru*) the rhythms of the *shamisen*, declaiming each syllable in a regular pattern timed to a chord of the *shamisen* accompaniment. Another technique that presents a serious challenge to the most experienced actors is the *yakuharai*, the subtle delivery—according to a hardly noticeable cadence—of poetical text written in the Japanese metrical form of alternating seven and five syllable verses (*shichigochō*).

More obvious to Western students has been the importance of the second requirement, movement, which has been described in detail, in the West, by such authors as Ernst, Gunji, Leiter, and Pronko.[15]

From the very beginnings dance has been an essential factor in the great success of *kabuki*. The free style of the pre-Genroku dance had been a conscious break from the established rules of other dance traditions in favor of eccentric glamour. Soon, however, it gave way to a process favoring the creation of sophisticated movement patterns (*kata*) which became a most precious heritage left by famous actors to their disciples for the interpretation of roles they had created. The term *kata* literally means "forms," and is used to describe fixed dance patterns as well as all conventional forms of performance, ·especially those referring to acting. *Kata* are learnt through observation and imitation of the masters, and sometimes are also described in writing, which often provides interesting notes regarding the genesis of particular stage business. In most cases, however, *kata* are learnt by rote, without discussion of meaning or motivation. Most actors grow up in the atmosphere of a *kabuki* family, and naturally memorize the *kata* they will use almost spontaneously in their dance and in their acting.

Kabuki's stylized movement can be construed as sequences of *kata* which move (solemnly and intensely in the *aragoto* style or graciously and sensually in the *wagoto* style) from one statuesque position to the next, interspersed with pauses (*ma*) until the climactic sequence suddenly freezes in a uniquely expressive pose called *mie*.

The concept of *ma* is a fundamental one in Japanese performance esthetics, as it represents the emptiness of time/space from which movement appears and into which it dies. In practical use, *ma* also includes the important meaning of "timing." The art of mastering *ma* always has been considered as extremely difficult and elusive, its secret being that of knowing its "degree" or "extent" (*hodo*), something that can only partially be taught and is supposed to be dictated by an artistic instinct similar to the *kokoro* of *nō* esthetics.

The *mie* pose reached at climactic moments summarizes with great intensity the feelings to be expressed, and represents one of the most characteristic high points of *kabuki* art. Moving in accord with a clearly established rhythm, the actor takes an imposing body position, rotates his head slowly, gives it a final snap, and freezes his expression into an intensely powerful stare, usually with the eyes crossed. Besides the most spectacular individual *mie* that crown the finales of scenes or plays on a grand scale with all the underpinnings of music and the striking of wooden clappers, there are several other types of *mie*; these are performed by individual actors or by two or three together to form a beautiful picture, in domestic as well as in historical plays. They all serve the same purpose of highlighting the finale of a sequence of movements.

Spectacular forms of movement in *kabuki* are the techniques of stage fighting and stage acrobatics that are known as either *tate*, which include some two hundred precisely stylized patterns, or *tachimawari*, a more generic term describing all fighting movements. The importance of martial arts in Japan's life during the Tokugawa era is hardly to be imagined in today's society. Recent interest in Japanese martial arts has revealed to the West a lesser-known reality of militaristic training and soldier-like atmosphere of life under the hegemony of over 400,000 *samurai* families, who lived at the expense of the state as an immense army always ready to sustain the artificial fabric of Tokugawa society.[16] The lack of real battle-fields had multiplied the need for artificial training situations in the martial arts, which could provide the proud *samurai* with advanced skills in sword-fighting and/or self-defense techniques of the most disparate types, with or without weapons. *Kabuki* reflected that reality through a generous use of stylized martial arts techniques, which became a must for the *kabuki* actor. Spectacular stage combats and complexly choreographed fighting scenes are an important part of almost all *kabuki* roles, and even female roles are not spared from the need to perform deadly fights or deeds of suicidal self-sacrifice according to the rules of military etiquette.

The old tradition of acrobatics in Japanese show business has found in *kabuki* a spectacular haven, not only within the choreography of stylized stage combat, but also in the imitation of animals and in other non-human roles, and especially in techniques of flying, either above the stage or over the audience (*chūnori*).

The techniques of stage entrances and exits make use of special dance steps to meet the audience's high expectations at the first appearance of the star on the stage, or at the moment of the finale. *Roppō* is one such technique. The meaning of the word is "six directions." It developed from a special step used for entrances imitating the dashing way the *otokodate* swaggered around Edo. Eventually several kinds of *roppō* developed as steps used especially for spectacular exits, from the *tobi roppō* or flying *roppō* for certain *aragoto* bravura exits, to the *kitsune roppō* which imitates the movements of the fox (*kitsune*), or the *yūrei roppō* for the ghosts, and so on.

The history of *kabuki* dance is strictly intertwined with the history of *kabuki* itself, and each epoch left its mark on today's movements. Influences from a number of traditions are present, and sometimes traceable back to *furyū*, *nembutsu odori*, *nōgaku*, and a number of popular dances that provided the seedbed for a splendid development of *kabuki buyō* (*kabuki* classical dance). Without betraying its popular origins and its being geared to the tastes of large audiences, *kabuki* dance succeeded in assimilating the different styles and providing for them a basic common denominator that makes the originally very divergent styles all recognizable as genuine *kabuki buyō*.

As an element of *kabuki*, *mai*, the general term for dance, acquires the specific meaning of designating pieces derived from *nōgaku*; *odori*, on the contrary, designates dances of popular origin. The term *furi* is used for pantomimic movements in *kabuki*, taken from many different sources, among which one of the most characteristic is the *ningyō-buri* in which the dancer imitates the movements of the puppets. Realistic mimetic movements are named *monomane-buri*, while sequences of abstract mimic movements are called *fuzei-buri*.

Most of *kabuki buyō* is accompanied by *shamisen* music which collected and popularized a number of aspects from all previous forms of Japanese music, from *gagaku*, *kagura*, *nō*, down to the folk and fashionable songs of the day. The most popular *shamisen* music was called *nagauta* (long song) which reached a golden age in the first half of the nineteenth century as dance music for the *henge mono* or "quick change pieces." *Nagauta* music is very flexible, can be performed by one *shamisen* or by the entire orchestra of twenty musicians, of which ten are *shamisen* players, while others play flutes and drums. In *nagauta* dance pieces the musicians (*hayashigata* or *narimonoshi*) are seated on the stage in full view, on upstage platforms (*hinadan*) blending with the background or covered with red carpet. The musicians playing in full view are called *debayashi* or *debayashigata*. In many plays the musicians play inside the *geza*, a bamboo-screened room located at stage right, from which they can see what happens on the stage without beeing seen by the audience. In that case the musicians form the *kage hayashi* or in-the-wing orchestra. Task of the musicians is not only to provide the musical accompaniment of the shamisen (*aikata*) but also, when required, to sing, to produce sound effects such as rain and wind, and to play a number of other instruments—in some cases more than thirty—including the most common ones taken over from the *nō*; that is the flute (*fue*), the small drum held in one hand by ropes around its frame and played with the other hand (*kotsuzumi*), the waist drum (*ōtsuzumi*), and the stick drum (*taiko*).

The development of costume had a decisive influence in the making of *kabuki* dance. While early *kabuki* had emphasized the new sensual freedom of the body itself, the introduction of the *onnagata* and of refined stylization favored a transition to an emphasis on the beauty of the costume and on its dance use as a means to conceal the body, the sex, and often the age of the *onnagata*. The new fashion of long sleeves was emphasized and built into dance movements to express shyness and other emotions, and the wave-like rhythm of the long kimono was used to establish walking movement patterns which remained a trademark of *kabuki*'s graceful elegance.

Dance as a prerogative of leading male roles (*tachiyaku*) was present from the beginnings of *kabuki*, but made especially strong advances from the end of the eighteenth century with the establishment of *buyō-geki* (dance drama with accompaniment of *jōruri* music).

Personal attractiveness is, besides voice and movement, the third element the actor is supposed to bring to performance. In *kabuki* the special actor-audience relationship assumes a very unique flavor in that the actor as a person is always present, together with his role, in the consciousness of the audience. There is no attempt, as in the realistic western theatre, to "disappear" in the role. On the contrary, several customs seem rather to be aimed at capitalizing on the entertaining game of the actor's shifting from his role to his own person—and vice-versa: on-stage costume changes, formal announcements of the actors' names at the beginning of the play, serving a cup of tea on stage to the actor after an exhausting scene, and wearing costumes bearing the crest of the family, which instantly identify the actors to knowledgeable fans. The fans are accustomed to this direct relationship to the star: in sign of their approval they do not clap their hands but shout the name of the artist himself, or compliments related to his family such as "like your father!" This custom, however, is rapidly disappearing, and barely survives today, being superseded by applause.

Costumes and Make-up

Costumes and make-up are an essential complement in the pictorial beauty of *kabuki* performance. They are carefully planned to give relief to the actors' movements and facial expression, and to help orchestrate subtle or magnificent choreographic effects based on combinations of colors and forms typical of *kabuki* tradition. Colors are, in general, bold and rich, and used without fear of contrasts that often go beyond conventional taste. Some garish tones approach kitsch in their gaudy and surprisingly effective celebration of the bawdy atmosphere of the red light districts.

Two broad categories of costumes correspond to the two basic categories of plays: the *jidaimono* or historical plays, and the *sewamono* or domestic plays. While domestic play costumes match the historical clothes of the Tokugawa period townspeople, the costumes for the historical plays are "non-historical," that is, they do not correspond to historical truth. They follow fixed conventions that make recognizable to the audiences the rank of the role in the feudal hierarchy, and at the same time contribute to the theatrical effects that real *samurai* outfits would not have provided.

A special case of stylized costumes are those used in *jidaimono* for super-human roles, the *hito-kami* or the *kami* in human form, who perform extraordinary deeds in exaggerated *aragoto* style. The oversize costume for the hero of *Shibaraku* is a typical example; it requires several times the amount of material needed for a normal *kabuki* costume, and two assistants must help the actor move around with it on stage, especially in the famous final *mie* in which they hold the two enormous square sleeves kept rigid by bamboo or (more recently) steel ribbing.

Another spectacular effect is the quick on-stage costume change. When the character undergoes a deep interior transformation—as does for example the holy man in *Narukami* after being seduced by the beautiful noble lady—the technique called *bukkaeri* is used: special threads in the upper half of the costume are removed, and the parts of the costume above the sash (*obi*) fold over the lower part of the previous costume, matching with the pattern revealed and thus giving the impression of a change of the whole costume. If the change happens simply to provide visual beauty and variety in a dance piece, *hikinuki* is used, a technique which allows the stage assistant to whip off the upper kimono, basted on top of one or more layers of other costumes, with a pull of strategically positioned buttons. The stage assistants, usually dressed in black to signify their non-existence on the stage, in the *shosagoto* dance pieces wear the formal kimono called *kamishimo*, consisting of the *kataginu* top and the divided long *hakama* trousers.

The striking pictorial effect of the costumes is completed by *keshō*, the *kabuki* make-up. The base for the make-up is mostly white, although many shades between white and red are also used. The eye lines and lip styles are standardized according to a long established tradition for each role in each play. This is also true for the most characteristic of *kabuki* make-up styles, the *kumadori*. At first glance very similar to the Chinese *l'ien pu* make-up for Beijing opera, and probably influenced by Chinese models, the *kumadori* is differentiated by its tendency to emphasize, rather than cover, the actor's facial expression. The one hundred or so different types of *kumadori* consist of systems of strong lines—basically black, red, and blue, but occasionally also brown, gold, purple, and red ochre—that represent, according to color and shape, such different qualities as righteousness (red) or fear and evil (blue).

Theatre Buildings, Stage, and Decor

The first stages used by *kabuki* at the time of Okuni were built according to the measurements and shape of those used for the large audiences of *kanjin nō*, the *nō* performances given to raise charitable contributions for temples and shrines. Paintings of early *kabuki* show a colorful backdrop—made of either hanging cloth or screens—which covered, or substituted for, the *matsubame* (the painted pine tree of the *nō* stage); the upstage floor, where the musicians squatted, was furnished with red patterned carpets. The measurements of the square main stage, which maintained the gable roof and pillars typical of the *nō* stage into the eighteenth century, were first twelve by twelve feet, and later eighteen by eighteen. The need for a larger acting space because of the revue-type performance introduced by *onna kabuki* was met with a substantial widening of the original *hashigakari*—a process that eventually led, step by step, to the broad and spacious stage of modern *kabuki*, which fills the entire width of the theatre building. The frequent fires and relocations and rebuilding of the theatres made possible a relatively unnoticeable but constant adaptation of the basic shape of the wooden stage to the expanding requirements of an increasingly spectacular choreography, and a substantial growth in the size and capacity of the buildings themselves, comparable to that of the London theatres in the eighteenth century.

In the earliest times the audience spread straw mats and sat on the ground in the *doma* (the pit in front of the main stage and the enlarged *hashigakari*), unsheltered from the rain. The sheltered side galleries (*sajiki*) were considered the best seats. The *doma* was later divided into square sections (*masu*), first by ropes and then by wooden partitions, which were used as a pathway by vendors to reach the crowded areas of the pit with food and drinks. Only after the Meiji Restoration in the last decades of the nineteenth century were the first chairs introduced; eventually, all partitions were eliminated in favor of a western-type orchestra with only armchairs as seats in the house; however, some remaining *sajiki* were retained with traditional *tatami* for those spectators who prefer to sit in traditional style.

The side galleries soon expanded to up to three levels. In early *kabuki* the *sajiki* opened at the rear into elegant tea-house rooms with free direct access to the stage. This arrangement made possible the notorious parties with beautiful actors behind the drawn bamboo curtains concealing the *sajiki* interiors from the public at large. The noisy merrymaking in the theatre was prohibited by the authorities on several occasions, and strict enforcement eventually led to the removal of the bamboo curtains.

In the first decades of the eighteenth century the construction of a wooden roof over the *doma* was finally allowed by the authorities, and consequently the *kabuki* theatre became for the first time a building fully sheltered from the elements. At the same time the *hanamichi* began to be used as an acting area. It is not precisely known when the *hanamichi* made its initial appearance in *kabuki*, although it was probably a passageway to the stage for the purpose of presenting gifts to the actors. It originally ran on a diagonal from center of the stage to one side, a fact supporting the theory that the *hanamichi* is a development of the steps in the center of the *nō* stage leading down to the orchestra where admirers placed flowers (*hana*) for the *nō* performers. At present the usually five-foot-wide *hanamichi* runs from stage right to the back of the orchestra, and in some plays it is complemented by a narrower, sometimes temporary *hanamichi* that runs parallel to it from stage left. The present *kari hanamichi* (temporary *hanamichi*) is a feature that used to be built permanently from the 1770's into the next century. The *hanamichi* is equipped with a *suppon* (literally: snapping-turtle), a stage trap and lift located at a point called *shichi-san*, three-tenths of the way from the stage; it is used for the entrance of unusual characters such as ghosts and sorcerers. The *hanamichi* is covered with white or blue stage cloth when suggesting snow or water; a smooth dance surface (*shosabutai*) is laid upon it when used as an extension of the main stage's dance floor for dance plays (*shosagoto*). The entrance curtain (*agemaku*) to the *hanamichi* is located at the back of the orchestra. A complex lighting plot is today used to enhance the stage effects of the action on the *hanamichi*, which is usually equipped with footlights. Before the introduction of electricity, stage hands used to hold candles close to the actors' face on long flexible wands (*sashidashi*).

The *hanamichi* became central to *kabuki* acting and choreography as a place enhancing like a frame the high points of solo performances by the stars, spectacular entrances and exits, and parades of courtesans and *samurai*, among other effects. For example, plays in *aragoto* style require the main actor to exit from the *hanamichi* executing a *roppo*; as part of the exit an elaborate *mie* is performed at the end of the *hanamichi*, which becomes at the moment the only center of audience attention, while the main curtain is drawn across the stage.

From the beginning of the eighteenth century the stage itself acquired the technical equipment for spectacular changes of decor, which were performed in front of the audience and became a traditional part of the show. At this time the playwright Nakamura Denshichi devised a primitive revolving stage built as a platform on wheels that could be turned manually from the side of the stage. In 1758 a more sophisticated platform was built by Namiki Shōzō, using an axle through the floor and capable of being maneuvered from beneath the stage. Finally in 1793 at Edo's Nakamura-za, the first permanently installed revolving stage (*mawari butai*) was cut into the stage surface itself and provided with a mechanism which until the advent of electricity was operated by a team of workers under the stage.[17]

Around the middle of the eighteenth century the pillars used to support the gable roof above the main stage were eliminated, opening the way for a larger and more flexible acting area. The subsequent building of traps and mechanical lifts made possible even the lowering and lifting of an entire elaborate setting.

Kabuki scenery, in Okuni's time merely a simple drapery used as a backdrop, developed into a very colorful decor which presents strikingly realistic characteristics. The setting became standardized in its parts and methods of construction. Although the audience's general impression is that of an accurate theatrical reconstruction of the play's required settings, *kabuki*'s decor does not intend primarily to reproduce realistically a locale but merely to indicate it, providing a "background against which, rather than in which, the actor plays."[18] A number of conventions are used, such as the cloth floor coverings (white for snow, blue for water, dark grey for dirt), or straw mats to indicate interiors, bare planks to indicate exteriors. Black background is used where the painted or built decor ends. No shadows are painted on and no cyclorama is used. The interiors are apparently more realistic, because of their sparse use of furniture and their sliding doors, but the same basic concepts of indicating place and providing a background for the actor are respected.

In general the use of properties is more extensive than in *nō* or *kyōgen*. Because of the quasi-realistic style of *sewamono* a great number of objects such as fans, umbrellas, a variety of paper goods, lanterns, and the like, corresponding to the historical reality of the Tokugawa world are used. More characteristic on the contrary are the exaggerated *kabuki mono*-like props still to be seen in such plays as the *jidaimono* featuring superhuman heroes or demigods, especially when the main actor engages in grand *aragoto* style scenes. The oversize swords, halberds, arches with arrows, hatchets, and other weapons match the spectacular exaggeration of the costumes, the enormous wigs and head ornaments, the necklaces of egg-sized beads, the *kumadori* make-up, and the special compressed vocal tones that create *kabuki*'s unique excitement.

Kabuki *and* Jōruri *Playwrights*

The social position and the *modus operandi* applying to professional playwrights attached to *kabuki* and *jōruri* companies were very similar. Many playwrights wrote for both genres, and oftentimes the plays written for one genre were adapted for the other.

In *kabuki* the first playwrights were the actors themselves. During the earliest period, Okuni is probably to be credited with the original adaptation of the structure of a *mugen nō* (consisting in the conjuration of a ghost, its appearance, a dialogue between shaman and ghost, and the appeasement of the ghost through the workings of the shaman) to her extravagant new show; moreover, she put the ghost of a recently deceased notorious *kabuki mono* in the place of traditional ghost-heroes as the protagonist of her play.

The additions/developments by the *onna kabuki* and *wakashu kabuki* were such revue-style numbers as chorus-girl line-ups, erotic dances, the *yūjo-kai* (buying a prostitute) scene in the tea-house, the *furoagari* (bathhouse) scene, and the *saruwaka kyōgen* (comical antics scenes), all of which hardly required the efforts of a professional playwright, but did utilize the skills of actors who adapted their experience in a number of other performing arts, such as *kyōgen* and *furyū*, to the requirements of the new entertainment.

A professional playwright became necessary with the development of full length plays in the *yarō kabuki*, when the revue-style entertainment was severely curtailed by the shogunate and *kabuki* was renamed *monomane kyōgen zukushi*. The first playwrights' names appearing on *kabuki* programs—as distinguished from those of the actors—are Miyako Dennai of Edo and Fukui Yagoemon of Osaka in the 1661-1662 season.

As a member of the company, the playwright was not esteemed on a high literary level, but was rather employed as an artisan at the level of the backstage helpers. His task was that of putting together plots and dialogues conceived as "vehicles" for the actor. Rather than stressing the dramatic structure and the value of the play in itself, *kabuki* playwriting strictly followed the function of suiting the star's whims. This was one of the major reasons why the best playwrights turned to the puppets, where—without the interference of the actors—their script would be performed unchanged. The method of putting the scripts together was mostly via a collaboration between the main playwright (*tatesakusha*) and his assistants, who would take care of minor scenes or even entire acts not considered central to the action. The final approval of the text belonged to the main actor of the company, who would freely introduce the   modifications he wanted for his histrionic purposes.

It would have been far from the concern of *kabuki* playwrights to publish their playscripts for readers. Texts of *kabuki* plays began to be published only after the Meiji Restoration, towards the end of the nineteenth century, at the same time as the phenomenon of independent men of letters becoming *kabuki* playwrights emerged in Japan.

The social status of the professional playwright was also reflected in his earnings, which were on a level with those of a costumer, and far below the earnings of an actor.

The first playwright given credit as such in the program of a *kaomise kōgyō* ("face showing performance," the important annual show at the beginning of the theatre season introducing the company for the year) was Tominaga Heibei (fl. 1673-1697) in 1680. Heibei started his career as an actor but changed to playwriting. Eight of his plays remain, all of them belonging to the *oie-mono* (great family strife) genre, which deals with the succession to the inheritance of a *daimyō* family, usually usurped by a villain, and eventually restored to the rightful heir. This genre provided popular situations that fostered the development of certain roles; among these were the situation of the weak young lord in distress, his "golden hearted" courtesan/mistress sacrificing herself to help him out of his misery, the faithful retainer giving his life for the young lord, the cruel villain plotting the ruin of the innocent, and so on.

The dramatization of contemporary events was forbidden, but the *kabuki* artists not only found a way around the prohibition via the transparent, but face-saving, transferral of the action to a past period of history, but also made out of "disguise" a most entertaining and quite sophisticated characteristic of *kabuki* playwriting. The game of building plays and roles on two levels, obvious and concealed, became an essential esthetic factor, always leaving a sense of double-entendre, typical of drama in periods of strict censorship.

Parallel to the process of placing contemporary events in the past was the transferral of the old to the new, offering to the actor the possibility of modernizing and bringing within the realm of actuality historical figures and legendary heroes. The appearance on the stage of the typical contemporary Edo dandy type, the *otokodate* Sukeroku, was seen by the Genroku audience both as a celebration of the latest fashions in the red light districts and as the transparent revival of the famous medieval hero Soga no Gorō seeking to take revenge on his father's murderer. While the middle-class *otokodate*'s triumph over the wicked *samurai* Ikyū pleased the mostly middle-class audience, the true identity of the historical *samurai* hero reinforced the Tokugawa values of *samurai* ethics and superiority. There was always a layer that satisfied the censorship, and one that satisfied the audience at large in a subtle, always face-saving, and shifting game. The taste for the game of double identity was highly appreciated by the Edo audiences. It was also extended to the interpretation of the choreography of climactic multiple *mie*, when the final tableau would represent, besides the obvious positions of the actors relative to each other as a result of the action, a beautifully arranged symbolic picture, such as a crane, (symbol of long life and prosperity), a suggestion of other animals, trees, or of natural phenomena which were transparently meaningful to the Edo audience. The Japanese words for the "dual identity-double meaning" game are *yatsushi* and *mitate*—an esthetic key to the appreciation of both playwriting and performance.

Kabuki Jūhachiban

Western literary scholars have echoed the Japanese specialists in praising the *kabuki* plays adapted from *jōruri*, extolling the beauty of their language and the sophistication of their dramatic structure, often overlooking the importance of the plays written for *kabuki* only; i.e., the "performance" texts' born and developed as vehicles for actors' bravura and spectacular dance choreographies. Recently, however, a number of western scholars, e.g., Brandon and Leiter,[19] have applied to *kabuki* the present-day interest of theatre historians for theatrical values and for dramatic structures of plays that are born from, and fit for, special types of performance

—independently from their literary value. This process of revision has generated a greater understanding and proper evaluation of *junsui kabuki* (plays written for *kabuki* only), among which are masterpieces that made *kabuki* famous the world over because of their excellence as performance texts, which provide what living *kabuki* artists only, and not the puppets, can deliver. The best known plays of this group are the *Kabuki jūhachiban* (The *Kabuki* Eighteen), a collection put together by the actor Ichikawa Danjūrō VII (1791-1859). The criteria for the choice reflect the Ichikawa family's preference for *aragoto* style, which offers plenty of opportunities for highly theatrical effects and spectacular costuming. Typical is, for example, the play *Shibaraku* by Mimasuya Hyōgo (pen name of Danjūrō I) that had its premiere at the Nakamura-za in Edo in 1697. The name of the play is derived from a several times repeated shout of the hero, Kamakura Gongorō Kagemasa, that stops the evil Lord Uke's attendants from executing two innocent characters, guilty only of opposing Uke's nefarious will. Right at the moment of the execution, the shout *shibaraku* (wait a moment!) is heard from the *hanamichi*, where the hero Gongorō appears in one of the most spectacular costumes of the entire *kabuki* wardrobe, bearing the Ichikawa family crest; he brandishes an enormous sword and his *kumadori* (facial make-up) shows, on a white base, powerful red lines, the color of righteousness. After a long speech in which he brags about his name, he cuts off the heads of a large group of Lord Uke's guard, liberates the innocent victims, and exits again through the *hanamichi* with great stylized dignity dancing a splendid bounding *roppō*. Independently from literary considerations, the play is one of best structured for spectacular effects in the *kabuki* repertory, and has become almost a symbol of *kabuki* itself. Another masterpiece belonging to this group is the above mentioned *Sukeroku: Flower of Edo*, which concentrates on the adventures of the *otokodate* Sukeroku (his double identity is that of the famous hero Soga no Gorō) in his attempt to revenge his father's death and in his scheme to retrieve his family's heirloom sword. This play, that opened at the Yamamura-za in Edo in March 1713, has also a relatively simple plot, the scheme of the hero being to linger in the red-light district and to provoke as many suspects as possible to drawing their sword, thus making an identification of the stolen treasure possible. Of course, the real interest of the play is in the acting of the main characters, mainly the dashing hero, Sukeroku, and the villain, Lord Ikyū, who is in possession of the stolen sword and is eventually killed by Sukeroku: all against the splendid, colorful background of the red-light district, where courtesans in magnificent costumes and elaborate wigs parade in procession scenes, where stylized but animated sword fights occur, and the public can enjoy Sukeroku's famous plunging into a vat filled with water and laugh at plenty of slapstick when Sukeroku and his brother Shinbei oblige passersby to crawl between their legs. Again, the spectacular choreography, "sensuality, vitality, optimism, and good-natured fun," (Brandon) and the acting bravura required in the central scene of the confrontation between Sukeroku and Ikyū; that is, the building of tension in the action and the skillful blend of *aragoto* and *wagoto* styles—and not sophisticated poetical values of the language—made this play one of the most successful and typical vehicles for the greatest actors of *kabuki* history.

A number of "performance" plays, which are unique to *kabuki* and which made the genre famous in Japan and abroad, belong to the group of dance plays (*shosagoto*), for example *Kanjinchō* and the *Dōjōji mono* (plays and dances centered on the legend of the temple Dōjō). Both examples are adaptations, for the *kabuki* stage and style of dance (*buyō*), of classic *nō* plays of the same title that dramatize and choreograph legends familiar to Japanese audiences. *Kanjinchō* (1840) was the first *kabuki* to borrow liberally from a well-known *nō* play (*Ataka*), which narrates an episode of the superhero Yoshitsune during his escape from the persecution of his powerful brother Yoritomo. At the barrier of Ataka the officer in charge of checking all passersby eventually allows Yoshitsune to pass, impressed by the total dedication of his four retainers and their leader, the warrior-priest Benkei, all disguised as *yamabushi* mountain priests. This play, which inherited from its model a highly emotional climactic recognition scene and some beautiful lines, in its *kabuki* version is primarily focused on Benkei's dances and his spectacular *roppō*, which made it one of the most often performed plays in the *kabuki* repertory. In a similar way, the *Dōjōji mono* present variations on the legend of beautiful Kiyohime's frustrated love for a young priest, and her transformation into a serpent in quest for revenge: the elegant dance of Kiyohime in disguise, during which she changes her costume nine times, her trasformation into a demon, and the spectacular fights against her demonic powers provide plenty of occasions for famous dances and spectacular effects.

Geidan: *Actors' Memoirs*

Among the important sources for the study of *kabuki* are numerous memoirs of actors (*geidan*, or talks about the craft of the actor). They contain precious insights drawn from episodes of famous actors' stage careers, as well as advice to younger fellow actors on how to acquire special skills, and general principles about artistic training. These memoirs were generally transmitted only to a restricted number of members of the family, as was the case for Zeami's and Zenchiku's treatises on the secret tradition of the *nō*. In recent years, however, especially since World War II, even in the secretive *nōgaku* world a number of famous performers became willing to make their "talks-on-art" public, thus providing wide audiences with published *geidan* by such great *nōgaku* artists as Kita Roppeita (*Roppeita geidan*), Umewaka Manzaburō (*Manzaburō geidan*), and Nomura Manzō (*Kyōgen no michi*).

Kabuki- and *jōruri*-related *geidan* by famous actors from the Genroku period to the present are by far less systematic and less theoretical than the classic treatises on the nō; they are rather fragmentary and occasional, and aim at instructing about specific acting problems or at recording episodes which illustrate specific accomplishments, rather than at speculating about the ultimate nature of art.

The most famous among *kabuki*-related *geidan* is the *Yakushabanashi* (also known as *Yakusha rongo* and translated as The Actors' Analects), which collects seven major pieces by different authors of the Genroku era.[20]

The first piece, *Butai hyakkajo* (One Hundred Items on the Stage, by Sugi Kuhei, the teacher of the famous *kabuki* actor Sakata Tōjūrō I), opens the series as a general introduction to such problems as the lowering of contemporary artistic standards, the feelings an actor has to bring to a role, the need for teamwork among actors, and so on. The writings that follow in this collection develop in more detail the items touched upon by Kuhei.

The second short treatise, *Gei kagami* (Mirror for Actors, by Tominaga Heibei) is a very important source of information for the history of pre-Genroku *kabuki*. Its four short chapters outline simple dramatic sketches of successful early *kabuki* shows which reflect the atmosphere of the red light districts, where the subject of male and female prostitution is taken for granted as a background for humorous situations.

The best known among the seven pieces is the third, the already mentioned *Ayamegusa* (Words of Ayame), set down by Fukuoka Yagoshirō as a guide for the *onnagata*, to be kept in the highest secrecy. Yoshizawa Ayame (1673-1719) is considered as the model and the great master of *onnagata*. His teachings and memoirs fill twenty-nine chapters, which contain, among many other pointers, the often quoted advice to the *onnagata* to behave in private as he does when performing on the stage. The *Ayamegusa* is also important as a source of information about Ayame's life and his artistic career, and, in general, because of the many details on how to achieve the best artistic results when performing as an *onnagata*.

The fourth and fifth pieces, the *Nijinshū* (Dust in the Ears, written down by the playwright Kaneko Kichizaemon), and the *Zoku nijinshū* (Sequel to Dust in the Ears) collect a number of episodes and sayings about and by the great Sakata Tōjūrō and other famous *kabuki* actors of the Genroku period. What Ayame did for the *onnagata* in the *Ayamegusa*, Tōjūrō did for the male lover's roles in the *Nijinshū*.

The sixth treatise, *Kengaishū* (The Kengai Collection, recorded by Somewaka Jūrobei) expands on the personality of Tōjūrō, his excellent intuition as an actor, his respect for his fellow performers, his collaboration with Chikamatsu, and his skills as a manager.

The *Analects'* last piece, *Sadoshima nikki* (Sadoshima's Diary), contains information about the life of the actor Sadoshima Chōgorō (1700-1757), followed by the *Shosa no hiden* (The Secret Tradition of the Kabuki Dance), which consists of eleven short items of practical advice on how to perform *kabuki* dance.

The tradition of transmitting *geidan* as a precious heritage from generation to generation has continued to the present time. Unfortunately, important materials for the understanding of the craft, style, and direction of *kabuki*, such as *Sadanji geidan* (by Ichikawa Sadanji II, 1880-1940), *Onnagata no koto* and *Ume no shitakaze* (by Onoe Baikō VI, 1870-1934), *Gei*, *Odori*, and *Rokusei Kikugorō geidan* (by Onoe Kikugorō VI, 1885-1949), and many others, are not available in translation. For most western readers, however, the loss is not relevant, because the topical nature of those writings makes them meaningful only for students who are familiar with the jargon and the daily life of the *kabuki* world.

NOTES

[1]Webber, *The Essence of Kabuki: A Study of Folk Religious Ritual Elements in the Early Kabuki Theatre*, 76, and *passim* for further information on the subject. See also Jackson, "Kabuki Narratives of Male Homoerotic Desire in Saikaku and Mishima," 464, for an interpretation of the verb *kabuku* as "to bend forward" and "to be aberrant," with clear suggestion of the strong homosexual component present in the *kabuki* world from its very beginning.

[2]Ortolani, *Das Kabukitheater: Kulturgeschichte der Anfänge*, 24-31.

[3]Shively, "Bakufu *versus* Kabuki," 326-356.

[4]The above quoted dissertation by Webber, *The Essence of Kabuki*, is the first systematic study of the subject in English.

[5]Webber, *Ibid.*, 93-98, gives an English translation of the document, the title of which she reads *Kunijo kabuki eshi*. A German translation is to be found in Ortolani, *Das Kabukitheater: Kulturgeschichte der Anfänge*, 69-74.

[6]Webber, *Ibid.*, 191.

[7]Ortolani, *Das Kabukitheater*, 108-117.

[8]Hibbett, *The Floating World in Japanese Fiction*, gives an excellent picture of *ukiyo*, the "floating world" of the red light districts.

[9]Webber, *The Essence of Kabuki*, 130.

[10]Webber, *Ibid.*, 130-131.

[11]Dunn and Torigoe, tr. *The Actors' Analects* contains both the Japanese text and the English translation of Ayame's treatise.

[12]See the paragraph on "Theatre Buildings, Stage and decor," for further information on the subject.

[13]Kawatake Toshio, "A Crisis of Kabuki and Its Revival right after the World War II," 36-42.

[14]Brandon, *Kabuki: Five Classic Plays*, 40-41.

[15]See for example Leiter, *The Art of Kabuki*, where he describes all major movements of the actors for the performance of the plays translated in that volume.

[16]Ratti and Westbrook, *Secrets of the Samurai*, provides a frightening panorama of the oppressive militaristic atmosphere in Tokugawa Japan, and of the extensive training in the martial arts within that system.

[17]According to Sugino Kitsutarō, "Tōzai mawari-butai to sono sōshisha," *Waseda shōgaku*, 126 (1957): 147-182, the person responsible for the 1793 first permanent revolving stage in the Nakamuraza was a stage technician named Jūkichi.

[18]Ernst, *The Kabuki Theatre*, 127.

[19]See Brandon, *Kabuki: Five Classic Plays*, 1-47, and Leiter, *The Art of Kabuki*, ix-xii.

[20]See an English translation in Dunn and Torigoe, trs., *The Actor's Analects*.

CHAPTER VIII

THE PUPPET THEATRE

The Words Jōruri *and* Bunraku

The literal meaning of the word *jōruri* is "pure crystal."[1] During the last decades of the sixteenth century a puppet play dramatizing the brief love story between the beautiful Lady Jōruri and Yoshitsune, the legendary hero of the Minamoto clan, became so popular that the name of the heroine began being used as a synonym for the puppet theatre. The basic plot of the story—set during the time of the civil wars in the twelfth century—is the following: Young Ushiwakamaru (boyhood name of Yoshitsune) happens to pass by the mansion where Jōruri lives and catches a glimpse of her beauty. By playing the flute from a distance, he succeeds in drawing Jōruri's attention, which leads to an exchange of poems and eventually to a night of secret, passionate love, followed by the inevitable cruel separation at the break of dawn. On his travel Ushiwakamaru becomes mortally ill on the beach, but is miraculously revived because of Jōruri's prayers and care. Finally, after the hero's full recovery, moving vows of eternal love are exchanged before they part again forever. These are the main elements of a story that underwent many variations in its numerous versions both as a narrative and as a successful puppet theatre plot.[2]

The word *bunraku* derived from the name of a famous puppeteer, Uemura Bunraku-ken (1737-1810). His real name was Masai Kahei, and he came from the island of Awaji, which is considered the homeland of Japanese puppetry. He conceived and successfully carried out a courageous plan of reviving the languishing art of the puppets in Osaka (in the time between 1780 and 1871 when the Bunraku-za was

opened in Osaka, no theatre existed in Japan exclusively
dedicated to the puppets). The name *bunraku* has been very
popular since that time. As a matter of fact, it is more
commonly used than the older designations such as *jōruri*,
ningyō jōruri (puppet *jōruri*), or *ningyō shibai* (puppet show).

History of Jōruri

Jōruri was born towards the end of the sixteenth century
as the successful synthesis of three separate arts: puppetry,
storytelling/chanting, and *shamisen* music. Starting from the
last decades of the seventeenth century, the decisive
contribution of dramatic masterpieces by some of the foremost
Japanese playwrights in conjunction with the extraordinary
achievements of master chanters, puppeteers, and musicians
brought *jōruri* to the foreground of the popular performing
arts. The result was the form of puppetry preserved to the
present time, considered by many critics as probably the most
sophisticated achievement in the world history of puppets.

A) *Puppets in Japan.* The origins of Japanese puppets are
not known. Scholars have reached very different conclusions in
their interpretation of the vague available evidence about the
beginnings. It is generally assumed that since the days of
ancient ritual puppets were used for religious purposes, to
transmit prayers to the gods and/or as a medium by which the
shaman/medium became "possessed" by the gods. Puppets were
also used as protection against children's diseases. These uses
are not completely extinct in remote villages and shrines,
especially in the northwest of Japan.

The first documented Japanese name for puppets—found
in a gloss of the eighth century—is *kugutsu*. Its derivation has
been controversial. Some scholars find connections with
Chinese, Gypsy, Turkish, and late Greek terms for puppets.
The similarity of the words is sometimes striking, and is often
invoked to support a theory of derivation from Asia Minor
through gypsy puppeteers to China, Korea, and eventually
Japan. Whichever the origin, it is a fact that puppets are found
scattered all over the Japanese islands, and that puppets were
used in ancient Shinto rituals. The use of puppets for
entertainment was documented from the eighth century as part
of the imported *sangaku*.

The puppets were very simple and operated by one hand, far removed from the sophisticated mechanical dolls which by the tenth century had conquered the fancy of Chinese emperors because of the marvellous robot-like ingenuity of their complex mechanisms. In Japan the few imported mechanical dolls do not seem to have stimulated the interest and the skill necessary for a meaningful development until the late sixteenth century. They probably inspired, however, the process that eventually led to the transformation of the small, primitive, eighth-century puppets into the remarkably complicated and life-like eighteenth-century *jōruri* puppets.

A variety of puppets has been used in Japan at different times: string marionettes, stick puppets operated by one hand on a miniature portable stage, hand-puppets held above the head of the concealed operator, and puppets maneuvered by one or more puppeteers in full view of the audience on a stage comparable in size to that of living actors. Priceless old puppets representing a variety of sizes and forms—the remnants of a rich past—are found in a number of villages throughout Japan. In most cases the puppets are preserved in museums or public places such as a shrine or the municipal buildings. In several villages they are still used at least once a year for actual performances by local talent.

The transformation of the *jōruri* puppets happened gradually, reaching the present final stage towards 1740. Only a few decades before that date, at the time when Chikamatsu's masterpieces were presented for the first time, the puppets were smaller and much less sophisticated (and also less cumbersome) in their movements, allowing faster changes and more fantastic passages from one scene to the other. In remote places such as the island of Sado such puppets, operated by only one man, are still used for performances of older types of *jōruri*, called *noroma*, *bunya-bushi* and *sekkyō-bushi*.

Today's *bunraku* puppets are classified according to different criteria. A first division is based on the number of puppeteers necessary to operate a puppet. The puppets used for the major roles require three puppeteers, while most secondary roles—such as servants, soldiers, bystanders, and animals—are performed by puppets requiring only one operator.

Another division is based on the sex and age of the roles. Male characters are played by large puppets up to almost four feet tall, which require a relatively heavy frame made out of a flat, thin, and straight wooden board for the shoulders, connected to a light metal or bamboo ring (staying for the waist line) by thick pasted paper or cloth which gives the shape of the torso. The all-important head is inserted into the wood of the shoulder line, while the arms and the legs are suspended with a string at the padded cotton extremities of the same wooden board. The whole body frame is usually fully covered by the costume. In the few cases in which the chest and arms are shown, a cotton cloth is fashioned and painted in a rather realistic way, including tattoos if the character requires them. The puppets for female roles, with one or two exceptions, have neither legs nor feet. They are smaller, built in a simpler and lighter way, without the bamboo rod at the ring of the waist line and with a weighted cloth pouch hanging from the waist ring to help—in the absence of the legs—in the manipulator's shaping of the leg line when the puppet sits.

The head of a puppet is mounted on a wooden grip supplied with levers and springs to move eyes, eyebrows, and mouth. With his left hand the leading puppeteer controls this ingenious, complex mechanism which allows an astonishing expressiveness of the accurately sculptured and painted features of the face. There are at least thirty basic types of puppet heads—with several variations within each type—which are classified according to the names of the characters. While some heads are interchangeable, allowing them to be used for different characters with similar characteristics, others are unique for a specific role; this is especially notable in the case of roles which require specific transformations obtained through a special mechanism which changes the head's appearance as, for example, from a woman to a demon. Great care is given to the eyebrows which can move and be made in different ways according to the role; to the eyes, which can rotate, be opened, and closed; and to the wigs, permanently attached to the heads and made of real hair arranged in dozens of complicated fashions requiring special styling for every performance.

The mechanism for the movements of eyes, eyebrows, and mouth is placed inside the head of the puppet after the block of wood is roughly carved and split into two halves. The two halves are then glued together, and the carving and painting is completed. Hands and feet are specifically crafted for the roles. There are nine basic types of hands with twenty-four variations, and four kinds of feet for male puppets. The movements of the fingers are regulated through levers with strings: depending on the type of hand, either only the thumb can be moved, or the thumb and the wrist, or the thumb, the wrist, and a set of fingers which are usually carved in one or two pieces.

The costumes of the puppets are often very ornate and costly, representing splendid old court attire, *samurai* armour, colorful courtesan kimonos, and the more modest but accurate fashions of the Edo merchant class.

B) *The Puppeteers*. Documents of the Heian period (794-1185) testify to the existence of gypsy-like *kugutsu-mawashi* (puppeteers) who made a living primarily as hunters, wandered around the provinces without a fixed abode, setting up their tents wherever they found a convenient place, and were considered outcastes. They operated small, primitive hand puppets within a miniature stage—a wooden box hanging from the neck—presenting a type of simple, one-man puppet show still to be found in a few remote villages. Their womenfolk, according to a famous description by the eleventh century scholar Oe Masafusa, were skilled in dances, entertainments, divination, and magic tricks, and had a reputation of enticing travelers to spend the night with them. Masafusa's description fits the stereotype of the "alien gypsy" with amazing precision. The connection of puppetry with outcaste status and prostitution is also confirmed by the fact that many of the recent discoveries of older puppets occurred in villages known to be the old *sanjo*, that is, outcaste communities where *sangaku*, *shirabyōshi*, and other performers were ordered to live, together with prostitutes and other categories of outcastes. Moreover, the very term *kugutsu*—the first in old Japanese to designate the puppets—was later used in the popular language for prostitutes.

It is therefore safe to conclude that, from the time of the gypsy puppeteers of the eleventh century through the Meiji Restoration, puppet operators were, in general, equated socially with other outcaste entertainers such as *kabuki* actors and prostitutes. The low social status of the puppeteers also was reflected in the fact that even in very recent times a number of the most accomplished operators were illiterate and incapable of speaking a polished, standard Japanese; instead, they expressed themselves in the rough dialect of the Osaka working class. Their training was extremely harsh, in most cases almost brutal, with bodily punishment for errors or negligence, and long, painful hours of hard work under the strict surveillance of a pitiless master.

It is traditionally taught that a puppeteer needs ten years to learn how to operate the feet, another ten years to learn the movements of the left arm, and ten years to learn how to operate the head and the right arm—a total of thirty years before he is allowed to perform a leading role.[3]

Three operators are used for the main puppets. The main operator (*omozukai*) controls the head and the right arm, the second operator (*hidarizukai*) the left hand, and the third operator (*ashizukai*) the feet. The main operator's left hand has access to the frame of the puppet through an opening of the costume under the *obi*, while his right hand reaches the operating mechanism through the upper part of the puppet's right sleeve. With the left hand he maneuvers the head and body as a whole—suggesting the movements of walking, running, fighting, and breathing—and also the strings that command movements of the eyes, eyebrows, and mouth. The puppeteer's right hand is used to operate a toggle that regulates the whalebone springs in the puppet's right hand.

The second operator cannot have the same proximity to the puppet as the first, and therefore he uses a fifteen-inch long stick with a toggle to which are attached the cords that regulate the movements of the left hand. The third operator is in charge of the legs and feet of the male puppets, or simulates their presence under the costume of the female. He has the difficult task of perfectly synchronizing the movements of the lower extremities with those of the torso as set by the principal puppeteer, also providing the sounds that create the illusion of walking, running, stamping, and so on.

While the second and third operators usually wear completely black costumes and have their heads covered with a see-through black hood, the principal puppeteer in most cases performs without a hood and in an elegant formal costume, which is brightly colored and certainly not meant to conceal the operator. Reasons for this breach in the code of anonymous service to the puppets include the ambition or ego of the artists and the demand of audiences to see the famous puppeteer's face.

It is no wonder that *bunraku* in the last decades has faced a serious problem in recruiting young people willing to submit themselves to the hard discipline required of puppet operators, despite the fact that training conditions have become more humane in recent years. Puppet operators still come primarily from families of puppeteers. Exceptions, however, are now welcome in an art which no longer attracts enough recruits to continue its highly demanding traditions.

C) *The Chanters*. The *bunraku* chanters have always enjoyed a very special recognition and respect as a kind of aristocrat/intellectual elite among the puppet artists, probably because their skills require a wide knowledge of the literary texts and familiarity with the complexity of the musical tradition. Some chanters, who provided important contributions into the research of old *jōruri* texts and the reconstruction of forgotten music, reached the status of nationally respected scholars. During the Tokugawa period the outstanding chanters were usually honored with the official title of *Jō* by the imperial court, thus being entitled to the treatment due honorary *samurai* status. This was reflected in the official documents of the shogunate which referred to chanters as human beings, while the counting of *kabuki* actors and other artists officially belonging to the outcastes was routinely done with the numeral used for animals.[4]

The art of storytelling through chanting with the accompaniment of a string instrument has a long history in Japan. Already around the eleventh century chanters were popular; they accompanied their narration of stories about the origins of shrines and temples, or about Buddhist and other legends with the *biwa*, an instrument with four to five strings, similar to the lute.[5]

In the following centuries the *biwa hōshi* flourished; they were blind monks who, to the accompaniment of the *biwa*, chanted the *samurai* epics from the *Heike monogatari* (*Tale of Heike*), much in the way as the minstrels who, accompanied by the lute, sang the *chansons de gestes* in Europe at approximately the same time. The legendary, heartbreaking events of the defeat of the Taira clan, underlined by the harsh, emotional sound of the *biwa*, achieved a great popularity during the long centuries of *samurai* strife and struggles. By the sixteenth century, however, the fashion changed because of the great popularity of the Jōruri story and the introduction and the rapid diffusion of a new musical instrument, the *jabisen* or *shamisen*, which was lighter and could produce sounds that were perceived as exotic, more harmonious, more modern, and smoother than those produced by the *biwa*. The original *shamisen*, introduced to Japan from the Ryūkyū islands during the Eiroku period (1558-1570), was covered with snake-skin. The short supply of such material in Japan suggested the use of the skin of female cats or dogs; this became standard in the definitive adaptation of the instrument, which was especially common in the red light districts of Kyoto, Osaka, and Edo during the Tokugawa period. There the ubiquitous sound of the *shamisen* could be heard in the tea-houses, where it accompanied the entertainment provided by the courtesans, in the *kabuki* theatres, where the *shamisen* had become the prevalent instrument in the orchestra, and, of course, in the puppet theatres where the *shamisen* was the standard and only accompaniment for the chanters.

It is not sure whether the first chanter who gave up the *biwa* for the *shamisen* was Sawazumi Kenkyō or Takino Kōtō. They were both blind monks, reciters of the Heike *biwa* tradition, and both certainly constitute the important link between the blind monks playing the *biwa* and the professional *jōruri* chanters accompanied by the *shamisen*. The disciples of such pioneers were the first to accomplish the fusion of *jōruri* chanting, *shamisen* music, and puppetry. A disciple of Sawazumi, Menukiya Chōzaburō, teamed up with a puppeteer from the island of Awaji. Kenmotsu, a disciple of Takino, joined forces with Jirōbei, a puppeteer from Nishinomiya on the Inland Sea. Both Awaji and Nishinomiya are still considered in Japan as the cradle of the puppet theatre, and to this day preserve the living puppetry tradition. The birth of *jōruri* as a new form of entertainment is usually attributed to Chōzaburō, who was not a blind monk, but a master craftman in the art of making hilt ornaments for swords; he was a townsman who brought to the new art his class's down-to-earth vitality and taste for subject matter other than the traditional episodes from the *Tales of Heike*.

There is no official date of birth for *jōruri* as a composite art of chanting, shamisen music, and puppetry. The fusion of the three arts happened in the last decade of the sixteenth century, about ten years before Okuni started the dances that began *kabuki*. It was the same decade in which the first opera was produced in Italy by the *Camerata fiorentina*, and the Elizabethan theatre in England was reaching with Shakespeare the height of its accomplishments.

The history of the *jōruri* chanters, especially during the first period of the *ko jōruri* (old *jōruri*)—which covers the years from the beginnings to the first masterpieces by Chikamatsu—is documented primarily in the surviving texts of plays printed as *shōhon* (certified true versions, the accuracy of which was attested by the chanter) between 1620 and 1686. According to the calculations of Dunn at least eight hundred such books—of which we know of about one half—were actually printed during the fifty odd years of the history of old *jōruri*.[6] Pictorial evidence and the records of female names among the early *jōruri* chanters testify to the interesting phenomenon that in Kyoto in the early years the role of the narrator was sometimes taken over by women chanters, who performed in full display above the puppet stage. Women chanters, however, probably disappeared with the prohibition of the women entertainers of the *onna kabuki* in 1629.[7]

The most important chanter-playwright at the start of this period (the pre-*Kimpira* time) was Satsuma Jōun, a disciple of Sawazumi Kenkyō. He moved to Edo and built a theatre there, where he died in 1669.

Jōun catered to the taste of the Edo audiences, which swarmed with military people, and was very successful in the development of plays full of violent action, which he performed with matching energy. His fame obscured that of Sugiyama Tango, a disciple of Takino, who is credited with developing a softer, more flexible style, less to the taste of the Edo audience. The plays of this time already presented material which could be divided into historical subject matter deriving from 1) the tradition of the *Tale of Heike*; 2) the miraculous religious subject matter of both Buddhist and Shinto origin; and 3) the *oie sōdō* describing the troubles of the great *samurai* families. A rather large number of plays also treated the theme of abduction into slavery, which gave the chanter an opportunity to evoke compassion among the spectators.

Jōun's generation was followed by a generation of his disciples, all raised in Edo and catering, with the style of the plays they wrote and their method of chanting, to a taste for extreme violence. The action was usually set in times of warfare with plenty of fighting, extraordinary heroic deeds, enemies' heads flying off in great numbers, dismemberment of horrifying monsters, and the like. The superhero is Kimpira, gifted with extraordinary powers, who gave his name to the genre. The *Kimpira* plays use simple language with no literary pretensions. The behavior of each role is completely predictable and simplistic, almost as in the comics, or in animated cartoons, with a minimum of emotion and plenty of spectacular action. The *Kimpira* style is believed to have influenced the famous *kabuki* actor Ichikawa Danjūrō I in introducing his *aragoto* style into *kabuki*. The most famous chanter/playwright of the *Kimpira* style was Sakurai Tamba, who became legendary for the frenzy of his chanting, during which—not unlike today's equally popular rock singers—he would smash the puppets to pieces.

The great fire of Edo in 1651 destroyed the theatres. While a number of puppeteers migrated to the Kyoto-Osaka area, those involved in the *Kimpira* style remained. Tamba built his new theatre in the newly established entertainment district in Edo's Sakai-chō area; it became the main center of the *Kimpira* style. The extraordinary popularity of *Kimpira* plays after the Edo fire is traced to the increased need for escape by the distressed townspeople, and to the character of Kimpira himself, who presented endearing Edo characteristics of irresponsibility and fallibity joined to a habit of cracking grim jokes, all qualities which brought him very close to the Edo townspeople and lower-ranking *samurai*.

From the many reprints of *Kimpira* playbooks it is evident that the popularity of the *Kimpira* chanters continued into the beginning of the eighteenth century. An attempt to revitalize the disappearing fortunes of the *Kimpira* chanters was made by Naishō Toranosuke, later known as Tosa no shōjō, who started as a puppeteer, then became a famous chanter and playwright. In his approximately fifty known plays an effort is evident to strive for a higher degree of dignity and loftiness, giving up the crudeness of the typical *Kimpira* style. Among the famous chanters of the Kyoto-Osaka area three are especially important: Yamamoto Kakudayū, Inoue Harima, and Uji Kaga no jō. Kakudayū became famous because of the style of delivery to which he gave his name, and because of his ingenious use of mechanical dolls and string puppets. He used these in his plays for special effects of transformations, such as changing a fox into a woman, for example in *Shinoda-zuma* (The Wife of Shinoda), a play which also employs a magic re-assembling of body parts and the resurrection of a man. The fame and success of Kakudayū continued into the time of the new *jōruri*.

Inoue Harima was probably born in 1632 in Kyoto, and died in 1685, one of the few chanters of old *jōruri* whose precise death year is recorded. His training in the *nō* not only gave his voice a special power, but also inspired his abundant use of themes taken from *nō* plays. Scholars estimate that about a hundred of his plays were published. Chikamatsu did some of his early work for him. Harima is credited with restraining the *Kimpira* style and avoiding the continuous introduction of monsters and strange miraculous *deus ex machina* interventions, reintroducing a more realistic and human dimension, and therefore opening the way for the taste which made the success of Chikamatsu's new *jōruri* possible.

The last important chanter/playwright of the old *jōruri* is Uji Kaga no jō, like Harima a student of *nō* who could not develop as a *nō* actor because he did not belong to a *nō* family. Kaga gave employment to a talented young chanter, Gorōbei, who was destined to obscure his fame. Gorōbei is a boyhood name of the artist known in history as the legendary partner of Chikamatsu: Takemoto Gidayū (1651-1714), the first "star" singer of the new *jōruri*, and, after 1685, destined to overshadow his employer. Kaga continued the process of adaptations from the *nō*. He changed the style of the *jōruri* scripts, providing notations which indicate through symbols the details of the performance for the chanter. He also introduced a rounder, clearer, less cramped style of calligraphy in the *daihon*, the texts used professionally by the chanters. In the prefaces to his *daihon* Kaga made an attempt to adapt Zeami's esthetics to the art of *jōruri* chanting, striving thus to elevate *jōruri* to the artistic level of the *nō*. He cut most of the *kimpira*-like exaggerations, increased the more human and symbolic aspects of those plays, borrowing heavily from *nō* texts, and developed a style of *jōruri* chanting similar to that of the *nō*, but adapted to the *shamisen* accompaniment. Kaga was a very prolific and versatile playwright, experimenting not only in the imitation of the *nō* but also developing themes that foreshadow the genres of historical and domestic plays

218

(*jidaimono/sewamono*) as defined in the work of Chikamatsu. The dramatic structure of Kaga's plays shows a great improvement over previous playwrights, and a high degree of sophistication. He is considered the major individual responsible for the change in the structure of a *jōruri* play from twelve parts constituting six *dan*, consisting of two parts each, to five *dan*, just as a day of *nō* was traditionally made out of five plays (the length of one *dan* of a *jōruri* play corresponds more or less to the length of a *nō* play). This structural change was motivated by an effort to transform the loose episodic structure of most puppet plays—as inherited from the performance of episodes from the *Tales of Heike*—into a more coherent dramatic unit with a beginning, middle, and end. This was equivalent to the application of the *jo, ha, kyū* structure of *gagaku* music and *nō* plays to the *jōruri* dramatic structure.

A consideration of Kaga's work in its totality places him as the bridge between the old and the new *jōruri*. The characteristics of his work definitely overcome the limitations of the old *jōruri* and introduce a variety of styles, a new realism, and a higher literary quality already heralding the new *jōruri* of the master playwright, Chikamatsu Monzaemon.

Kaga was the last great chanter of the old *jōruri* who either wrote personally the plays he performed, or strictly supervised the writing of his plays by the company's playwright, as in the case of the several plays Chikamatsu wrote for him during the latter's apprenticeship. Takemoto Gidayū began the tradition of chanters who left the task of writing plays to the resident playwright, and concentrated completely on the art of delivery and on giving the puppets an almost human dimension. In this task Gidayū was helped by the depth and complexity of Chikamatsu's characters and his refusal to indulge in the overuse of extraordinary and miraculous effects.

In the history of the chanters Gidayū remains the most influential and the most celebrated. He belonged to a family of farmers, an unlikely beginning for a career in the arts. His voice was so outstanding that he succeeded in becoming a disciple of one of the best chanters of his time, Kiyomizu Rihei (hence his first stage name, Ridayū). His innovative approach created a new synthesis out of the styles of Harima, Kaga, *sekkyō-bushi*, and the fashionable new songs. Once established as an artist, he changed his name to Takemoto Gidayū, and, in 1684, he founded his own theatre in Osaka, the Takemoto-za, which was to become the most important center for the triumphs of the puppet theatre. In 1685 he hired Chikamatsu as head playwright, and the very first play born out of their collaboration was the extraordinarily successful *Shusse Kagekiyo* (Kagekiyo the Victor) which is considered the beginning of a new epoch in *jōruri* history, marking the end of the old *jōruri* and the beginning of the new *shin jōruri* (also called *gidayū jōruri*). The successful collaboration of Gidayū with Chikamatsu continued through the great masterpieces of the double suicides plays at the beginning of the eighteenth century until Gidayū's death in 1714. The style of delivering the *jōruri* narrative introduced by Gidayū became the standard for the art, and is still referred to as *gidayū bushi*.

The importance of the chanter in influencing the content and style of the plays has been remarked by scholars, who have noticed profound shifts in Chikamatsu's playwriting according to the change of the chanter for whom he was writing.[8] There is no doubt that the playwrights tailored their plays to the special talents and demands of the chanters.

A formidable rival to Takemoto Gidayū was Toyotake Wakadayū, who established in 1703 the Toyotake-za, a new puppet theatre in competition with Gidayū's Takemoto-za.

A number of chanters achieved fame in the time of the puppets' great successes, until the fall into quasi-oblivion after 1780. The tradition of excellent chanters was reestablished after the opening of the Bunraku-za in 1871 and has continued to the present time.

The training of a chanter is highly demanding and the chanter's world still expects of the apprentice the observance of a rigid etiquette of great respect for the teacher. The apprentice usually starts his training as a child in the household of a master who gives him a name traditionally used in his school at the beginning of a career. The training used to be extremely harsh, requiring long hours of practice in the biting cold of winter, and, in general, an almost cruel discipline of continuous vocal exercise. Today the discipline is still very strict. The end result must be an incredibly resilient voice and enormous breath control, with the greatest adaptability to the different roles and circumstances of the plays, and the capability of transmitting deep emotions. The chanter acts like a fully trained actor who manifests the emotions of all the roles he alternatively impersonates. He wears a *kamishimo* ceremonial costume and squats on a stage-left podium behind the stand on which the text is always placed, even when not necessary for the performance, as is the case when the chanter is blind.

While in most areas of the Japanese theatre world it is customary to transmit an art within the family, this is usually not the case among chanters, probably because the vocal talent needed for success is very rare.

D) *The Playwrights.* The recognized master of playwriting for the *jōruri* and *kabuki* stages is Chikamatsu Monzaemon (1653-1724). Western scholars recognize Chikamatsu's greatness and sometimes use the appellation "the Shakespeare of Japan" when describing his position in Japanese playwriting. Unfortunately, however, they have dedicated a very modest amount of solid research to his life and work.[9] The western neglect represents a sharp contrast with the plentiful literature in Japanese on every aspect of Chikamatsu's work.

Chikamatsu spent all his life in a country that had been completely sealed off from any meaningful foreign presence. His literary activity occurred at a time completely dominated by the new Tokugawa order and was primarily spent in writing plays for the puppets, aiming at the favor of an audience that was gathering in the red light districts for the specific purpose of being entertained. His premises are therefore quite different from those of contemporary European playwrights, and his frame of reference should always be kept in mind for a fair understanding of his art.

Chikamatsu's life illustrates the peculiar situation of floating mobility for the *rōnin*, the masterless *samurai* who neither had a position with the shogunal government nor was at the service of a *daimyō*. We do not know where he was born. Several villages in the vicinity of Kyoto claim the honor of being the birth place of Japan's greatest dramatist. Born as the second son of the minor *samurai* family Sugimori, he was first called Nobumori, a name he changed to Chikamatsu, possibly because of the Chikamatsu temple where he stayed for some time before dedicating himself to the theatre. We know very little about the years of his youth beyond the tradition of his staying at the Buddhist monastery where he probably learned the religious doctrines he shows such knowledge of in his plays. Surviving documents prove that from at least his nineteenth year he was in the service of a Kyoto nobleman, Ogimachi Kimmochi (1653-1733), who held a high rank at court and was known as a writer of puppet plays for the chanter Uji Kaga no jō. This seems to be Chikamatsu's first contact with the world of the puppets. The influence of Chikamatsu's highly educated employer is usually considered decisive for the young dramatist in the development of his theatrical talents; it probably also figured strongly in providing Chikamatsu with the high degree of literary and classical knowledge which are at the foundation of his plays. Probably the separation from his protector placed before Chikamatsu the necessity of finding work. It was at this time that he decided to "step down" socially and join a theatre company as playwright. Chikamatsu's direct personal experience of the different worlds of the *samurai*, the nobility, the clergy, townspeople, and *kabuki* and puppet artists gave his genius an unusually wide background within the limited Genroku society.

Japanese experts have not found evidence to establish which was Chikamatsu's first play, nor do they know how many plays he wrote for either *kabuki* or *jōruri* at the start of his career. Most probably he began as an assistant to the main playwright who was considered the author of the play. None of the approximately forty texts Chikamatsu wrote directly for *kabuki* has survived, but we know the contents of about twenty of them. Their usual theme is similar to those in the works of Tominaga Heibei; that is, an *oiemono* plot of struggle within a *daimyō* family with built-in scenes involving courtesans and the colorful red light districts. While Heibei had stressed intrigue and plot, Chikamatsu developed the psychological and poetical insight into the struggling, complex human heart, a trait which appeared in its full maturity in his double-suicide plays, the *shinjūmono*. There, perhaps in its highest tragic expression, we find the classical conflict of Japanese drama between the feelings of one's heart (*ninjō*) and the severe duties of feudal ethics (*giri*).

Chikamatsu's work is usually divided into four periods, the first being that of his early *kabuki* contributions, from the unknown time of his debut to about 1684. The most famous play of this period, according to some authors, is *Fujitsubo no onryō*, a play attributed—but not unanimously—to Chikamatsu. The play scored a great success because of an effective coup-de-théâtre, the on-stage transformation of Lady Fujitsubo's ghost from a wisteria flower into a snake.

The first great success of Chikamatsu as a playwright for the *jōruri* came at the beginning of his second period; the play, *Shusse Kagekiyo* (Kagekiyo Victorious, 1684), marks the end of the crudely structured puppet plays of the *ko jōruri* (old *jōruri*) and the beginning of the *shin jōruri*, the new kind of puppet plays that led the way to the series of masterpieces which made *jōruri* a formidable competitor of *kabuki*. The innovation Chikamatsu introduced into the primarily narrative *ko jōruri* was the use of *kabuki*'s dramatic structure and living dialogue.

As Chikamatsu collaborated with the great *kabuki* actor Sakata Tōjūrō, between 1684 and 1705, he wrote a number of *kabuki* plays, which extended into the third period (1703-1724). From 1705, however, he began to write exclusively for the puppets, and moved the following year to Osaka as staff playwright (*tatesakusha*) of the Takemoto-za, managed by Takeda Izumo I (?-1747), in which the famous chanter Takemoto Gidayū (1651-1714) was active. The genre of puppet plays for which Chikamatsu became especially famous, the *shinjūmono*, debuted with his *Sonezaki shinjū* (The Love Suicides at Sonezaki) in 1703. The event that prompted Chikamatsu to write it occurred just one month before the performances began. Other famous love-suicides plays are *Shinjū mannensō* (The Love Suicides at the Women's Temple, 1708), and *Shinjū ten no Amijima* (The Love Suicides at Amijima, 1721). These outstanding examples of *shinjūmono* show three different spiritual attitudes to self-inflicted death in the souls of the protagonists. The oldest play interprets death as a simple escape to paradise; the second presents a darker sense of doubt about the afterlife; and the third stresses the sense of death as a specter affirming the preciousness of life.[10]

Love Suicides at Amijima belongs to the last and final period of Chikamatsu's activity, which is usually dated from the death of Gidayū in 1714 to Chikamatsu's death in 1725. Another well known work of this period is *The Battle of Coxinga* (*Kokusenya kassen*), a very complex play that combines heroic and fantastic elements with moving love elements and an obligatory happy ending, after touching sacrifices in the name of the Tokugawa ethics.

Chikamatsu's puppet plays were written with a deep poetic feeling for the intricate ambivalence of the human heart. The multifaceted characters were difficult for the puppets to interpret adequately; at the time they were changing in size and complexity of manipulation, requiring slower timing in the dialogue and more explicitly "black-and-white" role characterizations. As a consequence, Chikamatsu's plays were soon replaced by new dramas tailored for the new needs.

Although Chikamatsu remains as the literary giant of Japanese playwriting, his successors, especially Takeda Izumo II (1691-1756) and Namiki Sōsuke (1695-1751) succeeded in bypassing the master's technical skill in dramatic structure, and producing the most successful and famous of all Japanese plays, *Kanadehon Chūshingura*.

Among all Japanese plays the most translated and commented on by non-Japanese scholars is *Kanadehon Chūshingura*, also written first for *jōruri* and then adapted for *kabuki*.[11] Literally *kanadehon* means "copybook of the Japanese syllabary," which stands for "model, standard"; and *chūshingura* means "storehouse of loyalty." The play has been, however, translated with many different titles, such as *The Forty-seven Models of Loyalty*, *The Forty-Seven Samurai*, *The Forty-Seven Ronin*, and *The Treasury of Loyal Retainers*.

The authorship of this complex eleven-act drama is shared by three playwrights. Scholars are not able to determine with certainty who wrote which part. Although the name of Takeda Izumo II is almost always mentioned first, contemporary scholarship accords to Namiki Sōsuke credit for the general organization of the play. The weaker acts are usually attributed to Miyake Shōraku, who has the reputation of a hack. Credit for the effective style of the major part of the play is given to the creative and talented playwright Takeda.

Chūshingura dramatizes an episode of loyalty to a feudal lord even beyond his death and at the cost of the retainers' own lives. It summarizes all the elements of both the *jidaimono* and *sewamono* because it mingles its characters on the level of the great *samurai* families and on that of the red light district brothels. It is one of the most transparent

examples of the "disguise" technique of transferring a
sensational event of the present to the past; in other words, it
presents one of those forbidden topics which could only be
performed under assumed names and in the setting of a non-
Tokugawa period. The play's extraordinary success is also
attributed to the combination of the subject matter with the
timing of its appearance. Within the drab reality of the rather
meaningless and dull *samurai* life following a century of peace
under the Tokugawa police state, the news of the vendetta
carried out on the fourteenth day of the twelfth month, 1702,
by forty-seven *rōnin* to avenge the honor of their feudal lord,
the *daimyō* Asano Naganori (1667-1701), spread like fire. It
was like a sudden rediscovery of the reality of those *samurai*
ideals that had been preached endlessly, and also had
penetrated the world of society's lower strata as a recognized
code of morality.

The leader of the long planned and successfully realized
vendetta, Oishi Kuranosuke, placed the severed head of the
villain Kira Yoshinaga on the grave of the defunct lord, and
gave himself up to the police, together with the other forty-six
rōnin. The shogunate punished the slaying with death, but in
recognition of their noble motives the defendants were given
the honor of committing suicide by *seppuku*. The forty-seven
avengers became national heroes and were referred to as *gishi*
(righteous warriors) rather than as plain *rōnin*. The subject
matter was immediately picked up by playwrights, and a
number of *jōruri* and *kabuki* and plays were written about it.
Chikamatsu also wrote a puppet play on the subject, *Kenkō
hōshi monomiguruma* (The Sightseeing Carriage of the Priest
Kenkō), followed by a sequel, the still preserved one act play
Goban Taiheiki, and introduced most of the slightly changed
names which were later used in the more successful play by
Takeda, Namiki, and Miyoshi.

Most of the many plays that were actually written on the
subject are no longer extant. The single masterpiece,
Kanadehon Chūshingura, seems to have capitalized on all the
possible theatrical situations that such an involved and
emotionally rich subject could offer. The variety of
backgrounds, shifting from the palaces of the powerful to the
brothels and the shrines, as well as the country spring and
winter outdoor scenes, are effectively used to underline the

highlights of the plot developing over eleven parts and occupying an almost impossibly long performance time. While not reaching the poetic individuality and refined psychological insights of Chikamatsu's mature dramatic masterpieces, *Chūshingura* succeeds in providing melodrama at its best, with sharply defined black-and-white characters, highly emotional heroic sacrifices of personal honor and life, clear-cut conflicts, highly theatrical battle scenes, and the eventual punishment of the villain, followed by the final triumph of both official governmental justice and personal ethics, through the heroes' honorable death.

Bunraku *after the Meiji Restoration*

From its beginnings *bunraku* had been an art that depended on the support of popular audiences for survival, without recourse to the patronage of the powerful in times of non-commercial viability. The shifting of popular support from *jōruri* to *kabuki* at the end of the eighteenth century resulted in the closing for almost a century of all theatres dedicated solely to the puppets. The successful efforts of Bunraku-ken in the first decades of the nineteenth century revived popular support in the Osaka area, but did not achieve the same in Edo, where *bunraku* was perceived as a provincial left-over from a past in need of modernization. Moreover, in Edo there was a sense of mistrust and antagonism between *kabuki* and *bunraku* artists, which precluded, for instance, the use of *kabuki* theatres for visiting *bunraku* performances.

While *kabuki* was prompt to accept the 1872 order of the Tokyo authorities to change the fictional names in the historical plays to the actual names corresponding to historical fact, and also began experimenting almost immediately with plays featuring actors in western clothes and western haircuts, *bunraku* was much slower in trying out similar ideas, which, moreover, only rarely met with audience approval.

During the Meiji period (1868-1912) *bunraku* did flourish in Osaka, to the point that after the opening in 1884 of a new puppet theatre, two such theatres, the Bunraku-za and the Hikoroku-za, were operating in sharp competition. Bad management of the Bunraku-za forced that company in 1909 to sell all its assets to the Shōchiku brothers, who at the time were beginning their gradual monopolization of theatrical management for both *kabuki* and *bunraku*.

Bunraku was left without a home after the 1926 fire which destroyed the theatres as well as invaluable and irreplaceable old puppet heads. The need to find a home for performance, however, worked out to the advantage of *bunraku*, which at the time included splendid artists such as the famous chanters Toyotake Kōtsubodayū (born 1878), Yoshida Bungorō (1869-1962) and Yoshida Eiza (1872-1954). *Bunraku* had no choice but to travel, and the audiences of Tokyo this time were impressed with Kōtsubodayū's extraordinarily colorful performances and the very high standards of the traveling troupe. The new theatre in Osaka was opened at the end of 1929, almost on the brink of the Manchurian war. Patriotic plays which presented the puppets in contemporary soldiers' uniforms and tried to capitalize on the feelings stirred by the conflict had a limited success, but *bunraku* would have disappeared without governmental financial support. This happened in the form of a bill passed by the Diet in 1933, marking the first official legislation of a modern Japanese government aimed at preserving a popular performing art, and the recognition of its value as a national cultural treasure. Notwithstanding the modest governmental subsidy *bunraku* went through very difficult years during the thirties, but resumed its popularity during World War II because of increased official support for it as a purely Japanese form of art.

An almost complete destruction of theatre and equipment followed the air raids over Osaka in 1945. Shortly after the war in 1946, a makeshift theatre became the temporary home for a resurrected *bunraku* group, which eventually found a beautiful new playhouse in 1956 in Osaka's Dōtombori district. The postwar period also saw the development of a movement to modernize the ultra-conservative world of the chanters and, in general, the entire organization of *bunraku*. The young forces of *bunraku* joined a labor union and caused a temporary split in the *bunraku* world, but this came to an end with the formation of the Bunraku Kyōkai (Bunraku Association) in 1963.[12]

The Bunraku Association, a non-profit organization which took over the Shōchiku Company's managerial responsibilities for *bunraku*, began an era of relative stability, which culminated with the recent opening of the luxurious, marvellously equipped National Bunraku Theatre in Osaka, and the building of a similarly equipped small hall dedicated to *bunraku* performances in Tokyo's National Theatre (where, however, *bunraku* performances are presented no more frequently than every other month). In the meantime the government adopted the policy of designating the main performing artists of such traditional theatre forms as *nō*, *kabuki*, and *bunraku* as "Human Cultural Treasures," a practice that—combined with great successes abroad—drew much needed attention to *bunraku*'s unique cultural value.

In a time of national prosperity and pride in purely Japanese artistic traditions, the economics of *bunraku*'s viability has not been an overwhelming preoccupation of postwar experts. Instead, the question is continually raised concerning the willingness of new generations of university-educated puppeteers and chanters to submit themselves to the harsh discipline necessary to master the subtly difficult techniques. A training program which was started at the end of the seventies at the National Theatre in Tokyo is now carried on in Osaka. So far the facts have shown that *bunraku* has found enough young men to keep the tradition alive and healthy.

The Stage

Bunraku is performed in Japan today primarily in two theatres, the National Bunraku Theatre, opened in 1984, in Osaka, and the smaller hall of the National Theatre in Tokyo. Both theatres are built according to the most modern guidelines for western-style theatre architecture and decor, including standard western-style seating, air-conditioning, computerized lighting, and electronic sound and stage machinery. The general appearance of the stage is similar to that in recently built *kabuki* theatres which present a much wider stage opening than was usual in the traditional Tokugawa buildings. Modern *bunraku* has borrowed the *hanamichi* from *kabuki*; it is built with a deep floor to partially conceal the puppeteers. The general style of the scenery also is borrowed from *kabuki*: the painted backdrops present the same kind of colorful, conventional, non-illusionistic decors, without chiaroscuro or shadows, built in proportion to the height of the puppets, and therefore giving the impression of a scaled-down *kabuki* stage design. An important difference is that of the stage floor, which in *kabuki* is quite visible and essential for a number of effects and conventions but is not visible in *bunraku*, because it must serve the all-important function of providing space for the complex traffic of several operators involved in each scene at various levels and depths. In many plays in which the illusion must be created of one or more floor levels for the puppets, the stage floor where the operators perform is divided into three sections: forestage, center stage and rear stage. They are usually divided by wooden boards, which can be arranged in different fashions according to the needs of the set. Most of the action usually takes place in the central area, which is often defined at the front by a board about three feet high providing the illusion of the floor level for the audience sitting in the orchestra (unfortunately, this does not work properly for those who sit in the balcony or galleries). The rear stage is usually occupied by scenic constructions representing whatever is required by the play, such as a gate, a palace, a room, the interior of a mansion, and so forth. This third area can also be used by the operators of the puppets acting, for example, inside an upstage room.

In general *bunraku* makes less use than *kabuki* of complex machinery. The revolving stage, a standard feature of *kabuki*, is traditionally not used in *bunraku*. Changes of scenery are often obtained through a system similar to the baroque shifting of painted wings and backdrops, which are placed one in front of the next. Traps and lifts are occasionally used for puppets and operators. The effect of a long journey is sometimes created through the use of painted scenery rolled slowly behind the traveling puppets.

Props are used sparingly, but are essential in the performance of a number of plays: these include swords, letters, musical instruments, fans, lanterns, and the like. Most are built in proportion to the height of the puppets.

Bunraku *Aesthetics*

Chikamatsu tried to define the difference between a simple narration of episodes from the heroic tradition of the past—as was usual in the old *jōruri*—and a fully developed art of playwriting for the puppets, in terms of "restraint" or control, or, even better, stylization. He explained this concept as a correction both to the intent of complete realism (or exact copy of reality) and that of uncontrolled fantasy. He called the result of this correction "a certain something in the slender margin between the real and the unreal."

Chikamatsu's plays are admirable examples of literary success in creating this "certain something." In the performance of the traditional *bunraku* this ideal has been translated into the typical stylization—between the real and the unreal—of the puppets' movements and of the art of the chanters. The illusion of life, so essential in the art of puppetry, is achieved through sophisticated movements that, over the centuries, have reached an extraordinary degree of both simplification and intensification. The conventional stylization of everyday movements and gestures (*furi*) is alternated with the stylized patterns (*kata*) corresponding to those of *kabuki* acting and dancing. All *bunraku* roles are performed according to a fixed routine of sequences of *furi* and *kata*, which have been established by the masters and have in themselves the unique rhythm of their art—"in the slender margin between the real and the unreal." Accordingly, a similar process of stylization by the chanters has produced an extraordinary capacity to infuse a constantly high degree of artistic life into the puppets. This traditional respect for proven sequences of stylized puppet movements and stylized chanters' performances explains why only great masters dare—and then only very rarely—to introduce slight changes in such areas.

NOTES

[1]Dunn, *The Early Japanese Puppet Drama*, 7. See also 109-110 for an analysis of the word *jōruri* and its connection with Buddhist contexts.

[2]*Ibid.*, 29-41.

[3]This rule is not always strictly adhered to in modern *bunraku*.

[4]Komiya, *Japanese Music and Drama in the Meiji Era*, 21.

[5]A description of different types of *biwa* is in Harich-Schneider, *A History of Japanese Music*, 513-515.

[6]Dunn, *The Early Japanese Puppet Drama*, 75.

[7]The names of the principal chanters of the old *jōruri* and their known accomplishments are recorded in Dunn, *The Early Japanese Puppet Drama*, 76-107.

[8]Keene, *Bunraku: The Art of the Japanese Puppet Theatre*, 42-43.

[9]In English, after Keene's pioneer work of translation and introduction of Chikamatsu's major plays in 1961 no major book-length study was dedicated to him until the recent *Circles of Fantasy: Conventions in the Plays of Chikamatsu* by Gerstle.

[10]Gerstle, *Ibid.*, 152-153.

[11]The literature in Japanese about the play is enormous. In English, a recent abridged *kabuki* acting version is in Brandon, *Chūshingura: Studies in Kabuki and the Puppet Theatre*, while Keene's translation of the original *jōruri* text remains the best suited for reading.

[12]The dissertation *The Bunraku Puppet Theatre since 1945 to 1964: Changes in Administration and Organization*, by Julianne K. Boyd includes important information about the period of formation of the Bunraku Kyōkai.

CHAPTER IX

THE MODERN THEATRE: SHIMPA

Origins of the Shimpa Movement: Sudō Sadanori

The word *shimpageki* means "new school drama" and is used (mostly in its abbreviated form *shimpa*) to designate a specific form of theatre, the first to develop outside the *kabuki* world after the Meiji Restoration as an attempt to modernize and westernize Japan's drama. The name began to appear in the newspapers starting from the very first years of our century to distinguish the drama of the "new school" from that of the "old school" (*kyūha*), that is, of *kabuki*.[1]

It was unavoidable that the theatre would join the general movement of change that swept Japan after the opening of the country to western influence. The efforts of the *kabuki* and *bunraku* professionals to modernize their art produced only sporadic results of short duration, and certainly did not transform those genres into forms of westernized spoken theatre. They instead generated today's *kabuki* and *bunraku*, which present a change from the pre-Meiji outlook something like that accomplished in the performances of many operas in the West in which music, libretto, and basic acting style have remained much the same, while modern technical resources have been incorporated.

The lack of participation by professional actors in the creation of a modern theatre resulted in amateurism and low levels of acting skills in the courageous pioneers. Not much could be expected from the first groups that dared to present themselves to the public without acting training and without a clear idea of what a modern style should look like; this was largely because the only experience of theatrical performance in Japan was that of the traditional performing arts, and direct experience of western theatre was not yet available to the young amateurs.

Despite the lack of professionalism and a model for modernization, one thing was very clear in the mind of Sudō Sadanori (1867-1907), who is considered the founder of *shimpa*: theatre was to be an instrument of political propaganda against the conservative regime.

The first expressions of this goal occurred in conjunction with a tense political situation. In 1884 the conservative government dissolved the major opposition force, the Liberal Party (*Jiyūtō*), of which Sudō was a militant member, and forbade all political rallies. A group mostly made up of young militants decided to continue the fight against the government with the means left at their disposal, such as lectures, newspaper articles, and, eventually, the theatre. These young people called themselves *sōshi*, a word that means both "courageous young man" and "political bully" or "henchman." Several *sōshi* were lawless ruffians, who did not shy away from violent revolutionary actions, and often got into trouble with the police. Their political aims of freedom were unfocused, and their unrest was expressed primarily as a manifestation of a sense of frustration with the conservative leadership, rather than as the execution of a clear and systematic plan of action.

A group of *sōshi* came together under Sadanori's leadership and formed the Dainippon Geigeki Kyōfūkai (Great Japan Society for the Reformation of the Theatre), one of the many "improvement societies" born in the middle eighties to promote the westernization of some aspect of life or culture, this time, however, with the aim of using theatre for the purpose of liberal political opposition against the conservative government. The first performance took place in Osaka in December 1888.

Rather than epoch-making events, this and similar performances were generally considered by contemporaries as a kind of a curiosity, an odd attempt by amateurs to present theatre outside the monopoly of the *kabuki* establishment. Many failed to recognize until much later the importance of a movement that broke the ice in the process of thrusting Japan into the stream of contemporary spoken drama, introduced new theatre customs such as darkened auditoriums and elaborate stage lighting, added the new dramatic subject of social and political struggle, re-introduced women to the stage, and, above all, showed the possibility of surviving outside the traditional theatre monopoly.

The founder of *shimpa*, Sudō Sadanori—a Kyoto policeman turned journalist, a *sōshi*, and eventually a full time actor—spent twenty years of his short life mostly touring the provinces, but reaping only scattered success in the big cities where he could not last long in competition with both the professional *kabuki* theatre and the offspring of his own reform, such as the more aggressive and better organized troupe of Kawakami Otojirō. Sudō died at forty, in the dressing room of a Kobe theatre. On the memorial erected in his honor in 1937 in the cemetery of the Tennōji temple of Osaka an inscription describes him as the "father of the new theatre."

Kawakami Otojirō

If Sudō was the first to show the possibility of survival outside the *kabuki* world, Kawakami Otojirō (1864-1911) succeeded in proving much more: that stardom and financial reward independent from *kabuki* were possible even for a man of obscure origins without any family connections with the professional theatre world.

Kawakami's life reads like a fast-paced adventure novel, a sequence of continuous changes, failures, new enterprises, and a series of "firsts" in the Japanese theatre world.[2] Though he never achieved greatness in the quality of his performances as an actor, his role as a catalyst in the process of forming Japan's new theatre was unique. Kawakami's family had served for generations as official purveyors under the feudal lords of Hakata in Kyūshū. He left home at fourteen and started a series of diverse experiences: among others, as an apprentice in a Buddhist temple, as a pupil of the famous scholar Fukuzawa Yūkichi at Keiō University, as a policeman, and as a political propagandist. In 1887, he was on stage with *kabuki* actors in Kyoto, his role being to improvise outside the curtain at those points where the text broke off. In 1888, he became the disciple of a famous Osaka *rakugo* storyteller, Katsura Bun'nosuke, and used his new skill to put together his original

Oppekepe bushi, a satirical ballad sung to a very popular tune composed by Katsura Tōbei, a storyteller of the same school. The ballad's onomatopoeic name derived from the sound of the trumpet which opened its refrain. The ballad made Kawakami famous three years later, when he performed in Tokyo in 1891 with his new company formed in imitation of Sudō's *sōshi* theatre. He appeared at the Nakamura-za in plays not worth remembering, gaining his success because of his entr'acte performance of the *Okkepeke bushi*, which he sang while dashing like a swashbuckler in front of a golden screen with a Japanese flag in his hand. His success was so great that even the major *kabuki* stars went to see him.

Kawakami is responsible for the introduction of such "sensations" from the West as the changing of scenery in darkness, the new system of lighting the stage while the orchestra is darkened, and the "authentic reportage" drama in which in a relatively realistic way he presented war episodes from the Chinese campaign of 1894/95. His war plays were enormously successful, gaining a better public reception than the corresponding war plays done by *kabuki* actors. To enhance the patriotic atmosphere he had soldiers and sailors fight in formal uniform, and instructed the audience to bow when the name of the Emperor was mentioned. He traveled to Korea to inspect the front-line and then produced his most successful play, *Kawakami Otojirō senchi kembunki* (Kawakami Otojirō Reporting from the Battle Field, 1894) in which he played himself in the role of a reporter at the front line witnessing the valiant deeds of the Japanese heroes. For the first time, *shimpa* won over *kabuki*, and for the first time the most important *kabuki* stage, Tokyo's Kabuki-za, was at *shimpa*'s disposal.

Kawakami was also the first to present Japanese theatre abroad. He toured with his company to America, England, France, Germany, and Russia. As a consequence of his experiences abroad Kawakami introduced western-style tickets and shortened the duration of his shows. He pioneered childrens' theatre in 1903. Also in 1903 he began the presentation of western masterpieces: he began by staging his adaptation of *Othello*, and followed it between 1903 and 1906 with *Hamlet*, *The Merchant of Venice*, and plays by Maeterlinck and Sardou.

Contemporary sources agree in judging rather harshly the quality of Kawakami's performances. It is clear that his forte was sensationalism, not art. In his war plays the secret of his success was a rhetorical, sentimental appeal to patriotism, and an ostentatious, one-sided glorification of valiant Japanese heroes. Photographs of the time show cheap operetta-like sets and exaggerated, melodramatic gestures. In the play *Itagaki-kun sōnan jikki* (The True Story of Itagaki's Misfortunes, 1891) during the scene of the attempted murder of the famous liberal politician, Itagaki Taisuke, he had actors in police uniforms suddenly appear on the *hanamichi*, so that the audience momentarily believed in a real intervention by the police. His presentation of western masterpieces could hardly give an idea of the originals; he often relied on western curiosities such as introducing Hamlet by having him make a sensational entrance on a bicycle.

It is doubtful whether the type of Japanese theatre shown by Kawakami abroad was a service to the cause of international exchange. The purpose of his foreign trip originally had been to study the western theatre, not to perform. An enterprising theatre manager in San Francisco, however, induced him to go on the stage with his fellow actors. Part of the mixed success was due to his wife, Kawakami Sadayakko (1872-1946), who was not an actress, but, before her marriage, had been a professionally trained, high class *geisha*. She was therefore capable of fascinating European audiences who had never seen the live performance of a *geisha*.[3]

It is clear that Kawakami was successful both in Japan and abroad as long as he could capitalize on spectacular or emotional elements which did not require real acting skills. Their very lack of acting skills, however, gave to the performances of his troupe a freshness unknown to the stereotyped traditional models. While most *kabuki* plays repeated themes that were becoming increasingly obsolete, Kawakami's presentations exploited the hottest issues of the day. While the language of *kabuki* was sounding more and more like something from the past, Kawakami's colloquialisms reflected the latest, rapidly changing expressions of "modernized" society. Kawakami did not abolish the convention of female impersonation in *shimpa*, but selectively used actresses for certain female roles, thereby initiating a new tradition of female stars on the Japanese stage. In 1908 he established the first modern school for actresses, the Teikoku Joyū Yōseijo (Imperial Actresses School), which was headed by his wife Sadayakko. His last enterprise was the building of a new theatre, the Teikokuza, in Osaka, which he hoped would become the center for the "true theatre." Shortly after opening the new house in 1911 he died, aged forty-seven.

Seibikan and Other Companies

During Kawakami's time, realization of the need to improve the quality of acting and the standards of the plays was at the root of efforts by several of the most serious theatre reformers. Several groups were formed, those especially worthy of mention being the Seibikan, the Seibidan, the Isami-engeki, and the Hongōza.

The Seibikan was short-lived; it performed only one program in Tokyo in 1891. It was the brainchild of Yoda Gakkai (1833-1909), a scholar and theatre critic who gave to the company the purpose of high artistic ideals exclusive of political concerns. It was the Seibikan who introduced young Ii Yōhō (1871-1932), an actor who was to become very famous as a *shimpa* star for decades; the troupe also was the first to break the ban on theatrical companies comprising both men and women.

The Seibidan also was a short-lived effort to stress quality over sensationalism. It was founded in 1896 by an ex-member of Kawakami's troupe, Takada Minoru (1871-1916), who is credited, with such collaborators as Kitamura Rokurō (1871-1961) with having set the standards for the best achievements of *shimpa*. In 1898 the name Seibidan disappeared from the records, but Takada's teaching about the importance of *iki* (breathing) and his exemplary dedication to the art of acting as a technique of realistic expression had great importance in the process of finding a serious new professionalism within *shimpa*. Takada died at forty-six, in 1915. Kitamura, an offshoot of the Seibidan, founded a school of acting which continued the same methods.

The Isami-engeki was formed in 1895 by the actors Ii Yōhō, Satō Toshizō (1869-1945), and Mizuno Yoshimi (1863-1928; the name I-Sa-Mi was formed with the initial syllable of each actor's name). Ii was the most popular among the *shimpa* actors. A very handsome and talented performer, Ii is also remembered for his serious effort to rediscover for the new theatre treasures of traditional playwriting or new interpretations of Japanese legends as presented by important contemporary authors. Famous are his cycle of eight plays, *Chikamatsu kenkyū-geki* (Research Plays on Chikamatsu), and *Tamakushige futari Urashima*, novelist Mori Ogai's philosophical adaptation of the Urashima Tarō legend. The contribution of such talented modern writers as Mori Ogai (1862-1922), and the dramatization of famous contemporary tragic novels such as Tokutomi Roka's *Hototogisu* (The Cuckoo) and Ozaki Kōyō's *Konjiki yasha* (A Demon of Gold) provided the *shimpa* stage with a new repertory representative of contemporary Japanese culture, quite different from whatever Kawakami had been dressing up to display his showmanship.

The Golden Age of Shimpa

The first decade of the twentieth century was a period of prosperity and busy activity for *shimpa*. The death of the two major *kabuki* stars Kikugorō and Danjūrō in 1903 had left a great vacuum in the Tokyo theatre. The beginning of the Russo-Japanese War in 1904 inspired *shimpa* to revive the genre of war plays which had been extremely well received at the time of the Sino-Japanese War. The success of war plays by different *shimpa* groups was such that an invitation was extended to *kabuki* actors to produce one of them jointly. The invitation was not accepted, but *kabuki* actors did themselves produce a *shimpa* war play—a sign of the new importance reached by *shimpa* on the Tokyo scene. *Shimpa* was taking a vigorous leadership in the professional theatre world not only by choosing timely themes for its plays (war plays and plays adapted from successful novels and newspaper serials), but also because of the input of serious and well trained actors such as Ii and the female impersonator Kawai Takeo, son of a *kabuki* actor and therefore belonging by birth to the traditional theatre establishment. This "great age" of *shimpa* saw times in which *shimpa* plays were simultaneously presented at three different Tokyo theatres: a famous example is that of the three competing productions of *Hototogisu* running at the same time a few blocks away from each other.

In 1907 two hundred thirty *shimpa* actors formed a Grand Coalition of New Actors (*Shinhaiyū daidō danketsu*), which lasted only two months, but was a clear indication of the strength and diffusion reached by the *shimpa* movement in a period of two decades. Novelists whose work had been dramatized for *shimpa* use began to write original dramas. The most important among them was Mayama Seika (1878-1948). A number of successes of this period are still performed as "classics" of the *shimpa* repertory: an example is the play derived from Izumi Kyōka's novel, *Onnakeizu* (A Woman's Chronicle), a tragic love story with strong sentimental overtones, that opened in 1909.

The Decadence of Shimpa

The beginning of *shimpa*'s decadence coincides with the rise of *shingeki*. The function of *shimpa* as a catalyzer of new theatrical energies seemed soon to be exhausted. Attempts to revive audience interest, such as Inoue Masao's production of western plays with his new Shinjidaigeki Kyōkai (Association for the New Epoch Theatre, founded 1911), or Kawai Takeo's production of such plays as Hofmannsthal's *Elektra* with his Kōshū Gekidan (Public Theater Company, founded 1913), were unsuccessful.

Shimpa went through very difficult years during the Taishō period (1912-1926). Even the most popular stars such as Ii and Kawai could hardly survive; the famous female impersonator Hanayagi Shōtarō, however, scored some success with his *geisha* roles, which became and have remained very important in the *shimpa* repertory.

In 1929 the Shōchiku Company took the initiative of bringing together all *shimpa* performers and managing regular performances. *Shimpa* was slowly taking its place in the Tokyo theatre establishment, in a new position, well defined by Inoue Masao in 1937, of *chūkan engeki*, the "theatre in-between" *kabuki* and *shingeki*.

Around this time the actress Mizutani Yaeko (born in 1905), whose long career saw her rise to legendary status, was already enriching *shimpa* with her great acting and introducing a repertory of sentimental dramas with melodramatic heroines against the backdrop of the *demi-monde*.

Shimpa *from World War II*

During World War II three *shimpa* companies were active, Engekidōjō (The Theatre Studio) directed by Inoue Masao; Geijutsuza (Art Theatre), directed by Mizutani Yaeko; and Honryū Shimpa (Main Stream Shimpa), directed by Kitamura Rokurō and Kawai Takeo. The revival of patriotic plays helped the fortunes of *shimpa*, but the end of the war opened a serious crisis of survival. The great post-war boom of *shingeki* attracted some of the best *shimpa* actors to the rival field, making the *shimpa*'s situation even more critical. Finally, in 1950 all remaining *shimpa* performers came together in a company called Gekidan Shimpa, which relied heavily on the fame of Mizutani Yaeko and Hanayagi Shōtarō for a hoped-for revival. The famous Kubota Mantarō, Kawaguchi Matsutarō, and Nakano Minoru wrote some successful plays for *shimpa*. *Shimpa* became a synomym for light, sentimental, old fashioned drama, geared above all to an audience made up primarily of housewives, and performed in a style in between the realism of *shingeki* and the traditional stylization of *kabuki*.

Shimpa was born in the Meiji period, during which time it reached the zenith of its success. There have been recent attempts to introduce *shingeki*-like plays and performance style into *shimpa*. In a true sense, however, *shimpa* still reflects the uncertain period of Japan's early modernization, and embodies a nostalgia for what today is felt as the old-fashioned, strangely distant, mixed esthetic tastes of a period when Japan was being introduced to the culture of the West.

NOTES

[1]Komiya, ed. *Japanese Music and Drama in the Meiji Era*, 270.

[2]Ortolani, "Nō, Kabuki and New Theatre Actors in the Theatrical Reforms of Meiji Japan (1868-1912)," 113.

[3]See an attempt to interpret the importance of Sadayakko's performances in Europe in Savarese, "La peripezia emblematica di Sada Yacco."

CHAPTER X

SHINGEKI: THE NEW DRAMA

The Period of Trial Plays (1906-1913)[1]

The pioneers of *shimpa* had shown little interest in the serious study of western drama as a literary genre and as a guiding light in the process of modernizing the Japanese theatre. The occasional performances of great western plays by *shimpa* companies previous to *shingeki*'s beginnings were experiments in superficial sensationalism; even in the golden era of *shimpa*, the repertory remained made up primarily of makeshift Japanese plays which did not even try to achieve literary value. *Shimpa* was born in the ebullient arena of active, sometimes violent, political confrontation, developed in a commercial direction, and stabilized under the management of the very same Shōchiku company that ruled the *kabuki* world.

Shingeki, on the contrary, was born around two major Tokyo universities. From the very beginning the serious study, translation, and performance of western dramatic literature, as well as the development of a Japanese dramatic literature comparable in value to that of the West, have been central to the *shingeki* effort at creating a modern theatre in Japan. These principles were essential to at least some of the *shingeki* pioneers, who shunned commercialism, and worked mostly outside Japan's professional entertainment world.

A) *Tsubouchi Shōyō*. The establishment of the Bungei Kyōkai (Literary Association, 1906) by Tsubouchi Shōyō (1858-1933) at Waseda University, and of the Jiyū Gekijō (Liberal Theatre, 1909, centering around Keiō University) by Osanai Kaoru, are usually considered by historians as the starting point of *shingeki*. The two leaders and the movements

243

they originated represent two very different approaches to the same ideal of modernizing the Japanese theatre.

Tsubouchi was a man of many activities and many merits. His concerns were broader than the theatre: they encompassed the wide spectrum of modernizing literature in general, although focusing especially on the novel and the drama. Early in his career he became the leading literary critic of his time, and pioneered the study of the nature of the western novel in his *Shōsetsu shinzui* (The Essence of the Novel, 1885). Besides being considered with Osanai one of the two founding fathers of *shingeki*, and having produced and directed the very first *shingeki* performances, he wrote a number of novels, translated the entire dramatic work of Shakespeare, authored a few important plays of his own, published essays on the new esthetics, was the editor with Shimamura Hōgetsu of one of the most influential literary journals of the time, the *Waseda bungaku*, and was a highly esteemed university professor, and the recognized founder of theatre research in Japan.

Tsubouchi's basic approach to the complex problem of modernization was that of using the serious study of the western masterpieces as a means to his end of reforming contemporary Japanese literature. His main purpose in translating Shakespeare was not so much to capture his spiritual message, but rather to learn his masterful playwriting technique and use it for the reform of *kabuki*.[2] From the commencement of his activity to his death Tsubouchi was concerned with the continuity and improvement of the existing forms of Japanese literature, including drama. As a theatre historian, Tsubouchi had no doubt that *kabuki* was *the* theatre of Japan, and that the problem therefore was not whether to abandon *kabuki* or not, but how to reform *kabuki* for the new times. He had been disillusioned by Danjūrō's *kabuki* experiments with the historical accuracy of the *katsureki* plays, and was convinced that the way to modernize *kabuki* was by providing new literary texts that would satisfy the needs of a contemporary psychological approach.

Tsubouchi did not consider himself a playwright; wanting, however, to give an example of what he meant, he wrote in 1884, when he was only twenty-five, *Kiri no hitoha* (A Leaf of Paulownia). The protagonist of this historical play—a famous sixteenth-century warrior, Katagiri Katsumoto, caught in the struggle between his master Hideyoshi and the future ruler of

Japan, Ieyasu—offered an ideal case to demonstrate the new technique of dealing with psychological insight into a complex character facing extremely difficult circumstances; the traditional *kabuki* would simply have handled such a character as a villain. Despite the favorable reception by the critics who read the play in *Waseda bungaku*, the *kabuki* actors did not feel confortable with the implications of the new style. The play was not performed for twenty years until 1904, when it became a great success with both critics and audiences.

More important is Tsubouchi's second play, *En no gyōja* (The Hermit), published in several versions between 1914 and 1921 and written under the influence of Ibsen, whom Tsubouchi in the meantime had discovered. The subject matter is a poetic re-telling of a legend about a Buddhist hermit and his deep disillusion caused by the failure, because of a woman, of his beloved disciple to follow his path of living. The personal emotion of loss and betrayal caused by the desertion of the actor Shimamura Hōgetsu from Tsubouchi's company gives the play a sincere autobiographical touch, and, even more than in his preceding play, a dimension of profound psychological insight.

Tsubouchi's importance is not limited to his contribution to a renewal of playwriting. Even before establishing his Literary Association, Tsubouchi had started a playreading group to teach proper methods of elocution. He continued his mission as guide to the new generation of actors through his new association, the purpose of which more and more became that of training amateurs for the new plays. Tsubouchi had lost the hope of reforming the professional *kabuki* actors, and therefore concentrated his efforts on preparing a new breed of professionals from the ranks of amateurs having no family connections with the traditional theatre world.

Beyond his efforts as a teacher and founder of a school for actors which gave Japan some of its finest *shingeki* artists—such as the renowned actress Matsui Sumako and the actor/entrepreneur Sawada Shōjirō, who became famous because he founded the theatrical group Shinkokugeki (New National Theatre, very popular in the twenties)—Tsubouchi is very important as a pioneer in producing and directing plays that remained as landmarks in the history of the new theatre. At the beginning of his producing/directing activity Tsubouchi had single acts or scenes from Shakespearean plays performed in between *kabuki* plays, of which the first was the court scene from the *Merchant of Venice*, presented at the Kabukiza theatre (1906). After a few performances of *Hamlet* at the actors' school, he directed in 1911 a very successful production of Ibsen's *A Doll's House*. This led to an invitation to perform at the Imperial Theatre, then the most modern and best equipped stage in Tokyo. This recognition of *shingeki* can be considered as the highpoint of the Bungei Kyōkai as a producing company, and a landmark in the history of the modern Japanese theatre.

The unfortunate romance between Tsubouchi's disciple Shimamura Hōgetsu and the leading star Matsui Sumako provoked a crisis in the Bungei Kyōkai which led to its dissolution in 1913, after a final performance of Shakespeare's *Julius Caesar* at the Imperial Theatre.

B) *Osanai Kaoru.* While Tsubouchi had championed continuity and gradual reform, Osanai Kaoru (1881-1928) became the promoter of a complete break from the past and of a new start according to the models of the contemporary western theatre. Tsubouchi had programmatically avoided professional actors and placed his hopes for the future in the transformation of amateurs into professionals through his school. Osanai, on the contrary, with his collaborator, the *kabuki* actor Ichikawa Sadanji (1880-1940, the first among the *shingeki* pioneers to visit Europe), wanted to re-educate professional *kabuki* actors into non-professional *shingeki* performers. Tsubouchi had aimed at a renewal of drama, music, and dance without ever abandoning his ideal of a modernized *kabuki*. Osanai had no interest in music and dance—which he dismissed as entertainment for the masses— and concentrated on the inception of a realistic, psychological drama, according to what he considered to be the real message of the most important modern western playwrights. While Tsubouchi had given equal importance to Shakespeare and Ibsen, Osanai placed every western author before Ibsen at the same level as *nō* and *kabuki*, and therefore considered them irrelevant to the efforts to speed up the modernization of Japan. While the morally conservative Tsubouchi had not particularly appreciated certain Ibsenian attitudes—such as those exemplified by Nora's behavior in *A Doll's House* —Osanai loved controversial plays which scrutinized values taken for granted in the past.

246

The first production of the Jiyū Gekijō was Ibsen's *John Gabriel Borkman*, only thirteen years after its premiere in Copenhagen.[3] This production, considered by many as the first real *shingeki* performance, was staged on November 27, 1909, at the Yūrakuza, then probably the most up-to-date theatre in Tokyo. Despite the fact that the female roles were performed by *kabuki onnagata*, and that Sadanji interpreted the intense guilt feelings of the typical Northern introverted main character with the falsetto tones of traditional *kabuki* diction, audiences were deeply moved and perceived that a new kind of drama was being offered for the first time in Japan.

Osanai organized his theatre according to the model of the Stage Society of London, which his associate Sadanji had experienced during his stay in London. Each year he presented only a couple of new productions to a limited membership until the group ended in 1919. His repertory consisted primarily of non-Anglo-Saxon authors such as Ibsen, Maeterlinck, Gorkij, Hauptmann, Wedekind, and Pirandello.

During the early years of *shingeki* the performance style of both the Bungei Kyōkai and the Jiyū Gekijō troupes remained closely related to that of *kabuki*, especially in the matter of diction. Tsubouchi had studied closely the technique of *jōruri* singing, and Osanai had been involved with *kabuki* actors from the onset of his *shingeki* activity. The definite step in the direction of a realistic acting method was taken after Osanai's trip abroad in 1912-1913, during which he experienced the work of Max Reinhardt in Berlin and of Stanislavskij in Moscow, each of whom remained lifelong models for his work.

The Period of Commercialization (1914-1923)

The years that followed the dissolution of the Bungei Kyōkai saw a number of *shingeki* companies coming together and falling apart without any special achievement as far as the quality of performances was concerned. Tsubouchi was silent and hurt. Osanai, fresh from his experiences abroad, did not hide his disillusionment at the poor quality in the performances of the period's best troupes, including the Geijutsuza (formed by Shimamura Hōgetsu and Matsui Sumako after the dissolution of the Bungei Kyōkai). The Geijutsuza had a great success in 1914 with the production of Tolstoi's *Resurrection*, which went on tour all over Japan, but the critics insisted that popularity had come at the price of quality and accomodation to the taste of the masses. The death of Shimamura in 1918 and the suicide of Matsui in 1919 marked the end of the Geijutsuza.

According to the critics, *shingeki* of this period had lost the enthusiasm and inherited the defects of its early days. The division into numerous, mostly short-lived, small companies did not help the cause of quality. "The intellectuals of that time found pleasure in the mere sight of red-haired people with pipes in their mouth and their shoulders against the mantelpiece, engaged in philosophical discussion, or just cutting meat with their knives and forks."[4] This statement by playwright Takada Tamotsu expresses the feeling of those contemporaries who became very critical about the exaggerated hopes of intellectuals looking to the West as a saviour. At this point several critics began to divorce themselves from a *shingeki* that was slipping into a superficial acting-out of western curiosities.

On the positive side, *shingeki* playwrights such as Yoshii Isamu, Nagata Hideo, Kurata Momozō, and others began to write *shingeki* plays that achieved success. Kurata Momozō's *Shukke to sono deshi* (The Monk and His Disciple, 1916), a drama about an idealized Shinran Shōnin, the famous thirteenth century Buddhist reformer, provides a touching example of the search for a new synthesis between Japanese and imported ideals.[5]

The Early Tsukiji Little Theatre Movement (1924-1927)

The years between the great Tokyo earthquake of 1923 and the death of Osanai Kaoru in 1928 are dominated by the opening of the first theatre exclusively dedicated to *shingeki* and by the activities of Osanai's final years. The vast destruction in the capital provided Tokyo with an opportunity to modernize its appearance: new buildings, new streets, and new theatres. Hijikata Yoshi (1898-1959), who was in Germany at the time of the earthquake to study contemporary theatre movements, immediately returned to Tokyo at the news of the earthquake and financed the building of the Little

Theatre at Tsukiji (Tsukiji Shōgekijō), in an area close to the Ginza and far away from Asakusa, the entertainment quarter where most of the previous *shingeki* performances had taken place. The move to Tsukiji meant catering to a more exclusive audience, limited in number, and conscious of being an intellectual elite interested in ideas in foreign plays. Osanai became the soul of the new five-hundred-seat theatre, which was designed according to the latest developments in western theatre architecture and provided with excellent equipment for lighting and scenic effects. He conceived the new theatre as an experimental laboratory where the various western styles, from realism to expressionism, from impressionism to symbolism, and all avant-garde novelties were to be tried out and presented to a public eager to become acquainted with them. The Tsukiji Shōgekijō became the center of *shingeki* activity, the place where a new generation of *shingeki* theatre people was formed.

Osanai had been especially influenced in Europe by the importance of the director, as exemplified by the period's two European directorial giants, Max Reinhardt in Berlin and Stanislavsky in Moscow. The work of the Russian maestro in building an ensemble remained in Osanai's memory as probably the most important model to imitate in his future work in Japan. This explains why he did not give much importance to the development of new Japanese plays, which he considered inferior—his own plays included—and which he completely neglected for several years; he instead concentrated all his enormous energy on building the "cult of the director" as applied to the production of translations of the best contemporary western plays. In this period about fifty major western plays were produced, against very few original works by new Japanese playwrights.

The difference in taste between Osanai and Hijikata became more and more evident. Osanai preferred authors who were primarily interested in an artistic message, especially those in the psychological-naturalistic vein such as he had experienced during the time he spent with Stanislavsky. Hijikata, on the contrary, during his Russian trip had particularly admired Meyerhold's brilliant combination of vivid theatricalism, daring stylization, and political message; hence his preference for expressionistic and politically involved plays. Hijikata became more and more part of a trend towards socialism which was to take over most of the *shingeki* world as soon as Osanai's leadership was brought to an abrupt end by his premature death in 1928. Tsubouchi's and Osanai's battle against Marxist infiltration into the *shingeki* world—they never showed any understanding of or inclination toward socialism—was lost.

The Leftist Propaganda Plays (1928-1932)

In the economic crisis of the twenties trade unionism and other leftist workers' movements developed in Japan, but were severely repressed by the conservative government. A number of leftist intellectuals rallied around *shingeki* theatre companies to continue their political battle for socialism. In 1921 Hirasawa Keishichi started the Rōdō Gekidan (Worker's Company), and in 1925 the Toranku Gekijō (Trunk Theatre, inspired by the European Agit-prop theatre), began its performances. Its founders were to give life to a number of leftist companies, such as the Zen'ei Gekijō (Avant-garde Theatre) and the Proretaria Gekijō (Proletarian Theatre). After the death of Osanai, Hijikata left the company of the Tsukiji Theatre and started the Shin Tsukiji Gekidan (New Tsukiji Company), which became, with the Sayoku Gekijō (Leftist Theatre, a company that had coalesced out of smaller leftist groups) the main force of the *shingeki* world.

The leftist movement was sharply criticized by non-socialist historians, who found the plays and performance style of this period dull, repetitious, and devoid of artistic inspiration; theatrical values were replaced by propaganda slogans inciting to class struggle, and the proletarian plays offered classes in Marxist ideology instead of genuine poetical drama. Leftist critics, on the other hand, consider this time as the fervent years of *shingeki*; the plays of such leftist playwrights as Murayama Tomoyoshi (born 1901), Kubo Sakae (1901-1958), and Miyoshi Jurō (1902-1958) are thought of as typical, important examples of *shingeki* political theatre. There is no doubt that there were no geniuses among those talented authors who tried to succeed at the difficult task of joining political propaganda and playwriting: it would be unjust, however, to dismiss their contributions, in difficult circumstances, as worthless. The leftist companies did rely almost exclusively on Japanese scripts, thus providing for the first time the place for new Japanese plays that Osanai had refused. However, Osanai's "cult of the director" had deeply penetrated the mental attitude of the leftist leaders, who relegated the playwright to the inferior position of a scenario-writer subject to the demands of an omnipotent director—thus perpetuating the old *kabuki* traditions of the playwright being mainly a hack in the service of a leading actor.

The Marxist political dominance of *shingeki* could not go unnoticed by the military authorities, who began to censor "subversive" leftist propaganda, jailed leaders like Murayama, and eventually suppressed the principal leftist *shingeki* companies.

The Artistic Period (1933-1940)

The harassment of the leftist companies by the authorities reached a point at which plays were censored and occasionally forbidden, leaders and actors sometimes arrested and jailed, and spectators attending the plays had to face the risk of being held and interrogated by the police. The Nihon Proretaria Gekijō Dōmei (Japan Proletarian Theater Federation), which had succeeded in obtaining control of most of *shingeki* by 1930, was finally dissolved in 1934. Meanwhile, a group of anti-leftist *shingeki* actors and playwrights had come together in 1932 as the Tsukijiza, a company with an artistic program which introduced two new important elements to the *shingeki* structure: first, the elimination of the all-dominant figure of the company leader in favor of a collective leadership by actors, and, second, a preference given to serious, original Japanese plays as the backbone of the repertory. This is a time during which a number of important playwrights developed new Japanese plays of lasting value. Among them the important contribution of Kishida Kunio (*Mama sensei to sono otto*, Professor Mama and Her Husband, *Ushiyama Hoteru*, Ushiyama Hotel), Kubota Mantarō (*Fuyu*, Winter, *Kadode*, Leaving Home, *Odera gakkō*, Odera School), Satomi Ton (*Ikiru*, Living), Tanaka Chikao (*Ofukuro*, Mother), and others.

Kishida (1890-1954) was educated as a specialist in French literature, and in France he learnt the technique of the French conversation plays.[6] Upon his return to Japan in 1923

251

he began to work in small *shingeki* companies. He played an important role in the formation of the Tsukijiza, supporting the two major actors, Tomoda Kyōsuke and Tamamura Akiko, and providing leadership in the choice of the repertory. He was a major factor in switching the main focus of attention of the *shingeki* people from the German, Scandinavian, and Russian dramatists—who had been the favorite of Osanai and of the leftist groups—to the French and English authors. In France Kishida had learnt to admire Copeau's work, and had nurtured the ideal of transferring to Japan Copeau's intention of renovating the dramatic literature. Kishida, moreover, hoped to assume a mission in Japan as *shingeki*'s teacher-theoretician-reformer, much as Copeau had been for the contemporary French theatre. Kishida's achievements, however, were not as high as his ideals. He succeeded, though, in leading a number of the best *shingeki* talents to a serious pursuit of non-political, purely literary, and theatrical values in the plays, and of artistic integrity in their performance. These ideals became the program of the Bungakuza, the company he was instrumental in forming (1936), which became the longest lasting group in *shingeki* history.

After the suppression of the major leftist companies, Murayama Tomoyoshi, who had been in prison until 1933, rallied some of the left-over politically involved *shingeki* people and formed the Shinkyō Gekidan (Collaboration Company) in 1934. It was a time in which Socialist Realism was enforced in the Soviet Union over "formalistic deviations," and the Japanese Marxists followed the new party line. The best plays in this style were *Kazanbaichi*, by Kubo Sakae, which criticizes capitalistic farm policies, and *Hokutō no kaze* (North-East Wind) by Hisaita Eijirō.

Meanwhile, the government had become less and less tolerant of any activity "unsuitable to the national feeling." The leftist companies took refuge in the performance of western classics and the training of their actors according to the Stanislavsky method. They tried not to attract the attention of the hostile authorities, but it was to no avail. On August 19, 1940, the two remaining leftist *shingeki* troupes, the Shinkyō Gekidan and the Shin Tsukiji Group, were dissolved and a number of their members arrested. The only survivor during the war years was the Bungakuza, which had no political affiliation and quietly continued the pursuit of its "art for art's sake" ideal. Those *shingeki* actors who were released from jail could perform during the war only under the supervision and control of the nationalistic authorities.

Shingeki *after World War II (1944-1994)*

Immediately after the war the American occupation authorities favored *shingeki*. They were distrustful of the "feudalistic" traditional drama of *kabuki* and *nō*, which was censored and subjected to special control, while complete freedom and support was given to the new westernized drama as a potential instrument of democratization. All prominent veteran *shingeki* actors joined forces and in December 1945 opened with a production of the old favorite of Japanese audiences, Chekhov's *The Cherry Orchard*. Soon a number of companies were organized, and an extraordinary torrent of productions followed, with a success that for a short while seemed to indicate a possible assumption by *shingeki* of the leading role among post-war theatrical genres.

Among the post-war companies one of the most important is the Haiyūza (Actors Theatre, founded in 1944), centered around the director/actor Senda Koreya. Senda has been for many years one of the main leaders of *shingeki* activity; he had a great influence also as the founder of an actors' school in which numerous successful recent *shingeki* performers were trained. Senda had been involved with the leftist theatre movement for years before starting the new company with the director Aoyama Sugisaku, the actors Tōno Eijirō and Ozawa Sakae, and the actresses Higashiyama Chieko and Kishi Teruko.

Also important is the Tōkyō Geijutsu Gekijō (Tokyo Art Theatre), the major members of which formed, after its dissolution, the Gekidan Mingei (People's Art Theatre, founded in 1950) around Unō Jūkichi. The Bungakuza flourished after the war, continuing its artistic mission, while companies like the Haiyūza, Mingei, and Murayama's reconstitued leftist Shinkyō Gekidan showed a renewed Marxist involvement. The honeymoon between *shingeki* and the occupation authorities was soon over. Marxist propaganda began to appear more dangerous than the "feudalistic" traditional plays—which were actually admired by audiences not because of their remote contents but for the enjoyment of politically harmless stylized theatricalism. While the censorship of *kabuki* plays was being eased, and eventually abolished, the official backing of *shingeki* soon became a policy of the past. *Shingeki* was on its own, and the wave of initial enthusiasm gradually leveled off. Numerous companies came and went, many of them lasting only a short time. In an average year in the fifties and the sixties there might have been in Tokyo forty to fifty such companies producing about a hundred plays yearly.

The *shingeki* companies, as a rule, have no fixed place of performance; for each production they rent for their production a hall, proportionate in size and importance to their means and their hope of public reception; these places range from large modern theatres to small private or public halls, or even locales comparable to off-off Broadway lofts. In 1954 the Haiyūza Company built its own 400-seat theatre called Haiyūza Gekijō, which was rebuilt in 1980. The ensemble, however, no longer uses that facility for its major shows because it would not be financially possible to produce an expensive play for such a small audience.

Most *shingeki* actors have traditionally supported themselves with work outside their company, especially in television and other commercial jobs, both acting-related and not, because it has been well known since *shingeki*'s birth that "you cannot make a living with *shingeki*." For the great majority of *shingeki* people their many years of hard work in the theatre has been an act of faith in political and/or artistic ideals with minimal financial reward. As a matter of fact, the actors have been in the habit of contributing their earnings to the company so as to be able to produce plays, *shingeki* never having been granted state support, and high rents, taxes, and low returns creating a constant economic strain.

In recent years, however, greater flexibility and interchangeability among the various fields of the performing arts has increasingly blurred the border between the despised "commercial"[7] and the revered "artistic" and/or "politically committed" theatre. The beginnings of this process were seen as early as the fifties and the sixties, when it became fashionable to experiment with the use of stars of one genre for performances in another. Important companies like Kumo (The Clouds), founded in 1963 by Fukuda Tsuneari (born 1912), one of the most important critics and leaders of *shingeki* from the sixties to the present time, made use of famous *kabuki* actors in the interpretation of the major Shakespearean roles. *Kyōgen* and *nō* actors like Nomura Mansaku and Kanze Hideo became part of avant-garde experimental groups, and important *shingeki* actors like Akutagawa Hiroshi or even avant-garde directors like Suzuki Tadashi became famous in the so-called commercial circuit of the theatre or through the movies.

Moreover, an important development inside the *shingeki* world is represented by the enormous diffusion of both government and commercial television networks in Japan, especially since the seventies. Entire *shingeki* productions have been broadcast and followed by millions of viewers, opening for the best *shingeki* actors the wide market of television popularity, which greatly enlarges the range previously reached by the work of a few *shingeki* actors in films.

Shingeki actors and directors are also hired along with movie and television stars for the so-called "commercial" productions of hit plays often transferred from Broadway and West End theatres to the Tokyo stages—thus increasingly blurring the boudaries of what defines *shingeki*.

Since the fifties a number of *shingeki* groups have come and gone; only a few still survive to the present (1988) or have left a lasting mark in Japan's theatrical landscape.[8] Among them is the group Gekidan Shiki (Theatre Four Seasons), founded in 1953 and directed since its beginning by Asari Keita (b. 1933), who was inspired by the ideals of playwright Katō Michio (1918-1953). Katō was deeply influenced by the French literature and the French way of acting, and this explains why the repertory of Gekidan Shiki consisted almost exclusively of French plays—especially those by Giraudoux and Anouilh. Since 1972 Shiki has ventured into the production of large scale musicals, among which the recent *Cats* and *Phantom of the Opera* were immensely popular.

The Kumo company—established by Fukuda as a part of his Modern Drama Foundation— specialized in performing Fukuda's translations of the major Shakespearean plays. Kumo sought to realize the high aspirations of its demanding leader for a literary theatre, in contrast with the overtly political and ideological aims of groups like the Haiyūza and Mingei, and in opposition to the flatness of a style inspired by socialist realism. Kumo's inheritance was taken over by the company Subaru (The Pleiades), founded by Fukuda in 1976 after the dissolution of Kumo.

The Hayūza company still maintains a position of leadership in the *shingeki* world. Veteran actor-director Senda Koreya (b. 1904, real name Itō Kunio) continued his important mission of training hundreds of actors at his Research Institute of Actor's Theatre until 1967, when the training work was transferred to the newly established theatre department at To ‾hō Gakuen. The Bungakuza company, the longest living *shingeki* group established in 1937, continues, notwithstanding a number of painful secessions, its non-political performances of valuable, literary texts. Gekidan Mingei, the spiritual heir to the proletarian theatre of the leftist tradition, solidly anchored in realism, is still—with the Hayūza and the Bungakuza—one of the three major *shingeki* companies.

Probably the most interesting achievement of *shingeki* in the last few decades has been the maturation of playwrights of sustained distinction, some of whom recently have achieved a deserved international recognition. Outstanding among them is Mishima Yukio (1925-1970) whose modern *nō* plays are frequently produced by many companies all over the world. Most of Mishima's plays, which followed an almost morbid and decadent "art for art's sake" estheticism before he became involved in his dream of the restoration of ultratraditional samurai values, were premiered by Tokyo's Bungakuza in the fifties and in the sixties.

Also important is the work of Kinoshita Junji (b. 1914), whose play *Yūzuru* (Twilight Crane) is a delicate masterpiece of the poetic-symbolic genre, and an important break from the realistic *shingeki* tradition. *Yūzuru* was also adapted for *kabuki*, *nō*, and opera performance. Besides his plays centered on the theme of folklore, such as *Hikoichibanashi* (Tales of Hikoichi) and *Akai jimbaori* (The Red Tunic), Kinoshita has written successful plays on social themes, such as *Furō* (Wind and Waves) and *Otto to yobareru Nihonjin* (A Japanese Called Otto).[9]

256

Tanaka Chikao's (b. 1905) lifetime work spans many periods of *shingeki* history. In his many plays, from *Ofukuro* (Mother, 1933) to the more mature *Maria no kubi* (Mary's Neck), Tanaka shows a delicate and profound insight into the intricacies of modern Japanese interior struggles, not only, as so often had been the case, on a political level, but primarily on the individual and religious levels as well.

The break from the realistic/naturalistic style, even in leftist *shingeki* companies, began with the introduction of Brecht in the fifties. In the sixties the advent of absurdism sharpened the discussion about the place of theatrical elements (*engekisei*), ideological elements (*kannensei*), and literary elements (*bungakusei*) in theatre, with the result that there was, at least theoretically, an acceptance of the importance of theatricality in the new absurdist plays by Japanese authors such as Abe Kōbō (b. 1925).

Abe already had become known abroad because of the filming of his novel *Suna no onna* (The Woman in the Dunes, 1962). His many avant-garde plays, starting with *Doreigari* (Slave Hunting) in 1955, through the more recent plays such as *Tomodachi* (Friends) and *Suichū toshi* (Underwater City) baffled Japanese critics because of their pitiless and unconventional vivisection of the contradictions in today's society. Abe's plays also have been presented abroad, in an avant-garde style typical of the sixties by his own company, the Abe Sutajio (Abe Studio), which was founded in 1973, and continues in Tokyo with performances in repertory of the plays by its leader.

It was unavoidable, in the wake of a renewed nationalism and pride in the value of the Japanese tradition, that *shingeki* artists would "rediscover" the importance of *nō* and *kabuki* as a source of inspiration for new plays and for actor training. Mishima, taking a hint from the modern adaptation of the Greek classics by French playwrights, had opened the way by using themes from the classical *nō* for his modern *nō* plays. Kinoshita had found in *kyōgen* inspiration for his folkloristic plays. A further step in this direction was to be taken by the new generation of post-*shingeki* theatre groups, that are now known under the common denominator of underground theatre, or *angura*.

During the last few years of the Shōwa period (ca. 1985-1989), after the gradual fading away of the underground theatre movement (1960-1985, see next paragraph), *shingeki* has shown little artistic vitality. The healthy number of companies, productions, and new theatre buildings reflects the extraordinary prosperity of the Japanese economy. The Japanese critics, however, lament *shingeki*'s lack of direction and its widespread escapism, deprived of serious inspiration, as exemplified by the great number of senseless, superficial comedies. They cannot avoid the comparison with the "commercial" shows, which follow production patterns similar to those of Broadway or the West End and often succeed in reaching higher quality and greater success, while employing, also in competition with the media, an increasing number of the best *shingeki* talent. The role of the traditional *shingeki* companies and, in general, the characteristics of *shingeki* in the pluralistic Japanese theatrical scene of the next decades, remain, at the beginning of the new period of Japanese history, Heisei, difficult to foresee.

The Underground Theatre Movement (1960-1985)

While *shingeki* was finding its place among the legitimate forms of the Japanese theatre, the function of protest and avant-garde experimentation was being taken over by the underground movement (*angura*).[10] Although born from an explicitly anti-American protest, the *angura* developed a following in the manner of the off-off Broadway theatre and of the "happenings" in New York in the sixties, with the same purpose, that of creating a new counterculture. Its origins were in the violent demonstrations led by the leftist Zengakuren student organization against the renewal of the United States-Japan Security Treaty in 1960. The fact that the *shingeki* groups—even those that openly proclaimed themselves pro-communist—failed to react seriously to the treaty renewal caused deep disaffection among the young protesters with what they sneeringly started to call the "Old Left." They also felt alienated from the powerful leftist Rōen (acronym for Rōdōsha engeki hyōgikai, The Workers' Council on Theatre), which had deteriorated, in their eyes, into a champion of conservativism concerned only with the profitable recruitment of audiences and with the preservation of its own power. Politically, a number of the young protesters wanted neither the alliance with the United States, favored by the government, nor a new one with the Soviet bloc, favored by the pro-communist leftist organizations. They were fighting for a complete "independence" of Japan, in a non-aligned, neutral position.

Most of the protest-inspired youth produced rather poor, overwritten plays and sophomoric acting, often displaying grotesque elements in costume and make-up, shocking nudity, loud music, and so on; they thus were akin to a part of the avant-garde work being done in the radical New York theatre of the sixties. Among bursts of exuberant and often confused anti-*shingeki* energy some important common characteristic traits emerged in the work of a number of representative post-*shingeki* playwrights, who deserve special consideration.

After World War II the major *shingeki* groups had developed—notwithstanding differences in artistic and political ideals—a silent consensus in accepting the following characteristics typical of much western modern theatre: a commitment to realism; the principle that theatre must be based on a text, which both actor and director cooperate to correctly intepret on the stage; a deep conviction that the theatre "educates" the audience, which takes therefore the passive attitude of a pupil towards his master; and the use of a conventional proscenium stage. The commitment to realism took the shape of a thorough effort to completely secularize drama in Japan, ignoring the existence of, and replacing the native gods and demons—omnipresent in pre-Meiji drama—with imported psychology and Marxist slogans. The better *angura* artists began to question the above *shingeki* tenets, and eventually rejected them, one by one, in the attempt to create a new, original, non-western contemporary Japanese theatre, rooted again in the native tradition. Goodman calls this process of re-rooting "the return of the gods"[11] and warns that such return is not meant as a religious revival, but as a process to liberate Japanese ghosts (i.e., the Japanese gods, as a symbol of the Japanese archetypal, aesthetic, and sociopsychological heritage) "not to affirm them, but to aknowledge and negate them."

Most *angura* groups, including the first inspired by the new ideals, the Seinengeijutsu (1959), had a very short life, lacked professionalism, and relied more on shocking the audiences than on learning the necessary acting techniques. The five groups that succeeded in achieving results worth mentioning are the Kurotento 68/71, the Jōkyō Gekijō, the Tenjō Sajiki, the Tenkei Gekijō, and the Waseda Shōgekijō.

The theoreticians of the Kurotento 68/71 (called in English Black Tent Theatre, or BTT 68/71) are Tsuno Kaitarō (b. 1938) and Saeki Ryūkō (b. 1941), who gave shape to the criticism against *shingeki* shared by most *angura* groups.[12] Instead of using the typical proscenium stage in a conventional *shingeki* theatre, the BBT 68/71 built in 1970 an enormous black tent where any kind of stage could be set up. The tent made possible a complete independence from the organized network of traditional *shingeki* theatres, confined mostly within the Tokyo metropolitan area. Instead of traditional realistic plays, a number of performances were presented, including "songs, dances, one-liners, agit-prop, promotions, readings, record concerts, film screenings, standup comedy, slapstick, Noh and Kyōgen, through lectures and panel discussions, to demonstrations, carnivals, parties, and mass meetings."[13] Instead of catering almost exclusively to the Tokyo *shingeki* audiences, the BTT 68/71 began traveling extensively all over Japan, performing in a great number of centers which had never been reached by *shingeki*, and trying always to involve the audience in the action. BTT 68/71 also performs sophisticated theatrical extravaganzas/new plays by such playwrights as Satoh Makoto, Katō Tadashi, and Yamamoto Kiyokazu, in a small locale called the Red Cabaret in Tokyo. Instead of preserving the *shingeki* cult for European style, the BTT 68/71 has increasingly leaned towards the creation of an Asian style, going back to *nō* and *kyōgen* and assimilating elements from other Asian countries such as China, Korea, India and the Philippines.

While the BTT 68/71 always tried to draw its repertory from a number of new playwrights, the Jōkyō Gekijō (Situation Theatre) orbited around the work of its charismatic leader, the playwright Kara Jūrō (b. 1940). Also departing from *shingeki* tenets, Kara led his troupe to perform in most unusual environments, using "public toilets, railroad stations, and even lily ponds (from the waters of which the cast make their entrances and exits) as the setting for his plays."[14] Kara was the first to use a tent for his performances (1967), and his red tent in the precincts of the Hanazono Shrine in Shinjuku became a symbol of revolt against environmental abuses. Searching for inspiration in the Japanese tradition, especially in *kabuki*, Kara called his actors *kawara kojiki* ("river-bed beggars," the name by which Tokugawa era *kabuki* actors were called), and found in the *kabuki* techniques models for a non-realistic acting style, while also the content of his plays leaned more on traditional *kabuki* themes than on the modern western models. A prolific playwright, Kara received the Kishida Prize for his *Shōjo kamen* (Virgin Mask, 1969), and was honored also with the important Akutagawa Prize for literature (1983). Among the best of his plays is *Ai no kojiki* (John Silver, The Beggar of Love, 1970),[15] a typical example of retreat of the avant-garde from the political and social action of the sixties into the individual consideration of human fragmentation and a search for a world of fantasy and poetry typical of the seventies and the eighties. Kara also pursued an Asian ideal of independence from western models, and traveled often with his company to third world countries, remaining on purpose aloof from a pursuit of fame in the industrialized countries of the West. Recently Kara has begun directing "commercial" productions in Tokyo, joining therefore other avant-garde artists like Suzuki Tadashi who have, in recent years, capitalized on their fame to be hired by the once despised corporate establishment.

The third group, Tenjō Sajiki, owes its existence to one man, Terayama Shuji (1935-1983) who produced a large amount of avant-garde work not only in the theatre, but also in poetry, film, photography, television, radio scripts, and children's theatre.[16] His happening-like underground theatre provided hallucinatory visual and sound experiences for an audience invited to share in the continuing search for a more intense and meaningful reality than that of everyday routine. Terayama, born in the poor and mountainous Aoyama region, grew up with the hard memories of the postwar years, as an underprivileged and sickly youth: eventually he had to drop out of Waseda University and struggle for the balance of his short life because of poor health. This partially explains his poetic and escapist vivid imagination, never tired of creating happenings, street theatre, and theatrical events, one of which,

Jinriki hikōki soromon (The Man-Powered Airplane, Solomon, 1970) for example, required the spectators to go to different places in Tokyo at a variety of times, making therefore the experience different for each individual. Terayama did participate with his troupe in a number of European and American Festivals and became therefore well known abroad because of his "scandalous" style.

The post-*shingeki* reaction against the foreign dogma of realism is especially represented by the work of Ota Shōgo (b. 1939), founder and director of the Tenkei Gekijō (Theatre of Transformation), founded in 1968 and disbanded for financial non-viability in 1988. Ota is especially known for his three-part play, *Mizu no eki* (Water Station), *Chi no eki* (Earthhill Station), and *Kaze no eki* (Wind Station), and for his work as a critic and theoretician (*Doshi no in'ei*, Shades of Verbs, and *Geki no kibō*, The Hope of Drama). *Mizu no eki* is a two-hours play in which not a word is spoken: the wordless intense performance by actors trained to perform with almost blank facial expression and slow movements, impressed public and critics in Japan and abroad because of its successful attempt to rediscover the *nō*'s secret of the moments of non-action.[17] The tendency to silence is also evident in *Komachi fūden* (Tale of Komachi Told by the Wind, 1977), one of the few contemporary plays that uses a *nō* stage and has a protagonist a heroine who does not speak throughout the play. Ota believes that "only what is difficult to convey is worth artistic expression," and therefore drama should emphasize the power of "passivity," that is of being, instead of the easier to convey power of "activity," that is of doing. Silence and quiet are a great part of human "being," and should therefore be prominent on the stage instead of word and action. In the early nineties Ota has switched to a new period of his creativity, as the artistic director of the new Civic Theatre, a municipal theatre in Fujisawa, a suburb of Tokyo. His play *Sarachi*, which premiered there in 1992, presents speaking characters and confirms Ota's preoccupation with simple daily life: "dispossession, wandering, a search for for connectedness; questioning and reaffirmation of life."[18] Ota is basically apolitical, like a growing number of today's leading theatre people belonging to the surviving *shingeki* companies or to whatever is left of the post-*shingeki* movement; he is, however, concerned with an intercultural approach that furthers experiments with foreign artists—an approach that he shares with the abroad better known theatre directors Suzuki Tadashi and Ninagawa Yukio.

The Waseda Shōgekijō (Waseda Little Theatre, since 1984 called SCOT, Suzuki Company of Toga) rooted in the student theatre at Waseda University, developed around the personalities of the already mentioned leader, Suzuki Tadashi, and of the gifted playwright Betsuyaku Minoru (b. 1937). Betsuyaku is the author of the first play of some importance written for the post-*shingeki* movement, *Zō* (The Elephant)[19] produced in 1962 by the group which at the time was called Jiyū Butai (Free Stage), before taking the name Waseda Little Theatre in 1966. *Zō* shows evident influences of Beckett, and repeats the lack of action, the sense of futility and hopelessness of man trapped in life, the darkness and pessimism expressed through the poetical helplessness of a clown, so typical of numerous avant-garde/absurdist plays since *Waiting for Godot*. The deceptive simplicity of the language had also a great influence on the stage language of the *angura* plays.[20] The return to Japanese traditional *nō* theatre for inspiration is also typical of Betsuyaku's work, as much as it is in some aspects of Suzuki' s method of training. The Waseda Little Theatre did not limit itself to Betsuyaku's plays, on the contrary it was responsible for presenting to the public the two important works *Atashi no biitoruzu aruiwa sōshiki* (My Beetles and the Funeral, 1966) by Satoh Makoto, and the already mentioned *Virgin Mask* (1969) by Kara, both directed by Suzuki Tadashi. In collaboration with the actress Shiraishi Kayoko, Suzuki developed a series of collages titled *Gekiteki naru mono o megutte* I, II, III (On the Dramatic Passions, I, II, III) which gave Suzuki the chance to develop his synthesis of an acting style founded in severe discipline, the martial arts, and *kabuki* and *nō* techniques.[21] Of all the post-*shingeki* groups, the Waseda Little Theatre was the one that received the greatest attention in Europe and in the United States, because of the keen interest in finding a bridge between eastern and western traditions and solving the practical problem of making the experience of classical Japanese acting techniques meaningful for today's performers of western plays. The success of Suzuki's production of *The Trojan Women* both in Japan and in the tours abroad is to be explained in view of this special interest of elites. In imitation of Jerzy Grotowski's Laboratory Theatre in Wroclaw, Poland, Suzuki moved with his troupe to a small village, Togamura, far away from every important cultural center, and began there a five-year period of intense training that lasted until 1980. Togamura has become since an important center, where yearly groups of professional actors from many countries are trained, and theatrical events of international interest take place.

The vitality of the *angura* movement appears to have subsided since the onset of the eighties, to the point that many critics have declared it as practically finished by 1985, notwithstanding the fact that most of its major playwrights are still very prolific. It is still premature to attempt a definition of its historical position and value. In the long range, the phenomenon of *angura* might end up in the history of Japanese theatre as a short and not very relevant offshoot of the *shingeki* movement, or as the turning point for a new, yet to be named, post-*shingeki* period. Today, at the beginning of the Heisei era (began 1989), it becomes ever more difficult to draw the lines of demarcation between *shingeki* and *angura*, and between *shingeki* and the commercial theatre. Suzuki's career is an example of the blurring of borders among the genres of the modern Japanese theatre. He began as a student at Waseda University during the politically activistic anti-*shingeki* underground theatre movement of the sixties, then started to reevaluate the treasures of the Japanese tradition after discovering the power of the *nō* at a 1972 international festival in France. From an avant-garde position he developed his own group into a conservative, highly disciplined unit that many would probably categorize as a form of contemporary *shingeki*; at the same time, Suzuki directed commercial productions of Broadway-like plays for major Japanese producing companies, and made his mark on the international scene both through the presentation of his productions and the teaching of his method abroad, as well as by organizing his international school and festival in the mountains at Togamura.

The increased mobility of several performers and directors from one to the other genre of the pluralistic Japanese scene, with the consequent blurring of the borders among the genres themselves, might well be the most characteristic development of the Japanese theatre of the eighties and beginning nineties.

NOTES

[1]The division of *shingeki* history follows with few modifications the one proposed by Toita Yasuji in his *Shingeki gojūnen*, (Fifty years of *shingeki*), Tokyo: Jijitsūshinsha, 1956.

[2]Ortolani, "Fukuda Tsuneari: Modernization and Shingeki," 484-488. See also Rimer, *Toward a Modern Japanese Theatre: Kishida Kunio*, 17-27.

[3]Rimer, *Ibid.*, 29. Tokyo: Shinchōsha 1958, 221.

[4]Words by the playwright Takada Tamotsu during a conversation with Fukuda, referred to by Fukuda himself in his essay "Nihon shingeki-shi gaikan (Outline of Japanese *shingeki* history)," in *Watakushi no engeki hakusho* (My theatre confessions), Tokyo: Shinchōsha, 1958: 221.

[5]See a summary of this play in Ortolani, "Das japanische Theater," in Kindermann, ed. *Einführung in das Ostasiatische Theater*, 401-403.

[6]See Rimer, *Toward a Modern Theater: Kishida Kunio*, 57-71, and passim, for a thorough discussion of Kishida's life and accomplishments.

[7]See Tsubaki, "Bunraku Puppet Theatre, Kabuki, and Other Commercial Theatre," 100-102, for a listing of the most important companies producing "commercial" theatre, among which the two giants are Shōchiku and Tōhō.

[8]See Tsubaki and Miyata, "Shingeki, The New Theatre of Japan," 103-110, for a listing of the major *shingeki* companies operating at present in Japan. See also *Theater Japan 1989. A Companion to the Japanese Theater: Companies and People*, the most up-to-date information available in English on the subject.

[9]Ortolani, "Shingeki: The Maturing New Drama of Japan," 174-178.

[10]*Angura* was the name mostly used in Japan to describe the movement during the 1960s and 1970s. Other descriptive name is *shōgekijō undō*, or little theatre movement, which refers to the small theatres used by most companies involved. Other terms used in recent publications are "post-*shingeki*" and "alternative Japanese drama." See Goodman, *Japanese Drama and Culture in the 1960s*, 26, note 26, and Rolf and Gillespie, eds., *Alternative Japanese Drama*. These two recent books made available in translation important plays by major authors of this period not discussed in this book, such as Satoh Makoto, Akimoto Matsuyo, Fukuda Yoshiyuki and Shimizu Kunio.

[11]Goodman, "The Post-Shingeki Theatre Movement in Japan," 11-112. See also the rest of the article for an overview of the major *angura* companies since the sixties, and his Japanese Drama and Culture in the 1960s, 5-8.

[12]About Tsuno's and Saeki's ideas see Goodman, *Japanese Drama and Culture in the 1960s*, 345-359.

[13]Quoted in Goodman, "The Post-Shingeki Theatre Movement in Japan," 115.

[14]Goodman, "The Post-Shingeki Theatre Movement in Japan," 116.

[15]See Sorgenfrei, *Shuji Terayama: Avant Garde Dramatist of Japan,* 84-90.

[16]*Ibid.*, 91.

[17]See a translation of *The Water Station* by Mari Boyd in *ATJ*, 7/2 (Fall 1990), 150-183. About Ota's affinity for *nō* theatre see Brandon, "Contemporary Japanese Theatre: Interculturalism and Intraculturalism," 92-93.

[18]See Robert T. Rolf, "*Sarachi*: A Play by Ota Shōgo," p. 134.

[19]About Betsuyaku see Rolf and Gillespie, eds, *Alternative Japanese Drama*, 15-23. The book contains also the translations of Betsuyaku's *The Little Match Girl* and *The Cherry in Bloom*. See a discussion of *Zō* in Sorgenfrei, *Shuji Terayama*, 74-83.

[20]Goodman, "The Post-Shingeki Theatre Movement in Japan," 120.

[21]Suzuki's theories, summarized in his book *Ekkyō suru chikara*, were recently translated into English by Thomas Rimer as *The Way of Acting: The Theatre Writings of Tadashi Suzuki*.

CHAPTER XI

MODERN MUSIC AND DANCE THEATRE

Opera

Soon after the Meiji Restoration, the government began a campaign for the diffusion of western music, as a means of promoting the desired modernization of the country. At first, however, western music did not find the same enthusiastic reception which had greeted the introduction of other novelties from the West. A substantial change in the attitude of the new generation began when, in 1898, the study of western music became a compulsory subject in all schools. A gradual familiarization with the new sounds and the new rhythms followed, leading eventually to the great diffusion of western music in twentieth century Japan.

Operatic music and the singing of famous arias from classical operas were a part of this process, and eventually reached a wide audience. The history of opera production, however, shows a slow and difficult development, from its amateur beginnings in the 1890s to the sophisticated stagings of recent decades. High production costs, made more prohibitive because of opera's restricted appeal and the lack of government support, always have been the main reason for the limited activity of Japanese opera companies.

Opera production was introduced to Japan in the excerpted performance of a work that took place in 1894 in Tokyo as part of a benefit program for the Japanese Red Cross: the first act of Gounod's *Faust* was performed by a group of foreign amateurs who sang the leading roles in collaboration with students of the Tōkyō Ongaku Gakkō

(Tokyo School of Music), who provided the chorus, and with the musicians of the Imperial Household Ministry conducted by Franz Eckert (1852-1916).

In 1902 the Kageki Kenkyūkai (Opera Study Society) was formed by students of the same Tokyo School of Music and of the Imperial University. On July 23, 1903, this group sponsored the first complete opera performed in Japan, Gluck's *Orfeo ed Euridice*, which produced a loud echo in the Japanese music world and inspired Japanese composers to enter the new field of opera. The libretto was translated into Japanese for the occasion. Because of the lack of an orchestra the production had to make do with a simple piano accompaniment. The sets were prepared by students of the Bijutsu Gakkō (Fine Arts School). The single performance incurred a huge financial loss and provoked a series of controversies which reached the Ministry of Education, with a consequent official warning to the School that discouraged the continuation of such pioneering opera activities.[1]

The first attempt at a Japanese opera was *Roei no yume* (Dream in Camp, libretto and music by Kitamura Kisei), presented in 1905 at the major *kabuki* theatre of the time, the Kabukiza, between *kabuki* plays, on the same program. *Kabuki* actor Matsumoto Kōshirō VII—employing traditional *kabuki* vocalization—performed the leading role of this operatic composition written in unaccompanied monotones with orchestral intermezzi. Kōshirō was supported by *kabuki* actors who also recited their parts in *kabuki* style. Rather than an opera it was actually a play with spoken parts and connecting songs.

The *shingeki* pioneers, Tsubouchi Shōyō and Osanai Kaoru, were involved in the first phase of operatic development. In 1904 Tsubouchi published the first theoretical work about Japanese opera, the *Shingakugekiron* (Theory of the New Music Drama), in which he envisioned original Japanese operas free from imitation of foreign models and inspired by Japanese tradition. As an example of his theory he wrote the libretto for *Tokoyami* (Eternal Darkness, music by Tōgi Tetteki), whose performance was the first sponsored by the Bungei Kyōkai. The first opera greeted by Japanese critics as a successful fulfillment of Tsubouchi's ideal was *Hagoromo* (The Feather Robe, 1908, inspired by the homonymous *nō* play, music by Komatsu Kōsaku). In addition, Osanai Kaoru arranged and staged *Chikai no hoshi* (The Star of the Oath, music by Yamada Kōsaku).

The opening in 1911 of the Teikoku Gekijō (Imperial Theatre, often called Teigeki) with an opera department (begun in 1912) under the direction of the Italian Giovanni Vittorio Rossi offered new hopes for a development of opera in Japan. The reality, on the contrary, remained rather modest. Only single acts, or abridged versions of light operas, were performed between plays in the fashion of typical *kabuki* programming. The director of the opera department was actually a ballet master who had been primarily active in the field of operetta in London. In his tenure from 1912 to 1916 he produced only some light opera/operettas such as Donizetti's *La Figlia del Reggimento* and Planquette's *Les Cloches de Corneville*. The production of serious classical opera at the Imperial Theatre was still far from being commercially and artistically viable; an enormous effort would have been necessary to support the development of singers and orchestras, not to mention audiences.

The task of popularizing operatic music and arias was accomplished by the popular theatres in Asakusa between 1916 and 1920, when up to three theatres at a time were playing "opera," that is, a variety of mostly western-looking plays with music and songs. Together with operetta, selected parts of the famous classical operas were also popularized through the Asakusa stages.

The next important event in the history of classical opera was the nineteen day visit in 1919 of the Russian Opera from Vladivostok for nineteen days at the Imperial Theatre. For the first time Japanese audiences could witness fully staged productions of such works as *Aida*, *Carmen*, *La Traviata*, *Tosca*, and *Boris Godunov*, with a singer of the caliber of the world famous soprano Bulskaja. The great success of these foreign guests inspired several more attempts to organize Japanese performances of opera, but with sparse results.

Eventually, a series of radio programs of western music directed by Iba Takashi between 1927 and 1930—during which fifteen operas were broadcast with accurate introductions and with enormous audience success—helped greatly in creating an atmosphere in which the first important Japanese opera company was founded by the tenor Fujiwara Yoshie in 1934.

The Fujiwara Kagekidan (Fujiwara Opera Company) has survived to the present time as probably the most important producer and promoter of serious opera—in spite of the many financial problems that have plagued its life as well as those of other opera companies such as the Nagato Miho Gekidan and the Nikikai Opera Company.

Despite the great progress in the diffusion of opera and in the level of artistry during recent decades, there is still no opera house in any of the big cities in Japan. The various companies must rent a theatre or a suitable hall for their performances.

In the post-war era a great number of the world's best opera ensembles have visited Tokyo, where every year at least one or two such groups usually perform to sold-out houses.

The Takarazuka Revue Company

A special place in the history of Japanese popular musical entertainment is occupied by the Takarazuka Revue Company, which for three quarters of a century has been a most successful and unique phenomenon in the Japanese performing arts world. The present average of four troupes of about one hundred performers each, all consisting of unmarried women, performing almost constantly in enormous theatres in Takarazuka (located in the Kyoto-Osaka area) and Tokyo, and on tour all over Japan, gives an idea of the scale of this enterprise.[2]

The founder, Kobayashi Ichizō (1873-1957), had started his all-girl company in 1914 with the hope that it would evolve into a uniquely Japanese form of grand opera for large, popular audiences. His efforts were always directed at providing morally unobjectionable and financially affordable theatre entertainment for the average Japanese family. A very successful industrialist who also eventually climbed the political ladder, becoming Minister of Commerce and Industry, Kobayashi was a man of many large-scale initiatives, such as creating the "Terminal Culture;" that is, commercial development of terminals with huge restaurants, department stores, and mass entertainments near the new railroad lines he had planned; he founded, moreover, Tōhō Films, of which he was the president (Kurosawa's *Seven Samurai* and the popular

271

Godzilla films were produced under his leadership). His genius for meeting the needs of the Japanese populace also guided him in changing a small, quiet town, Takarazuka, into a busy entertainment center, with a famous music school and a three-thousand-seat Grand Theatre. He eventually adapted his dream of grand opera to the reality of a more popular, extremely successful, and unique synthesis of revue/operetta/musical theatre which over the decades won an important share of popular entertainment throughout the entire country.

Kobayashi was the founder and the soul of the famous Music School—a convent-like training ground for thousands of Takarazuka performers, which became a legend among Japan's teenage girls, and is still highly respected and much in demand. He personally set the strict rules for the *seito* (students, the name all Takarazuka girls share, even after they reach stardom) and made sure they would be closely observed, thus maintaining a deserved reputation of high moral standards and thorough dedication.[3]

As a first step towards the establishment of his school, Kobayashi put together the Takarazuka Shōtakai (Takarazuka Chorus), a group of sixteen girls aged twelve to sixteen who gave their first concert in 1913. It soon became the Takarazuka Shōjo-Kageki Yōsei Kai (Girls Opera Training Society), which debuted as an entertainment for the Takarazuka spa in 1914. This naive show concocted of fairy tale operettas and dances is now considered the first official performance of the Takarazuka girls.

During the early years the girls performed rather childish adaptations of nursery tales, such as *Urashima Tarō*, and cut-and-paste stories from foreign sources, many of which were prepared by Kobayashi himself. Their success was based on the charm of innocence and inexperience, which exercised a surprisingly magnetic attraction on steadily growing audiences.

Additions of theatre professionals to the staff of the School resulted in a profound change in the training, which produced accomplished performers ready for more ambitious programs. The great successes in the Osaka-Kyoto region were extended to the capital, with performances at the Imperial Theatre in 1918.

In 1919 the Shōjo-Kageki Yōsei Kai became the Takarazuka Ongaku Kageki Gakkō (Takarazuka Music Opera School), which has served to the present time—under the simpler name of Music School—as the only training ground for girls who aspire to become stars in the Takarazuka company. In 1923 the upper age of the girls admitted to the school was changed from fifteen to nineteen, thus making possible the transition from basically childish programs to adult and professional-looking shows.

In 1924 Kobayashi built in Takarazuka the largest theatre in the Orient, the Daigekijō or Grand Theatre, seating three thousand (the previous largest theatre in Japan had been the Imperial Theatre, seating sixteen hundred). Soon the need for new programming was felt, and the writer-director Kishida Tatsuya was sent abroad for inspiration. He came back in 1927 with the idea of adapting the French revue. The first show in the new style was *Mon Paris*, a series of numbers tied together by the trip of a honeymoon couple stopping in exotic places such as India, Egypt, Shanghai and, of course, Paris. The chorus line now counted eighty girls, scenery and costumes were lavish and sparkling, and the splendidly glossy French-style revue—tamed by a typical Takarazuka sense of family style decency—conquered the fantasy and hearts of innumerable full houses. A new era for the Takarazuka *à la Parisienne* had begun.

The 1930 trip of Shirai Tetsuō to New York, London, and Paris brought to Takarazuka the latest techniques of Broadway musicals. The result was a stunning success of the revue *Parisette* which shared with enormous audiences in all major Japanese cities the lessons learnt from such masters as Maurice Chevalier, Josephine Baker, and the Ziegfield shows; however, nudity and sex were conspicuous by their absence. While never relinquishing the principles of popular family entertainment the Takarazuka company created a formula that has been the source of constant success: an eclectic composite of romantic musical comedy and revue, a mixture of western and Japanese themes and styles, with a heavy emphasis on dance, large-scale choreography with the participation of enormous chorus lines, glitter and gorgeous costumes, and all the trimmings that today are usually identified with the Las Vegas style—minus an emphasis on sex, which is carefully avoided and substituted by a subtler eroticism.

The building in 1934 of the new Tokyo Takarazuka Theatre, which was followed during the next decade by new theatres in Yokohama, Kyoto, Nagoya, Shizuoka, and Hiroshima seemed for a while to establish Takarazuka as a kind of national popular theatre of Japan, a dream shattered by the war.

Success was not limited to Japan. Pre-World War II tours abroad, both to Europe and America, were greeted with general enthusiasm except for the New York performances during a time of political tension preceding the beginning of the conflict between the two countries.[4]

The war in China and World War II saw the company entertaining the Japanese soldiers in Asia and at home with patriotic productions exalting the war effort. The company dropped the word "girls" (*shōjo*) from its name and became the Takarazuka Kageki, (literally Takarazuka Opera), a misleading but official name which is reflected in the logos including the English initials TOC, for Takarazuka Opera Company.

As soon as the war ended the Grand Theatre in Takarazuka was soon repaired; it reopened in 1946. The Takarazuka Theatre in Tokyo, on the contrary, was taken over by the occupation authorities who turned it into a G.I. entertainment center until 1955, when it reopened as the Tokyo center for Takarazuka revues.

The success of the post-war revues was immense, probably because they provided a bright moment of escape in a particularly hard time. A Takarazuka style *Carmen* had an enthusiastic reception, and was followed by a series of hits, among which those worth remembering include a spectacular *Gubijin* (The Beautiful Gu, 1951, located in imperial China) and *Genji Monogatari* (The Tale of Genji, 1952). The repertory of the Takarazuka revues shows that there is hardly any area of successful world drama, novel, opera, operetta, ballet, musical comedy, and so on which has not been adapted for the Takarazuka stage, from *Hamlet* to *Tristan and Isolde*, from *Turandot* to *The Arabian Nights*, from *Coppelia* to *The Merry Widow*, from *West Side Story* to *Carousel* and so forth, to the recent (1987) *Me and My Girl* and a version of the Dracula story.[5]

In 1958 Emperor Hirohito and the imperial family attended a Takarazuka benefit performance, and starting in the late fifties a number of foreign dignitaries, including royal personages, visited the Takarazuka shows during their stay in Japan. Coveted official recognition of the artistry reached by Takarazuka performers was achieved in 1958, when for the first time the prestigious Purple Ribbon Medal of Merit (Shijuhōshō) and the Fine Arts Festival Prize (Geijutsusaishō) were awarded to Takarazuka stars. Many other important awards were earned in the following years. Recognition came also in the form of favorable reviews by major world critics on the occasion of successful tours abroad, for example during the recent performances at Radio City Hall in New York City (1989).

Kobayashi Ichizō died in 1958. To ensure the continuity of his company after his death—despite the enormous production expenses and the relatively low cost of tickets—Kobayashi placed the fiscal responsibility for the school and the productions in the hands of the trustees of the prosperous Hankyū railway system, who always have taken good care of the Takarazuka Company's finances.

At Kobayashi's funeral over three hundred artists filled the stage of the Grand Theatre in Takarazuka, and admirers in the thousands honored the man who had pursued the dream of making theatrical entertainment available to everyone. His dream, however, reached only a section of the general population. Apart from a small percentage, the audiences of the Takarazuka revues have become almost exclusively female, the majority of whom are very young.[6] The typical Takarazuka fan has become almost a synonym for a dreamy teenage girl, infatuated with the glossy fantasy-world of an *otokoyaku* star (an actress playing male roles), and romantically sharing the ideals of the Takarazuka girls, *kiyoku, tadashiku, utsukushiku* (be pure, be right, be beautiful).

Revue, Operetta, Miscellaneous Entertainments

The great success of the Takarazuka revues did not long remain without competition.[7] Only three years after the first performance of the Takarazuka girls, the Tōkyō Shōjo Kageki (Tokyo Girls Opera, later renamed the Osaka Girls Opera, abbreviated as OSK) started its performances about six months before the Tokyo debut of the Takarazuka company. In 1928, the powerful Shōchiku organization joined the field with the Shōchiku Kageki Dan (Shōchiku Opera Company, usually abbreviated as SKD), which, until World War II, was almost as successful as the Takarazuka. It was characterized by sophisticated dances and lavishly decorated stages, with liberal use of the latest mechanical technology for special effects. After World War II, however, only Takarazuka succeeded in recapturing a wide following, while OSK and SKD reduced their activity to three or four programs a year. The SKD used to perform, until its closing in 1982, at the Kokusai Gekijō in Asakusa, catering to an audience mostly of adults of both sexes from mixed social backgrounds, very different from Takarazuka's audiences swarming with teenage girls from upper and middle class families. Since 1982 the SKD has given some performances at the Kabukiza and other Tokyo theatres; it has been, however, recently inactive because of financial problems.

The efforts of ballet master Rossi at the Imperial Theatre resulted in the production of western operettas performed by Japanese artists between 1912 and 1916. When the Opera Department was closed, Rossi tried to continue the production of operettas at a small Theatre, the Royal-kan; after two years, however, he had to give up, and went back to London.

Very successful, on the contrary, was the so-called Asakusa Opera (1919-1923), performed at up to four Asakusa theatres at the same time with programs changing every ten days. Broad concessions to popular taste produced a genre which is difficult to define, but which certainly made the arias of famous operettas and classical operas well known all over Japan.

The epoch of the Asakusa Opera was brought to a sudden end by the Tokyo earthquake of 1923, which destroyed the theatres. For a while Asakusa was dormant as a theatrical center, until a revue theatre, the Casino Folly (Kajino Fōri), opened in 1929. It introduced to Japan a popularized and magnified night club-style revue based on low comedy and the sex-appeal of scantily clad girls. The most remarkable comedian of this genre was Enoken (Enomoto Ken'ichi, 1904-1970), who became very famous, while the erotic shows found a very large following, largely because of their escapist values for depression audiences. Enoken later joined the Tōhō company and was part of the development of the Nichigeki

Dancing Team (NCT), which made the new theatre, Nihon Gekijō (usually called Nichigeki, built in 1933), famous because of the popular Nichigeki Shows, partly inspired by the presentations at the glamorous Radio City Music Hall of New York.

After World War II Enoken's effort to revive the revue were unsuccessful. For a while the large popular adult audience was preoccupied by strip shows, which developed a following disproportionate to that of any other country; at one point, they were seriously considered by Japanese theatre historians as a significant chapter in the history of the nation's popular entertainment. The major centers of such sex shows were the Teito Theatre in Shinjuku and the Nichigeki Music Hall in Yūrakuchō.

Butō *and the Phenomenon of Circularity*

Among the contemporary Japanese contributions to theatrical arts a post-modern dance genre, *butō*,[8] deserves a brief mention because of its international influence which goes beyond the field of dance. The pioneers of *butō* are Ono Kazuo, who is still (1989) active as the grand old man of *butō*, and an avant-garde dancer, Hijikata Tatsumi (who died in 1986 at 57 years of age). In the late fifties they created a new type of dance which had its roots in Hijikata's dadaistic and surrealistic experiments, and in a need to express in a subversive manner the feeling of anguish and terror experienced during the wartime destruction of Japan. There are some common characteristics in the variety of *butō* artists and companies: the intensity of training, the surrealistic and hallucinatory atmosphere of unconventional, overcontrolled, and mostly slow movements, near-naked bodies painted white, shaved heads, rolled-upwards eyes, wide-open mouths, and the presentation of several spectacular outdoor pieces, such as the one performed by the Dai Rakuda Kan company, in which the dancers are lowered by ropes from high above while expressing a slow unfolding from a fetal position.

Butō, like the achievements of Suzuki Tadashi in the formation of actors, presents an example of the phenomenon of "circularity" in present-day Japanese performing arts. Educated by western teachers who had been deeply impressed and influenced by the classical theatre arts of Japan, young Japanese artists trained in western performing arts, while at the same time "rediscovering" the treasures of their own traditions. The most creative artists went back to the sources of their Japanese training, but only *after* the western experience had left an indelible mark on them.

Some results of the new synthesis are of the highest caliber and allow the hope that, in general, the encounter between East and West may become an important factor in the improvement of the performing arts during the next century.[9]

NOTES

[1]Komiya, *Japanese Music and Drama in the Meiji Era*, 499.

[2]Berlin, *Takarazuka: A History and Descriptive Analysis of the All-Female Japanese Performance Company*, is the major source for this subject in English.

[3]*Ibid.*, Appendix 3, 327-328, provides a translation of the regulations for *seito* entering the organization.

[4]*Ibid.*, Appendix 1, 311-312, provides a list of tours abroad.

[5]*Ibid.*, Appendix 4, Table 4, 329-344, provides a list of plays based on western sources and other familiar material.

[6]*Ibid.*, Appendix 2, 313-326, provides a survey of fans and audiences.

[7]*Ibid.*, 128-129.

[8]Vicki Sanders, "Dancing and the Dark Soul of Japan: An Aesthetic Analysis of *Butō*," 148-162 and Maria Pia D'Orazi, "Kazuo Ohno: Alle radici del Butō," 121-148.

[9]Ortolani, "Il teatro occidentale alla ricerca dell'energia profonda, «rilassata e composita» dell'oriente", 192-194.

CHAPTER XII

HISTORY OF WESTERN RESEARCH ON THE JAPANESE THEATRE

From Mid-Sixteenth to Mid-Nineteenth Century

The fortuitous landing in Japan of Portuguese traders in 1542 and the beginning of missionary activity by **Saint Francis Xavier** in 1549 mark the beginning of the flow of letters, diaries and reports by merchants, missionaries and travelers which contain the first western documentation about Japanese performing arts. There we find mostly brief mentions of unspecified dances, scattered among a variety of news and descriptions of exotica. In a few cases, however, surprisingly detailed eye-witness reports also appear, about *kagura* and *furyū*, *nō* and *kyōgen*, the new church-sponsored Christian mystery plays and, in the beginning of the seventeenth century, *kabuki* and *jōruri*. The available sources for the period between the middle of the sixteenth century and the closing of Japan at the beginning of the seventeenth include several published and unpublished collections of letters such as the *Cartas que os Padres e Irmãos da Companhia de Iesus escreverão dos Reinos de Iapão (1598)*; works by historians such as the Jesuit **Luis Frois** (*Historia de Iapam, 1549-78*); official reports such as the *Relación del Reino de Nippon* by the Spanish merchant **Bernardino de Avila Girón**; and diaries such as *The Diary of Richard Cocks, Cape-Merchant in the English Factory in Japan 1613-23*.

The fierce persecutions of Christianity in the first two decades of the seventeenth century and the ensuing almost total official closing of Japan to foreign visitors marked the end of the predominantly Spanish and Portuguese sources. Descriptions by western eye-witnesses of the now blossoming *kabuki, jōruri* and other performances became restricted to writings by merchants belonging to, or occasional travelers associated with, the Dutch trading post on the island of Dejima near Nagasaki—the only official remnant of western presence in Japan. Once a year, when the renewal of the Dutch trading privileges was due, a Dutch delegation, with an occasional guest traveler, had the (for westerners of the time) unique chance of witnessing theatre performances in Edo, Osaka and Kyoto on the way to the court of the Shogun. The most important witnesses of this period are **Engelbertus Kämpfer** (1651-1716), **Carl Peter Thunberg** (1743-1828) and **Philipp Franz von Siebold**. Kämpfer, the German physician who spent two years (1660-62) with the Dutch colony and succeeded in visiting Edo and being received by the Shogun Tsunayoshi, eventually wrote a *Geschichte und Beschreibung von Japan* (two volumes, 1677-79) in which he testifies to the variety and daily occurrence of theatrical performances in Edo. The Swedish botanist Thunberg, author of a diary about his one-year stay in Japan (like Kämpfer as physician of the Dutch colony), in his *Voyages de C.P. Thunberg au Japon....(1796)* left some descriptions of theatre buildings, costumes, plays and acting conventions. His few critical remarks, however, reveal a condescending attitude and little understanding of the dramatic contents.

Only at the beginning of the nineteenth century, when also the first detailed descriptions by Japanese authors about *kabuki* start to appear, we find more accurate reports of the performances in the writings of a westerner, the German scientist von Siebold. Siebold can be considered as the "discoverer" of the value of Japanese theatrical arts and of the greatness of its performers. Also a physician to the Dutch colony, Siebold resided in Japan for several years and developed a much deeper understanding and a sincere appreciation of Japanese culture. In his important *Archiv zur Beschreibung von Japan und dessen Neben- und Schutzländern* (1832-58) he expresses his genuine admiration for the great artistry of the *kabuki* performers in their various roles, and is the first to recognize that such skill would command the applause even of a sophisticated European audience. Siebold was intrigued by the art of the *onnagata*, by the richness of the costumes, and even attempted a comparison between the chorus of ancient Greece and the *gidayū*-narrator of the *jōruri*.

The available partial studies about the western reports on Japanese performing arts before the reopening of Japan in mid-nineteenth century agree in concluding that—in general and with very few exceptions as in the case of Siebold—the occasional critical remarks by westerners of this time share a lack of serious interest beyond the curiosity for exotic novelties. They show neither real understanding for the drama nor appreciation for the stylized acting conventions, nor an effort to systematize and distinguish the various types of theatrical traditions then alive in Japan. It appears also evident that the actual witnessing of theatrical events happened casually and that, during the period of seclusion under the Tokugawa regime, high quality performances were *de facto* accessible only to the very few foreigners who visited, just for a few days and in most cases only once in their lifetime, the three major centers of theatrical activity, Edo, Osaka and Kyoto.

From the Mid-Nineteenth Century to Shōwa

The trade delegations which visited Japan right after the opening of the country in the mid-nineteenth century did not have access to the major theatres of Edo because of the unrest caused by the still unsettled political conditions in the capital. They left no substantial descriptions or critical remarks about the performances in Yokohama which were accessible to them.

Within the following twenty years, two diplomatic representatives from European countries wrote well-informed, eye-witness accounts about Japanese performances. The first British ambassador to Japan, Lord **Rutherford Alcock**, in his *The Capital of the Tycoon: A Narrative of a Three Years Residence in Japan* (two volumes, 1863), accompanied his descriptions of *kabuki* with some critical remarks—not concealing his victorian moralistic disapproval of extravagant excesses in erotic and violent *kabuki* scenes. To the Swiss ambassador **Aimé Humbert**, however, who resided in Japan for ten months in 1863 and published his *Japon illustré* in 1870, goes the merit of pioneering, even ahead of his Japanese contemporaries, the process of critical recognition of basic facts about *kabuki*. He acknowledged that, although the literary value of *kabuki* plays is generally weak, the performance has the hability to create a powerful poetic atmosphere and the actors succeed in expressing deep human passions. He also noticed the absence in Japan of strictly historical plays in the fashion of the European tradition. He was the first to remark that *kabuki* is the theatre of the middle class and not of the nobility, and that the lavishly expensive *kabuki* productions in theatres comparable in size to the big European opera houses are not dependent, as in Europe, on state subsidies, but are financially self-supporting. He also predicted great changes in the theatrical world of Japan in connection with the rapid general process of modernization, and expressed the wish that Japanese plays be translated so that the deepest essence of the Japanese soul might be understood by westerners.

Humbert's wish began slowly to become a reality in the last decades of the century, during which a number of (often partial) translations, adaptations and paraphrases of *nō*, *kyōgen*, *kabuki* and *jōruri* plays appeared in German, French, English, Italian, and other European languages. Pioneers in this process were **A. Pfizmaier** (*Ueber den Text eines japanischen Dramas*, 1870), **Frederick Victor Dickins**, (*A Japanese Romance, Chiuschingura, or the Loyal League*, 1876), **Basil Hall Chamberlain** (*The Classical Poetry of the Japanese*, 1880), **F. A. von Langegg**, (*Vassallentreue Chiu-shin-gura-no-bu*, 1880), **L. De Rosny** (*Le couvent du Dragon vert. Une comédie Japonaise*, 1893).

At the beginning of our century **Karl Florenz**, in his pivotal *Geschichte der japanischen Litteratur* (2 volumes, 1905) presented *nō*, *kyōgen*, *jōruri* and *kabuki* in the context of Japanese literary culture. Florenz did not show much appreciation for the literary or other value of the Japanese plays in general. On the other hand Chamberlain wrote in his classic *Things Japanese* (1905) some of the most insightful remarks about the difficulty of properly translating the drama of Japan, the literary beauty of the *nō*, and the importance of *kabuki* as a symbol of the bourgeois culture of the Tokugawa period.

The work of translation during the rest of the Meiji (1868-1912) and Taishō (1912-1925) periods reached a high degree of sophistication. The most important contribution to

the study of the *nō* in this period might well be the work of
Noël Peri, whose excellent translations and critical remarks,
first published starting from 1909 in the *Bulletin de l'École
Française d'Extrème Orient*, were put together twenty years
after his death in a volume which became a classic (*Le Nō*,
1944).

In English, after the "Translations from the No" by **George
Sansom**, in *Transactions of the Asiatic Society of Japan*, (1911)
and *Plays of Old Japan: The Nō together with Translations of
the Dramas* (1913), by **M. Stopes** and **J. Sakurai**, two works
have had a lasting influence in introducing generations of
westeners to the *nō*: *Noh, or Accomplishment, a Study of the
Classical Stage of Japan* (1916), by **Ezra Pound** and **Ernest
Francisco Fenollosa** and *The Nō Plays of Japan* (1921), by
Arthur Waley. In the early twenties translations of *shingeki*
plays began to appear, which made it possible for the West to
become acquainted with some of the most successful new
westernized drama. Important among them are translations by
Glenn Shaw, *Kurata Hyakuzō, The Priest and his Disciples*
(1922), *Kikuchi Kan, Tōjūrō's Love and Four other Plays*
(1925) and, later, *Yamamoto Yūzō, Three Plays* (1935).

The Shōwa Period to the End of World War II

The first two decades of the Shōwa period (beginning in
1925) saw the development of a number of serious studies
dedicated to the various forms of Japanese performing arts,
although the vast majority of publications still continued to be
occasional writings of little consequence. Fundamental for the
study of *kabuki* in general was the pioneer work of **Zoë
Kinkaid**, *Kabuki, the Popular Stage of Japan* (1925). Important
general introductions were *Le Théâtre Japonais* by **Albert
Maybon** (1925), *An Outline History of the Japanese Drama* by
Frank Allison Lombard (1928) and *Japanisches Theater* edited
by **Curt Glaser** (1930). Lombard was the first to begin the
history of the Japanese theatre with an extensive treatment of
kagura. **Friedrich Perzynski** began the important task of
exploring in depth specific areas within genres with his two

volumes about masks: *Japanische Masken, No und Kyogen* (1925), while **Wilhelm Gundert** began the studies of specific themes within a genre with his *Der Shintoismus im japanischen Nō Drama* (1925).

It is important to remember that most of the studies above mentioned are primarily concerned with the drama rather than with the performance element of the theatrical art, and are written by scholars accustomed to considering theatre as literature, or by authors extensively evaluating the theatre because of its importance for philosophical or sociological insights. It is out of such interests that several scholars and artists, especially poets and novelists such as **Paul Claudel** and **Pierre Loti** wrote, and France's leading Japan scholar **Serge Elisséeff** co-authored with **A. Jacovleff** the beautifully illustrated *Le Théâtre Japonais: Kabuki*, (1933).

In the years which preceded World War II and during the conflict, western publications about Japanese theatre continued at a moderate pace, producing still more translations and studies, among which the following should be mentioned: *Le Théâtre comique des Japonais* by **André Beaujard** (1937), an introduction to the study of *kyōgen*; the several translations and specialized articles published in the journal *Monumenta Nipponica* and by the Deutsche Gesellschaft für Natur und Völkerkunde Ostasiens in Tokyo; and the studies in Italian by **Corrado Pavolini** (*Teatro giapponese classico*, 1941) and **Enrico Fulchignoni** (*Teatro giapponese: Sette Nō*, 1942).

Following World War II

The research activity on the Japanese theatre by westerners increased substantially after World War II, when several American scholars joined the European experts, and Japanese studies became more and more institutionalized in universities around the world. Also, the number of periodicals publishing scholarly research on Japanese performing arts increased. Prestigious journals dedicated to Oriental studies such as *The Journal of Asian Studies*, the *Harvard Journal of Asiatic Studies*, and the *Journal of the American Oriental Society* were added to *Monumenta Nipponica*, the *Bulletin de la Maison Franco-Japonaise*, the *Bulletin de l'École Française d'Extrème Orient*, the *Nachrichten aus der Deutschen*

Gesellschaft für Natur und Völkerkunde Ostasiens in the important function of occasionally publishing serious studies on the Japanese theatre. Moreover, the major journals dedicated to theatre research in several languages began to publish articles about the Japanese theatre, and even to dedicate entire issues to it, as in the case of *Maske und Kothurn* (1961, Heft 1 and 1981, Heft 1) and the 1984 annual issue of the *Mime Journal* dedicated to *Nō/Kyōgen Masks and Performance*. The first periodical entirely dedicated to oriental performing arts, the *Asian Theatre Journal*, has become since 1984 the natural forum for the increasing research on the topic. An increasing number of dissertations—often later published in book form—have been steadily enriching the research with more specific explorations into aspects of the theatrical phenomenon in Japan.

It is not the purpose of this survey to mention all the western scholars who have contributed to our knowledge of the field since the new fervor for Japanese studies developed after World War II. Only those contributions will be briefly described which appear to have left a major mark, or to have a special meaning in the effort of research.

An Italian translation of the *Chūshingura*, which remains standard for that language, was published by **Mario Marega** (*Il Ciuscingura: La vendetta dei 47 Rōnin*, 1948). Also in Italian, the volume by **Marcello Muccioli**, *Il Teatro giapponese* (1962), remains to date one of the most complete presentations of the whole spectrum of the Japanese theatre. In French, **Gaston Renondeau** brought to the attention of scholars the importance of a variety of forms of Buddhism in *nō* (*Le Bouddhisme dans le Nō*, 1950; he also published the more comprehensive *Le Nō*, 1954). In German, **Hermann Bohner** collected a vast amount of information about the *nō* in general, and the individual plays, which still remains unmatched in western languages (*Gestalten und Quellen des Nō*, 1955; *Nō: Die einzelnen Nō*, 1956; *Nō: Einführung*, 1959). Bohner also began the important work of translating into German Zeami's secret tradition of the *nō*, publishing between 1943 and 1961 four volumes of translations of Zeami's major treatises. The enterprise of making Zeami's treatises available in English had been pioneered by **Wilfrid Whitehouse**, who, in collaboration with **Shidehara Michitarō**, prepared in 1941, under the title "Seami Jūroku Bushū: Seami's Sixteen Treatises," a translation of the *Kadensho*. A further important contribution to the translation and interpretation of Zeami's work was published by **Oscar Benl** (*Seami Motokiyo und der Geist des Nō-Schauspiels*, 1952) who made available in German the *Kadensho* and the *Kyūi-shidai*. Benl also, in collaboration with **Horst Hammitzsch**, provided a study important for the understanding of the spiritual background of the Japanese plays (*Japanische Geisteswelt: Vom Mythos zur Gegenwart*, 1956) and continued the translation of Zeami's work in his *Die geheime Überlieferung des Nō* (1961). Hammitzsch edited the *Japan Handbuch* (1981) with many updated articles by specialists on genres and aspects of the Japanese theatre. In English, **Richard McKinnon** published a summary of his dissertation on Zeami's theories, "Zeami on the Art of Training" (1953) which was influential in the interpretation of Zeami's thinking. In French, **René Sieffert** provided a scholarly and almost complete translation of Zeami's treatises with commentary (*La Tradition secrète du nō*, 1960).

In the fifties three publications by American authors became widely used as textbooks for courses including *kabuki*: *Japanese Theatre* (1952) by **Faubion Bowers**, *The Kabuki Theatre of Japan* (1955) by **Adolphe Clarence Scott** and *The Kabuki Theatre* (1956) by **Earl Ernst**. While Bowers' book filled the need for a smoothly written and easy-to-read introduction, Ernst's work has remained as probably the best conceived and most reliable book-length account of *kabuki* as a theatrical art. Also in the fifties **Donald Shively** began his translations and scholarly contributions to the study of special aspects of Japanese theatre and its socio-political implications (*The Love Suicide at Amijima: A Study of a Japanese Domestic Tragedy*, 1953; the articles "Chikamatsu's Satire on the Dog Shogun" and "Bakufu versus Kabuki" both 1955; "The Social Environment of Tokugawa Kabuki" 1978; and "Tokugawa plays on Forbidden Topics," 1982).

To **Donald Keene** goes the merit of translating Chikamatsu's masterpieces (*Major Plays of Chikamatsu*, 1961); providing splendidly illustrated introductions to the puppets and to the *nō* (*Bunraku: The Art of the Japanese Puppet Theatre*, 1965 and *Nō: The Classical Theatre of Japan*, 1966); editing a collection of translations of *nō* plays (*20 Plays of the Nō Theatre*, 1970); and in general providing a solid literary context for the understanding of both the drama and the theory of the major Japanese forms of classical theatre within his fundamental works on Japanese literature (e.g. *World within Walls*, 1976).

P. G. O'Neill started the process of inquiry by western scholars into the formation of the *nō* with his *Early Nō Drama*, (1958), and "The Social and Economic Background of Nō," (1981). This process was continued by **Hagen Blau** (*Sarugaku und Shushi*, Wiesbaden 1966) and **Benito Ortolani** ("Le Origini del teatro Nō," 1973; "Shamanism in the Origins of the *Nō* Theatre," 1984). Blau investigated the history of popular performing arts before the beginning of *nō*, especially during the Heian period (794-1185) and brought to the attention of western scholars the probable function of the *shushi* in the formation of the chain of performers that eventually gave birth to the *nō*. Ortolani studied the various theories on the birth of the *nō* and the function of shamanism in the process; brought to the attention of the West the importance of Zenchiku as a theoretician of the *nō* ("Komparu Zenchiku und die Metaphysik der Nō-Schauspielkunst," 1964; *Zenchiku's Aesthetics of the Nō Theatre*, 1976; "Spirituality for the Dancer-Actor in Zeami's and Zenchiku's Writings on the *Nō*," 1983); explored the beginnings of *kabuki* (*Das Kabukitheater: Kulturgeschichte der Anfänge*, 1964) and the phenomenon of *shingeki* ("Shingeki: The Maturing New Drama of Japan," 1963; and "Fukuda Tsuneari: Modernization and Shingeki," 1971).

Research on the origins of the puppet theatre and the early *jōruri* drama was published by **Charles J. Dunn** (*The Early Japanese Puppet Drama*, 1966), who also translated primary sources for the study of the early *kabuki* actors, *The Actor's Analects*, edited with Torigoe Bunzō (1969). **Peter Kleinschmidt** provided a thorough analysis of the *gigaku* masks (*Die Masken der Gigaku, der Ältesten Theaterform Japans*, 1966).

In the field of research on music as an essential element of most forms of Japanese theatre the publications of **Hans Eckardt, Eta Harich-Schneider,** and **William P. Malm** are fundamental. Eckardt explored the sources of *gagaku* music and *bugaku* performances in his *Das Kokonchomonshū des Tachibana Narisue als Musikgeschichtliche Quelle* (1956), and in his "Konron: Reste kontinentaler Mythologie in der japanischen Bugaku" (1960). Harich-Schneider published a series of scholarly articles mostly related to court music, and summarized the results of her life-long research in two important books, *The Rhythmical Patterns in Gagaku and Bugaku* (1954) and the comprehensive *A History of Japanese Music* (1973). Malm provided several publications about theatrical music, of which the most important are his two books, *Japanese Music and Musical Instruments* (1959) and *Nagauta, the Heart of Kabuki Music* (1963); he also authored "Music in the Kabuki Theatre" (1978); and "A Musical Approach to Jōruri" (1982). Recently **Andrew C. Gerstle** (*Circles of Fantasy: Conventions in the Plays of Chikamatsu*, 1986) indicated the necessity of considering the musical patterns as an essential element in the very foundation of the dramatic structure of Chikamatsu's masterpieces, as well as in all *jōruri* and *kabuki* plays.

Literary analysis of *nō* plays was developed in such works as *Ono no Komachi: Gestalt und Legende im Nō Spiel* (1960) by **Peter Weber-Schäfer**, *The Legend of Semimaru, Blind Musician of Japan* (1978), by **Susan Matisoff**, and her two articles "*Kintōsho*: Zeami's Song of Exile" and "Images of Exile and Pilgrimage: Zeami's *Kintōsho* (both 1979);" the recent *Zeami's Style: The Noh Plays of Zeami Motokiyo* (1986) by **Thomas B. Hare**; *The Artistry of Aeschylus and Zeami: A Comparative Study of Greek Tragedy and Nō*, by **Mae J. Smethurst** (1989); *Noh Drama and The Tale of Genji* (1991), a study and translation of fifteen *nō* plays related to the *Genji monogatari* by **Janet Goff**. Weber-Schäfer also translated into German numerous *nō* plays (*Vierundzwanzig Nō-Spiele*, 1961).

The availability in English of Zeami's texts on the secret tradition of the *nō* greatly improved because of the translations by **Mark Nearman**, which appeared with scholarly commentary starting from 1978, and also because of the work of **Thomas Rimer** who published in collaboration with Yamazaki Masakazu the most complete English translation of Zeami's theoretical writings to date: *On the Art of the Nō Drama: The Major Treatises of Zeami* (1984). Rimer also introduced to the west the key personality of the *shingeki* theatre of the twenties, the playwright Kishida Kunio (*Toward a Modern Japanese Theatre: Kishida Kunio*, 1974), and two plays of the contemporary *shingeki* playwright Yamazaki Masakazu (*Mask and Sword*, 1980). Zenchiku's main treatises were translated with erudite introduction and commentary by **Arthur H. Thornhill III** in *Six Circles, One Dewdrop: The Religio-Aesthetic World of Komparu Zenchiku* (1993).

James Brandon in his *Kabuki: Five Classic Plays* (1975) introduced a system of description of the action on the stage which attempts to visualize the *kabuki* conventions for the western reader. Brandon also published essays on *kabuki* ("Form in Kabuki Acting" 1978, and "The Theft of *Chūshingura*: or the Great Kabuki Caper," 1982); he is the editor of the *Asian Theatre Journal* which since 1984 regularly publishes studies on the theatre of Japan. **Samuel Leiter** has pioneered the difficult task of translating and adapting for the use of western students important theatrical reference works (*Kabuki Encyclopedia: An English-Language Adaptation of Kabuki Jiten*, 1979). Leiter is also the author of a number of articles about *kabuki* and of the book *The Art of Kabuki: Famous Plays in Performance* (1979), which all stress the performance approach in the description of actors and *kabuki* stage conventions. A similar approach is followed by the articles on *kabuki* by **Leonard Pronko**, who is also the author of *Theater East and West: Perspectives toward a Total Theater* (1967)—an early discussion of the problem of intercultural exchanges in the field of drama and theatre. The colorful world of *kabuki* costumes was studied by **Ruth Shaver** (*Kabuki Costume*, 1966). A new German translation with introduction and commentary on the classic *Yoshitsune senbonzakura* was published by **Eduard Klopfenstein** (*Tausend Kirschbäume- Yoshitsune: Ein klassisches Stück des japanischen Theaters der Edo-Zeit*, 1982).

Thomas Immoos introduced the study of early influences of Japanese themes on western Baroque theatre ("Japanese Themes in Swiss Baroque Drama" 1963; "Japanische Helden des europäischen Barocktheaters" 1981). Immoos has also studied the origins of the Japanese theatre, and summarized his ideas on the importance of the religious/magic element in "The Birth of the Japanese Theatre" (1969) and in his illustrated book, *Japanisches Theater* (1975). The study of the folk beliefs influencing the birth and development of Japanese theatre arts was also pursued by **Frank Hoff** and **Jacob Raz**. Hoff translated important documents by the Japanese authority on *kagura*, Honda Yasuji. He published a study on the subject, *Song, Dance, Storytelling: Aspects of the Performing Arts in*

Japan (1978), and in collaboration with Willi Flindt he also translated Yokomichi Mario's analysis of the structure of *nō*, *The Life Structure of Noh* (1973). Raz published the article "Chinkon—From Folk Beliefs to Stage Conventions" (1981), and *Audience and Actors: A Study of Their Interaction in the Japanese Traditional Theatre* (1983).

A detailed analysis of the movements in the performance of the *nō* was published by **Monica Bethe** and **Karen Brazell** (*Dance in the Nō Theater*, in three volumes, 1982). **Günter Zobel** studied the staging, dramaturgy, and etnological background of the *nō* in his *Nō Theater: Szene und Dramaturgie, volk- und völkerkundliche Hintergründe* (1987). **Don Kenny** published *A Guide to Kyogen* (1968) which provides convenient outlines of the plays in the current repertory, as well as a recent (1989) translation of thirty plays, *The Kyogen Book*.

The field of the sources left by the missionaries and other early visitors to Japan, especially about church sponsored theatrical activities, was researched by **Thomas Leims** (*Die Entstehung des Kabuki: Transkulturation Europa-Japan in 16. und 17. Jahrhundert*, 1990). Important additions to the translations of *bunraku* plays were provided by **Stanleigh Jones** with his "Miracle at Yaguchi Ferry: A Japanese Puppet play and its Metamorphosis to Kabuki" (1978) and *Sugawara and the Secrets of Calligraphy* (1984). The backstage life of *bunraku* was described by **Lydia Brüll** in "Die Bewegungstechnik der Figuren im japanischen Puppentheater" (1962) and by **Barbara Adachi** in the book *The Voices and Hands of Bunraku* (1978); **Julianne K. Boyd** wrote a dissertation on the managerial aspects of recent *bunraku* (*The Bunraku Puppet Theatre since 1945 to 1964: Changes in Administration and Organization*, 1986). **Johannes Barth** described performance aspects of the Japanese theatre in *Japans Schaukunst im Wandel der Zeiten* (1972).

Information about recent developments within *shingeki* and the *angura* movement was made available by **Manfred Hubricht** (*Shuji Terayama: Theater contra Ideologie*, 1971); **Carol Jay Sorgenfrei** (*Shuji Terayama: Avant Garde Dramatist of Japan*, 1978); **David G. Goodman** ("The Post-Shingeki Theatre Movement in Japan," 1986, and *Japanese Drama and*

Culture in the 1960s: The Return of the Gods, 1989); **Robert T. Rolf and John K. Gillepsie** (*Alternative Japanese Drama: Ten Plays*, 1992).

Japanese Contributions to Western Languages

An overview of research about Japanese performing arts in western languages would not be complete without mentioning contributions by Japanese authors—some of them also second generation Japanese, naturalized or living outside Japan. As is the case with many western publications, a great majority of the titles by Japanese authors do not deal with scholarly research, but rather present introductory materials for the use of foreign non-specialists—often prepared for occasional performances or exhibitions, or simply as guides for visitors to Japan, by such organizations as the Japan Travel Bureau or the Kokusai Bunka Shinkokai. To this category belong a number of translations/adaptations of plays. Although very little original research was published by Japanese scholars in western languages, their contribution fulfilled as a whole the important function of making available basic materials to non-Japanese-reading students, and presenting the points of view and the conclusions of Japanese scholarship on a number of questions related to their interpretation.

This process began in the last decade of the nineteenth century. **Inouye Jukichi** published a partial translation of *Chushingura or the Loyal Retainers of Akao* (1894; Inouye later completed this partial translation and published it under the title *Chushingura, or the Treasury of Loyal Retainers*, 1917). In the periodical *The Far East*, between 1896 and 1898, a series of short articles/translations was published among which are those by **G. Fukuchi** ("The Rise and the Progress of the Japanese Drama", four short articles in 1894) and **T. Owada** ("The Noh Performance," in two short installments in 1898). In French, **G. Yoshida** translated *Le cerisier de Soma; Théâtre japonais, drame en cinq actes et six tableaux* (1898). At the beginning of the 20th century **T. Kitasato** translated into German the popular *Sakura Giminden* by Segawa Jokō III (*Sakura Sogo, Drama aus der japanischen Geschichte in 5 Akten*, 1901); and **N. Okamoto** translated *Tsubosakadera, oder die wunderbare Gnade der Göttin Kwannon,* *ein monodisches Drama* (1903). Remarkable are the translations by **Noguchi Yone** (*Ten Kyogen in English*, 1907; *Twelve Kyogen*, 1911; *Ten Japanese Noh Plays*, 1920); and by **Miyamori Asatarō** (*Tales from Old Japanese Dramas*, 1915 and *Masterpieces of Chikamatsu, the Japanese Shakespeare*, 1926). A French translation of the *Chūshingura* was published by **Shinobu Jumpei** (*Tchūshingoura ou le trésor des vassaux fidèles, d'après la représentation théâtrale*, 1918). The *nō* scholar **Nogami Toyoichirō** began his publications in English in the early twenties with a short essay in *The Japan Magazine*, "Some Observations on the Noh Drama,"(12, 1921/22); in the 30's, he published *Japanese Noh plays, How to See Them* (1934), *Masks of Japan: the Gigaku, Bugaku, and Noh Masks*, (1935), *Noh Masks: Classification and Explanation* (1938); later he published in Italian *Il dramma Noh* (1940), and again in English *The Noh and Greek Tragedy* (1940), and *Zeami and His Theories of Noh* (1955). **T. Miyajima** wrote a *Contribution à l'étude du théâtre de poupées* (1928). The *kabuki* historian **Kawatake Shigetoshi** provided a number of publications in English centered on the history of *kabuki* (*Development of the Japanese Theatre Arts*, 1936; *An Illustrated History of Japanese Theatre Arts*, 1956; *Kabuki, Japanese Drama*, 1958); in German he published "Kabuki und Bunraku," (1964). **Sugino Masayoshi** gave an account of the origins of the Japanese theatre in "Die Anfänge des japanischen Theaters bis zum Nospiel"(1940). In the 50's **K. Kitayama** published *Noh Masks Treasured in the Kanze Family* (1954). The *nō* scholar **Toki Zemmaro** prepared an introduction to the *nō* for foreigners, *Japanese Noh Plays* (1954). In the same spirit of providing a scholarly introduction to the *nō* a group of Japanese specialists produced three volumes of translations with accurate commentary and introductions, and small sketches which make it easier to understand the basic position of the *shite* during the performance of the thirty selected *nō* plays (*Japanese Noh Drama: Ten Plays Selected and Translated from the Japanese*, 1955/59/60). A collection of essays on *kabuki* by well known Japanese theatre authors was translated into English by **F. Takano** (*Kabuki*, by Y. **Hamamura, T. Sugawara, J. Kinoshita, and H. Minami**, 1955). An important source of information on drama in the Meiji period, which remains to date a valuable source in English for such items as *shimpa* and beginning *shingeki* is a book edited by **Komiya Toyotaka**, *Japanese Music and Drama in the Meiji Era*, translated and adapted by Donald Keene and Edward Seidensticker, 156). **Saito Seijirō**, *et al.* edited a book on the *bunraku* puppets (*Masterpieces of Japanese Puppetry: Sculptured Heads of the Bunraku Theater*, 1958); **Sakanishi Shio** published translations of numerous *kyōgen* (*Kyogen: Comic Interludes of Japan*, 1958). In the sixties **Tsubouchi Shōyō** and **Yamamoto Jirō** published a *History and Characteristics of Kabuki, the Japanese Classic Drama* (1960). The scholar of Japanese literature **Hisamatsu Sen'ichi** published a concise introduction to the main concepts of Japanese literary aesthetics which are basic for the understanding of dramatic literature (*The Vocabulary of Japanese Literary Aesthetics*, 1963). **H. Ishibashi** contributed a comparative study of *Yeats and the Noh: Types of Japanese Beauty and their Reflection in Yeats' Plays* (1966). **Hironaga Shuzaburō** published a convenient guide to Bunraku (*Bunraku: Japan's Unique Puppet Theatre*, 1964).

In German, two general introductions to *kabuki* were published by **Senzoku Takayasu** (*Kabuki, das Theater des altjapanischen Bürgertums*, 1964) and **Miyake Shutarō** (*Kabuki, Japanisches Theater*, 1965).

In French, **Nomura Mansaku** published *Kyōgen no michi. La voie du Kyogen* (1968) and **Nonomura Kaizō** authored *Théâtre de noh hier et aujourd'hui* (1968).

The *kabuki* scholar **Gunji Masakatsu** provided the text for the beautifully illustrated *Kabuki* (1969, new edition 1986) and for the volume *Buyō: The Classical Dance* (1970) in the series Performing Arts of Japan. In the same series **Nakamura Yasuo** wrote *Noh: The Classical Theater* (1971), **Tōgi Masatarō** wrote *Gagaku: Court Music and Dance* (1971), **Toita Yasuji** wrote *Kabuki: The Popular Theatre* (1970), and **Andō Tsuruo** wrote *Bunraku: The Puppet Theatre* (1970)—all reliable introductions to the main performing arts of Japan, with beautiful illustrations and a perspective on the present state of those arts.

In the early seventies the journal *Concerned Theatre Japan* published a number of articles by leading Japanese performing artists and critics, such as **Kanze Hideo** and **Satoh Makoto**, on the classical performing arts and the experimentations of the Japanese avant-garde.

The theatre historian **Inoura Yoshinobu** prepared in English an abridged version of his Japanese opus, *A History of Japanese Theatre I: Noh and Kyogen* (1971) which remains to date an important source of information for the history of the Japanese theatre previous to *kabuki*. Volume II of that history was written by **Kawatake Toshio** (*A History of Japanese Theatre II: Bunraku and Kabuki*, 1971: Vol. I and II are now available as one book). Kawatake Toshio also authored, in collaboration with Benito Ortolani, the special issue of *Maske und Kothurn* dedicated to the Japanese theatre (7/1961), and a number of introductory and comparative writings mostly related to *kabuki*. **Tamba Akira** published the only book which is totally dedicated to the music of the *nō* theatre (*La Structure musicale du Nō*, 1974). **Iwabuchi Tatsuji** published a number of articles primarily on *shingeki*, and **Nakamura Tetsurō** introduced the results of his research on the history of the western discovery of *kabuki* in "Die Entdeckung des Kabuki durch den Westen" (1981). Several materials on *nō* architecture and music were made available through the book *The Noh Theater: Principles and Perspectives* (1983) by **Komparu Kunio**, a professional *taiko* player turned architectural critic.

Important scholarly contributions by authors who are either Japanese or of Japanese origin but residing abroad are the research by **James Araki** (*The Ballad Drama of Medieval Japan*, 1964); the essays on Zeami, Toraaki and Chikamatsu by **Ueda Makoto** (*Literary and Art Theories in Japan*, 1967); the doctoral dissertation by **Frank T. Motofuji** (*A Study of Narukami, an Eighteenth Century Kabuki Play*, 1964) and his translation of a *kabuki* play by Kawatake Mokuami (*The Love of Izayoi and Seishin*, 1966); the analysis by **Kenneth Yasuda** of *nō* plays (*Masterworks of the Nō Theater*, 1989); the first anthology of contemporary drama including five representative *shingeki* plays, translated and introduced by **Ted T. Takaya**, *Japanese Drama: An Anthology*, 1979); and the study on the origins of *kabuki* as rooted in folk religion by **Akemi Horie Webber** (*The Essence of Kabuki: A Study of Folk Religious Ritual Elements in the Early Kabuki Theatre*, 1982). A Korean scholar teaching in Vienna, **Lee Sang-Kyong**, published in German a study of the relationship between *nō* and European theatre (*Nō und europäisches Theater*, 1983).

An overview of the Japanese theatrical events of the year is provided by the *Theatre Year-Book*, an annual volume published in English by the International Theatre Institute, Japan Center. Recently (1989) the Japan Foundation has made available the publication *Theater Japan 1989. A Companion to the Japanese Theater: Companies and People* (edited by **Tsuboike Eiko**) which offers updated basic information about a great number of theatre groups, individuals, facilities, and production organizations active at the end of the Shōwa era.

GLOSSARY

Amaterasu 天照 Also: Ama-terasu-ō-mi-kami, or "Heaven-Illuminating Great Deity." The sun goddess, venerated as the main Shinto *kami*, progenitor of the Japanese people.

Angura アングラ The Japanese underground theatre movement (1960-1985). It was partly inspired, in its efforts of developing a counterculture, by the off-off Broadway theatres and the happenings in New York.

Aragoto 荒事 In *kabuki*, the style of the oversize, supernatural, rough hero, especially loved in the Edo area, as opposed to *wagoto*, the gentle style beloved in the Kyoto-Osaka area.

Ashikaga 足利 Family name of several Shogun who played an important role in the history of the *nō* during the Ashikaga period (1392-1568).

Asobi 遊 Entertainment. Sometimes used for *kamiasobi*, entertainment for the gods.

Asobi-be 遊部 At the time of the beginning of the *nō*, a group of outcastes who specialized in funeral rites.

Asura nō 阿修羅 能 Also called *shura mono*, from the name of the Buddhist underworld, where warriors killed in battle were believed to wander without peace. In *asura nō* the *shite* usually performs the role of the ghost of a famous *samurai*.

Ato-za 後座 The rear-stage, where the *nō* musicians sit.

Ba 場 In the structure of a *nō* play, it corresponds to a western act. Most *nō* are in two *ba*, the first act being called *mae-ba*, and the second *nochi-ba*.

Bakufu 幕府 Shogunal government.

Bangaku 番楽   A name used generically for *yamabushi kagura*, or *kagura* of the *shishi* tradition.

Bangakumai 番楽舞 A group of about thirty warrior pieces in the repertory of the *yamabushi kagura*.

Biwa 琵琶   Japanese term for the Chinese *p'i-p'a*, a pear-shaped lute. The *biwa* was imported during the eighth century and became a very popular instrument, until it was largely replaced by the *shamisen* at the end of the sixteenth century.

Bodhisattva (In Japanese, *Bosatsu* 菩薩   ) A Buddhist holy savior, who was believed to help the faithful to reach salvation.

Bon-matsuri 盆祭   The summer festival of the dead; the lantern festival.

Bon-odori 盆踊   Popular dance performed by the participants in the *bon-matsuri*.

Bugaku 舞楽   Literally "dance-music" or "dance-entertainment." One of the major genres of Japanese theatre, introduced from China in the eighth century A.D. and still performed in a substantially unchanged form. The term is the Japanese reading of the Chinese characters for the "correct and elegant" music of the court, pronounced *ya-yüe*.

Bunraku 文楽   Popular name for the puppet theatre, derived from the famous puppeteer Uemura Burakuken. Since the late eighteenth century, this name has replaced in the common use the older term *jōruri*.

Bunraku Kyōkai 文楽 協会   The Bunraku Association, founded in 1963.

Butō 舞踏   Post-modern dance genre, with roots in dadaistic and surrealistic experiments, born to express in a subversive way the feelings of anguish and terror experienced during the wartime destruction of Japan.

Buyō 舞踊　　　　　Dance. Used often as *kabuki buyō* with the meaning of traditional *kabuki* dance.

Buyō geki 舞踊 劇　In *kabuki*, plays featuring primarily dance, with accompaniment of *jōruri* music.

Chidō 治道　　　　The leader of the procession at the beginning of a *gigaku* performance.

Chinkon 鎮魂　　　Repose of souls; soul appeasing.

Chinkonsai 鎮魂祭　A service for the repose of the departed souls; soul-appeasing ceremony.

Chinkonsha 鎮魂者　　　A professional performer of rites for the repose of deceased souls.

Dadaiko 大太鼓　　Large *gagaku* drum.

Daihon 台本　　　In *bunraku*, the textbooks used professionally by the chanters.

Daikagura 太神楽　Street performances of a lion dance and jugglery; also a grand performance of sacred music and dancing at the Ise shrine.

Daimyō 大名　　　A feudal lord.

Dan 段　　　　　In the structure of a *nō* play, a subdivision of a *ba*. Each *ba* is made out of five *dan*. A *dan* corresponds to what today would be called a "scene."

Dengaku 田楽　　　Rice-field entertainment. Original purpose of songs and dances performed by farmers was to pray for the fertility of the fields. *Dengaku* was later performed by professionals, who were organized in guilds (*za*). During the fourteenth century it developed parallel to *sarugaku* into *dengaku nō*, an important theatrical tradition contemporary to the beginning classical *nō*. *Dengaku nō* practically disappeared in the sixteenth century.

Dogū 土偶　　　　　Clay figurines of the Jōmon period (ending ca. 250 B.C.).

Dōkeyaku 道化役　　　Comical role, especially in *kabuki*.

Doma 土間　　　　　In early *kabuki*, the pit in front of the main stage, unsheltered from the rain.

Edo 江戸　　　　　Name of the capital of the Tokugawa shogunate (the present-day Tokyo) during the Edo Period (same as Tokugawa period, 1600-1867).

Engaku 燕楽　　　　Banquet music.

Ennen 延年　　　　Originally prayers for longevity, later banquets honoring the guests of the temple or shrine after the services. Entertainments were added to the banquets; eventually the banquets disappeared, and the performance element grew with the addition of numbers borrowed from several traditions. *Ennen nō* reached a period of splendor in the fifteenth century, at the same time as the classical *nō*.

Fuebashira 笛柱　　　The pillar of the *nō* stage near the seat where the flute player performs.

Furi 振　　　　　In *bunraku* and other performing arts, conventionally stylized everyday movements and gestures.

Furoagari no asobi 風呂上りの遊び　　　Erotic bathhouse scene in early *onna kabuki*.

Furyū 風流　　　　Originally the word meant something elegant. The original purpose of the performance of folk dances known as *furyū* was to avoid pestilences. From the end of the Heian period through the Kamakura period *furyū* indicated parades, processions and group dancing which were characterized by colorful and fancy costumes.

Furyū nō 風流 能　　　*Nō* plays characterized by dance rather than dramatic plot; dance pieces.

Fūshi-kaden 風姿花伝　　　See *Kadensho*.

Gagaku 雅楽　　　Classic court music imported from China during the eighth century. In common use, the word *gagaku* often designates also the *bugaku* court dances.

Gagakuryō 雅楽寮　Japan's first imperial academy of music, instituted in 701.

-gaku 楽　　　In the composition of many Japanese entertainment terms often translated into English as "music." Its meaning, however, is usually broader, and corresponds rather to "entertainment."

Gakunin 楽人　　Court musicians of the imperial household.

Gakuya 楽屋　　Dressing rooms; green room.

Geidan 芸談　　Actors' memoirs.

Geisha 芸者　　A professional entertainer, skilled in several arts, such as singing and dancing.

Geki nō 劇 能　　*Nō* plays with a dramatic plot.

Gempuku 元服　　Ceremony of shaving the front hair (*maegami*) which marked the coming of age for a young man.

Genzai nō 現在 能　*Nō* plays about the world of the living, featuring a living person (and not a ghost) as *shite* in the main role.

Geza 下座　　A bamboo-screened room for the *kabuki* musicians located at stage right.

Gidayū bushi 義太夫 夫節　　The style of delivering the *jōruri* narrative introduced by Takemoto Gidayū.

Gigaku 伎楽　　Music and entertainments for Buddhist religious services imported from South China in early seventh century A.D.

301

Giri 義理   The severe duties imposed by feudal ethics.

Gongen 権現   A sign of the presence of the deity, usually an object kept in the tabernacle of a shrine.

Gozagae no shinji 茣蓙替神事   In *kagura* of the Izumo tradition, the ritual of changing the old straw mat inside the sanctum of the shrine with a new one.

Gyōdō 行道   Processional ritual consisting in carrying arourd a Buddha statue while Buddhist monks and the faithful chant prayers.

Haikai 俳諧   Same as *haiku*, a seventeen syllabled poem.

Haiku 俳句   A short poem of seventeen syllables.

Hakama 袴   Divided skirt for man's formal wear.

Hakobi 運   In *nō*, the basic movement of walking.

Hana 花   The flower. The result of successful interaction between the actor and the audience. It happens when the performance is deeply fascinating (*omoshiroki*) and unexpectedly new (*mezurashiki*). *Hana* can be temporary (*jibun no hana*) or true and permanent (*makoto no hana*). Among the types and ranks of *hana* the highest is the flower of the miraculous (*myōkafū*), an undescribable experience unifying performer and audience in some degree of direct perception of the Absolute.

Hanamatsuri 花祭   Festival of flowers, celebrating Buddha's birthday at the time of the cherry blossoms.

Hanamichi 花道   The "flower path." A bridge connecting stage right with the rear of the orchestra. The *hanamichi* is widely used in *kabuki* for spectacular entrances and exits.

Haniwa 埴輪   Fired clay statuettes found in grave sites of the Kofun period (250-710).

Hannya 般若   The horned mask of the demoness of jealousy.

Hashigakari 橋掛   In *nō*, a roofed bridgeway connecting the main stage with the mirror room.

Hayato 隼人   In early Japan, the name of a clan which was subjugated by the Yamato clan.

Heian 平安   Name of period of Japanese history (794-1192) during which *bugaku* reached its splendor.

Hikimaku 引幕   Draw curtain used in *kabuki*.

Himiko (Queen) 卑弥呼   Ruler of the Yamato clan in the third century A.D., famous because of her shamanistic powers. Also Pimiko, or Pimiku.

Hinoki 檜   Japanese cypress.

Hito-kami 人神   Literally: "man-god." In *kabuki* plays, super-heroes were considered as more than valiant men. In a state of *kamigakari* (divine possession) they had extraordinary powers, such as defeating alone legions of villains and appeasing powerful *onryō*.

Honbutai 本舞台   The main stage.

Hōshi 法師   A Buddhist priest or monk. *Sarugaku hōshi* and *dengaku hōshi* were professional performers at the service of a temple.

Hōshibara 法師原   Professional performers of *sangaku* and *sarugaku*, who donned the habit and wore the haircut of monks, pretending to belong to a monastery or a temple to avoid conscripted labor in the fields and high taxes. Although they were actually gypsy-like outcastes without any formal connection with a religious institutions, they were hired by shrines and temples in the provinces for the major festivals because of their skills in performing acrobatics, magic, comic *monomane*. They are probably the main responsible for beginning and developing the process of using religious subjects and masks which eventually lead to the serious plays of the *nō* tradition.

Ichibun 一分   Traditional *samurai* ethical principle of individualistic integrity and honor. See also *iji*.

Iemoto 家元   In several traditional arts, the head of a school. The name *iemoto* was applied to the world of the artists in the eighteenth century, but the institution can be traced back to the Heian period. The *iemoto* has extensive powers and provides for the preservation of the tradition in his art. In the *nō*, the *iemoto*, also called *sōke*, became a kind of teacher/king, immensely respected and faithfully served by his disciples. He decides who is performing what, the use of masks and costumes, and the financial matters of the school.

Iji 意地   Traditional *samurai* ethical principle of "pride" which, usually together with *ichibun*, allowed, and even imposed a change of allegiance or rebellion when the sovereign went against "the will of heaven" (*ten-mei*).

Illud tempus   Latin for "that time"; that is, the timeless frame ouside our time, valid for the supernatural world belonging to the "other" dimension ouside our space. *Illud tempus* and "other" dimension are brought into our world through the representation of ritual which actualizes the timeless myth into our time and space.

Ishō 衣装   Theatrical costumes.

Izumi School 和泉   One of the two surviving schools of *kyōgen*.

Jidaimono 時代物   In *kabuki* and *jōruri*, period pieces based on historical or semi-historical material.

Ji-utai 地謡   The chorus of the *nō*.

Jo, ha, kyū 序 破 急   In *gagaku*, the standard musical movements, often translated as exposition, development, and climax. The *jo, ha, kyū* principle was applied to other

Japanese performing arts, especially the *nō*.

Jōmon 縄文   Earliest period of Japanese history, from the Neolythic to approximately 250 B.C.

Jōruri 浄瑠璃   Name of the heroine of a puppet play, extremely popular since the last decades of the sixteenth century. The name was widely used for the genre of the puppets until the beginning of the nineteenth century, when the name *bunraku* took its place.

Ka-bu-isshin 歌舞一心   Literally: song-dance-one-heart. Zenchiku's theory of unity of poetry and dance.

Kabuki 歌舞伎   Traditional form of popular theatre which began at the end of the sixteenth century, and soon became the most successful theatre entertainment in the red light districts of the great cities. With the *nō*, to the present time it is considered the most important Japanese contribution to world theatre.

Kabuki mono 歌舞伎者   During the early Tokugawa period, individuals who expressed their anti-conformism through a series of extravagant protests against the strict order of the Tokugawa society.

Kadensho 花伝書   The Book of the Transmission of the Flower, a fundamental treatise of *nō* esthetics by Zeami. Although the title *Kadensho* is more popular, many scholars prefer, as more correct, the title *Fūshikaden*. It was written about 1402, and completed by 1418.

Kagami no ma 鏡の間   The mirror room, where the bridgeway (*hashigakari*) of the *nō* stage begins.

Kagura 神楽   Euphonic contraction of *kamu-kura*, the seat of the deity; entertainment of, or for, the gods; music, dance, and pantomimic performances mostly performed in Shinto shrines.

Kaidanmono 怪談物   A group of early nineteenth century *Kabuki* plays focused on grotesque supernatural events.

Kakegoe 掛声   Literally, "attached calls." In *nō*, the strange, guttural sound of the drummers' shouting. Originally they were probably part of the conjuration for the descent of the spirits; they presently serve as integral part of the *nō* music. The human voice, in this form of syllables which the drummers shout, hum, or moan, is considered as a fifth instrument, added to the flute and the three drums, with an essential function in the building of the unique atmosphere of the *nō*. There is no improvisation, the *kakegoe* are strictly indicated as part of the score.

Kakyō 花鏡   A Mirror Held to the Flower, 1424. Important treatise of the secret tradition of the *nō* by Zeami.

Kamakura 鎌倉   Capital of the shogunate during the Kamakura period (1192-1333).

Kamae 構   In *nō*, the basic posture of the dancer.

Kamen 仮面   A general term for theatrical masks.

Kami 神   A term widely used for gods, deities, superior beings, both singular and plural.

Kamiage 神上   Dismissal of the gods in the early morning at the end of the *mikagura*.

Kamigakari 神懸   Divine inspiration; divine possession; the person who is possessed by the god.

Kami mono 神物   See *waki nō*.

Kamioroshi 神降   Descent of the deity.

Kamishimo 上下   Formal kimono for men consisting of a stiff sleeveless robe (*kataginu*) as a top and the divided long *hakama* trousers.

Kamiza 上座   The place where the deity temporarily resides.

306

Kangengaku 管弦楽 Purely orchestral music of *gagaku*, as opposed to music accompanied by dance (*bugaku*).

Kanjin nō 勧進能 *Nō* performances to raise funds for such pious purposes as the construction of a new temple or the repair of an old one.

Kannushi 神主 Shinto priest.

Kaomise kōgyō 顔見世 興行 "Face showing performance." In *kabuki*, the annual show introducing the company of the year to the audience.

Kata 形 A term widely used in classical dance and in the description of traditional theatrical movement, with the general meaning of "pattern," "form." In the most common meaning *kata* refers to fixed patterns of performance, mostly related to acting, but applicable also to other production elements. *Kata* are inherited and transmitted as precious legacies of famous performers, especially in *kabuki*.

Katakiyaku 敵役 In *kabuki*, the role of a villain.

Katari 語 Telling of a story by a shaman.

Katsura mono かつら物 Wig plays. Name of a group of *nō* plays which feature women in the *shite* role. Also *onna mono* (women pieces).

Katsurekimono 活歴物 After the Meiji Restoration, *kabuki* plays which presented historically accurate names, events, and costumes.

Kawaramono 河原者 People of the riverbed. During the Tokugawa period, *kabuki* actors were called *kawaramono*, or *kawara kojiki* (beggars of the riverbed), because of the place where they originally set up their stages.

Kazura かづら Same as *katsura*. Wig.

Keisei 傾城   A courtesan. Same as *yūjo*.

Kemari 蹴鞠   Court kickball.

Ken 間   Measure corresponding to six Japanese *shaku*. One *shaku* is equal to .994 foot; 1 ken=1.99 yards or 1.82 centimeters.

Keshō 化粧   Generic term for *kabuki* make-up.

Kimpira 金平   Name of a superhero of the *kojōruri* plays, gifted with extraordinary powers. Kimpira became very popular in Edo, and a series of plays took their name after him.

Kiri nō 切能   Final *nō*. Plays performed at the end of a program, in which the *shite* role belongs to the mythological world of demons, monsters, and goblins.

Kizewamono 生世話物   Early nineteenth century *kabuki* plays dedicated to the depiction of the poor, the wretched, and the underworld. Also called *masewamono*.

Kofun 古墳   Period of Japanese history (250-710) following the Jōmon.

Kojiki 古事記   *Records of Ancient Matters*, with the *Nihongi* the oldest Japanese written source for Japanese history (eighth century).

Kōjin 工人   The artisans, one of the four classes of Japanese society during the Tokugawa period.

Kojōruri 古浄瑠璃   Old *jōruri*, before the reform introduced by Chikamatsu.

Kokata 子方   In *nō*, a role performed by a child actor, in most cases as a *tsure*; that is, as a companion to the *shite*. *Kokata* are used for such lofty roles as that of an Emperor, or of Yoshitsune.

Kokoro 心　　　　The heart. Zeami uses this term to indicate the ultimate foundation of the art of the *nō*; that is, the source of the impact upon audiences, of genuine *yūgen*, and of the highest levels of sublime (*myō*) performances. The invisible *kokoro* is rooted in the very essence of all things, the Buddha-nature, and unites all powers of the performer and of the audience.

Kongō 金剛　　　A popular guardian god of the Buddhist pantheon. With Rikishi, he stands at the entrance of many temples. Also, a major character of a *gigaku* dance.

Konoe 近衛　　　Name of a unit of imperial guards, the Konoe-fu (during the eighth century, some four hundred men strong) which served as bodyguards for the Emperor, and also as performers and supervisors of music and dance.

Konron 崑崙　　　(also Kuron). Main character in a *gigaku* dance. The Konron mask is dark or black, a fact supporting the interpretation of being that of a dark complectioned villain from the South Seas.

Kotsuzumi 小鼓　　　In *nō*, the small hand drum.

Ko-uta 小唄　　　Since the tenth century, "small songs," prevalently amorous or reflective of personal feelings. In *nō*, the traditional style of music—about which little is known—before Kan'ami's introduction of the *kusemai* style.

Kuge 公家　　　The nobility of the imperial court, as distinguished from the *samurai* aristocracy.

Kugutsu 傀儡　　　Ancient term for puppets. The puppeteers were called *kugutsumawashi*.

Kumadori 隈取　　　Make-up style created for the *aragoto* roles in *kabuki*. There are about one hundred types of *kumadori*, consisting of systems of strong lines of different colors, which represent such qualities as righteousness (red) or fear and evil (blue).

Kusemai 曲舞　　　Type of dance and music about which little is known, but important because it influenced Kan'ami in the creation of the *nō*.

Kyōgen 狂言　　　The word *kyōgen* has a very wide use, alone and in association with other words, in several traditions, including the *kabuki*. It indicates often the comical form of traditional theatre which developed parallel with the *nō* and is still performed mainly between the plays of a typical *nō* program.

Kyōran mono 狂乱物　Madness pieces. *Nō* plays about tragically insane protagonists. They belong to the fourth group pieces.

Kyū-i 九位　　　The Nine Levels, a treatise by Zeami on the different levels of achievement by *nō* actors.

Ma 間　　　　　Pause. Important concept of Japanese performance esthetics, representing the emptiness of time/space from which movement appears and into which it dies. It also includes the meaning of "timing."

Mai 舞　　　　Dance. In *nō*, a dance of an abstract type, accompanied only by the orchestra, and performed at the end of the play. The term *mai* is used in many other performing arts, for instance *kusemai*, *shishi mai*, and so on.

Manyōshū 万葉集　A monumental anthology of poetry from the end of the eighth century.

Masaki 柾　　　A spindle-tree.

Matsubame 松羽目　The painted pine-tree backdrop of the *nō* stage.

Mawari butai 回舞台 Revolving stage.

Meiji 明治　　　Historical period (1868-1912) named after Emperor Meiji. The Meiji Restoration marked the end of the Tokugawa shogunate, the re-opening of Japan to international trade, and the beginning of the process of modernization and westernization in all areas, including the theatre.

Metsukebashira 目付柱 The pillar of the *nō* stage which serves as orientation for the masked performer.

Mibu kyōgen 千生狂言 Masked, mute pantomime performed at the Mibu temple in Kyoto.

Michiyuki 道行 At the beginning of a *nō* play, the travel scene.

Mie 見得 In *kabuki*, the final pose reached at climactic moments, summarizing the special feelings of the actor.

Mikagura 御神楽 The *kagura* performed inside the precincts of the imperial palace by the court musicians of the imperial household.

Miko 神子 Originally a sorceress; a medium; today the term designates mostly young women at the service of Shinto shrines. See also: shaman.

Miko kagura 神子 神楽 *Kagura* performed by *miko*.

Mimashi 味摩之 Came to Japan in 612 from Kudara (Korea) and introduced *gigaku* under the patronage of Prince Shōtoku.

Minzoku geinō 民族 芸能 Term widely used for popular performing arts of various traditions, including *kagura*, *dengaku*, and *furyū*.

Momoyama 桃山 (also Azuchi-Momoyama). Name of period of Japanese history (1573-1600), during which the first *kabuki* dances took place.

Monomane 物真似 Literally imitation, mimesis. It was the specialty of the Yamato *sarugaku*, that stressed what we would call today realistic acting, as opposed to the Omi *sarugaku*, which stressed elegant dance and singing.

Monomane kyōgen zukushi 物真似狂言尽   New name for *kabuki* after the abolition of the *wakashu kabuki* in 1652.

Mugen nō 夢幻能   *Nō* plays about dreams and phantasms, featuring beings from the other dimension, such as gods, ghosts, demons, or spirits of animals and plants appearing in a dream or dreamlike experience.

Muromachi 室町   Name of historical period (1333-1573) of Japanese history. The Muromachi period overlaps with the Ashikaga period (1392-1568), and also the Namboku (1336-1392) and Sengoku (1467-1568) periods. It is particularly significant for the theatre because of the birth and development of *nōgaku*.

Myō 妙   Peerless charm; the marvelous; the sublime. It is achieved by the actor at the top of his artistry, when he performs without effort, above any artifice, in union with the world of nature.

Nagauta 長唄   "Long song." The most popular music for *shamisen*. It reached a golden age in the first half of the nineteenth century. *Nagauta* music is the heart of *kabuki* music.

Nara 奈良   Ancient capital of Japan, which gave the name to the Nara period (710-794).

Nembutsu 念仏   Repetition of the prayer *Namu Amidabutsu*, often translated as "Homage to Amida Buddha," which was very popular in the Amidistic sects of Buddhism. The *nembutsu odori* was a dance during which the *nembutsu* was chanted. Okuni's adaptation of a *nembutsu odori* at the end of the sixteenth century is considered to be the beginning of *kabuki*.

Netori 音取   Formal tuning of the *gigaku* orchestra.

Nikite 和幣   In early Japan, cloth symbols of rice and fruit offerings which later became the strips of white and colored papers still used in Shinto shrines.

Nihongi (or *Nihon shoki*) 日本紀 *Chronicles of Japan*, together with the *Kojiki*, the oldest (eighth century) written source of Japanese history.

Ningyō 人形 A puppet. A doll. The term *ningyō shibai* is used for puppet show, as a synonym of *jōruri*.

Ninjo 人長 Principal male performer in some *kagura* and *bugaku* dances.

Ninjō 人情 The feelings of the heart, as contrasting with *giri*, the duties of feudal ethics.

Niwabi 庭火 A garden fire.

Nō 能 The word means skill, talent. Genre of dance theatre developed within the *sarugaku* tradition by Kan'ami and Zeami during the fourteenth century. It has flourished to the present time as one of the major forms of Japanese classical drama. See also *sarugaku*.

Nōgaku 能楽 A word indicating both the classical *nō* and *kyōgen* as two facets of one tradition.

Nōkan 能管 In *nō*, the flute.

Nōmin 農民 The peasants, one of the four classes of Japanese society during the Tokugawa period.

Nyōbō sarugaku 女房猿楽 *Sarugaku* performed by amateur women.

Obi 帯 A sash.

Odōgu 大道具 In *kabuki*, the large stage properties.

Odori 踊 Dance. This term is used for many types of dances in several traditions, among which the most important is *kabuki*.

Oie-sōdō 御家騒動 In *kabuki*, the house-strife pattern; that is, plays about the succession to power in a feudal house.

Okina 翁 The popular image of Okina is that of a godly old man bestowing long life and fertility. However, depending on the different traditions, the interpretation of the Okina roles varies from a Shinto *kami* to sophisticated Buddhist personifications. The *Okina* play is performed at the beginning of the year and in the occasion of solemn inaugural festivities.

Okina sarugaku 翁 猿楽 Form of *sarugaku* developed during the thirteenth century, considered as an important connection between the primitive *sarugaku* and the *sarugaku nō*.

Okura School 大倉 One of the two surviving schools of *kyōgen*.

Okuni 阿国 The legendary founder of *kabuki*, who flourished at the end of the sixteenth and the beginning of the seventeenth century. A *miko* from the Izumo shrine in the Shimane province, she is credited with the first *kabuki* dances and the original adaptation of *nō* dramaturgy to *kabuki*.

Okuni kabuki 阿国 歌舞伎 The period of the origins of *kabuki*, approximately from the last few years of the sixteenth century to the beginnings of the seventeenth.

Omi *sarugaku* 近江 猿楽 A style of *sarugaku* which stressed the element of *monomane*.

Omozukai 主遣い In *bunraku*, the main puppet operator.

Onnagata 女形 In *kabuki*, a male performer of female roles. Same as *oyama*.

Onna kabuki 女 歌舞伎 Women *kabuki*. From the beginning of the seventeenth century to 1629. This phase of *kabuki* history is characterized by the *kabuki* performed by prostitutes (*yūjo*, hence the name *yūjo kabuki*) which focused on extravagant and sensual dances.

Onna mono 女物 See *katsura mono*.

Onryō mono 怨霊物 *Nō* plays about revengeful ghosts, belonging to the fourth group pieces.

Otokodate 男達   In general, a man of chivalrous spirit. In *kabuki*, *otokodate* roles represented idealized commoners as heroes who bravely dared to stand up against injustice in defense of the weak and the oppressed.

Otsuzumi 大鼓   In *nō*, the larger hand drum.

Oyama 女形   Same as *onnagata*.

Rakugo 落語   Popular art of storytelling.

Rambu 乱舞   Literally: disorderly dance. The term was used during the Middle Ages as synonym for the *sarugaku* of the professional *sarugaku hōshi*. In some cases the word indicated probably comical dances, performed by non-professional members of the court.

Rikishi 力士   A guardian god of the Buddhist pantheon. His statue is usually revered at the entrance of temples, in a pair with Kongō's statue.

Rōei 朗詠   Chinese poems chanted as court entertainment.

Rōjaku 老弱   The quiet beauty of old age. Important esthetic concept used by Zeami to indicate the reduction to the essence of the *nō* beauty in the performance of the role of an old person by a great master.

Rokurin ichiro 六輪一露   Zenchiku's theory of the six wheels and one dew drop.

Rōnin 浪人   Masterless *samurai*.

Roppō 六方   Technique of stage entrance or exit. Several different *roppō* steps are used, especially for spectacular exits, for example the *tobi roppō*, or flying *roppō*.

Sahō-no-gaku 左方の楽   In *gagaku*, music of the left. Includes music of Chinese, Indian, and Japanese origin. Also called Tōgaku, or T'ang music.

Sahō-no-mai 左方の舞 In *bugaku*, dances of the left. They are accompanied by *sahō-no-gaku*, music of the left.

Saibara 催馬楽 In *gagaku*, popular folk songs.

Saibari 前張 In *kagura*, musical entertainments for the gods. Probably originated as songs of the grooms, or, according to other opinion, as songs to excite horses.

Sajiki 桟敷 The sheltered side galleries in the early *kabuki* theatre building.

Sakaki 榊 *Cleyera ochnacea* or *cleyera japonica*; a glossy leaved evergreen considered sacred in Shinto cult.

Samurai 侍 The warriors. The military class which dominated Japanese society from the twelfth to the nineteenth century.

Sangaku 散楽 Miscellaneous entertainments imported from the mainland in several waves starting from the eighth century. They included a variety of acrobatics, juggling, games, magical acts, comical sketches, folk dances and songs, etc.

Sanjo 散所 Special villages where the outcaste performers of *sangaku*, *sarugaku*, *shirabyōshi*, and many other performing arts were ordered to reside.

San-yüe 散楽 (transcribed also as *san-yüo*) Chinese collective name used after the sixth century A.D. for a variety of popular entertainments. Many of them were imported by the Japanese starting from the eighth century, thus giving birth to *sangaku*. *San-yüe* entertainments had developed in China from miscellaneous arts imported from Central Asia. The Chinese characters for *san-yüe* are read in Japanese *sangaku*.

Sarugaku 猿楽 or 甲楽 "Monkey music," or "monkey entertainment." By the end of the tenth century the word *sarugaku* took over the functions of the word *sangaku*, indicating the same variety of miscellaneous entertainments. *Sarugaku* increased the comical-pantomimic element of *monomane* (imitation), and eventually developed into *sarugaku*

316

nō, the tradition from which—by the middle of the fourteenth century— the classical *nō* was born.

Sarugaku hōshi 猿楽 法師　　　Often translated as *sarugaku* monks. Professional *sarugaku* performers were attached to Buddhist temples and considered as members of the temple community.

Sarume 猿女　　　Name of the clan to which belonged the women who succeeded the goddess Uzume in the official task of performing the soul-appeasing (*chinkon*) rites. They eventually merged with the *miko*.

Saruwaka 猿若　　　A comical role in early *kabuki*.

Sasa 笹　　　Bamboo grass; bamboo leaves.

Sasara 簓　　　A serpentine clapper made of many small pieces of wood.

Satokagura 里神楽　　*Kagura* performed outside the compound of the imperial palace.

Satori 悟　　　The Buddhist enlightenment.

Seito 生徒　　　A disciple, a student. In the Takarazuka world, all girls, even the most famous stars, are called *seito*.

Semmin 賤民　　　The outcastes, to which also most performers belonged until the Meiji Restoration.

Seppuku 切腹　　　Suicide by disembowelment.

Sewamono 世話物　　In *jōruri* and *kabuki*, domestic plays; that is, plays reflecting the life of commoners in the Tokugawa period.

Shaji 社寺　　　Lit. "shrines and temples," used collectively for the clergy of Shinto and Buddhism.

Shaman シャーマン　A medicine man, who can travel in spirit to the "other" dimension and function both as a medium and as a healer. Since time immemorial, in Japan the most wide-spread type of shaman was the *miko*, a professional practitioner of ecstasy. The *miko*, as well as Shinto priests, Buddhist monks, and other ascetics, entered into communication with deities, souls of the deceased, and spirits of animals, became possessed by them, and acted as a medium of supernatural communication from that "other" dimension.

Shamanism   Folk religion embracing the belief in powerful spirits that can be influenced only by a shaman. Since time immemorial present in Japan, shamanism permeated early Shinto rituals and had a very important place in the practice of popular Buddhism. Shamanistic rituals are an important source of Japanese performing arts, especially of *kagura* and *nō*.

Shamisen 三味線   String instrument that became very popular from the second half of the sixteenth century, and took the place of the *biwa* in early *jōruri*. It is the prominent instrument in *kabuki* music. Also *jabisen*.

Shigoto 仕事   In a *nō* play, what the *shite* does; that is, the centerpiece of the action of the play.

Shikigaku 式楽   Ceremonial, official entertainment, consisting mainly of *gagaku* music and *bugaku* dances.

Shikibutai 敷舞台   In *bugaku*, a temporary stage built of Japanese cypress, usually consisting of two platforms connected in the middle.

Shimpa 新派   New school drama, a form of theatre which developed after the Meiji Restoration as an attempt to modernize and westernize Japan's drama independently from the *kabuki* tradition.

Shingeki 新劇   The new theatre movement, which began in 1906 and has dedicated itself to the ideal of the creation of a modern, westernized theatre, stressing the care of literary and theatrical values independently from the main stream of commercial theatre.

Shin kabuki 新歌舞伎　　　　　New *kabuki*. A movement of early twentieth century dramatists who wrote original plays for the stagnating *kabuki*.

Shinjūmono 心中物　Double-suicides plays.

Shin sarugaku 新猿楽　　　　　New *sarugaku*. Flourished between the second half of the tenth and the end of the thirteenth century. Its characteristics, as compared to the old *sarugaku* (*ko sarugaku*), were an emphasis on *monomane* (mimicry) and comic-farcical roles, and its appeal to urban audiences.

Shinto (*shintō* 神道　) The way of the gods; the indigenous religion of Japan.

Shirabyōshi 白拍子　Literally: white rhythm. It indicates both a special type of dance and its performers, popular from the Heian through the Muromachi period.

Shiranamimono 白浪物　　　　Nineteenth century *kabuki* plays about petty thieves, who use blackmail or other crooked means to help the poor.

Shishi 獅子　　　　Originally a term for wild animals whose meat can be eaten, became eventually the official term for lion.

Shishi kagura 獅子　神楽　　　　A tradition of *kagura* including two main groups, the *daikagura* (mainly acrobatic) and the *yamabushi kagura*.

Shishimai 獅子舞　Lion dance. One of the most ancient and wide-spread dances, which took different forms in a number of traditions, including *kagura*, *gigaku*, *sarugaku*, and so on.

Shishi-ko 獅子　子　Children who accompany the lion in the *shishi* dance.

Shite 仕手　　　　In *nō* and other performing arts, the main actor.

Shitebashira 仕手柱 The pillar at the entrance of the *nō* main stage where the *shite* usually stays.

Shogun (*shōgun* 将軍) The head of the military goverment called shogunate (1185-1868). The Shogun held a dictatorial power under the nominal authority of the Emperor. The Shogun's court, first in Kamakura and later in Kyoto, became the most important center of the new *samurai* culture. The favor of Shogun Yoshimitsu was decisive for the development of the *nō*, and the policies of the Tokugawa shogunate had great influence in determining the course of development of such theatrical forms as *kabuki* and *jōruri*.

Shō-hichiriki 笙篳篥 Popular name for *gagaku*.

Shōmin 商民 The merchants, one of the four classes of Tokugawa society.

Shōmyō 唱声 Buddhist chanting of the sutra.

Shosagoto 所作事 In *kabuki*, plays which consist only or primarily of dance. Dance plays.

Shōtoku taishi 聖徳太子 Prince Regent Shōtoku (574-622) was very important for his decisive patronage of the newly imported Buddhist culture, including *gigaku*.

Shōwa 昭和 Name of the recent period of Japanese history under Emperor Hirohito, which started in 1926, and ended in early 1989.

Shōzoku 装束 Theatrical costumes. This term is used primarily for the *nō* costumes, while the term *ishō* is used for *kabuki*.

Shugen 修験 A tradition which gave birth to *shugen nō*, or *nō* performed by the *yamabushi*.

Shugendō 修験道 The way to achieve supernatural powers through training. A religion combining a pre-Shinto mountain cult with elements of Shinto, Buddhism, and Taoism, and stressing a severe training of its itinerant monks, the *yamabushi*.

Shura mono 修羅物   See *Asura nō*.

Shushi 呪師   The term means magician, master of conjuration and exorcism. Probably they were temple servants who performed ceremonies of exorcism, divination, and magic. Later they added theatrical skills to their performances.

Sōshi 壮士   Courageous young man, and/or political bully. After the Meiji Restoration, a group of *sōshi* came together to use the theatre for political purposes, and gave birth to the *shimpa* movement under the leadership of Sudō Sadanori.

Suppon すっぽん   Stage trap and lift in the *hanamichi*.

Ta-asobi 田遊   Rice-field entertainment. Originally the dances were both a prayer for a good harvest and entertainment for the farmers.

Tachimawari 立回   Stage fighting movements.

Tachiyaku 立役   Main male role in *kabuki*.

Taiko 太鼓   In *nō*, the stick drum.

Taishō 大正   Recent period in Japanese history (1912-1926) named after Emperor Taishō.

Takabutai 高舞台   In *bugaku*, the standard open-air high stage.

Takusen 託宣   Divine utterance by the *miko* possessed by a spirit.

Tama 玉   The vital element of both man and *kami*. The soul. The difference between man and *kami* is not substantial, but in "quantity" or "power" of the *tama*. Also, a round jewel.

Tamafuri 玉振　　　Literally: shaking of the *tama*. A ritual aimed at the infusion of fresh vital energy.

Tamai 田舞　　　Rice-field dances. Originally performed as a prayer for a good harvest, they were also meant as a conjuration of the spirits of the fields. *Tamai* developed into *dengaku*.

Tamashizume 鎮魂 Literally: appeasement of the *tama*. A ritual aimed at appeasing the soul of the deceased.

Tanka 短歌　　　A poetic composition of 31 syllables, consisting of five verses following the scheme of 5-7-5-7-7 syllables.

Tatami 畳　　　The traditional strawmats used in most Japanese homes as floor covering.

Tate 殺陣　　　In *kabuki*, techniques of stage fighting, including some two hundred stylized patterns.

Tatesakusha 立作者 In *jōruri* and *kabuki*, the main playwright.

Tokugawa　徳川　　Family name of a dynasty of *daimyō* and Shogun. The Tokugawa shogunate gave the name to the Tokugawa period (1603-1868), also called Edo period, during which *kabuki* and *jōruri* reached their artistic splendor.

Torimono 採物　　Objects held in the hand during a *kagura* performance; during the divine possession they were believed to become the temporary abode of the *kami*.

Tsukurimono 作物　Stage properties.

Tsure 連　　　A companion to the *shite*. Also called *shitezure*.

Uhō-no-gaku 右方の楽　　In *gagaku*, music of the right. Includes musical compositions of Korean and Manchurian origin, and the elements assimilated from *gigaku*. Also called *Komagaku*.

Uhō-no-mai 右方の舞 In *bugaku,* dances of the right. They are accompanied by *uhō-no-gaku,* music of the right.

Ukiyo 浮世 During the Tokugawa period, the "floating world" of the red light districts, which became the new center of the Edo culture. *Ukiyo-e* are the wood-block prints and other forms of paintings portraing that world.

Umisachi 海幸 (also Umi-sati-bito, or Powori) The godly fisherman. The first professional actor, as distinguished from the shaman, who is mentioned in a Japanese document.

Uta 歌 A poem; a song; a *tanka.*

Uta-awase 歌合 Poetry competition.

Utagaki 歌垣 In ancient Japan, festivals of songs and dances—characterized by sexual promiscuity—held on beautiful hillsides.

Utai 歌 Chanting of a *nō* drama text.

Uzume 細女 [Ame-no Uzume-no-mikoto]. The mythical performer of the first *kagura* recorded in Japanese sources. Uzume's dance lured the sun-goddess Amaterasu from the cave, thus giving back the sun to the world.

Wa 和 In ancient Chinese records, the early name for Japan.

Wagon 和琴 A musical instrument with six strings, similar to the modern *koto.*

Wagoto 和事 In *kabuki,* the style of the gentle, soft, romantic hero, as opposed to *aragoto.*

Waka 和歌 A thirty-one syllable poem; same as *tanka.*

Wakaonna 若女　　In *nō*, the mask of a young woman.

Wakaoyama 若女形　In *kabuki*, the role of a beautiful young woman.

Wakashu 若衆　　A young man before the ceremony of coming of age; i.e., before the shaving of the front hair. *Wakashu kabuki* designates a period of early *kabuki*, from the prohibition of the *onna kabuki* in 1629 to 1652, during which the dances of young male prostitutes became very popular in the red light districts of the main cities.

Waki 脇　　In *nō* and *kyōgen*, the supporting actor; deuteragonist.

Wakibashira 脇柱　The pillar of the *nō* stage under which the supporting actor (*waki*) usually sits.

Waki nō 脇能　　Group of about thirty-nine *nō* plays named after the supporting role, the *waki*. In these plays the *shite* represents a deity, hence the alternate name of *kami mono* (plays about gods).

Waki-za 脇座　　The side-stage, where the chorus of the *nō* sits.

Wazaogi 俳優　　Comic pantomime. Performer of same.

Yakkogata 奴形　　The role of a servant.

Yamabushi 山伏　　Ascetics associated with an indigenous mountain worship (see: *shugendō*). They used to spread their faith through performances of *yamabushi kagura*, a tradition rich in colorful rituals, acrobatics, sword dances, magic with fire, and masked plays.

Yamasachi 山幸　　(Also Yama-sati-bito, or Powori). The godly hunter, brother of Umisachi.

Yamato 大和   Name of the clan which succeeded in obtaining the supremacy among the primitive clans of early Japan. Yamato became a synonym for Japan. Also, a province in the proximity of Kyoto, where the *Yamato sarugaku* began. Yamato is also the name of a period of early Japanese history (300-710).

Yatsushi やつし   With *mitate*, the Japanese for "dual identity-double meaning," an esthetic key for appreciation of *kabuki* playwriting and performance.

Yayoi 弥生   Early period of Japanese history (ca. 250 B.C.-300 A.D.)

Yarō kabuki 野郎 歌舞伎   The *kabuki* performed by adult men, which followed after the abolition of the *wakashu kabuki* in 1652.

Ya-yüe 雅楽   Chinese for "correct," "elegant," formal" music, used for the ceremonial music of official Confucian rites. In Japanese, the same characters are read *gagaku*.

Yudate 湯立   In *kagura* of the Ise tradition, ritual of boiling large couldrons of water as an act of worship, and sprinkling the audience as a means of purification.

Yūgen 幽幻   In Zeami's time, a complex principle of literary esthetics fashionable at court in judging the beauty of poems. Zeami applied it, with the meaning of refined elegance, to the performance of *nō*. In his later writings Zeami gave to the term a deeper meaning, including a profound, mysterious sense of the beauty of the universe, and eventually also of the sad beauty of human suffering.

Yūjo 遊女   A prostitute. The *yūjo kai* (whore-buying) scenes were very popular in the *onna kabuki*, which was also called *yūjo kabuki*.

Yūzaki za 結崎座   The *nō* company founded by Kan'ami, which later became the Kanze *za*.

Za 座 A theatrical company; a school (of *nō*); a theatrical guild during the middle ages; a theatre (in composition with the name of the theatre; for example, Nakamuraza, Meijiza).

Zangirimono 散切物 After the Meiji Restoration, *kabuki* plays in which actors adopted short-cropped western style hair fashion.

Zōmen 蔵面 In *bugaku*, white rectangular silk masks with highly stylized, abstract features painted in black.

BIBLIOGRAPHY

The following selective bibliography includes books, articles, and dissertations in English, French, German, and Italian. When occasional citations of sources in other languages occur, essential bibliographical information is provided in the notes. This bibliography is divided into five sections:

Abbreviations

ATJ	*Asian Theatre Journal*
BOAS	*Bulletin of the School of Oriental and Asiatic Studies*
Diss.	Dissertation
ETJ	*[Educational] Theatre Journal*
HJASt	*Harvard Journal of Asiatic Studies*
MN	*Monumenta Nipponica*
MOAG	*Mitteilungen der Deutschen Gesellschaft für Natur- und Völkerkunde Ostasiens*
MuK	*Maske und Kothurn*
NOAG	*Nachrichten der Deutschen Gesellschaft für Natur- und Völkerkunde Ostasiens*
OAG	Deutsche Gesellschaft für Natur- und Völkerkunde Ostasiens
TASJ	*Transactions of the Asiatic Society of Japan*
TDR	*The Drama Review [Tulane Drama Review]*
Tr[s].	Translator[s] or translation
Univ.	University
UP	University Press

SECTION 1: Comprehensive Studies and General Bibliographies

ARNOLD, PAUL. *Le théâtre japonais d'aujourd'hui*. Paris: La Renaissance du Livre, 1974.

ARNOTT, PETER D. *The Theatres of Japan*. London: Macmillan, 1969.

BARTH, JOHANNES. *Japans Schaukunst im Wandel der Zeiten*. Wiesbaden: Steiner, 1972.

BÉNAZET, ALEXANDRE. *Le théâtre au Japon, ses rapports avec les cultes locaux*. Paris: Ernest Leroux, 1901.

BEONIO BROCCHIERI, PAOLO, et al. *Alle radici del sole: Teatro, musica e danza in Giappone*. Turin: E.R.I., 1983.

BOWERS, FAUBION. *Japanese Theatre*. New York: Hermitage House, 1952.

BOWERS, FAUBION. *Theatre in the East: A Survey of Asian Dance and Drama.* New York: T. Nelson, 1956.
BRANDON, JAMES R. *Asian Theatre: A Study Guide and Annotated Bibliography.* Washington D.C., 1980.
----------, ed. *Traditional Asian Plays.* New York: Hill and Wang, 1972.
----------"Theatre East and West: An International Congress." *ATJ*, 2/1 (Fall 1985): 231-233.
----------"A New World: Asian Theatre in the West Today." *TDR*, 33/2 (T 122, Summer 1989): 25-50.
----------, ed. *Cambridge Guide to Asian Theatre.* Cambridge: Cambridge UP, 1993.
COBIN, MARTIN. "Traditional Theatre and Modern Television in Japan." *ETJ*, 21 (May 1969): 156-170.
CRUMP, J. I. and MALM, WILLIAM P., eds. *Chinese and Japanese Music-Dramas.* Ann Arbor: Center for Chinese Studies, Univ. of Michigan, 1975.
DE VOS, GEORGE and WAGATSUMA, HIROSHI. *Japan's Invisible Race: Caste in Culture and Personality.* Berkeley and Los Angeles: Univ. of California Press, 1966.
DUNN, CHARLES J. "Comparative Dramatics and Japanese Dramatic History." *Transactions of International Conferences of Orientalists in Tokyo*, 12 (1967).
----------"Religion and Japanese Drama." In *Drama and Religion,* Themes in Drama 5. Cambridge: Cambridge UP, 1983: 225-37.
DURNELL, HAZEL. *Japanese Cultural Influences on American Poetry and Drama.* Tokyo: Hokuseido Press, 1983.
EDWARDS, OSMAN. *Japanese Plays and Playfellows.* London: William Heinemann, 1901.
ERNST, EARL. "The Influence of Japanese Theatrical Style on Western Theatre." *ETJ*, 21 (May 1969): 127-138.
---------*Three Japanese Plays from the Traditional Theatre.* New York: Grove, 1960.
FLORENZ, KARL. *Geschichte der japanischen Literatur.* 2 vols. Leipzig: Amelangs, 1905.
GLASER, CURT, ed. *Japanisches Theater.* Berlin: Würfel, 1930.
GÖSSMANN, ELIZABETH and ZOBEL, GÜNTER, eds. *Das Gold im Wachs: Festschrift für Thomas Immoos zum 70. Geburtstag.* Munich: Iudjcium, 1988.
GUIMET, EMILE and REGAMEY, FÉLIX. *Le théâtre au Japon.* Paris: Le Cerf, 1886.
HAAR, FRANCIS. *Japanese Theatre in Highlight: A Pictorial Commentary.* Text by Earle Ernst. Rutland, VT. and Tokyo: Tuttle, 1952.
HAMMITZSCH, HORST, ed. *Japan Handbuch.* Wiesbaden: Steiner, 1981.
HARICH-SCHNEIDER, ETA. *A History of Japanese Music.* London: Oxford UP, 1973.
HAYASHIYA, TATSUSABURO. "Ancient History and Performing Arts." *Acta Asiatica*, 33 (1977): 74-90.
----------"Historical Review and Studies and References on Japanese Performing Arts." *Acta Asiatica*, 33 (1977): 74-90.

HISAMATSU, SEN'ICHI. *The Vocabulary of Japanese Literary Aesthetics*. Tokyo: Center for East-Asian Cultural Studies, 1963.
HOFF, FRANK. "Killing the Self: How the Narrator Acts." *ATJ*, 2/1 (Spring 1985): 1-27.
IMMOOS, THOMAS. *Japanisches Theater*. Zürich: Orell Füssli, 1975.
---------"The Birth of Non-verbal Theatre in Shinto Ritual." *MuK*, 29 (1983): 301-306.
INOURA, YOSHINOBU. *A History of Japanese Theater I: Noh and Kyōgen*. Tokyo: Kokusai Bunka Shinkokai, 1971.
---------- and KAWATAKE, TOSHIO. *The Traditional Theatre of Japan*. Tokyo: The Japan Foundation, 1981 (A reprint of the above with Kawatake's part II).
I.T.I. JAPAN CENTER, comp. *Theatre Year-book: 1987*; *Theatre Year-book: 1988*; *Theatre Year-book: 1989*. Tokyo: Japan Center, International Theatre Institute, 1987-89 (Annual publication).
ITO, KISAKU. "Stage Design in Japan." *Japan Quarterly*, 99 (Spring 1967): 301-308.
IZUTSU, TOSHIHIKO and TOYO. *The Theory of Beauty in the Classical Aesthetics of Japan*. The Hague: Martinus Nijhoff, 1981.
JAPANESE NATIONAL COMMISSION FOR UNESCO, comp. *Theatre in Japan*. Tokyo: Printing Bureau, Ministry of Finance, 1963.
----------, ed. *Proceedings of the International Symposium on the Theatre in East and West*. Tokyo, 1965.
JAPANISCHES KULTURINSTITUT KÖLN, ed. *Klassische Theaterformen Japans: Einführungen zu Noo, Bunraku und Kabuki*. Köln and Vienna: Böhlau, 1983.
KAWATAKE, SHIGETOSHI. *Development of Japanese Theatre Art*. Tokyo: Kokusai Bunka Shinkokai, 1935.
KAWATAKE, TOSHIO. "Einführung in die Feldtheorie des Theaters." In Gössmann and Zobel, eds., *Das Gold im Wachs*. Munich: Iudicium, 1988: 207-222.
---------- and ORTOLANI, BENITO. "Zur Theatergeschichte Japans." *MuK*, 7/11 (1974): 1-88.
KEENE, DONALD. "Realism and Unreality in Japanese Drama." *Drama Survey*, 3 (1964): 332-351.
KOKUSAI BUNKA SHINKOKAI, comp. *Bibliography of Standard Reference Books for Japanese Studies with Descriptive Notes*. vol. 8 (B), Theatre, Dance and Music. Tokyo: Univ. of Tokyo Press, 1961.
KUSANO, EISABURO. *Stories Behind Noh and Kabuki Plays*. Tokyo: Tokyo News Service, 1962.
LEIMS, THOMAS. "Japanisches Theater." In *...Ich werde deinen Schatten essen: Das Theater des Fernen Osten*. Berlin: Frölich und Kaufmann, 1985: 169-194.
LOMBARD, FRANK ALANSON. *An Outline History of the Japanese Drama*. London: Allen and Unwin, 1928.
LORENZONI, PIERO. *Storia del teatro giapponese*. Firenze: Sansoni, 1961.
LOVEL, JOHN. "Theatre Audiences of Japan." *Theatre Survey*, 5 (Nov. 1964): 99-106.

MAGNINO, LEO. *Teatro giapponese*. Milano: Nuova Accademia, 1956.

MALM, WILLIAM P. *Japanese Music and Musical Instruments*. Tokyo and Rutland, VT: Tuttle, 1959.

----------, ed. *Essays on Asian Music and Theater*. New York: Asia Society: 1971-71.

----------*Six Hidden Views of Japanese Music*. Berkeley, CA: Univ. of California Press, 1986.

----------"Music Cultures of Momoyama Japan." In George Elison and Bardwell L. Smith, eds., *Warlords, Artists, and Commoners*. Honolulu: Univ. of Hawaii Press, 1981: 163-185.

MARKUS, ANDREW L. "The Carnival of Edo: Misemono Spectacles." *Harvard Journal of Asiatic Studies*, 45 (1985): 499-541.

MAROTTI, FERRUCCIO. *Il volto dell'invisibile: Studi e ricerche sui teatri orientali*. Roma: Bulzoni, 1984.

MAYBON, ALBERT. *Le théâtre japonais*. Paris: Henri Laurens, 1925.

MINER, EARL. "Our Heritage of Japanese Drama." *Literature East and West*, 15.4-16.2 (1971-72): 577-600.

MITCHEL, JOHN D. *Theatre: The Search for Style*. Midland, MI: Northwood Institute Press, 1982.

MITOMA SUSILO, JUDITH, ed. *Japanese Tradition: Search and Research*. International Conference Journal. Los Angeles: Univ. of California, College of Fine Arts, 1981.

MUCCIOLI, MARCELLO. *Il teatro giapponese*. Milano: Feltrinelli, 1962.

ORTOLANI, BENITO. "Das japanische Theater." In Heinz Kindermann, ed., *Einführung in das ostasiatische Theater*. Köln and Vienna: Böhlau, 1985: 317-426. (Revised edition of "Das japanische Theater," in Heinz Kindermann, ed., *Fernöstliches Theater*, Stuttgart: Kröner, 1966: 391-526).

---------"Iemoto." *Japan Quarterly*, 16/3 (July-September 1969): 297-306.

----------, ed. *International Bibliography of Theatre: 1982*. New York, NY: Theatre Research Data Center, 1985. *IBT:1983* (1986); *IBT:1984* (1987); *IBT:1985* (1989); *IBT:1986* (1991); *IBT:1987* (1992); *IBT:1988-89* (1993); *IBT:1990-91* (1994).

---------"Il teatro occidentale alla ricerca dell'energia profonda, «rilassata e composita» dell'Oriente." In Antonella Ottai, ed., *Teatro Oriente/Occidente*. Roma: Bulzoni, 1986: 185-195.

OTTAI, ANTONELLA, ed. *Teatro Oriente/Occidente*. Roma: Bulzoni, 1986.

OTTAVIANI, GIOIA. *L'attore e lo sciamano: Esempi d'identitá nelle tradizioni dell'Estremo Oriente*. Roma: Bulzoni, 1984. (Contains a comprehensive bibliography of Japanese theatre, 143-172.)

---------*Introduzione allo studio del teatro giapponese*. Firenze: Ponte alle Grazie, 1994.

PAVOLINI, CORRADO. *Teatro giapponese classico*. Roma, 1941.

PICONE, M. J. *Le maschere nelle rappresentazioni rituali dal Gigaku al Dai Kagura*. Firenze: Aistugia, 1980.

PIPER, MARIA. *Die Schaukunst der Japaner*. Berlin and Leipzig: Walter de Gruyter, 1927.

----------*Das Japanische Theater*. Societäts-Verlag, 1937.

PRONKO, LEONARD C. *Theater East and West: Perspectives Towards a Total Theater*. Berkeley and Los Angeles: Univ. of California Press, 1967.

----------*Guide to Japanese Drama*. Boston: G.K. Hall, 1973.

----------"Oriental Theatre for the West: Problems of Autenticity and Communication." *ETJ*, 20/3 (1968): 425-436.

RATTI, OSCAR and WESTBROOK, ADELE. *Secrets of the Samurai: A Survey of the Martial Arts of Feudal Japan*. Rutland, VT and Tokyo: Tuttle, 1973.

RAZ, JACOB. *Audience and Actors: A Study of Their Interaction in the Japanese Traditional Theatre*. Leiden: E. J. Brill, 1983.

RICHMOND, FARLEY. "Asian Theatre Materials: A Selected Bibliography." *TDR*, 15/3 (T50, Spring 1971): 313-324.

SADLER, ARTHUR L. *Japanese Plays. Nō-kyōgen-kabuki*. Sydney: Angus and Robertson, 1934.

SAKANISHI, SHIO. *A List of Translations of Japanese Drama into English, French, and German*. Washington, DC: American Council of Learned Societies, 1935.

SCOTT, ADOLPHE CLARENCE. *Theatre in Asia*. New York: Macmillan, 1973: 174-221.

SIEFFERT, RENÉ. "Bibliographie du théâtre japonais." *Bulletin de la Maison Franco-Japonaise*, Nouvelle Série, Tome III, 1953: 1-116.

----------"Le théâtre japonais." In Jacquot, Jean, ed., *Les théâtres d'Asie*. Paris: Editions du Centre National de la Recherche Scientifique, 1961: 133-161.

---------- and WASSERMAN, MICHEL. *Théâtre classique*. Arts du Japon. Paris: Maison des cultures du monde, Publications Orientalistes de France, 1983.

SILBERMAN, BERNARD S. *Japan and Korea: A Critical Bibliography*. Tucson: Univ. of Arizona Press, 1962.

TAMBA, AKIRA. "Gagaku." In *Encyclopédie permanente du Japon*, Oct-Nov , Paris: Publ. Orientalistes de France, 1977.

THEATRE YEAR-BOOK, 1989 (published yearly since, 1990, 1991, etc.). Tokyo: International Theatre Institute Japan.

TRAN, VAN KHE. "Le théâtre musicale en Chine, au Japon et au Viet-Nam." *Bulletin du Centre d'études de musique orientale*, 14-15 (1974-75): 1-13.

TSUGE, GEN'ICHI. *Japanese Music: An Annotated Bibliography*. Garland Bibliographies in Ethnomusicology 2. New York: Garland, 1986.

TSUNODA, RYUSAKU, et al., eds. *Sources of Japanese Tradition*. New York: Columbia UP, 1958.

UEDA, MAKOTO. *Literary and Art Theories in Japan*. Cleveland, OH: The Press of Western Reserve Univ., 1967.

UEDA, MAKOTO. "Japanese Idea of a Theatre." *Modern Drama*, 11 (Spring 1967): 348-357.

VARLEY, PAUL H. *Japanese Culture*, 3rd edition. Honolulu, Univ. of Hawaii Press, 1984.

WATERHOUSE, DAVID. "Actors, Artists, and Stage in Eighteenth-Century Japan and England." In J. D. Browning, ed., *The Stage in the 18th Century*. New York and London: Garland, 1981: 201-242.

WELLS, HENRY WILLIS. *The Classical Drama of the Orient*. New York: Asia Publishing House, 1965.

YAMAGUCHI, MASAO. "Theatricality in Japan." (tr. E. A. Walker) *Modern Drama*, 25/1 (1982): 140-142.

ZARINA, XENIA. *Classic Dances of the Orient*. New York: Crown, 1967.

SECTION 2: From the Beginnings to the Origins of the Nō

AKIMA, TOSHIO. "The Songs of the Dead: Poetry, Drama and Ancient Death Rituals of Japan." *Journal of Asian Studies*, 41 (May 1982): 485-509.

ARAKI, JAMES T. *The Ballad-Drama of Medieval Japan*. Berkeley: Univ. of California Press, 1964. Reprint: Rutland, VT: Tuttle, 1978.

ASAI, SUSAN MIYO. *Music and Drama in Nōmai of Northern Japan*. Ph. D. Diss. UCLA, 1988.

ASTON, WILLIAM GEORGE, tr. *Nihongi: Chronicles of Japan from the Earliest Times to A.D. 697*. London: Allen and Unwin, 1896. Reprint 1954.

BENAZET, ALEXANDRE. *Le théâtre au Japon: ses rapports avec les cultes locaux*. (Annales du Musée Guimet, tome 13). Paris: Ernest Leroux, 1901.

BLACKER, CARMEN. *The Catalpa Bow: A Study of Shamanistic Practices in Japan*. London: Allen and Unwin, 1975.

BLASDEL, CHRISTOPHER. "Anatomy of a Japanese Festival. *Hogaku*, 1/1 (1983): 113-119.

BLAU, HAGEN. *Sarugaku und Shushi: Beiträge zur Ausbildung dramatischer Elemente im weltlichen und religiösen Volkstheater der Heian-Zeit unter besonderer Berücksichtigung seiner sozialen Grundlagen*. Wiesbaden: Otto Harrassowitz, 1966.

BROWER, ROBERT H. *Japanese Court Poetry*. Stanford, CA: Stanford UP, 1961.

DALLA PALMA, SISTO, et al. *Alle radici del sole: Teatro, Musica e danza in Giappone*. Torino: E.R.I., 1983.

DORSON, RICHARD, ed. *Studies in Japanese Folklore*. Bloomington: Indiana UP, 1963.

ECKARDT, HANS. *Das Kokonchomonshū des Tachibana Narisue als musikgeschichtliche Quelle*. Wiesbaden: Otto Harrassowitz, 1956.

----------"Konron, Reste kontinentaler Mythologie in der japanischen Bugaku." *Oriens Extremus*, 7 (1960): 17-30.

ENDRESS, GERHILD. "Kagura." In Horst Hammitzsch, ed., *Japan Handbuch*. Wiesbaden: Steiner, 1981: 1850-1853.

FAIRCHILD, WILLIAM P. "Shamanism in Japan." *Folklore Studies*, 21 (1962): 1-122.

GABBERT, GUNHILD. *Die Masken des Bugaku. Profane japanische Tanzmasken der Heian- und Kamakura-Zeit.* Bd. 1: Hauptteil und Katalog. Bd. 2: Anmerkungen und Tafeln. Wiesbaden: Otto Harrassowitz, 1972.

GARFIAS, ROBERT. *Gagaku: The Music and Dances of the Imperial Household*. New York: Theatre Arts Books, 1959.

----------*Music of a Thousand Autumns: The Tōgaku Style of Japanese Court Music.* Berkeley: Univ. of California, 1975.

GILDAY, EDMUND THERON. *The Pattern of Matsuri: Comic Schemes and Ritual Illusion in Japanese Festivals.* Ph. D. Diss., Univ. of Chicago, 1987.

GRIM, JOHN and MARY E. "Viewing the Hana Matsuri at Shimoawashiro, Aichi Prefecture." *Asian Folklore Studies*, 41/2 (1982): 163-185.

HAGENAUER, CHARLES. "La dance rituelle dans la cérémonie du Chinkonsai." *Journal Asiatique*, 1930: 299-350.

HARICH-SCHNEIDER, ETA. *The Rhythmic Patterns in Gagaku and Bugaku.* Leiden: E. J. Brill, 1954.

---------*Rōei: The Medieval Court Songs of Japan.* Tokyo: Sophia UP, 1965.

---------"The Remolding of *Gagaku* under the Meiji Restoration." *TASJ*, ser. 3, 5 (December 1957): 84-105.

---------"Das Mikagura Hompu von 1332." In Lydia Brüll and Ulrich Kemper, eds., *Asien: Tradition und Fortschritt. Festschrift für Horst Hammitzsch.* Wiesbaden: 1971: 173-183.

HISAMATSU, SEN'ICHI. "The Characteristics of Beauty in the Japanese Middle Ages." *Acta Asiatica*, 8 (1965): 40-53.

---------*Zen and the Fine Arts*, tr. Tokiwa Gishin. Tokyo: Kodansha International, 1971.

HOFF, FRANK. *Song, Dance, Storytelling: Aspects of the Performing Arts in Japan.* Cornell Univ. East Asian Papers, 15. Ithaca, NY: Cornell China-Japan Program, 1978.

----------"Dance to Song in Japan." *Dance Research Journal*, 9/11 (Fall/Winter 1976-77): 1-15.

----------"The 'Evocation' and 'Blessing' of Okina." *Alcheringa Ethnopoetics*, n. s. 3.1 (1977): 48-60.

HONDA, YASUJI. "*Yamabushi Kagura* and *Bangaku*: Performance in the Japanese Middle Ages and 'Contemporary Folk Performances," tr. Frank Hoff. *ETJ* 26/2 (1974): 192-208.

----------"Reflections on Dance, Its Origins, and the Value of Comparative Studies." *Dance Research Annual*, 14 (1983): 99-104.

HORI, ICHIRO. "Shamanism in Japan." *Japanese Journal of Religious Studies*, 2 (1975): 231-287.

IMMOOS, THOMAS. "The Birth of Japanese Theatre," *MN*, 24 (1969): 403-414.

IMMOOS, THOMAS. "Das Mysterium von Feuer und Wasser im Schintō-Ritual (Yudate-Kagura)." In Baumgarten, Jakob, ed., *Vermittlung Zwischenkirchlicher Gemeinschaft. 50 Jahre Missionsgesellschaft Bethlehem Immensee*. Fs. Schönbeck-Beckenried, 1971: 143-162.
----------"Das Tanzritual der Yamabushi." *MOAG*, 50 (1968): 1-17.
----------"Ein Ritual der Wiedergeburt in den Yamabushi-Kagura." *MOAG*, 50 (1968): 19-25.
----------"Archetypen religiöser Erfahrung im Shintofest." In Wandelfels/Immoos, eds., *Fernöstliche Weisheit und Christlicher Glaube*. Festgabe für Heinrich Dumoulin, Mainz, 1985.
ISHII, TATSURO. "The Festival of the Kasuga Wakamiya Shrine." *Theatre Research International*, 12/2 (Summer 1987): 134-147.
KIM KWON, YUNG-HEE. "The Female Entertainment Tradition in Medieval Japan: The Case of *Asobi*." *ETJ*, 40/2 (1988): 205-216.
KIRBY, ERNEST THEODORE. "The Origin of *Nō* Drama. *ETJ*, 25/3 (October 1973): 269-284.
------------*Ur-drama: The Origins of the Theatre*. New York: New York UP, 1975.
KLEINSCHMIDT, PETER. *Die Masken der Gigaku, der ältesten Theaterform Japans*. Wiesbaden: Otto Harrassowitz, 1966.
KOBAYASHI, KAZUSHIGE. "On the Meaning of Masked Dances in Kagura." *Asian Folklore Studies*, 40 (1981): 1-22.
LUCAS, HEINZ. *Japanische Kultmasken*. Kassel: Erich Röth, 1965.
McCULLOUGH, HELEN G. and WILLIAM, trs. *A Tale of Flowering Fortunes: Annals of Japanese Aristocratic Life in the Heian Period*. Stanford, CA: Stanford UP, 1980.
MÜLLER, GERHILD. *Kagura: Die Lieder der Kagura Zeremonie am Naishidokoro. Übersetzung und Erläuterungen*. Wiesbaden: Otto Harrassowitz, 1971.
NISHIKAWA, KYOTARO. *Bugaku Masks*, tr. Monica Bethe. Tokyo: Kodansha International, 1977.
O'NEILL, P. G. "The Structure of Kusemai." *BOAS*, 21/1 (1958): 100-110.
ORTOLANI, BENITO. *Bugaku: The Traditional Dance of the Japanese Imperial Court*. Monographs on Asian Music, Dance, and Theater in Asia, vol. 5. New York: The Performing Arts Program of the Asia Society, 1978.
----------"Le origini del teatro Nō." In *Teatro Nō: Costumi e Maschere*. Roma: Istituto di Cultura Giapponese, 1970: 35-75.
----------"Shamanism in the Origins of the *Nō* Theatre." *ATJ*, 1/2 (Fall 1984): 166-190.
PERKINS, P. D. and FUJI, KEN'ICHI. "Gosechi no Mai or 'Five Notes on Dance'," *Cultural Nippon*, 7/3 (1939): 97-106.
PHILIPPI, DONALD L., tr. *Kojiki*. Princeton, NJ and Tokyo: Princeton UP and Univ. of Tokyo Press, 1969.
RAZ, JACOB. "*Chinkon*: From Folk Beliefs to Stage Conventions." *MuK*, 27/1 (1981): 5-18.

RUCH, BARBARA. "Medieval Jongleurs and the Making of a National Literature." In John Hall and Takeshi Toyoda, eds., *Japan in the Muromachi Age*. Berkeley, CA: Univ. of California Press, 1977: 279-309.

SADLER, ALBERT W." *O-Kagura*: Field Notes on the Festival Drama in Modern Tokyo." *Asian Folklore Studies*, 29 (1970): 275-300.

SCHNEIDER, RONALD. *Kōwaka-mai: Sprache und Stil einer mittelalterlichen japanischen Rezitationskunst*. Hamburg, 1968.

SUGINO, MASAYOSHI. "Die Anfänge des japanischen Theaters bis zum Nōspiel." *MN*, 3 (1940): 90-108.

SWANSON, PAUL L. "Shugendō and the Yoshino-Kumano Pilgrimage." *MN*, 36 (1981): 55-79.

TESSARI, ROBERTO. "Baubo: Frammenti di un mito di fondazione dello spettacolo comico." In Gioachino Chiarini and Roberto Tessari, *Teatro del corpo, teatro della parola: Due saggi sul «comico»*. Pisa: ETS, 1983: 3-20.

THOMPSON, FRED. "Archaische Raumordnung im Shintō-Fest (Matsuri): Shiraiwa und Kakunodate (Akita)." In Gössmann and Zobel, eds., *Das Gold im Wachs*. Munich: Iudicium, 1988: 81-92.

THORNBURY, BARBARA. "Kagura, Chaban, and the Awaji Puppet Theatre: A Literary View of Japan's Traditional Performing Arts." *Theatre Survey*, 35/1 (1994): 55-64.

TOGI, MASATARO. *Gagaku: Court Music and Dance*. Tokyo: Walker/Weatherhill, 1971.

TSUBAKI, ANDREW. "The Performing Arts of Sixteenth Century Japan." *ETJ*, 29/3 (1977): 299-309.

WOLZ, CARL. *Bugaku, Japanese Court Dance, with the Notation of Basic Movements of Nasori*. Providence, RI: Asian Music Publ., 1971.
----------"Bugaku Today." In Judith Mitoma Susilo, ed., *Japanese Tradition: Search and Research*. Los Angeles: Univ. of California, 1981: 115-124.

SECTION 3: Nō and Kyōgen

ALBERY, NOBUKO. *The House of Kanze*. New York: Simon and Schuster, 1985.

ARNOLD, PAUL. *Neuf Nō japonais*. Paris: Librairie Théâtrale, 1957.

BARTH, JOHANNES. "Nō Kyōgen: die mittelalterlichen Komödien Japans." *MOAG*, 44/2 (1963): 94-102.

BEAUJARD, ANDRÉ. *Le théâtre comique des Japonais. Introduction à l'étude du Kyoghén*. Paris: Maisonneuve, 1937.

BENL, OSCAR. *Seami Motokiyo und der Geist des Nō-Schauspiels*. Wiesbaden: Steiner, 1953.
----------"Zwei Spätschriften Seami Motokiyo's." *NOAG*, 73 (1952): 29-44.
----------*Die geheime Überlieferung des Nō*. Frankfurt/M: Insel Verlag, 1961.
---------- and HAMMITZSCH, HORST. *Japanische Geisteswelt: Von Mythos zu Gegenwart*. Baden Baden, 1956.

BERBERICH, JUNKO SAKABA. "Some Observations on Movement in *Nō*." *ATJ*, 1/2 (1984): 207-216.
BESLER, L., tr. "Chokubu Soga, a Noh Play." *MN*, 29/1 (1974): 69-81.
BETHE, MONICA and BRAZELL, KAREN. *Dance in the Nō Theatre*. 3 vols. Cornell Univ. East Asia Papers 29. Ithaca, NY: China-Japan Program, 1982.
----------*Nō as Performance: An Analysis of the Kuse Scene of Yamamba*. Ithaca, NY: Cornell Univ. East Asia Papers, 16, 1978.
BOHNER, HERMANN. *Gestalten und Quellen des Nō*. Tokyo/Osaka: OAG, 1955.
----------*Nō: Die einzelnen Nō*. Tokyo: OAG, 1956.
----------*Nō: Einführung*. Tokyo: OAG, 1959.
----------*Seami: Der Höchste Blume Weg*. Tokyo: OAG, 1943.
----------*Seami: Blumenspiegel (Kwakyō)*. Tokyo: OAG, 1953.
----------*Seami: Buch von der Höchsten Blume Weg (Shi-kwa-dō-sho)*. Tokyo: OAG, 1947.
----------*Seami: Der Neuen Stufen Folge (Kyū-i-shi-dai)*. Tokyo: OAG, 1943.
----------*Seami: Shū-dōsho, Kyakurai-kwa, Schriften der dritten Schriftumsperiode des Meisters*. Tokyo: OAG, 1961.
BRAZELL, KAREN. "Unity of Image: An Aspect of the Art of Noh." In Judith Mitoma Susilo, ed., *Japanese Tradition: Search and Research*. Los Angeles: Univ. of California, 1981: 25-43.
----------"Zeami and Women in Love." *Literature East and West*, 18/1 (1974): 8-18.
----------, ed. *12 Plays of the Noh and Kyōgen Theatres*. Ithaca, NY: Cornell Univ. East Asian Papers 50, 1989.
CALZA, GIAN CARLO. *L'incanto sottile del dramma nō*. Milano: Scheiwiller, 1975.
CHANG, SIK-YUN. "The Tragic Metaphor of the Nō Drama." *Theatre Annual*, 1968.
COLBATH, JAMES A. *The Japanese Drama and its Relation to Zen Buddhism*. Ph. D. Diss., Western Reserve Univ., 1963.
----------"The Noh and Its Relation to Zen Buddhism." *Theatre Annual*, 27 (1971-1972).
DE PORTER, ERIKA. *Zeami's Talks on Sarugaku*. Amsterdam: J. C. Gieben, 1986.
----------*Motoyoshi's Sarugaku dangi: A Description and Assessment with Annotated Translation*. Alblasserdam, 1983.
DE ROSNY, L. *Le couvent du Dragon vert: Une comédie japonaise*. Paris: 1893.
EMMERT, RICHARD. "Training of the *nō* Performer." *Theatre Research International*, 12/2 (Summer 1987): 123-133.
----------"Hiranori: A Unique Rhythm Form in Japanese Nō Music." In *Musical Voices of Asia: Report of Asian Traditional Performing Arts 1978*. Tokyo: Heibonsha, 1980.
FENOLLOSA, ERNEST FRANCISCO. *Certain Noble Plays of Japan: From the Manuscripts of E. F. Fenellosa Chosen and Finished by Ezra Pound, with an Introduction by W. B. Yeats*. Churchtown, Dundrum: The Cuala Press, 1916.

FENOLLOSA, ERNEST FRANCISCO. *"Noh" or Accomplishment: A Study of the Classical Stage of Japan, with the collaboration of Ezra Pound.* London: MacMillan, 1916.
FUJI TAKEO. *Humor and Satire in Early English Comedy and Japanese Kyōgen Drama.* Hirakata: KUFS Publications, 1983.
FULCHIGNONI, ENRICO. *Teatro giapponese: Sette Nō.* Roma, 1942.
GELLNER, WINFRIED. *Die Kostüme des Nō-Theaters.* Wiesbaden: Steiner Verlag, 1990.
GEORGE, DAVID E. R. "Ritual Drama: Between Mysticism and Magic." *ATJ*, 4/2 (Fall 1987): 127-165.
GOLAY, G. "Pathos and Farce. Zatōo Plays of the Kyōgen Repertoire." *MN*, 28/2 (1973): 1939-1949.
GOFF, JANET E. "The National Noh Theatre." *MN*, 39 (1984): 445-452.
----------*Noh Drama and The Tale of Genji: The Art of Allusion in Fifteen Classical Plays.* Princeton: Princeton UP: 1991.
GONTARD, DENIS. "Okina ou le nō absolu?" In Jaqueline de Jomaron, ed., *Dramaturgies.* Paris: Nizet, 1986: 435-439.
GUNDERT, WILHELM. *Der Shintoismus im japanischen Nō Drama.* MQAG, vol. 19. Tokyo, 1925.
---------"Über den Begriff 'Yūgen' bei Seami." *Festgabe der Deutschen Gesellschaft für Natur- und Völkerkunde Ostasiens zum 70. Geburtstag von Prof. Dr. K. Florenz.* Tokyo: 1935: 21-30.
---------"Gedanken über das Japanische Nō-Drama." In *Meiji Seitoku Kinen Gakkai Kiyo*, 27/28, Tokyo: 1926.
HARE, THOMAS BLENMAN. *Zeami's Style: The Noh Plays of Zeami Motokiyo.* Stanford, CA: Stanford UP, 1986.
----------*Zeami's Style: A Study of the "Mugen" Noh Plays of Zeami Motokiyo.* Ph. D. Diss., Univ. of Michigan, 1981.
HARRIS, A. J. *This Radical Nō.* Ph. D. Diss., Ohio State Univ., 1973.
HAYASHIYA, TATSUSABURO. "Ancient History and Performing Arts." *Acta Asiatica*, 33 (1977); 1-14.
HESSE, EVA, ed. *Nō, vom Genius Japans: Ezra Pound, Ernest Fenollosa, Serge Eisenstein.* Zürich: Verlag der Arche, 1963.
HOFF, FRANK. "A Community of Taste, Judgement and Interpretation Seen Through the Conversations of Zeami on Noh." In Judith Mitoma Susilo, ed., *Japanese Tradition: Search and Research.* Los Angeles: Univ. of California, 1981: 53-62.
----------"Dōjōji: A Woman and a Bell." *Dance Research Annual*, 14 (1983): 32-41.
----------"Sehen und Gesehen-werden im Nō." In Gössmann and Zobel, eds., *Das Gold im Wachs.* Munich: Iudicium Verlag, 1988: 187-206.
----------"The 'Evocation' and 'Blessing' of *Okina*: A Performance Version of Ritual Shamanism." *Alcheringa: Ethnopoetics*, 3/1 (1977): 48-60.
----------"Zeami on *jo ha kyū* Theory." *Proceedings: Preservation and Development of the Traditional Performing Arts*, 4 (1981): 217-228.

HOFF, FRANK and FLINDT, WILLI, trs. *The Life Structure of Nō. An English Version of Yokomichi Mario's Analysis of the Structure of Nō.* Tokyo: Concerned Theatre Japan, 1973.

HUEY, ROBERT, tr. "Sakuragawa." *MN*, 38/3 (1983): 295-312.

IMMOOS, THOMAS. "La teoria mistica della recitazione in Zeami." In Antonella Ottai, ed., *Teatro Oriente/Occidente.* Roma: Bulzoni, 1986: 213-229.

----------"Kyōgen—Worüber lachen die Japaner? Vom Mythos zum Kyōgen." *MuK*, 30/1-2 (1984): 41-62.

ISHII, TATSURO. "Zeami's Mature Thoughts on Acting." *Theatre Research International*, 12/2 (Summer 1987): 110-123.

----------"An Examination into the Mature Thought and Conceptual Framework Presented in the Later Treatises of Zeami." *Sangeet Natak*, 58 (1981): 45-68.

----------"Zeami on Performance." *Theatre Research International*, 8 (1983): 190-206.

ISHIKAWA, MINORU. *Zur Struktur des Kyōgen-Spiels."* Berlin: Kleine Schriften der Gesellschaft für Theatergeschichte, Heft 22, 1967.

JOHNSON, IRMGARD. "Priestly Nō at Chūsonji." *ATJ*, 4/2 (1987): 215-229.

----------"The Life of the Adult Nō Player in Japan Today." *Comparative Drama*, 18/4 (1984): 189-310.

----------"Women in the Man's World of Noh." *Journal of Asian Affairs*, 2/1 (1977): 1-8.

----------"Kurokawa New Year's Nō Festival: Ogi Matsuri" and "Governmental Nurture of the Nō Tradition." *The Japan Interpreter*, 13/1, 1980.

JONES, STANLEIGH H. Jr. "The Nō Plays Obasute and Kanehira." *MN*, 13/4 (1963): 261-285.

KADOWAKI, KAKICHI. "Die Taufe Jesu. Nō-Drama und Messe." In Gössmann and Zobel, eds., *Das Gold im Wachs.* Munich: Iudicium, 1988: 147-154.

KAISER, GERHARD. "Sprachlos im Nō-Theater." *Neue Deutsche Hefte*, 23/150 (1976): 273-285.

KOMIYA, TOYOTAKA. "Über die Nō-Spiel-Theorie von Seami." In Gustav Erdmann und Alfons Eichstaedt, eds., *Worte und Werte.* Berlin: de Gruyter, 1961: 169-176.

KANZE, HIDEO. "The Noh: Business and Art." *TDR*, 15 (1971): 185-192.

KATO, HILDA. *Kyōgen, ein Beitrag zur Funktion dieses Genres.* Ph. D. Diss., Univ. of Vienna, 1976.

KAULA, DAVID. "On Noh Drama." *TDR*, 5 (1960): 61-72.

KEENE, DONALD. *Nō: The Classical Theatre of Japan.* Tokyo and Palo Alto: Kodansha, 1966.

----------, ed. *Twenty Plays of the Nō Theatre.* New York: Colombia UP, 1970.

KENNY, DON. *A Guide to Kyōgen.* Tokyo: Hinoki Shoten, 1968.

----------, tr. *The Kyōgen Book.* Tokyo: The Japan Times, 1989.

KIM, MYUNG-WHAN. "Zenchiku's Philosophy of the 'Wheel' and the Yeatsian Parallel." *Literature East and West*, 15-16 (1971-72): 647-661.

KOMINZ, LAURENCE. "The Noh as Popular Theater." *MN*, 33 (1978): 441-446.

KOMIYA, TOYOTAKA. "Über die Nō-Spiel-Theorie von Seami." *Worte und Werte*, Berlin, 1961.

KOMPARU, KUNIO. *The Noh Theatre: Principles and Perspectives*. New York and Tokyo: Weatherhill/Tankosha, 1983.

KONISHI, JIN'ICHI. "New Approaches to the Study of the Nō Drama." *Tōkyō Kyōiku Daigaku Bungakubu Kiyō*, 5 (1960): 1-31.

----------"Michi and Medieval Writing." In Earl Miner, ed., *Michi and Medieval Writing*. Princeton: Princeton UP, 1985: 181-208.

LEE, SANG-KYONG. *Nō und europäisches Theater*. Frankfurt/M: Peter Lang, 1983.

MALM, WILLIAM P. "The Musical Characteristics and Practice of the Japanese Noh Drama in an East Asian Context." In Crump and Malm, eds., *Chinese and Japanese Music-Dramas*. Ann Arbor: Center for Chinese Studies, The Univ. of Michigan, 1975: 99-142.

----------"The Rhythmic Orientation of Two Drums in the Japanese Nō Drama. *Ethnomusicology*, 2/3 (1958): 89-95.

----------"An Introduction to Taiko Drum Music in the Japanese Nō Drama." *Ethonomusicology*, 4/2 (1960): 75-78.

MARTZEL, GÉRARD. *La fête d'Ogi et le nō Kurokawa*. Paris: Publications Orientalistes de France, 1975.

----------*Le Dieu masqué*. Paris: Publications Orientalistes de France, 1982.

MARUOKA, DAIJI and YOSHIKOSHI, TATSUO. *Noh*, tr. Don Kenny. Ōsaka: Hoikusha, 1969.

MATISOFF, SUSAN. "Images of Exile and Pilgrimage: Zeami's *Kintōsho*." *MN*, 34/4 (1979): 449-465.

----------"*Kintōsho*: Zeami's Song of Exile." *MN*, 32/4 (1977): 441-458.

----------*The Legend of Semimaru, Blind Musician of Japan*. New York: Columbia UP, 1978.

MATSUYAMA, YOSHIO. "Studien zur Nō-Musik." *Beiträge zur Ethnomusikologie*, vol. 18, Hamburg 1980.

McKINNON, RICHARD N. *Zeami on the Nō: A Study of 15th Century Japanese Dramatic Criticism*. Ph. D. Diss., Harvard Univ., 1951.

----------"Zeami on the Art of Training." *HJASt*, 16 (1953): 200-225.

----------*Selected Plays of Kyōgen*. Tokyo: Uniprint, 1968.

----------"The Nō and Zeami." *Far Eastern Quarterly*, 11/3 (May 1952): 355-361.

MELCHINGER, SIEGFRIED. "Das Theater der Stille." *Theater Heute*, 10 (1965): 18-23.

MINAGAWA, TATSUO. "Japanese *Noh* Music," *Journal of the American Musicological Society*, 10 (1957): 181-200.

MURAKAMI, UPTON. *A Spectator's Handbook of Noh*. Tokyo: Wanya Shoten, 1963.

NAKAMURA, YASUO. *Noh: The Classical Theater*, tr. Don Kenny. New York and Tokyo: Walker/Weatherhill, 1971.

NEARMAN, MARK J. "Zeami's *Kyūi*: A Pedagogical Guide for Teachers of Acting." *MN*, 33/3 (1978): 299-332.
----------, tr. and ed. "Kakyō: Zeami's Fundamental Principles of Acting." 3 parts, *MN*, 37/3 (1982): 333-74; *MN*, 37/4 (1982): 461-96; *MN*, 38/1 (1983): 51-71.
----------"*Kyakuraika*: Zeami's Final Legacy for the Master Actor." *MN*, 35/2 (1980): 153-197.
----------"Behind the Mask of Nō." In Rebecca Teele, ed., Nō/Kyōgen Masks and Performance. *Mime Journal*, 1984: 20-64.
----------"Zeami on the Goals of the Professional Actor." In Judith Mitoma Susilo, ed., *Japanese Tradition: Search and Research*. Los Angeles: Univ. of California, 1981: 43-52.
----------"Feeling in Relation to Acting: An Outline of Zeami's Views." *ATJ*, 1/1 (1984): 40-45.
NIPPON GAKUJUTSU SHINKOKAI, ed. *The Noh Drama: Ten Plays from the Japanese*. Rutland, VT. and Tokyo: Tuttle. Volumes 2 and 3 published as: *Japanese Noh Drama: Ten Plays Selected and Translated from the Japanese*. Tokyo: Nippon Gakujutsu Shinkōkai, 1959 and 1960.
NOBORI, ASAJI. "Zenchiku's Philosophy of Noh Drama." *Hiroshima Bunkyo Joshi Daigaku Kenkyū Kiyō*, 1 (1966): 24-37.
NOGAMI, TOYOICHIRO. *Zeami and His Theories on Noh*. Tokyo: Hinoki Shoten, 1955.
OGURA, SOEI. *Nō Masken*. Düsseldorf: Dumont-Lindemann-Archiv and Munich: Deutsches Theatermuseum, 1988.
OKANO, MORIYA. "Das Nō-Spiel und die Yuishiki-Lehre." In Gössmann and Zobel, eds., *Das Gold im Wachs*. Munich: Iudicium, 1988: 223-248.
OMOTE, AKIRA. "Nō und Nōforschung." In Harald Schneider, *Das japanische Nōtheater*. Ph. D. Diss. Ludwig-Maximilian-Universität, Munich, 1983: 388-403.
O'NEILL, P. G. *Early Nō Drama: Its Background, Character and Development, 1300-1450*. London: Lund Humphries, 1958.
----------"The Social and Economic Background of *Nō*." *MuK*, 27/1 (1981): 19-29.
----------*A Guide to Nō*. Tokyo: Hinoki shoten, 1964 (2nd edition).
----------"The Year of Zeami's Birth: A New Interpretation of *Museki Isshi*." *MN*, 34/2 (1979): 231-38.
----------"The Nō Schools and Their Organization." *Bulletin of the Japan Society of London*, 4/18 (1974): 2-7.
----------"The Nō Plays *Koi no omoni* and *Yuya*." *MN*, 10 (1954): 203-226.
----------"The Letters of Zeami. One Received from Jūni Gon-no-kami and Two Sent to Zenchiku." *Nōgaku kenkyū*, 5 (1979-1980): 150-134.
ORTOLANI, BENITO. "Il teatro Nō e il pubblico." In *Teatro Nō: Costumi e Maschere*. Roma: Istituto Giapponese di Cultura, 1970: 17-34.
----------"Zeami's Aesthetics of the No and Audience Participation." *ETJ*, 24/2 (May 1972): 109-117.

ORTOLANI, BENITO. *Zenchiku's Aesthetics of the Nō Theatre.* Riverdale Studies, 3. New York: Riverdale Center for Religious Research, 1976.
----------"Komparu Zenchiku: Ugetsu und die Metaphysik der Nō-Schauspielkunst." *MuK*, 10 (1964): 676-691.
----------"Spirituality for the Dancer-Actor in Zeami's and Zenchiku's Writings on the *Nō.*" *Dance Research Annual*, 14 (1983): 147-158.
----------"Nō." In Horst Hammitzsch, ed., *Japan Handbuch.* Wiesbaden: Steiner, 1981: 1862-1872.
----------"Kyōgen." *Ibid.*: 1855-1858.
----------"Il Ruzante e la teoria del Kyōgen di Okura Toraaki." In Giovanni Calendoli and Giuseppe Vellucci, eds., *Convegno Internazionale di Studi sul Ruzante.* Venezia: Corbo e Fiore, 1987: 117-128.
---------- and NISHI, KAZUYOSHI. "The Year of Zeami's Birth. With a Translation of the *Museki Isshi.*" *MN*, 20/3-4 (1965): 319-334.
PERI, NOEL. *Le nō.* Tokyo: Maison Franco-Japonaise, 1944.
--------*Cinq Nō: Drames lyriques japonais.* Paris: Bossard, 1921.
PERZYNSKI, FRIEDRICH. *Japanische Masken: Nō und Kyōgen.* Berlin: Walter de Gruyter, 1925.
PILGRIM, RICHARD B. "Some Aspects of *Kokoro* in Zeami." *MN*, 24/4 (1969): 393-401.
----------"Six Circles, One Dewdrop: The Religio-Aesthetic of Komparu Zenchiku." *Chanoyu Quarterly*, 33 (1983): 7-23.
----------"Zeami and the Way of the Nō." *History of Religions*, 12/2 (1972): 136-148.
PRETZELL, KLAUS and SEMBRITZKY, JOHANNES. "Das Ongyoku-seishutsu-kuden von Zeami: Ein Quellenbeitrag zur Nō-Forschung." *NAOG*, 93 (1963): 63-77.
QAMBER, AKHTAR. *Yeats and the Noh.* New York and Tokyo: Weatherhill, 1974.
----------"The Noh: Classical Dance Drama of the Shogunate Period." *Natya*, 4 (1963): 77-83.
RAZ, JACOB. "The Actor and His Audience: Zeami's Views on the Audience of the Noh." *MN*, 31 (1972): 251-274.
RENONDEAU, GASTON. *Le Bouddhisme dans le Nō.* Tokyo: Maison Franco-Japonaise, 1950.
----------*Le nō.* Tokyo: Maison Franco-Japonaise, 1954.
----------"L'influence bouddhique sur le Nō: La dévotion à Kwannon (Nō de Tomonaga)." In Jacquot, Jean, ed., *Les théâtres d'Asie.* Paris: Éditions du Centre National de la Recherche Scientifique, 1961: 163-184.
RIMER, THOMAS, tr. "Taema." *MN*, 25/3-4 (1970): 431-445.
---------- and YAMAZAKI, MASAKAZU, trs. *On the Art of the Nō Drama: The Major Treatises of Zeami.* Princeton, NJ: Princeton UP, 1984.
SAKANISHI, SHIO. *Japanese Folk-Plays: The Ink-Smeared Lady and Other Kyogen.* Rutland, VT and Tokyo: Tuttle, 1960.
SANSOM, GEORGE. "Translations from the Nō." *TASJ*, 38/3 (1911).

SATA, MEGUMI. "Aristotles' *Poetics* and Zeami's *Teachings on Style and the Flower.*" *ATJ*, 6/1 (Spring 1989): 47-56.
SCHNEIDER, HARALD. *Das japanische Nōtheater.* Ph. D. Diss., Ludwig-Maximilian Univ., Munich, 1983.
SCHNEIDER, ROLAND. *Kōwaka-mai.* Hamburg: DOAG, 1968.
SCOTT, JOSEPH WRIGHT. *The Japanese Noh Plays: The Essential Elements in its Theatre Art Form.* Ph. D. Diss., Ohio State Univ., 1949.
SEKINE, MASARU. *Ze-ami and his Theories of Noh Drama.* Gerrards Cross, 1985.
SESAR, CARL G. *Nō Drama and Chinese Literature.* Ph. D. Diss., Columbia Univ., 1971.
---------"China vs. Japan: the Noh Play *Haku Rakuten.*" In J. I. Crump and William P. Malm, eds., *Chinese and Japanese Music-Dramas.* Ann Arbour: Univ. of Michigan, 1975: 143-188.
SHIBANO, DOROTHY T. *Kyōgen: The Comic as Drama.* Ph. D. Diss., Univ. of Washington, 1973.
SHIDEHARA, MICHITARŌ and WHITEHOUSE, WILFRID, trs. "Seami Jūroku Bushū: Seami's Sixteen Treatises." *MN* 4/2 (1949): 530-565, and 5/2 (1950): 466-498.
SHIMAZAKI, CHIFUMI. *The Noh.* 3 vols. Tokyo: Hinoki Shoten, 1972, 1976: 1977.
SHIVELY, DONALD. "Buddhahood for the Non-Sentient: A Theme in Nō Plays." *HJASt*, 20 (1957): 135-161.
SIEFFERT, RENE. "Literary Sources of the Noh." *World of Music*, 17/3 (1975): 13-18.
----------"Mibu-Kyogen." *Bulletin de la Maison Franco-Japonaise*, Nouvelle Serie, 3 (1954): 117-151.
----------*Nō et Kyōgen.* 2 vols. Paris: Orientalistes de France, 1979.
----------, ed. *Les dances sacrées.* Paris: Le Seuil, 1963.
----------*La tradition secrète du nō.* Paris: Gallimard, 1960.
SCHOLZ-CIONCA, STANCA. "Der Granatapfel: Zur Feuer-symbolik des Tenjin im Nō." In Gössmann and Zobel, *Das Gold im Wachs.* Munich: Iudicium, 1988: 175-186.
SMETHURST, MAE J. *The Artistry of Aeschylus and Zeami: A Comparative Study of Greek Tragedy and Nō.* Princeton, NJ: Princeton UP, 1989.
SOEDA, H. "The Noh Stage." *Concerned Theatre Japan*, 1/4 (1971): 18-27.
STOPES, MARIE C. and SAKURAI, JOJI. *Plays of Old Japan: The Nō together with Translations of the Dramas.* London: Heinemann, 1913.
STUCKI, YASUKO. "Yeats' Drama and the Noh: A Comparative Study in Dramatic Theories." *Modern Drama*, 9 (May 1966): 101-122.
SUZUKI, BEATRICE LANE. *Nōgaku: Japanese Nō Plays.* London: John Murray, 1932.
TAMBA, AKIRA. *La Structure musicale du nō, théâtre traditionnel japonais.* Paris: Klincksiek, 1974.
----------*The Musical Structure of Nō*, tr. Patricia Matoréas. Tokyo: Tokai UP, 1981.

TAMBA, AKIRA. "Symbolic Meaning of Cries in the Music of Nō." *The World of Music*, 20, 3 (1978).

TEELE, REBECCA, comp. "Nō/Kyōgen Masks and Performance." *Mime Journal*, 1984.

----------"Recollections and Thoughts on Nō. An Interview with Kongō Iwao, Head of the Kongō School of Nō." *Ibid.*: 74-92.

TEELE, ROY E. "Translations of Nō Plays." *Comparative Literature*, 9 (1957): 345-368.

----------"Formal and Linguistic Problems in Translating a Noh Play." *Studies on Asia*, 4 (1963): 43-54.

----------"Comic Noh Essential to the Noh Theatre." *Literature East and West*, 11 (Dec. 1967): 350-360.

----------"The Structure of the Japanese Noh Play." In J. I. Crump, and William P. Malm, eds., *Chinese and Japanese Music-Dramas*. Michigan Papers in Chinese Studies, 19. Ann Arbor: Univ. of Michigan, 1975: 189-234.

----------, tr. with Nicholas J. Teele and H. Rebecca Teele. *Ono no Komachi: Poems, Stories, Nō Plays*. New York/London: Garland, 1993.

TERASAKI, ETSUKO. "Wils Words and Specious Phrases: *Kyōgen Kigo* in the Nō Play *Jinen Koji*." *HJASt*, 49/2 (Dec. 1989): 519-552.

----------"Images and Symbols in *Sotoba Komachi*: A Critical Analysis of a Nō Play." *HJASt*, 44/1 (June 1984): 155-184.

THORNHILL, ARTHUR H., III. "The Goddess Emerges: Shinto Paradigms in the Aesthetics of Zeami and Zenchiku." *Journal of the Association of Teachers of Japanese*, 24:1 (April 1990): 49-59.

--------- *Six Circles, One Dewdrop: The Religio-Aesthetic World of Komparu Zenchiku*. Princeton: Princeton UP, 1993.

TOKI, ZEMMARO. *Japanese Nō Plays*. Tokyo: Japan Travel Bureau, 1954.

TSUBAKI, ANDREW T. "Zeami and the Transition of the Concept of Yūgen: A Note on Japanese Aesthetics." *The Journal of Aesthetics and Art Criticism*, 30 (1971): 55-67.

----------"An Analysis and Interpretation of Zeami's Concept of Yūgen." Ph. D. Diss., Univ. of Illinois, 1967.

TSURUOKA, G. and ZÖBEL, GUNTER. *Nō und Kultisches Volkstheater*, Tokyo: OAG, 28, 1987.

TYLER, ROYALL. *Pining Wind: A Cycle of Nō Plays*. Ithaca, NY: Cornell Univ. East Asia Papers, 17, 1978.

----------*Granny Mountains: A Second Cycle of Nō Plays*. Ithaca, NY: Cornell Univ. East Asia Papers, 18, 1978.

----------, ed. and tr. *Japanese Nō Dramas*. London: Penguin Books, 1992.

UEDA, MAKOTO, tr. *The Old Pine and Other Noh Plays*. Lincoln: Univ. of Nebraska Press, 1962.

----------"Zeami on Art." *Journal of Aesthetics and Art Criticism*. 20/1 (1962): 73-80.

--------*Zeami, Basho, Yeats, Pound*. Hague: Mouton, 1965.

---------"Toraaki and his Theory of Comedy." *Journal of Asthetics and Art Criticism*, 24 (1964-65): 19-25.

WALEY, ARTHUR. *The Nō Plays of Japan*. London: Allen and Unwin, 1921.

WATSON, BURTON. "Mibu Kyōgen." *Japan Quarterly*, 6/1 (1959): 95-98.

WATSUJI, TETSURO. "*Yōkyoku ni awareta rinri shisō*. Japanese Ethical Thoughts in the Noh Plays of the Muromachi Period," tr. David A. Dilworth. *MN*, 24/4 (1969): 467-498.

WEBER-SCHÄFER, PETER. *Vierundzwanzig Nō-Spiele*. Frankfurt/M, 1961.

----------*Ono no Komachi: Gestalt und Legende im Nō -Spiel*. Wiesbaden: Otto Harrassowitz, 1960.

WELLS, HENRY D. "Japanese Farce and Japanese Art." *Literature East and West*, 11 (Dec. 1967): 345-349.

WILSON, WILLIAM RITCHIE. "Two Shuramono: Ebira and Michimori." *MN*, 24/4 (1969): 416-465.

WOLZ, CARL. "Dance in the Noh Theatre." *World of Music*, 17/3 (1975): 26-32.

----------"The Spirit of Zen in Noh Dance." *Dance Research Annual*, 8 (1977): 55-63.

WYLIE, KATHRYN. *An Analysis of the Concept of "Attitude" as a Basis for Mime*. Ph. D. Diss., City Univ. of New York, 1984. (Especially the chapter: "The Mime Dance of the Japanese Nō," 131-175.)

YAMAZAKI, MASAKAZU. "The Aesthetics of Transformation: Zeami's Dramatic Theories," tr. Susan Matisoff. *Journal of Japanese Studies*, 7 (Summer 1981): 215-258.

YANAGIT(D)A, KUNIO. *Vom Fest zur Feier, Matsuri kara Sairei e*. (In German and Japanese). Nakamura, Negishi, and Zöbel, eds. and trs., Tokyo: Waseda UP, 1975.

YASUDA, KENNETH. "A Prototypical Nō Wig Play: *Izutsu*." *HJASt*, 40 (1980): 399-464.

----------"The Structure of *Hagoromo*, a Nō play." *HJASt*, 33 (1973): 5-89.

----------"The Dramatic Structure of *Ataka*, a Nō Play." *MN*, 27 (1972): 359-398.

----------*Masterworks of the Nō Theatre*. Bloomington: Indiana UP, 1989.

YOSHIKOSHI, TATSUO and HATA, HISASHI. *Kyogen*, tr. Don Kenny. Osaka: Hoikusha, 1982.

ZEAMI. *Kadensho*, tr. Sakurai Chūichi et al. Kyoto: Sumiya Shinobe Publishing Institute, 1968.

----------*Kadensho: A Secret Book of Noh Art*, tr. Asaji Nobori. Osaka: Union Service, 1975.

----------*Birds of Sorrow*, tr. Meredith Weatherby and Bruce Rogers. Tokyo: Obunsha, 1947.

----------"Seami Jūroku bushu (Seami's Sixteen Treatises)," tr. W. Whitehouse and M. Shidehara. *MN*, 4 (1941): 204-239, and 5 (1942): 180-214.

----------"On Attaining the Stage of Yūgen," and other treatises, tr. Donald Keene. In Tsunoda Ryūsaku, et al., comps. *Sources of Japanese Tradition*. New York: Columbia UP, 1958: 283-303.

ZOBEL, GÜNTER. "Okina und Shishi. Zwei Themen kultischer Dramaturgie bei Thomas Immoos." In Gössmann and Zobel, eds., *Das Gold im Wachs*. Munich: Iudicium, 1988: 155-174.

ZOBEL, GÜNTER. *Nō-Theater: Szene und Dramaturgie, volks-
und völkerkundliche Hintergründe.* Tokyo: OAG, 1987.
----------*Die komischen Figuren des japanischen
Volkstheaters.* Reprinted from *Hikaku Bungaku.* Vol. 14,
Tokyo, 1970.

SECTION 4: **Kabuki, Bunraku,** *and* **Sixteenth/Seventeenth
Century School Theatre**

ADACHI, BARBARA. *The Voices and Hands of Bunraku.*
Tokyo: Kōdansha, 1978.
----------*Backstage at Bunraku.* New York and Tokyo:
Weatherhill, 1985. (Revised version of the above).
AKIMOTO, SHUNKICHI. "Kabuki Audiences, Past and
Present." *Japan Quarterly,* 3 (1962): 167-173.
ANDO, TSURUO. *Bunraku: The Puppet Theatre.* New York and
Tokyo: Walker/Weatherhill, 1970.
ATSUMI, SEITARO. "Kabuki Art of Make-up." *Contemporary
Japan,* (Feb. 1941): 203-213.
AZZARONI, GIOVANNI. *L'arte del Kabuki. Tredici lezioni di
Ichikawa Ennosuke III.* Firenze: Casa Usher, 1984.
BACH, FAITH. "New directions in Kabuki." *ATJ,* 6/1 (1989):
77-89.
----------*The Contributions of the Omodakaya to Kabuki.*
Ph. D. Diss., Oxford Univ., St. Anthony College, 1990.
BARTHES, ROLAND. "On Bunraku." *TDR,* 15/3 (T50, Spring
1971): 76-82.
BERRY, MARGARET. "ALMANZOR AND COXINGA."
Comparative Literature Studies, 22/1 (1985): 97-109.
BETHUNE, ROBERT. "Describing Performance in the Theatre:
Kabuki Training and the Western Acting Student." *TDR,*
33/4 (T 124, Winter 1989): 146-166.
BLAKENY, BEN BRUCE. "Rokudaime." *Contemporary Japan,*
18 (Oct./Dec. 1949).
BOYD, JULIANNE K. *The Bunraku Puppet Theatre since 1945
to 1964: Changes in Administration and Organization.*
Ph. D. Diss., City Univ. of New York, 1986.
BRANDON, JAMES R., tr. *Kabuki: Five Classic Plays.*
Cambridge, Mass.: Harvard UP, 1975.
----------, ed. *Chūshingura: Studies in Kabuki and the
Puppet Theater.* Honolulu: Hawaii UP, 1982.
----------"The Theft of *Chūshingura:* or The Great
Kabuki Caper." *Ibid.:* 111-147.
----------with MIWA TAMAKO, trs. *Kabuki Plays:
Kanjinchō and The Zen Substitute.* New York: Samuel
French, 1966.
----------, MALM, WILLIAM P, and SHIVELY,
DONALD H. *Studies in Kabuki: Its Acting, Music, and
Historical Context.* Honolulu: The UP of Hawaii, 1978.
----------"Form in Kabuki Acting." *Ibid.:* 63-132.
BRÜLL, LYDIA. "Chikamatsu Monzaemon in seinen
Ausserungen zum Puppentheater." *Oriens Extremus,* 8
(1971): 233-246.

BRÜLL, LYDIA. "Die Bewegungstechnik der Figuren im japanischen Puppentheater." *NOAG*, 92 (1962): 7-28.
CAVAYE, ROLAND. *Kabuki: A Pocket Guide.* Rutland VT: Tuttle, 1993.
DE VOS, PATRICK. "Onnagata—fleur de Kabuki." *Bouffonneries*, 15-16 (1987): 95-137.
DUNN, C. J. *The Early Japanese Puppet Drama.* London: Luzac, 1966.
---------- and TORIGOE BUNZO, trs. *The Actors Analects.* New York: Columbia UP, 1969.
ELZEY, JOHN M. "Awa *Ningyō Jōruri*: Provincial Puppet Theatre." *ATJ*, 4/1 (Spring 1987): 115-121.
ERNST, EARLE. *The Kabuki Theatre.* New York: Grove, 1956.
FAURE, P. *Le Kabuki et ses écrivains.* Paris: L'Asiathèque, 1977.
FLORENZ, KARL, tr. *Scènes du théâtre japonais: l'École du Village (Terakoya).* Tokyo: Hasegawa, 1900.
-----------*Japanische Dramen: Terakoya und Asagao.* Leipzig: Amelangs, 1900.
FROIS, LUIS. *Die Geschichte Japans* (1549-1578): tr. and comm. G. Schurhammer and E. A. Voretzsch. Leipzig, 1926.
GERSDORFF, WOLFGANG. *Terakoya: Die Dorfschule.* Berlin: Albert Abn, 1907.
----------*Japanische Dramen*, Jena: Eugen Diederichs, 1926.
GERSTLE, ANDREW C. *Circles of Fantasy: Convention in the Plays of Chikamatsu.* Cambridge, MA: Council on East Asian Studies, 1986.
----------"Flowers of Edo: Eighteenth-Century *Kabuki* and its Patrons." *ATJ*, 4/1 (1987): 52-75.
GOODMAN, DAVID. "Kabuki from the Outside: Interviews." *TDR*, 15 (1971): 175-184.
GUNJI, MASAKATSU. *Buyo: The Classical Dance.* New York: Walker/Weatherhill, 1970.
----------*Kabuki.* Tokyo: Kodansha, 1970.
----------*The Kabuki Guide*, tr. Christopher Holmes. Tokyo and New York: Kodansha, 1987.
HALFORD, AUBREY S. and HALFORD, GIOVANNA M. *The Kabuki Handbook.* Tokyo: Tuttle, 1961.
HAMAMURA, YONEZO, et al. *Kabuki.* Tokyo: Nakanishiya, 1910.
HIBBET, HOWARD. *The Floating World in Japanese Fiction.* New York: Oxford UP, 1959.
HIRONAGA, SHUZABURO. *Bunraku: Japan's Unique Puppet Theatre.* Tokyo: Tokyo News Service, 1964.
HIROSUE, TAMOTSU. "The Blind Kagekiyo: Beyond the Tragic." *Concerned Theatre Japan*, 1 (1970): 35-48.
----------"Ekin." *Ibid.*: 101-124.
----------"The Secret Ritual of the Place of Evil." *Ibid.*, 2: (1971): 14-21.
HIRSCHFELD-MEDALIA, ADELINE. "The Voice in *Wayang* and *Kabuki*." *ATJ*, 1/2 (Fall 1984): 217-222.
HOFF, FRANK. "Furyu Odori." In Ohta Saburō and Fukuda Rikutarō, eds., *Studies on Japanese Culture*, vol. 1 Tokyo: Japan P.E.N. Club, 1973: 623-629.
HUMBERT, AIMÉ. *Japon illustré.* Paris, 1870.

HUONDER, ANTON. "Zur Geschichte des Missionstheaters." *Abhandlungen aus Missionskunde und Missionsgeschichte,* 2. Heft. Aachen, 1918.

IACOVLEFF, A. and ELISSÉEF, S. *Le Théâtre japonais.* Paris: Jules Meynial, 1933.

IMMOOS, THOMAS. "Japanische Helden des europäischen Barocktheaters." *MuK,* 27/1 (1981): 36-56.

----------"Japanese Themes in Swiss Baroque Drama." In Joseph Roggendorf, ed., *Studies in Japanese Culture.* Tokyo: Sophia UP, 1963: 79-98.

INOUYE, JUKICHI, tr. *Chushingura.* Tokyo: Nakanishiya, 1910.

ITO, SACHIYO. "Some Characteristics of Japanese Expressions as They Appear in Dance." *Dance Research Annual,* 10 (1979): 267-277.

JACKSON, EARL Jr. "Kabuki Narratives of Male Homoerotic Desire in Saikaku and Mishima." *ETJ,* 41/4 (1989): 459-477.

JONES, STANLEIGH H. Jr. "Experiment and Tradition. New Plays in the Bunraku Theatre." *MN,* 36/2 (1981): 113-131.

----------"Miracle at Yaguchi Ferry: A Japanese Puppet Play and Its Metamorphosis to Kabuki." *HJASt,* 38/1 (1978): 171-224.

----------*Sugawara and the Secrets of Calligraphy.* New York: Columbia UP, 1984.

----------"Vengeance and Its Toll in *Numazu*: An Eighteenth Century Japanese Puppet Play." *ATJ,* 7/1 (Spring 1990): 42-75.

KAEMPFER, ENGELBERTUS. *The History of Japan... by Engelbertus Kaempfer...,* tr. J. C. Scheuchzer. 2 vols. London, 1727.

KAWATAKE, SHIGETOSHI. *Kabuki: Japanese Drama.* Tokyo: The Foreign Affairs Association of Japan, 1958.

----------*Development of the Japanese Theatre Arts.* Tokyo: Kokusai Bunka Shinkokai, 1936.

----------*Nihon engeki zuroku* (A Pictorial Record of Japanese Theatrical Arts) Tokyo: Asahi shimbunsha, 1956. (With partial English translation of explanations).

----------"Kabuki und Bunraku." *MuK,* 10 (1964): 692-708.

----------"Kabuki after the Opening of Japan." *Contemporary Japan,* 22 (1953): 62-72.

----------"Chikamatsu." In *Enciclopedia dello Spettacolo,* Roma: Le Maschere, 1955: 3: 658-661.

KAWATAKE, TOSHIO. "The Reaction of the Overseas Performances of Kabuki." *MuK,* 27/1 (1981): 85-96.

----------*A History of Japanese Theater II: Bunraku and Kabuki.* Tokyo: Kokusai Bunka Kenkyūkai, 1971.

----------"A Crisis of Kabuki and Its Revival Right after the World War II." *Waseda Journal of Asian Studies,* 5 (1983): 32-42.

----------*Das Barocke im Kabuki—das Kabukihafte im Barocktheater.* Thomas Leims, ed. and tr. Österreichische Akademie der Wissenschaften, Phil.-Hist. Klasse; Sitzungsberichte, vol. 382. Vienna: Verlag der Österreichischen Akademie der Wissenschaften, 1981.

KAWATAKE, TOSHIO. "Japanese Traditional Culture and Today's Japan: The Internationalization of the Kabuki Theatre and its Function in Modern Society." In Ian Nishi, ed., *Contemporary European Writing on Japan*, Woodchurch, Ashford, Kent, 1988.

KAY, HELEN V. *Kabuki: Eighteen Traditional Dramas*. San Francisco: Chronicle, 1985.

KEENE, DONALD. *Bunraku: The Art of the Japanese Puppet Theatre*. Tokyo: Kodansha, 1965.

----------, tr. *Major Plays of Chikamatsu*. New York: Columbia UP, 1961.

----------, tr. *Chūshingura: The Treasury of the Loyal Retainers*. New York: Columbia UP, 1971.

----------, tr. *The Battles of Coxinga*. London: Taylor Foreign Press, 1951.

----------*World within Walls: Japanese Literature of the Pre-modern Era, 1600-1867*. New York: Holt, Reinhart and Winston, 1976.

KENNY, DON, comp. *The Kyōgen Book: An Anthology of Japanese Classical Comedies*. Tokyo: Japan Times, 1989.

----------*A Guide to Kyōgen*. Tokyo: Hinoki Shoten, 1968.

KINKAID, ZOE *Kabuki: The Popular Stage of Japan*. London: Macmillan, 1925.

----------"Four Drama Forms of Kabuki." *TASJ*, 2nd series, 1 (1924): 83-99.

KLOPFENSTEIN, EDUARD. *Tausend Kirschenbäume (Yoshitsune sembon-zakura): Ein klassisches Stück des japanischen Theaters der Edo-Zeit. Studie, Übersetzung, Kommentar*. Bern: Peter Lang, 1982.

KOMINZ, LAURENCE. "Origins of *Kabuki* Acting in Medieval Japanese Drama." *ATJ*, 5/2 (Fall 1988): 132-147.

LADERRIERE, METTE. "The Technique of Female Impersonation in Kabuki." *MuK*, 27/1 (1981): 30-35.

LEABO, KARL, ed. *Kabuki*. New York: Theatre Arts Books, 1982.

LEE, SANG-KYONG. "Barocktheater und Kabuki." *MuK* 17 (1971): 48-72.

LEIMS, THOMAS. "Mysterienspiel und Schultheater in der japanischen Jesuitenmission des 16. Jahrhunderts." *MuK*, 27/1 (1981): 57-71.

----------"Europäische Mechanik auf der Kabuki- und Jōruribühne." *Bonner Zeitschrift für Japanologie*. 1 (1979): 263-274.

----------"Kabuki—Text versus Schauspielkunst." Japanisches Kulturinstitut Köln, ed., *Klassische Theaterformen Japans*. Köln and Vienna: Böhlau, 1983: 67-81.

----------*Die Entstehung des Kabuki: Transkulturation Europa-Japan in 16. und 17. Jahrhundert*. Leiden/New York: E. J. Brill, 1990. (A revised edition of his Ph. D. Diss., Universität Bonn, 1986).

----------"Japan and Christian Mystery Plays: Christian Kōwakamai Reconsidered". In Ian Nish, ed., *Contemporary European Writing on Japan. Scholarly Views from Eastern and Western Europe*, Woodchurch Ashford Kent: Paul Norbury, 1988: 206-210.

LEIMS, THOMAS. "Kabuki Goes to Hollywood: Reforms and 'Revues' in the 1980s." In E. Fischer-Lichte, et al., eds., *The Dramatic Touch of Difference*. Tübingen: Günter Narr Verlag, 1990: 107-117.

LEITER, SAMUEL L. *The Art of Kabuki: Famous Plays in Performance*. Berkeley: Univ. of California Press, 1979.

----------*Kabuki Encyclopedia. An English-Language Adaptation of Kabuki Jiten*. Westport, Conn: Greenwood, 1979.

----------"Keren: Spectacle and Trickery in Kabuki Acting." *ETJ*, 28/2 (1976): 151-188.

----------"Kabuki Jūhachiban." *Literature East and West*, 18 (1976): 346-365.

----------"Ichikawa Danjūrō XI: A Life in Kabuki." *ETJ*, 29/3 (1977): 311-318.

----------"Four Interviews with Kabuki Actors." *ETJ*, 18 (Dec. 1966): 391-404.

----------"The Frozen Moment: A Kabuki Technique." *Drama Survey*, (Spring 1967): 74-80.

----------"Authentic Kabuki: American Style." *Theatre Crafts*, 2 (Sept.-Oct. 1968): 6-14.

----------"The Depiction of Violence on the Kabuki Stage." *ETJ*, 21 (May 1969): 147-155.

----------"Onoe Kikugorō VII." *Asian Theatre Bulletin*, 3 (Fall/Winter 1973): 5-9.

----------*Tachimawari: Stage Fighting in the Kabuki Theatre*. Monographs on Music, Dance and Theatre in Asia, vol. 3. New York: Performing Arts Program of the Asia Society, 1976.

----------"Kumagai Battle Camp: Form and Tradition in *Kabuki* Acting." *ATJ*, 8/1 (Spring 1991): 1-34.

LEPSIUS, GITTA. "Das heutige japanische Puppentheater auf dem Lande und seine Vorgeschichte." *MOAG*, 50 (1968): 26-95.

LEVINE, NORMA. "The Influence of Kabuki Theatre on the Films of Eisenstein." *Modern Drama*, 12 (May 1969).

MALM, WILLIAM P. *Nagauta: The Heart of Kabuki Music*. Rutland, VT and Tokyo, 1963.

----------"Four Seasons of the Old Mountain Woman: An Example of Japanese *Nagauta* Text Setting." *Journal of the American Musicology Society*, 31/1 (1978): 83-117.

----------"Music in the Kabuki Theatre." In Brandon, James R., et al., *Studies in Kabuki*. Honolulu: East-West Center, 1978: 133-175.

----------"A Musical Approach to the Study of Japanese Jōruri." In Brandon, James R., ed., *Chūshingura: Studies in Kabuki and the Puppet Theatre*. Honolulu: Univ. of Hawaii Press, 1982: 58-111.

MAREGA, MARIO. *Il Ciuscingura: La vendetta dei 47 Rōnin*. Bari: Laterza, 1948.

MASEFIELD, JOHN. *The Faithful*. London: Heinemann, 1915.

MATISOFF, SUSAN K. "Nō as transformed by Chikamatsu." *Journal of the Association of Teachers of Japanese*, 11/2-3 (1976): 201-216.

MAY, EKKEHARD. "Monzaemon Chikamatsu: Sōshichis und Kojorōs Weg. Versuch einer integralen Ubersetzung." *Poetica*, 4/4 (1971): 513-553.

MITCHELL, JOHN D. and SCHWARTZ, E. K. "A Psycho-analytic Approach to Kabuki: A Study in Personality and Culture." *Journal of Psychology*, 52 (1961).

MIYAJIMA, TSUNAO. *Contribution à l'étude du théâtre de poupées.* Kyoto: Kansai Nichifutsu Gakkan, 1926. Revised edition, 1931.

MIYAKE, SHUTARO. *Kabuki Drama.* Tokyo: Japan Travel Bureau, 1961.

MIYAMORI ASATARO. *Tales from Old Japanese Dramas.* New York and London: Putnam's Sons, 1915.

----------*Masterpeces of Chikamatsu, the Japanese Shakespeare.* London: K. Paul, Trench, Trübner, 1926.

MOTOFUJI, FRANK T., tr. *The Love of Izayoi and Seishin: A Kabuki Play by Kawatake Mokuami.* Rutland, VT and Tokyo: Tuttle, 1966.

NAKAMURA, TETSURO. "Die Entdeckung des Kabuki durch den Westen." *MuK*, 27/1 (1981): 72-84.

ORTOLANI, BENITO. *Das Kabukitheater: Kulturgeschichte der Anfänge.* Tokyo: Sophia UP, 1964.

----------"Kabuki." In Horst Hammitzsch, ed., *Japan Handbuch.* Wiesbaden: Steiner, 1981: 1838-1850.

----------"Bunraku." *Ibid.*: 1819-1830.

----------"Okuni-kabuki und Onna-kabuki." *MN*, 12/1-4 (1962): 161-213.

----------"Das Wakashu-kabuki und das Yarō-kabuki." *MN*, 13/1-4 (1963): 89-127.

OUYANG, YU-CHIEN. "The Zenshin-za Kabuki Troupe." *Chinese Literature*, 5 (1960): 120-125.

PAULY, HERTA. "Inside Kabuki: An Experience in Comparative Aesthetics." *Journal of Aesthetics and Art Criticism*, 25 (1967): 293-304.

PIMPANEAU, JACQUES. *Phantômes manipulés.* Bibiothèque asiatique 30, Paris: Univ. de Paris-7, 1978.

PIPER, MARIA. *Die Schaukunst der Japaner.* Berlin and Leipzig; Walter de Gruyter, 1927.

----------*Das japanische Theater.* Frankfurt/M: Societäts-Verlag, 1937.

PRONKO, LEONARD C. "Kabuki and the Elizabethan Theatre." *ETJ*, 19/1 (1967): 9-16.

----------"Freedom and Tradition in the Kabuki Actor's Art." *ETJ*, 21 (1969): 139-146.

----------"Learning Kabuki: The Training Program of the National Theatre of Japan." *ETJ*, 23 (Dec. 1971): 409-430.

----------"What is wrong with Kabuki?" *Japan Quarterly*, 18 (1971): 330-333.

----------"Kabuki Today and Tomorrow." *Comparative Drama*, (1972): 103-114.

----------"Oriental Theatre for the West: Problems of Authenticity and Communication." *ETJ*, 20/3 (1968): 425-436.

----------"*Kabuki*: Signs, Symbols and the Hieroglyphic Actor." *Themes in Drama*, 1982: 41-55.